5P

THE GOTHIC WAR

THE GOTHIC WAR

ROME'S FINAL CONFLICT IN THE WEST

Torsten Cumberland Jacobsen

WESTHOLME
Yardley

Frontispiece: Print by Giuseppe Vasi (1710-1782) of the Porta
Pinciana in Rome c. 1747.

Westholme Publishing, LLC
Eight Harvey Avenue
Yardley, Pennsylvania 19067
Visit our Web site at www.westholmepublishing.com

First Printing May 2009
10 9 8 7 6 5 4 3 2 1

ISBN: 978-1-59416-084-4

Printed in United States of America

For my dearest wife, Katerina, without whose
support and encouragement this book
would never have been finished.

CONTENTS

PREFACE

THE AIM OF THIS BOOK is to describe some of the momentous military events that took place in the Roman world in the reign of Emperor Justinian during the sixth century AD, when he tried to regain the lost parts of the empire. I focus on the greatest and most important war, that against the Ostrogoths, who had taken Italy for themselves at the end of the fifth century, but I also touch upon the destruction of the powerful Vandals, the wars on the eastern border of the empire against the Persians, and the invasions of the Franks into northern Italy, as far as they influenced the overall military situation the empire faced. These wars were the last serious attempt by the Romans to return to the days of the old empire, and despite the immensity of the task, they almost succeeded.

The Gothic War changed Europe and the history of Europe. Two of the strongest barbarian nations—the Ostrogoths and the Vandals—ended up being destroyed, giving others a chance to enter the stage. The young Frankish kingdom enjoyed a period of respite to grow strong and transform Gaul into France. The small Lombard tribes took advantage of the weakened Roman Empire to take much of Italy in the late sixth century, thereby creating the foundations for medieval Italy.

Despite the great victory over the Ostrogoths and Vandals, the Roman Empire was critically weakened by its efforts and left itself vulnerable to attack. A hundred years later the Arab tribes would find it a tempting and easy target, conquering the former territories along North Africa and the Middle East, which gave Islam a chance to go from a local to a world-spanning religion. Therefore, the Gothic War and the period of Emperor Justinian are considered by some historians to mark the end of the Roman Empire and the start of the Byzantine Empire.

A major source for the period are the writings of Procopius, who was on the staff of the Roman General Belisarius, the officer who conducted much of the Gothic War. Procopius's vivid descriptions of the war and his curious observations on the life of the period continue to fascinate readers. Over the course of my research, I visited Italy on numerous occasions and was reminded further of the great struggle, whether in seeing the primitive graves of Lombard warriors in Fiesole above Florence or in the desperate repairs of the broken walls of Rome, where all manner of debris was used to cover the breaches made by the Ostrogoths. To read about events long gone while seeing the physical traces of them is always a stirring experience.

In addition to its historical importance, the Gothic War makes for a "good story," portraying the struggle between the last embers of the Roman Empire and the fierce barbarian Ostrogoths, with almost fairy-tale heroes and villains: Belisarius, considered to be one of the greatest generals in history; the young and strong Gothic King Totila, who, despite being outnumbered, defeated several Roman armies; and the austere and highly religious Emperor Justinian, intent on retaking the lost Roman lands. While Procopius and the other sources have a tendency to make matters more black and white than they were, Procopius can still be seen as a fairly objective historian who tried to recount both the good and the bad.

The Gothic War describes the conflict on an operational and tactical level, rather than a strategic level, which is well-covered by other books. It is, of course, impossible to ignore the strategic view altogether, and therefore this is brought up when required. I also present a brief history of the Ostrogoths to set the scene for the war, and address the military differences between the Roman and Ostrogothic armies. The sources at the end provide a list of the many authors on whose work I have based this book.

1

PRELUDE

THE SIXTH CENTURY AD brought many changes to the Roman world. After a long period of decline, Emperor Justinian (527–565) succeeded in stabilizing the borders following the violent barbarian invasions of the fourth and fifth centuries. Franks, Saxons, Vandals, Visigoths, Ostrogoths, and other lesser tribes were now settled on former Roman soil. All of the Western Roman Empire had been lost—Britain, Spain, Gaul, Italy, North Africa, and, worst of all, the city of cities, Rome. The stabilization meant Justinian could start preparing to reconquer the Western Empire. It was an ambitious plan to take back a territory larger than the existing Eastern Roman Empire with relatively few soldiers and resources, and with the constant pressure from foreign enemies who did not want to see a strong Roman Empire again. Yet despite all of this, Justinian would succeed in the next thirty years to hold off the energetic Persian Empire in the East and to retake Italy, Sicily, Sardinia, Corsica, North Africa, Dalmatia, and parts of Spain.

The strongest and most-organized enemies in the West were the Ostrogoths, who had taken Italy in 493. Thirty years later, the once great and feared tribes of the Ostrogoths and Vandals would be relegated to history.

JUSTIN AND JUSTINIAN

When Emperor Anastasius died in 518, there was much doubt about who would succeed him. After many deliberations, the Senate chose Justin, against the wishes of the *Scholares*—the Imperial Guard, who were known for making emperors—and others. Justin

Mosaic of emperor Justinian in the Church of San Vitale in Ravenna. The church of San Vitale was founded in 526 and dedicated in 548. (*Author*)

was an Illyrian peasant who had risen from the ranks and was now, at about age sixty-five, *comes excubitorium*, or chief of the palace guards. He had a respectable, if not distinguished, military career behind him, and he possessed neither culture nor administrative experience. There was even talk of him being illiterate.

Justin's favorite nephew was Petrus Sabbatius, whom he adopted and gave the name Justinianus. Already during the reign of Justin, Justinian was picked out for various important missions and was steadily promoted within the imperial administration.

In the spring of 527, Justin became dangerously ill, and the Senate asked him to crown Justinian as his colleague and thereby successor. The ceremony was performed on April 4, and on August 1, Justin died, leaving Justinian as sole emperor of the Roman Empire.

Justinian was enormously energetic, often working into the small hours of the night and fasting more than what was usual in the age. His legislation shows he was concerned with all details of government, and historians even criticized him for involving himself too much in administration instead of leaving it to his officials. He did, however, choose some able generals and ministers, whom he in some cases promoted from low station. He himself was an example of the opportunities open to even the poor peasants of Illyria and Thrace. His wife, Theodora, who played an important part in the administration, was a former dancer from a poor family.

Perhaps he did involve himself in too many details: the course of the war indicates that at times he was so engrossed in other matters of state that he did not ensure that enough troops and money were available for the Roman army operating in Italy and the other provinces at war.

Justinian was truly Roman, and he boasted that Latin was his native tongue—he did not even speak Greek up to the standards of the imperial court. He was well versed in Roman history and did much to revive old Roman customs while also trying out new ideas. Above all, he wanted to restore the Roman Empire to its ancient glory by recovering the Western Empire, and particularly Rome, the center of the ancient empire. And perhaps it would be the last chance to recover the lost provinces; time was passing, but still the citizens of the former Western Empire remembered the old days of the Empire when the barbarians were at the borders and not in the palaces. A generation later, few living persons would have experienced the Western Empire when the Romans ruled it, and the population would be less eager to support the return of the legions. It was time to act.

The Eastern Frontier

Although Justinian would fight to maintain the borders in the East against the Persians, he had no ambitions for conquest there. His general objective seems to have been to put enough military pressure on the Persians to avoid any major invasions and thus set him free to reconquer the lost provinces of the West. On his accession he acted according to these principles, actively carrying on the war against the Persians while continuing negotiations for a settlement.

One year after his accession, he started to set his grand plan into motion. He began a series of changes and furthered the efficiency of the Eastern military commands, and soon afterward the whole line of border defenses was moved forward. New fortresses were constructed close to the border to strengthen the Roman military presence. Construction of the fortress named Mindouos in Mesopotamia was put under the command of Belisarius, who would play a central role in the Gothic War and become famous as one of the greatest generals of history. The young officer, who came from Germana in Dacia, was at the time one of Justinian's bodyguards. This construction of a fortress so close to the border provoked the Persians, who attacked the Roman army defending it. Despite reinforcements from the provincial army of Lebanon, the

Romans were defeated and the fortress razed. But this setback did not change Justinian's plans.

Next he reinforced the Roman army of the East, bringing it up to about twenty-five thousand men, and appointed two new generals: Belisarius as general of the East, and Sittas, a young Armenian officer also from Justinian's bodyguard, as general in Armenia. Under the two new generals, the war, which had so far gone badly for the Romans, took a more favorable turn. In 530, Sittas defeated a Persian army at the Armenian towns of Theodosiopolis and Satala (Erzurum and Sadak in modern-day Turkey), and Belisarius won a great victory at Daras (Oguz in modern-day Turkey), a strongly fortified Roman city on the Persian border. Facing the Persian army of fifty thousand with his own twenty-five thousand, Belisarius beat them off with the loss of eight thousand Persians. The historian Procopius noted that it was the first time in many years that Roman arms had triumphed over the Persians in a major battle. The following year, however, the Persians invaded the Roman territory in the neighborhood of Callinicum on the Euphrates (Ar-Raqqah in modern-day Syria), with the aim of attacking Syria and the principal city of the East, Antioch.

BATTLE OF CALLINICUM

By skillful maneuvering, Belisarius forced the enemy to withdraw along the Euphrates, and he was content to shadow its movements and prevent pillaging. But his eager soldiers taunted him for not attacking the retreating Persians. So at the city of Callinicum on Easter Saturday, April 19, 531, Belisarius faced them with his army on the banks of the river. He placed his infantry on the left wing and his federate Saracens under their chieftain, Arethas, on the right, with his cavalry and himself in the middle.

The battle began with a furious discharge of arrows. While the Persians were trained to shoot more quickly, their bows had less strength than the Romans' and so caused fewer casualties. Two-thirds of the day passed with missile fire and single combat between the lines, when the Persians finally charged the Saracens on the right flank. The Saracens fled before the Persian troops and were later accused of treachery because of their quick escape. The Persian cavalry now moved to the rear of the Roman center and was slaughtering the inexperienced Roman troops. The remnants of the Roman cavalry retreated to the infantry, which formed a shield wall to protect against the Persian cavalry. The infantry succeeded in keeping the Persians away until nightfall, when the Romans could retreat to an island in the river. The defeat was severe for the Romans, who lost some three thousand soldiers. The Persians, however, had suffered much heavier losses and failed to take any Roman city or stronghold.

On returning to his homeland, Persian General Azarethes was asked to determine how many soldiers he had lost, in the customary Persian way: at the start of a campaign, each soldier would put an arrow in a basket, which was then closed. At the end of the campaign, the troops would march by the baskets and pick up an arrow. The remaining arrows would then show how many had been lost in the campaign. When Persia's King Cabades saw how many arrows were still in the baskets after the army had marched by, Azarethes was rebuked and punished for his costly victory.

Cabades died in the autumn of 531. His son, Chosroes, who wished to have his hands free for possible trouble at home, agreed in the spring of 532 to sign a Treaty of Eternal Peace. Territorially, the status quo before the war was restored. Justinian agreed to pay Chosroes eleven thousand pounds of gold for the latter's abandoning all claims to an old subsidy toward the defense of the strategic pass named the Caspian Gates. This was the traditional inroad of the northern barbarian tribes, and both nations were to defend it.

The death of Cabades and the expectation of a peace of at least some years on the Eastern frontier fit Justinian's plans perfectly. He was now free to start the first stage of the reconquest. Belisarius was recalled to the capital to prepare for the invasion of the Vandal kingdom in North Africa, and Sittas was appointed general of the East in his stead.

THE NIKA UPRISING

Belisarius would soon get a most-unexpected opportunity at Constantinople for retrieving his damaged reputation from

Callinicum. In January 532, an uprising started in Constantinople that soon assumed alarming proportions.

The Romans were great lovers of horse races, and in every Roman city four teams competed: the Blue, the Green, the Red, and the White, of which the latter two were of little importance. The Blue and Green teams were supported by factions who fought with each other at every opportunity. These gangs were known for their long hair and strange dress that imitated the Hunnish tribes. The uprising began as an ordinary riot of the factions, which local authorities quickly suppressed under the command of Eudaemon, the prefect of the city. Seven of the rioters from both factions were arrested and taken into custody to be executed. Five were executed, but the gallows had broken under the weight, and some monks had taken one Blue and one Green rioter, half–dead, to a church. The prefect insisted that they should receive their punishment. The two factions then declared a truce and united. On January 4 they stormed the prison, shouting "Nika!" ("Conquer!"), released all the prisoners, and sacked the hated city prefect's office. While the local citizens were fleeing across the straits, the rioters ran amok in the streets and began to set fire to public buildings.

Meanwhile, the emperor and parts of the Senate shut themselves up in the palace and remained quiet—probably in the belief that the riot soon would blow itself out.

Instead, the factions assembled in the Hippodrome the next day and demanded the removal of several unpopular ministers. Hoping to calm the mob, Justinian agreed, but this was not enough for the rioters, and the insurrection continued.

On the sixth day of the uprising, the factions sought out one Hypatius, a nephew of the late Emperor Anastasius's, and proclaimed him emperor against his will. Hypatius and some of the senators were then marched to the Hippodrome, and he was put in the imperial seat.

The situation was becoming increasingly dangerous, and Justinian began to contemplate leaving the city in boats. There were few troops in the capital, and many of them were biding their time, awaiting the outcome of the situation. Empress Theodora, however, talked Justinian into going on the offensive and quelling what was now a rebellion in the capital. By chance Belisarius and another general, Mundus, were in the palace with their personal retinue. Belisarius's bodyguards were veterans of the campaign in the East, and the Gepid barbarian Mundus, newly appointed general of Illyricum, had brought some of his fierce Herulian soldiers.

The generals led their troops to the Hippodrome, where the rioters had gathered. They surrounded it and attacked. The soldiers made short work of the unarmed rebels, and thirty thousand were said to have been killed in the fight. Hypatius was executed, and the other members of the Senate who had supported him were exiled and their property confiscated. Justinian later found out the reluctant role they had played in the uprising, and their property was restored to their families.

Belisarius had shown the emperor his loyalty and capabilities, and soon his next campaign would start.

During his stay in Constantinople, Belisarius married Antonina, who was later to have much influence on his military career and his standing at the imperial court. It was a surprising match: she was a widow with two grown children and some twenty-two years older than the young Belisarius. She would follow him through most of his campaigns and at times even guide his hand in political matters.

THE VANDAL WAR

In 530, the aged Vandal King Hilderic—who had proved unable to check the encroachments of the local African tribes, the Moors (not to be mistaken for the Muslim Berber and Arab tribes that settled in Spain in the eighth century)—had been dethroned and replaced by Gelimer, the next eldest descendant of the famous Vandal King Gaiseric.

Since then, Justinian had been working hard at diplomacy. He had promptly protested the deposition of a king who was in treaty relations with him and who, moreover, had abandoned the persecution of the African Catholics, and he was eager to use this pretext to attack the Vandal kingdom. This also made it possible for Justinian to claim that war was being made to reinstate the lawful king. Justinian's position was further strengthened by the will of

King Gaiseric (439–477), who, shortly before he died, had decreed that only the closest relative of his would rule the Vandal nation. Thus the Vandals saw the removal of Hilderic as a serious break with tradition. By a further stroke of luck, a Roman named Pudentius from Tripolis in Libya had rebelled from the oppressive rule of the Vandals and asked for troops to help him. Accordingly, Justinian sent General Tattimuth with a small force ahead of the main invasion force. When news reached the Vandals of the emperor's displeasure, a Goth in Vandal service, Godas, who was ruling Sardinia for Gelimer, sent a letter to Justinian asking for troops and then rebelled, setting himself up as king of Sardinia. The two rebellions severely weakened the Vandal kingdom at the worst possible time, particularly as Gelimer did not expect a serious Roman response so soon.

Justinian's generals and ministers greatly disliked the plan to attack the Vandals. They recalled the disastrous results of all previous attacks on Africa, such as the great expedition of General Basiliscus sixty-five years earlier, when the Vandals destroyed a great Roman fleet with fire ships. The plans were also openly opposed on financial grounds by elements at the imperial court headed by John the Cappadocian, the all-powerful praetorian prefect (in this period similar to a minister of finance). From a military point of view it was a dangerous undertaking, as there were no undefended harbors for the fleet in an area with stormy weather and no possibility of retreat if the army was defeated. It was also difficult to supply the expedition once it reached Africa, and the threat of the powerful and experienced Vandal fleet would be ever present. Earlier expeditions had been destroyed or defeated by these conditions.

Justinian was, of course, aware of the dangers of the undertaking, but several things were in his favor. The opportunity for a successful expedition rested in part on the fact that the Vandals had fallen out with their northern neighbors, the Ostrogoths, who held Sicily.

During the reign of Hilderic (523–530), the Vandals had suffered a serious defeat in one of the battles against the troublesome Moors. Because of the Vandals' weakness, there seems to have been plans by Ostrogoth King Theodoric the Great to take over their kingdom. In response, the Vandals killed the Goths in their kingdom and imprisoned Amalafrida, the sister of Theodoric and wife of the dead Vandal King Thrasamund. Theodoric could not respond to these misdeeds because the Ostrogoths did not have a navy capable of taking on the experienced Vandal fleet. So from then on the relations between Goths and Vandals were cold.

Accordingly, Justinian had asked Amalasuntha, the mother of Ostrogoth Boy-King Antalaric and de facto ruler of the Ostrogothic kingdom of Italy, if a market with provisions and horses could be made ready in Sicily to supply the Roman army on the expedition. The request was granted.

The strategic importance of Sicily for the African campaign was enormous, as it provided a base at which to resupply the army and get replacement horses for the cavalry, both of which were essential for the Romans. Sicily would also function as a resupply point for the Roman fleet, which would ferry supplies across to Africa. Otherwise, supplies would have to be sent from the ports of Greece.

The combination of events—peace with Persia, no immediate threats from the barbarians north of the Danube, the issue of the dethroned Hilderic, and the use of Sicily as a friendly base—would not be repeated. Justinian overruled all opposition, and in June 533 the expedition was ready to sail.

Troops were collected from the now-peaceful Eastern border, and the army was to be commanded by Belisarius, who had proved his loyalty in the Nika rebellion. The composition of the expedition is described in detail by the historian Procopius and gives a unique insight into the Roman preparations. The army was fairly large, comprising fifteen thousand regular and auxiliary troops and one thousand barbarian allies, as well as the core of the army—Belisarius's veteran bodyguard, which probably already numbered in the thousands. Of the fifteen thousand regulars, five thousand were cavalry and the rest infantry.

They were carried by a fleet of five hundred transports, manned by thirty thousand sailors and escorted by ninety-two small warships—*dromones* (Greek for "runners"), fast ships with one bank of oars—whose complement of marines totaled two thousand. The commanders of the auxiliaries were Dorotheus, general of the troops in Armenia, and the eunuch Solomon; the lesser commanders included Cyprianus, Valerianus, Martinus, Althias, John, Marcellus, and Cyril. The commanders of the regular cavalry were Rufinus, Aigan the Hun, Barbatus, and Pappus; while Theodorus, Terentius, Zaidus, Marcianus, and Sarapis commanded the regular infantry. A general named John was in overall command of the infantry. Apart from Aigan the Hun and Solomon, who was from Mesopotamia, almost all the other generals were from Thrace. Of the barbarian allies, the Herulian King Pharas commanded four hundred lightly armed Herulians, and Sinnion and Balas commanded six hundred Hunnish horse archers. Admiral Calonymus was in command of the fleet during the operation.

Belisarius was given full powers to conduct the war in the name of the emperor, as orders would take too long to reach him in Africa.

PROCOPIUS

Belisarius's secretary Procopius also accompanied him on the great expedition. During and after the wars, he would write about Belisarius's campaigns as he observed them first hand. It is to him and his vivid and detailed descriptions that we owe almost all our knowledge of one of the greatest Roman generals in history.

Procopius was born at Caesarea in Palestine late in the fifth century and became a lawyer. In 527 he was made legal adviser and secretary to Belisarius during his first command against the Persians. He went again with him in 533 against the Vandals, and in 535 against the Ostrogoths.

At some time after 540, his descriptions of the Gothic War become vaguer, and it is believed that he returned to Constantinople with Belisarius. It is, however, possible that he followed Belisarius to Italy on his campaign against Ostrogoth King Totila in 542. Procopius died sometime after 558.

His *History of the Wars* recounts the Persian Wars of Justinian down to 550, the Vandal War and the later events in Africa

(532–46), and the Gothic War against the Ostrogoths in Sicily and Italy (536–552). He also sketched later events to 554.

Procopius was a diligent, judicious narrator of facts and developments, although his knowledge of remote historical events was somewhat limited. He describes in detail peoples and places, and he boldly criticizes Emperor Justinian and his own master, Belisarius.

His two other extant works, *The Secret History* and *On the Buildings,* are somewhat different from the *History of the Wars. The Secret History* is a strong and bitter attack on Emperor Justinian and Empress Theodora's rule, and he describes the intrigues and scandals at the imperial court in the harshest terms. It is believed that *The Secret History* was meant to be published only after his death.

On the Buildings is, on the other hand, in the style of a fawning flatterer and lauds the great construction work Justinian undertook. It describes the public buildings, fortresses, roads, and bridges he constructed or restored. Despite its tendencies, it gives a good insight into Justinian's great military construction program.

THE SEA JOURNEY

At around the spring equinox, Belisarius's great fleet anchored off the emperor's palace in Constantinople. After the customary blessings, it sailed to Perinthus (Eregli in modern-day Turkey) where the emperor presented Belisarius with a gift of horses from the imperial stables. The army spent five days at Perinthus to organize itself for the journey. It then set sail for Abydus (Nara Burnu), where it was delayed four days because of contrary winds.

Discipline, especially among the federate Huns, was already a problem. In drunkenness (they were known for being constantly drunk), two Huns killed another in a brawl. Aware of the problems with discipline if things got out of hand, Belisarius impaled the two barbarians on a nearby hill in view of the whole army. The Hunnish contingent, and particularly the relatives of the impaled, complained that they were not subject to Roman laws and that it was wrong of the general to punish the two culprits so harshly. In response, Belisarius called an assembly of the Huns and the rest of the army where he scolded them for lack of discipline. It was not

Map 1. Europe and North Africa in 535.

only the murder he had punished but also the drunkenness. Chastened, the soldiers behaved more moderately.

At Abydus, Belisarius also solved the problem of keeping the fleet together while at anchor and while sailing. After some deliberations, the sails of the three ships in which he and his personal retinue were traveling were painted red, and poles were set up with lanterns for sailing at night. The pilots of the other ships were then ordered to follow these three ships. Furthermore, the pilots were instructed that when the fleet was about to sail from anchorage, trumpets would be used to announce the departure so that no ships would straggle behind the main body.

After taking these precautions, the fleet sailed for Sigeum and then to Malea, Taenarum, and finally Methone (Methoni in modern-day Greece), where it was to pick up Valerianus, Martinus, and their troops. As the wind had becalmed, Belisarius disembarked the army and camped until the winds would pick up again. During the stay at Methone, many soldiers died from eating spoiled food.

John, the praetorian prefect, had been put in charge of supplying the army with provisions for the voyage. Because of the length of the voyage, the soldiers had been issued double-baked bread. Bread baked this way stays preserved longer and weighs less, because the water in it has evaporated. For that reason, the Roman soldiers normally received one-fourth more bread for their rations, when such bread was distributed.

The praetorian prefect was, however, paid on the basis of the weight of normal bread, so to save money he calculated how he could reduce the amount of firewood used and how to pay the bakers less. Also, the reduced weight of the double baked bread was bothering him, as he was paid for ordinary bread. Instead of having the dough baked at the bakers, he brought it to the public baths of Achilles in Constantinople, in the basement of which there was constantly a fire burning to heat the water. Here his men baked it until it seemed somewhat cooked, then they threw it into bags and put it on the ships.

At Methone, the loaves had almost disintegrated into flour again and had become rotten and moldy. The rotten bread was dispensed to the soldiers, five hundred of whom became sick and died in the hot Greek weather. When Belisarius found this out, bread from the local bakers was bought and the matter reported to the emperor, who did not feel it was the right time to punish the powerful praetorian prefect.

From Methone, the fleet sailed to Zacynthus (Zakynthos), where water was taken on to cross the Adriatic Sea. The wind was again lacking, so it was only on the sixteenth day from Zacynthus that the army finally landed at a deserted place in Sicily, close to Mount Aetna. The voyage from Constantinople to Sicily had taken about two months.

THE LANDING IN NORTH AFRICA

The army had been demoralized by the long journey and greatly feared a possible naval battle with the Vandal fleet. Belisarius also wanted to know how prepared the Vandals were, how many soldiers they had, how they fought, and similar information. So he sent his adviser, Procopius the historian, to Syracusa (Syracuse in modern-day Italy) to look into matters. It turned out the Vandals were not even aware the Roman expedition had left Constantinople. Furthermore, King Gelimer was distracted by Pudentius's revolt in Tripolitania and another by his own governor in Sardinia. To subdue the latter, he had sent five thousand Vandal warriors under his brother Tzazon and, more importantly, one hundred and twenty warships. The king himself was at the head of the royal army at Hermione, four days away from the coast. Belisarius was thus able, after buying provisions and horses at the local markets, to land unopposed in Africa at Caput Vada (Chebba in modern-day Tunisia), about one hundred and thirty miles southeast of Carthage, the Vandal capital. About three months had now passed since the fleet left Constantinople.

After quickly establishing a fortified camp on the coast, Belisarius formed the plan of going straight to Carthage, while Gelimer was still inland. After several local revolts in the time of Gaiseric, the Vandals had razed all city walls in the kingdom except the one around Carthage. If the Roman army could gain control of Carthage, it would have a secure base of operations from which to fight the Vandals.

The Vandals were horsemen who fought with swords and lances, and they had little knowledge of the use of javelins and bows. Nor were they accustomed to dismounting and fighting as infantry. It was therefore best to fight them from a fortified city or camp to which it would be possible to retreat. Otherwise a rout would result in a total disaster for the Romans, who were mainly an infantry force.

The propaganda war was also immediately initiated: it was proclaimed that the Romans had come to remove the usurper Gelimer and restore the rightful king, Hilderic. They had not come to fight the Libyans (as they called the local Romans), but the men of Gelimer. The troops were given strict orders not to plunder the local inhabitants but to pay for the things they needed.

Belisarius sent on a vanguard of three hundred men commanded by John, an aide of Belisarius's (the popular Dorotheus had died in Sicily), and the allied Huns were sent to screen the left flank. The sea and the Roman fleet guarded the right flank. Meanwhile, Belisarius moved slowly with the main army along the coast road, passing through Leptis and Hadrumentum (Sousse—briefly renamed Justinianopolis after the war with the Vandals).

When Gelimer, who was in Hermione, heard of the Roman landing, he sent his brother Ammatas, who was in Carthage, to assemble as many Vandals as possible and prepare to ambush the Romans in the suburb of Ad Decimum (At the Tenth Milestone), about thirteen kilometers outside Carthage. Here they would trap Belisarius between the troops of Gelimer, who were following close behind the Romans, Ammatas coming from Carthage, and a detachment of two thousand Vandals under Gelimer's nephew Gibamund, who was moving parallel with the Roman main force.

Ammatas was also instructed to kill the imprisoned Hilderic, which he did immediately.

BATTLE OF AD DECIMUM

The Romans were made aware of the main Vandal army moving behind them when a series of nighttime skirmishes between scouts ensued. It was still not known, however, how many and how close the Vandals were.

Gelimer's plan was sound, and had Belisarius not taken precautions, the situation could well have ended in disaster for the Romans. The plan might even have succeeded if not for Ammatas, who went to Decimum ahead of time with only a small part of his forces, commanding the rest in Carthage to come as soon as possible. So, around September 13, 533, the small force of Ammatas came into contact with the vanguard of John at Decimum. Despite great personal bravery, single-handedly killing twelve Roman soldiers, Ammatas was killed in the fight, and his troops were routed. The remainder of Ammatas's army was coming along the road from Carthage in small bands of twenty and thirty warriors, and at the sight of the fleeing Vandals joined in the rout. John followed up his victory all the way to Carthage, slaughtering the barbarians in great numbers.

At the same time, Gibamund, with his two thousand Vandals, had reached Pedion Halon, about four and a half miles from Decimum. There he encountered the elite Hunnish cavalry, who made short work of his troops, quickly destroying them.

Meanwhile, Belisarius left his infantry in a fortified camp about four miles from Decimum and sent on his cavalry. His vanguard reached Decimum and saw the battlefield, where Ammatas lay. At the same time, Gelimer came up with his army and a fight ensued; the Romans were defeated and fled down the coastal road toward Belisarius.

The Vandals could still have won the day if Gelimer had followed up his victory against the army of Belisarius or moved against John's detachment, which had been disorganized by the pursuit of Ammatas's troops. Instead, when seeing his brother lying among the fallen, Gelimer broke down weeping and insisted on taking care of his burial on the spot.

Belisarius was not slow to receive his fleeing vanguard, and after organizing them he went immediately against the Vandal army at Decimum. Unprepared and in disorder, the Vandals were quickly put to flight by Belisarius's cavalry, and on September 13, he could rest his weary but victorious army on the battlefield. Meanwhile, Gelimer and his Vandals were in full flight toward Numidia and the plain of Boulla. It seems surprising that Gelimer did not move to

Carthage with his troops, but he considered that the city walls were in such disrepair that the city could not be held. Also, the civilian population was strongly in favor of the Roman cause. The other Vandals in the cities gave themselves up or fled.

On the day after the battle, Belisarius united with his infantry, cautiously moved toward Carthage, and camped outside the city. On the second day the Roman army entered the capital and was met by the jubilant inhabitants. It was found that Hilderic had already been killed on the orders of Gelimer. This strengthened the legitimacy of the campaign. Now the Romans would appear to be revenging the murder of the rightful Vandal king.

Belisarius billeted his troops in Carthage as in any other Roman city, and Procopius, somewhat surprised, notes that the troops were moving around in the city in an orderly fashion without taking advantage of the situation to plunder the inhabitants.

A Vandal attempt to get help from the Visigoths in Spain was rejected. The Visigoths stood behind the Ostrogoths in their attitude towards the Vandals, and the swift and decisive victory of Belisarius probably also weighed strongly. As a result of the victory at Ad Decimum, most of the Moorish tribes offered their allegiance to the Romans.

Meanwhile Belisarius was busy repairing the fortifications of Carthage and also had a ditch dug around the city walls. Pledges of safety were given to those Vandals who had sought sanctuary in the churches.

THE BATTLE OF TRICAMARUM

With the whole Vandal kingdom disintegrating before his eyes, Gelimer had little choice other than to march back to Carthage and fight Belisarius. He gathered his remaining Vandals, and some Moors who were still friendly to him. Despite now officially supporting the Romans, the Moors were still awaiting the outcome of the situation and sent no troops to Belisarius.

Tzazon, Gelimer's brother, had meanwhile defeated the rebels in Sardinia and soon received word from Africa of the grave situation. He and his army immediately set sail, landed on the coast of Africa, and marched to the plain of Boulla, some four days from Carthage, where Gelimer was organizing his troops. The reunion was an unhappy one, and Procopius relates how the two brothers fell on one another's necks and remained locked in a long, silent embrace, neither able to speak for tears.

The Vandals hoped for treachery among the Romans and so entered into secret negotiations with the Roman Hunnic allies, who decided to support the victor in the coming battle, be it Roman or Vandal. Meanwhile, Gelimer had moved close enough to Carthage to cut the aqueduct and block the roads. Belisarius, trusting in the open areas where his cavalry would be superior, sent his army against the Vandal king.

The two armies met at Tricamarum, some nineteen miles west of Carthage, where they deployed with a small stream between them. On the Roman side, Martinus, Valerianus, John, Cyprianus, Althias, and Marcellus held the left wing, and Pappas, Barbatus, Aigan the Hun, and the other cavalry commanders commanded the right wing. In the center was another John with the bodyguard of Belisarius and his standard. Belisarius also came to the center leading five hundred horsemen, leaving the infantry behind advancing at a walk. The Huns were stationed at the rear, as they disliked mingling with the rest of the Roman army if they could avoid it. This position was also particularly favorable to their plans to see who was winning before joining the fight.

The Vandal wings were led by the *chiliarchs*—a term for a high ranking Vandal officer—and the center was commanded by Tzazon, with the allied Moors in reserve. Gelimer himself moved around to urge on the troops where needed.

The armies stood waiting for a while, after which John attacked the Vandal center in three charges with the elite bodyguard of Belisarius. The Vandals repulsed the Romans in the first two charges, but in the third, Tzazon was killed and the Vandal center started to flee. With the rest of the Roman forces now crossing the stream, it soon turned into a full rout, and the undecided Huns joined the pursuit. The Vandals fled into their fortified camp, while the Romans stripped the Vandal dead of their valuables. The losses were eight hundred Vandals to fifty Romans.

Toward evening the same day, when the Roman infantry arrived, Belisarius attacked the Vandal camp. Gelimer fled at the onset with a small group of his kinsmen and left the rest of the Vandals to fend for themselves. When the camp was taken, the Romans were astonished by the amount of treasure in it; all the treasures the Vandals had taken from the sack of Rome in 455 and their constant raids on the Romans and Goths were there. The capture of the Vandals' camp happened three months after the Roman army had come to Carthage, on about December 15, 533.

The surviving Vandals were collected in Carthage so they could be sent to Constantinople in the spring for enrollment in the Roman army—a common thing to do with defeated barbarians in this period. The escaped Gelimer was shut up in a mountainous fortress by the pursuing Roman forces, and Pharas with his Herulians was sent to guard him, as it was too difficult to capture the place.

Meanwhile, Belisarius proceeded to occupy their outlying dominions, including Sardinia, Corsica, and the Balearic Islands, Minorca and Majorca, and even occupied Septem (Ceuta) opposite Gibraltar. The Moorish chieftains, who had caused much trouble to the Vandals and had awaited the outcome of the struggle, renewed their allegiance to the empire.

Troops were also sent to the city of Lilybaeum (Marsala) in Sicily, which had been given to the Vandals as dowry of the Ostrogoth Princess Amalafrida, when she had married the Vandal King Thrasamund (496–523). The Ostrogoths, who had already occupied the important city and its fortress, did not surrender it to the Romans, claiming it was now their possession. Sending troops there was a political move more than anything else. Belisarius was well aware that the Goths would not suffer the Romans to gain a secure foothold and a great harbor in Sicily. But Belisarius could now send an angry note to the Gothic commanders holding the city claiming that they had taken over a Roman possession, which the Romans had gained by defeating the Vandals and the usurper Gelimer. The threat was war, and not only for Lilybaeum, but for the entire Ostrogothic kingdom. On receiving this strongly worded note, the Gothic commanders brought it to Queen Amalasuntha,

Vandal coin of Gelimer from the mint at Carthage, depicting a soldier standing with spear and the head of horse. (*Author*)

who was governing the kingdom for her son, the young King Athalaric. She directed them to answer that they did not agree that the city was Roman, but that they were willing to bring the matter before the emperor for arbitration. The Romans were in all military matters eager to secure the moral high ground and have a just reason for a war, and by this apt maneuvering, Belisarius had already prepared the diplomacy for the war against the Ostrogoths. The Romans could now claim that the Ostrogoths had wrongfully taken over one of their cities.

At the start of spring 534, Gelimer was finally forced to surrender because of lack of provisions.

After ninety-five years of Vandal rule, North Africa was once more Roman. The Vandal nation had been crushed. Procopius estimated that the number of Vandals in Africa at the time of Belisarius was about eighty thousand men and that almost all perished in the war. There would be no Vandal rebellions, as there was no one left to fight.

For the Romans, it was an enormous success of strategic importance. In just a few months, North Africa had been taken without any damage to speak of. The great treasure of the Vandals was theirs and was to be sent to Constantinople to finance the coming operations against the Ostrogoths. The taking of Sicily and Italy and the destruction of the Ostrogothic kingdom—the strongest and most organized barbarian nation on former Roman soil—was now possible. The Roman fleet would be able to operate everywhere without fear of attack from the Vandal fleet, and provisions could be brought from North Africa when needed. Furthermore, Belisarius had studied the conduct of the war and was able to field a more efficient army. All the major battles had been won with the use of his five thousand cavalry, with the infantry not even being present. This arm was therefore strengthened greatly. The Vandals and Ostrogoths had similar troop types, so Belisarius had been able to study how to defeat the strong barbarian heavy cavalry. Particularly, the fight between the Hunnish horse archers and Gibamund's detachment of two thousand cavalry, in which the Vandals were destroyed with no loss to the Huns, was tactically interesting. Accordingly, the other Roman cavalry was trained further in these tactics, so as to be able to function as both shock cavalry and horse archers. It is particularly in his ability to study and adapt that Belisarius's military genius is seen at its strongest.

To the rest of the world, the prestige of the victory was great. One Roman general and five thousand cavalry had defeated the fierce and warlike Vandal nation, once the fear of all the Mediterranean. Justinian's preparations and gamble had paid off in full when he had taken advantage of a unique diplomatic and military situation.

The Reorganization of Africa

In 534, Justinian issued instructions for the civil and military organization of the reconquered provinces. Archelaus was appointed praetorian prefect of Africa, and Solomon was made master of the soldiers (*magister militum*, the senior commanding general in a praetorian prefecture) in Africa and was left with part of Belisarius's bodyguard. Because much of the frontier territory, including all the country west of Caesarea, had been lost to the Moors by the Vandals, the Roman generals were instructed to recover the lost territory and to re-establish the old *limes*—the military border—and to build up regiments of *limitanei*—local garrison troops—to patrol it as soon as possible in order to relieve the strain on the field army.

The great success did, however, cause some problems. Several of Belisarius's officers, perhaps envious, reported to the emperor that he was seeking to become king in Africa, now that he had the treasure of the Vandals. Accordingly, Justinian gave him the choice to either stay in Africa or to bring back the treasure to Constantinople personally. To stay would be seen as treason. The danger of a successful and rich general was not lost on Justinian, who was a keen student of the turbulent earlier Roman history. But there was no question of Belisarius's loyalty, so he prepared for his journey back to Constantinople.

He took with him the captured Gelimer and several thousand Vandal prisoners, who were enrolled in five regiments for use on the Eastern frontier. He also brought with him the enormous treasure of the Vandals.

On coming to Constantinople, he was granted a triumph, a special honor awarded to particularly successful generals. This was the first triumph celebrated by a Roman subject since the reign of Augustus (31 BC-AD 14), as only emperors and their close relatives were permitted so great an honor. It would also be the final triumph celebrated in the history of the Roman Empire. The occasion was celebrated with much pomp, and Belisarius went from his house in the suburbs to the Hippodrome, where the victorious general and the defeated king of the Vandals bowed before the emperor. He would receive further honors, and on January, 1, 535, he entered the consulate and on his procession through the streets of Constantinople scattered coins from the Vandal treasure to the jubilant populace.

Gelimer and his family were given lands in Galatia in Asia Minor and permitted to live there until they died, and Hilderic's children received great sums of money.

The stage was now set for the next and most important phase of the reconquest: the attack on the Ostrogothic kingdom in Italy. The emperor had decided that the time was ripe for the war, which he had long prepared for diplomatically, to start in 535.

2

THE
OSTROGOTHS

•

THEIR ORIGINS

Nothing much concrete is known about Ostrogothic history, especially not about the early periods. Even the name Ostrogoth is a
product of the late fourth and early fifth centuries, a long time after
Gothic society had been heavily influenced by contact with Roman
society. The Goths as a nation entered Roman history in the middle of the third century AD, but they had long existed far from the
eyes of Roman historians. The Gutones, a Germanic tribe, is mentioned in Roman sources from around AD 16–18. The first recorded instance of the Latin-Roman use of the name Goths is in 269,
when Emperor Claudius II (268–270) assumed the triumphal
name Gothicus. At least at the end of the first century, a people
called Goths were living somewhere in Northeast Europe, along
the limits of the Roman-Germanic world, where few Roman goods
were seen and fewer Roman traders had traveled. There the tribes
were living a simple and hard life. Over the generations, a sparse
population would travel from place to place and settle for some
years. They were living in small groups, rarely numbering more
than a hundred persons and perhaps only met in larger groups in
connection with religious festivals.

During the second and third centuries, these little groups were
slowly drawn toward the Roman Empire, with its luxurious goods
and great power and riches. It was not an organized migration of a
nation, but a slow filtering of families and individuals toward the

south, where they came into contact with the so-called Chernyakhov culture and, slowly over the years, became the dominant group in the region northwest of the Black Sea.

It is important to understand that there were no great wars and nations on the move, but a gradual aggregation of the local tribes and the newcomers under the name Goths. As the Goths slowly became a more territorial and political entity, they clashed with the other Germanic tribes in the region. Wars were fought against the Marcomanni, Quadi, and other tribes, such as the Gepids, with whom a feud arose that would echo in the myths of Gothic early history. Ethnicity in a tribe was fluid. To be a Goth or to be part of the Gothic confederation was more a question of attitude than a question of race and ethnicity. In this way the Gothic confederation consisted of changing tribes that either left the alliance or slowly lost their ethnic identity. Accordingly, a Hun or a Sarmatian could call himself a Goth, even if he would be considered otherwise with modern eyes. It was only later that the Goths could begin to challenge the empire. Not until the period of Emperor Traianus Decius (249–251) did the Romans meet an organized assault of a tribal coalition led by the Goths.

Roman coins perhaps best show the true nature of the barbarian attacks on the empire in the disastrous third century. The coins regularly celebrated an emperor's victories over the Germans in the traditional manner all through the third century. The names of wars and victories over nations they knew the names of were put on coins, such as *Victoria Carpica* (victory over the Carpi), who were members of the Gothic tribal coalition. But it was difficult for the Romans to distinguish the changing barbarian alliances from each other, and many victories are simply commemorated by the legend *Victoria Germanica*, without any precise ethnic attribution. The first coin with the legend *Victoria Gothii*, celebrating a victory specifically over the Goths, was struck under Claudius II. From then on the coins follow at increasing speed under Aurelian (270–275), Tacitus (275–276), Probus (276–282), and Constantine the Great (306–337). By reading the Roman coins, it can be gleaned that the struggle for power in the region of the Lower Danube was won by the Gothic tribal coalition around the middle of the third century.

By the time of Constantine, the region between the Dniester and Bug rivers was termed Gothia in Roman sources.

Even though the Goths lived some distance from the Roman border and therefore only rarely came into contact with the Romans, their chieftains were important enough to receive yearly tributes. This is seen perhaps as early as in 238, when Tullius Menophilus, general in the province of Moesia, tried to break the alliance between the Goths and Carpi. In 238, the Goths and Carpi crossed the Danube and devastated the area around the mouth of the Danube. The Romans bought the Goths off but offered nothing to the Carpi, who angrily replied that they were stronger than the Goths and therefore should be given more money. If they weren't, they threatened to continue the invasion. Until 248, the Carpi led a tribal coalition that included the Taifali, the Asdingi Vandals, the Peucini, and the Goths, when the Goths took over leadership of the loosely knit confederation.

In exchange for the annual payments that started in 238, the Goths had to supply the Romans with troops for their campaigns against the Persians. From 238 to 248, only Carpic invasions are reported in the historical sources. In 246 and 248, Emperor Philip I (244–249), surnamed "the Arab," defeated Carpic armies and celebrated triumphs over them.

THE CAMPAIGN OF 248–251

In 248, Philip felt strong enough to stop the annual payments and renounce the treaty with the now Gothic alliance. For a Germanic tribe, the act of giving gifts was almost sacred. To stop the gifts was in their eyes treason, and they immediately prepared for war.

Philip sent the able General Traianus Decius to Moesia to coordinate the Roman troops on the Danube and the defense against the Gothic confederation. Decius, however, soon made himself popular among the strong troop contingents stationed at the border and was proclaimed emperor by them. In the summer of 249, he marched to Italy to fight Philip, taking with him the Danubian army. The frontier was thereby left undefended, and the Goths, probably astounded, could make their threats real. In the spring of 250, the Gothic King Cniva crossed the Danube at the head of

Coin of Claudius Gothicus with the text "Victoriae Gothic" with a trophy and two captives on the obverse. (*Author*)

three columns of barbarians. The Goths were the dominant tribe, with the Carpi, Bastarnae, Taifali, and Vandals mentioned as other members of the alliance. The invasion was aimed at the provinces of Dacia and Moesia, which were soon plundered. Except for the siege of Marcianopolis (Devna in modern-day Bulgaria) in 248, and two years later Philippopolis (Plovdiv), the Goths avoided the Roman cities, which they did not know how to attack. The Romans brought their food into the cities, and without a system of supply, the Goths soon had to split up into several smaller groups to search for food.

Meanwhile, Decius had defeated Philip and hurried back to the troubled frontier. He quickly collected troops from the whole Balkan region and moved against the Goths. By marching against the war bands separately, he achieved several successes destroying them one by one. In late spring of 250, Decius was hard on the heels of Cniva, who was retreating through the Balkan Mountains. Decius hoped to relieve the beleaguered Philippopolis, which had been under siege for some time. While Decius was resting his troops at Beroea (Veria) after crossing the Shipka Pass, Cniva turned round and attacked the disorganized Romans, who had to retreat. Philippopolis was lost in the summer of 250, and Decius was unable to continue the campaign until the spring of 251.

The Goths wintered in Philippopolis and began the journey home in the spring of 251. The army was laden with the spoils of the campaign and huge numbers of slaves. Decius, however, was not

Traianus Decius's gold coin with the inscription "Victoria Germanica" on the reverse. The the emperor would be defeated and killed the year after this coin was minted. (*Author*)

satisfied with the Goths' leaving the region unmolested and moved after them. Unwilling to engage in a regular battle, Decius and his son Herennius Etruscus, who had just been named augustus and co-emperor, were harrying the rear of the unwieldy Gothic army and achieved several successes. Meanwhile, General Trebonianus Gallus was waiting at the Danube after having defeated several barbarian war bands. The Goths were in an uncomfortable position, with Roman troops at their front and back. Cniva, however, showed his tactical abilities again. In June 251, in the vicinity of Abrittus (Razgrad in modern-day Bulgaria), Decius and his army were ambushed in a swamp and severely beaten; the emperor and his son were left dead on the battlefield. The year before, coins had been minted with the now-ironic legend "*Victoria Germanica.*"

Trebonianus Gallus was proclaimed emperor by the troops, but he had to allow the Goths to return to their homelands with their rich spoils and thousands of captured Romans, and was even forced to promise annual payments to them. Trebonianus had no choice but to offer generous terms to end the war as soon as possible in order to secure his position as emperor. The Goths themselves were only too eager to accept the proposal, as they had suffered serious casualties during the campaign and wanted to bring back their loot without the danger of crossing the Danube against enemy troops.

The Decian strategy of defending the frontier and, if it was breached, re-establishing it behind the barbarians and fighting with inverted fronts could have caused the destruction of the invading barbarians and would later cause serious problems to the second great Gothic invasion in 253–254. At the same time, the previous invasions and the plague had devastated the frontier provinces so much that the barbarians no longer could live off the land as during previous invasions, and the Goths faced immediate supply problems after crossing the Roman frontier.

It can be difficult to understand what made the barbarians return again and again after often suffering horrendous losses or total annihilation. The answer is manifold; both the lure of the loot that some would bring back and the warrior culture of the Germanic tribes have been cited. The ones who stayed behind saw only the returning heroes.

Hunger was also one of the main causes for the migrations. The primitive subsistence farming in Barbaricum could not feed a great population, and most tribes were in an almost constant state of hunger due to overpopulation. The barbarians could either fight other tribes for food or raid the Roman Empire, with its fruitful and well-farmed lands.

The Gothic Invasion of 253–254

The next war with the Goths came in 253, when the governor of Moesia, Aemilianus, refused to pay the annual subsidies to the Gothic tribes. The Goths promptly invaded Moesia and Thrace, the provinces that had already suffered from the campaigns of 248–251. Aemilianus was, however, a capable general and had not stopped the payments without preparing for war. In a surprising move, he crossed the Danube and defeated the Goths in their own territory. This did not keep some war bands from plundering Moesia and Thrace, but there would be no talk of an organized Gothic invasion—or so it would appear.

The inherent instability in third century Roman society once again made itself felt. Following Aemilianus's victory, his troops proclaimed him emperor, and as was now almost a custom, he moved against Italy together with the Danube army, leaving the troubled frontier wide open. With their limited understanding of Roman politics and the scope of the vast Roman Empire, the Goths must have been flabbergasted at the sudden disappearance of the victorious Roman soldiers. The Goths soon recovered from the surprise and invaded the Roman provinces in 253. They were still recovering from the battle with Aemilianus and so did not cause much damage, but the undefended frontier was a beacon to all the tribes in the region, and in 254 the Goths invaded in strength at the head of a multitribe coalition. In the campaign of 254, they penetrated all the way to Thessalonica (Thessaloniki) in Greece, though they failed to take it.

SEABORNE INVASIONS

The general success of the invasions of 253 and 254 caused even more barbarians to try their hand at invading the empire. With the loss of the Roman Bosporan client kingdom on the Crimea to the Goths and Sarmatians, the Bosporan navy no longer patrolled the Black Sea. Instead, the barbarians used the Bosporan navy to raid the Roman coasts. After an initial defeat around 255 at Pityus (Pitsunda in modern-day Abkhazia/Georgia) on the slope of the Caucasus Mountains, a combined Gothic-Borani force sailed off in 256 to attack the sanctuary of Rhea Cybele at Phasis. The raid failed, but the barbarians attacked Pityus again, this time successfully. The great city of Trebizond (Trabzon in modern-day Turkey) was even sacked when the surprised garrison fled at the approach of the Goths. Letters of Bishop Gregorius Thaumaturgus of Neocaesarea (Niksar) in Pontus Polemoniacus show that many of the provincials actively supported the barbarians to get a share of the rich booty, or turned to plundering themselves.

In 257, the now seagoing Goths ravaged the southwestern coast of the Black Sea for the first time. Here the troops would march along the coast, while the fleet of small vessels and fishing boats would follow. The Goths could now ferry their army to the coast of Asia Minor to plunder the rich provinces there. Chalcedon (Kadiköy) was taken without a fight, and Nicomedia (Izmit), Nicaea (Iznik), Cius, and Apamea were sacked. A local Greek betrayed Nicomedia, and often internal treachery would help the Goths take the rich and untouched cities of Asia Minor.

These raids continued until 268, when a new barbarian invasion of unprecedented size began in the spring. A new tribe, the Heruli, had arrived on the scene, and the sources mention them as being part of the Gothic invasion. The Danubian border held, and Dacia was also successfully defended against the major invasion. The Goths and Heruli were not, however, put off by the defeats on land,

and they turned to the sea again. The Gothic fleet was initially beaten in a battle at Byzantium (Istanbul), but succeeded in forcing its way through the Roman fleet in a second attempt. The island of Lemnos was ravaged, and after this success the barbarian fleet split up into three squadrons that operated independently. Attica and possibly the Peloponnesus were attacked. The island of Scyrus (Skyros) was taken and sacked, and so were the cities of Athens, Corinth, Argos, Sparta, and Olympia, where desperate emergency fortifications had been excavated. Temples were torn down, and the columns and statues were used to make crude walls. In 269, another of the squadrons sacked Rhodes, Cyprus, Crete, Side, and the famous temple of Artemis at Ephesus (Efes)—one of the Seven Wonders of the World—although they were unable to take Ephesus itself. The fleet was said to consist of about two thousand smaller boats and suffered occasional losses from their lack of sea-worthiness.

The Romans did what they could to catch the barbarian war bands, and Emperor Gallienus (253–268) destroyed a mainly Herulian detachment northwest of Thessalonica, leaving three thousand Herulians dead on the battlefield and their leader captured. In Attica, a hastily formed militia under the local magnate Dexippus repulsed the barbarians. These battles did not, however, save the Roman cause, as the commander of the field army in Italy rebelled against Gallienus, and parts of the Roman troops in Greece also conspired against the emperor.

Gallienus was killed during the suppression of these rebellions, and Claudius II was established as emperor. While he was the first to be named Gothicus, more would soon follow, such as Aurelian, Tacitus, and Probus. At Naissus (Nish) in 269, the new emperor destroyed the barbarians who had been operating in Greece. Only scattered and broken war bands remained in the Balkan region, and they were later rounded up by Roman forces and taken into the Roman army or settled as *coloni*—dependent farmers—in the devastated regions south of the Danube.

Defeating these war bands had cost the Roman army two thousand legionnaires when the unsupported infantry attacked the Goths in Thrace. The almost complete destruction of the western groups of the invaders seriously weakened the Tervingi, the western Gothic tribes. The eastern part of the barbarians suffered from attacks by the Roman fleet and the eternal enemy of the barbarians, hunger, but many succeeded in returning to their homelands. Meanwhile, the Roman Empire continued its own destruction due to internal struggles for power, and while the Egyptian prefect Probus beat off the eastern Gothic invasion, the rich province of Egypt was lost to the rulers of Palmyra, Odenathus, and Zenobia.

Claudius II was not emperor long; he died of the plague in the winter of 269–270. The soldiers then made Aurelian, the commander of the court cavalry, emperor after the brief reign of Claudius's brother Quintillus. Aurelian immediately set about restoring the fortunes of the staggering empire. In 270 he defeated the Vandals and Iuthungi south of the Danube, and in 271 he marched east to subjugate the kingdom of Palmyra. On the way, Illyricum and Thrace were cleared of barbarian war bands, mostly Carpi. Crossing the Danube, Aurelian defeated the Goths repeatedly in some small engagements and finally won a great battle north of the Danube in which the Gothic King Canabaudes was killed, along with five thousand warriors. The victory gained Aurelian the triumphal title of Gothicus Maximus.

For the Goths, the horrendous losses of the past decades of constant campaigns had torn the heart out of the alliance, and there would be a long peace following the defeat. Despite being in complete control, Aurelian gave up the province of Dacia north of the Danube. Dacia was strategically difficult to hold, and the decision was wise, as the barbarian alliance soon after was dissolved, and fighting started over control of the old Roman province. The western Goths and the Taifali fought with their former allies, the Carpi, the Bastarnian Peucini, and the Vandals, and finally won control of the province.

In the course of the wars, the Bastarnae were repeatedly defeated, and in 280, Probus admitted the greater part of the tribe into the empire and settled them in the empty and devastated province of Thrace. The rest of the tribe followed in 295, and the nearly five-hundred-year history of the Bastarnae ended at the point of a Roman sword, as did that of so many other barbarian tribes. The

Carpi and Gepids would follow soon after, and both tribes were settled in the desolate frontier provinces.

TERVINGI AND GREUTHUNGI

Around 290, the development of the Gothic confederation reached a level where territorialized subgroups of the Gothic alliance could be identified. The tribes of the Greuthungi and Tervingi were different from the other elements of the Gothic confederation, such as the Taifali and the Heruli, in the sense that they were no longer migrating tribes, but were connected to geographic areas north of the Danube.

Tervingi, which may mean "men of the woods," lived in the forest belt from the modern city of Ploesti in the southwest to Copanca in the northeast—roughly west of the upper Dniester and lower Prut rivers. Greuthungi, which may mean "rulers from the steppes," lived further northeast on the open plains. When the Romans spoke of Goths in the fourth century, they meant Tervingi (the name is first mentioned in 291), with whom they were in contact at the frontier.

After Aurelian evacuated the Roman province of Dacia in 275, there were constant struggles in the region between barbarian tribes seeking to enter the power vacuum of the abandoned province. Gothic finds from this period exist and continue after 300, showing that the Tervingi spread their influence in the first decades of the fourth century from their core territories into Dacia.

Aurelian fought the various groups of the Tervingi confederation; some were beaten militarily, others were starved into submission. There was no organized group but a number of war bands under energetic warlords, and it was not possible to make peace with the Tervingi as a nation. Some were taken as slaves, and others were sent home after submitting and offering their services to the empire. At the start of the preparations for Aurelian's Persian campaign, the Tervingi came as promised, but when they found out Aurelian had been murdered and Tacitus made emperor in 275, they rebelled. For a German, loyalty was based on families and individuals—they probably did not even understand the concept of a state.

Map 2. The Roman Empire in 350.

Slavs

Burgundians

Vandals

Huns

ni

ava Quadi

Sarmatians

etio • Aquincum

Iazygians

Siscia Viminacium Goths

Sirmium

Salonae Singidnum • Marcianopolis

Naissus

Tomis
Durosturum

Philippopolis Adrianopolis
Hyzantium • Heraciea
Nicomedia

Thessalonica

Larissa

Athens • Ephesus

yracuse

Crete Cyprus

Persians

I T E R R A N E A N   S E A

Arabs

CIVIL WAR BETWEEN CONSTANTINE AND LICINIUS

Nevertheless, the following emperors would keep the Tervingi in their place by attacking the raiding war bands and driving them back across the Danube. Other groups were received into the empire and settled in the border provinces, many of which had been emptied of inhabitants because of the constant barbarian incursions and the plague. It became customary that Tervingi troops were supplied for major campaigns, as part of their treaty with the empire.

Under Constantine the Great (306–337) and Licinius (308–324), the Goths consolidated themselves further under the two regional tribes, the Tervingi and the Greuthungi.

The tetrarchy—with two senior augusti, emperors of West and East; and two junior caesars—which had brought stability to the Roman Empire, broke down during the civil war between Constantine and Licinius. On March 1, 317, the two rivals made peace and divided the empire. The diocese of Moesia went to Constantine and that of Thrace went to Licinius, thereby destroying the coherency of the Danubian frontier defenses. An effective defense against the Tervingi confederation could only be mounted if both emperors were united and trusted each other. Otherwise, the efficient movement of troops and uniting the armies was impossible.

The danger of the divided defense of the Danube was soon made evident. After Constantine defeated an Iazygian invasion in 322, he prepared for war against his rival. Licinius then withdrew his troops from the frontier, which caused a Tervingian invasion led by a noble named Rausimod. Although the Tervingi initially plundered Licinian territory, it was left to Constantine to push back the Goths. In 323, he crossed the Danube and destroyed the war band, and Rausimod was killed. But Constantine had been forced to enter Licinian territory to defend against the invasion, which gave Licinius a *casus belli* and the support of the Tervingi. The Tervingian warriors were led by a Prince Alica in the civil war. When Licinius was deposed, he sought to regain power with the help of the Tervingi, and when his plot was discovered and he was sentenced to death, he fled to the Tervingi. Licinius was caught in 324, and Constantine became sole emperor of the Roman Empire. And he was not about to forget the Tervingi support for his rival.

CAMPAIGNS OF CONSTANTINE THE GREAT AGAINST THE GOTHS

Constantine was busy elsewhere until the summer of 328, when he had a stone bridge built across the Danube at Sucidava (Celeiu in modern-day Romania). At the same time a fortress was built at Daphne (Spanţov in modern-day Romania) on the northern bank of the Danube in the territory of the Tervingi and Taifali, and a ferry established there. The stone bridge was a great change in the otherwise defensive Roman strategy toward the barbarians in the region. The Tervingi were forced away from the river, and a buffer zone was created along the Danube.

In 332 fights broke out between the Tervingi and the Sarmatians. Constantine took advantage of this and sent an army under his son, Constantine, the later Emperor Constantine II, across the Danube and into the area of the Tervingi. Attacking the preoccupied Tervingi in the rear, he inflicted a devastating defeat on them. The Tervingi group, which had penetrated into Sarmatian territory, had no means of returning, and the sources report that nearly one hundred thousand Tervingi starved and froze to death. While that number probably is overestimated, it still signifies a serious defeat of the Tervingi. It seems evident that Constantine's aggressive strategy of bringing back Roman influence into the regions north of the Danube and to establish barbarian client states to play out against each other was successful.

Peace was made in 332, and the Tervingi promised to provide troops in return for an annual payment, as had become the custom. Border traffic was mainly limited to the two crossing points established by Constantine. By providing the Tervingi nobles with annual payments, which could be withheld to the detriment of the nobility, Constantine created more stability in the region. Furthermore, the sons of Tervingi nobles were brought to Constantinople to experience the luxury of the Roman empire and to act as hostages. At peace with the Romans, the Tervingi turned to fighting the Vandals and Sarmatians north of the Danube, thereby further removing the pressure on the frontier.

The strategy was undermined by Constantine's death in 337, and after a breathing space, the Tervingi struck back in the 340s, when they chose a *iudex*—a form of dictator—to lead their united forces. Roman pressure had thereby created the first united military command among the Tervingi, who had before been ruled by a number of uncoordinated lesser kings and chieftains. There was no talk of a real invasion, but instead a number of raiding war bands. Constantius II (337–361) was busy against the Persians and so had to focus on that greater struggle rather than destroying the marauding Tervingi.

In 349, the old treaty was renewed, and the Tervingi received their traditional donatives. It was now relatively peaceful in the Danube region, but with a stronger Germanic influence than before. When the situation was settled, the position of *iudex* was dissolved, as it was no longer needed.

From the middle of the fourth century, conditions north of the Danube deteriorated. Inscriptions and coins disappeared, and the barbarians slowly gained more and more influence. At the same pace, the Romanized centers north of the Danube and along the Black Sea coast also deteriorated.

The emperors no longer had the strength to take and hold regions north of the Danube, so their strategy again became defensive and aimed to keep the various tribal alliances from being too powerful, and they strengthened the border defenses.

ULFILAS AND THE CONVERSION OF THE GOTHS

The Goths originally worshipped a number of traditional Germanic gods, such as Nerthus and Freyr, gods of agriculture; Wodan, the god of war; and similar deities. They also worshipped their forefathers and their spirits, sometimes personified in wooden statues. When Tacitus described Germanic society in the early second century, he wrote that only the priests—not warlords or even kings—were allowed to punish warriors. It appears that the nobility were the keystones in the actual cult practice, but we do not know if the Goths had holy sites as such or how they worshipped their gods.

The raids in the third century brought many Christian captives to the Gothic lands north of the Danube. They continued to worship during their slavery and inspired Goths to change their religion. Around 311, a Goth named Ulfilas was born into a family whose ancestors had been captured in the raids of the Goths, possibly in Cappadocia in Asia Minor. While the sources on the life of Ulfilas are difficult to use because of their different opinions on Arianism, it can be reconstructed that as a young man he made his first trip to Constantinople between 332 and 337, as a member of a delegation to the Romans.

The Romans found in him a strong Christian belief and a person who could spread Christianity among the Goths north of the Danube. During a later visit, in 341, Ulfilas was consecrated bishop by Eusebius of Nicomedia at the great Council of Antioch and sent back north of the Danube. He stayed there for seven years but was driven out during a persecution of the Christians and moved to Moesia, where he settled with other Christian Goths. There he translated the Bible into the Gothic language with an alphabet he invented using Greek, Latin, and runes.

The Goths did not immediately take to Christianity. The first persecution of Christians in the Gothic lands took place in 348, possibly after a war against the Romans. It might be that in the Christians, the Goths saw Romans. Several were martyred because they resisted worshipping the pagan gods, but otherwise it does not seem to have been a hard persecution. In 369, King Athanaric began a second persecution. This lasted four years, and again there were martyrs, but again it does not appear to have been a great persecution.

The missionary work by Ulfilas and his followers had its greatest impact on the Tervingi, who lived closest to the Danube, and less on the Greuthungi, who lived farther away. Many Greuthungi wouldn't be converted until fifty years after the Tervingi, and some never were. When the Huns came and forced the Goths to migrate into the empire in 376, many were more or less forcibly converted into Christianity by the Romans. Most likely the followers of Ulfilas helped this conversion. Ulfilas died in Constantinople in 383. While his impact on the conversion of the Goths is certain, particularly in his translation of the Bible, it is likely his impact was greatest on the nobility who could read and write and had the leisure to speculate over religion. The conversion of the common farmers would most likely take much longer and happen more gradually. Some parts of the Ostrogothic tribal confederation, such as the Bittuguric Huns, resisted completely and never adopted Christianity.

Arianism

Being an orthodox Christian in the fourth century required walking a narrow path. There were a host of heresies, such as the Monophysite, Dyophysite, Donatist, Manichee, and so on, some of them very localized. St. Augustine, the church father who wrote in the early fifth century, counted eighty-seven different heresies.

Arianism was the teaching of Arius, who lived in Alexandria, Egypt, in the early fourth century. His main point was that God and Jesus were not of the same substance, and that there had been a time when God existed and Jesus did not. His teachings were condemned as heretical at the First Council of Nicaea in 325, but they later regained acceptance. At the Second Ecumenical Council, in Constantinople in 381, Arianism was again decreed a heresy.

Ulfilas was an adherent of the Arian creed when it was well-accepted, and that was the Christianity he taught the Goths. From the Goths, Arianism spread to many other Germanic tribes, such as the Vandals, Burgundians, Heruli, and Lombards. So while Arianism had never been particularly popular within the Roman Empire, it became dominant among the Germanic tribes. The Franks were the only major tribe who were orthodox. The Ostrogoths kept to Arianism until the destruction of their kingdom.

So why did the Ostrogoths stay Arian throughout their later history inside the empire? It is doubtful that they really understood or appreciated the subtle differences between Arianism and the orthodox creed of Athanasius. Some modern historians believe it was a means of differentiating themselves from the other peoples in the empire and from the Romans. But it cannot be said that they were uninterested in Christianity. After all, it must have been somewhat important to them because the sources do not indicate there were ever any discussions of returning to paganism.

It can be argued, however, that the further they were from the royal court, the more the Goths became Christian in name rather than in deed. And not all noble Goths were Christian. Radagaisus, who invaded Italy in 405–406 with some twenty thousand warriors, was pagan and made human sacrifices, according to the sources. The Franks were orthodox Christians, but they did the same later during the Gothic War. And it is not unlikely that many Goths in the turbulent times during the Hunnish invasion faked their conversion in order to enter the empire but kept their pagan beliefs.

WAR WITH EMPEROR VALENS

In 364, at Naissus, Emperors Valentinian I (364–375) and Valens (364–378), his brother, divided the empire and army between them. Valentinian, who was older, took over the Western Empire, with his capital at Mediolanum (Milan in modern-day Italy), and Valens received the Eastern Empire, with its capital of Constantinople.

Valens immediately set about restoring his eastern frontier and marched toward Syria. On the march, somewhere in the province of Bithynia in the summer of 365, he received a message from his commanders at the Danube frontier that the Tervingi were forming a coalition and preparing to attack Thrace. Valens sent two elite cavalry and infantry units to the endangered frontier but continued his march to the east.

While the two units were marching through Constantinople, they were won over by the usurper Procopius to support him as emperor. With Valens still in Asia Minor, Procopius ordered the Tervingi to fulfill their obligations as Roman federates and send him troops. Procopius, who perhaps well understood the Germanic traditions, based his request on his kinship to Constantine the Great and Constantius. As loyalty to the Gothic tribes was based on people and families, the Tervingi dispatched three thousand veteran warriors to his aid. But they arrived too late; Procopius had been deposed and executed on May 27, 366. His relative Marcellus then tried to make himself emperor with the help of the Tervingi federates, but he failed.

Their task finished, the Tervingi started to march home, believing they were still allies of the Roman Empire and had performed the requested duty. The situation was a glaring example of the cultural misunderstandings that occasionally arose from the widely different civilizations and the limited Gothic understanding of the complex Roman politics. To the Tervingi, it appeared that the Roman emperor—a descendant of the great Constantine, with whom they had made a treaty—had requested help, which they had given. Whom or why they were fighting was probably rather unclear to the barbarians.

To Emperor Valens, it was treachery of the utmost form to support a usurper against him. The Gothic contingent marching home was overpowered by Roman troops without bloodshed and interned in various Thracian cities. As the churchman Eunapius writes: ". . . the king of the Scythians [the Tervingi are meant] demanded back these noble warriors. The case was embarrassing and difficult to settle justly." Meanwhile Valens sent envoys to Tervingi King Athanaric—one of several kings it appears, but who acted as spokesman for the Tervingi tribes—demanding an explanation of their support for Procopius. Athanaric showed the letter from Procopius requesting the aid of the Roman federates, but Valens did not accept the Tervingi explanations. The captives were not handed over, and nothing more is heard about them in the sources.

After consultations with his older brother, Valens prepared for a full-scale war against the Tervingi and put off his eastern plans. There could be no risk of barbarian tribes supporting usurpers to the imperial throne in the future.

In the spring of 367, the preparations were ready and Valens launched his campaign that was to last late into the summer of 369. A pontoon bridge was thrown across the Danube at the fortress of Daphne, and the Roman army crossed into the Tervingi territories. Athanaric, once again appointed *iudex,* or *kindins* in Gothic, and leader of the Tervingi tribal confederation, evaded the Roman army again and again while attacking Roman foragers and patrols and conducting the war in a guerrilla manner. The Roman forces were unable to catch the barbarian army and instead burned the Tervingi villages and drove off any captured livestock or Tervingi they happened to catch. At the end of the campaign season in 367, Valens returned across the pontoon bridge to Roman territory, having achieved little of consequence.

In 368, the Danube was flooded, and Valens was unable to cross the river. He wintered at Marcianopolis, having achieved nothing that year. The floods did, however, cause the Tervingi great problems. Roman troops had burned the harvest of 367, and floods destroyed the harvest of 368. Starvation became a serious problem to the Tervingi, who knew that Valens would continue his campaign the next year.

In 369, the emperor again crossed the Danube on a pontoon bridge at a new place, Noviodunum (Isaccea in modern-day Romania), and invaded what is now Bessarabia. Here his forces encountered a Greuthungian cavalry force that had been sent to aid the beleaguered Tervingi. This was the first direct Roman contact with the ancestors of the Ostrogoths. The Greuthungi withdrew hastily from the impressive imperial army, and the Romans marched on. As they penetrated deeper and deeper into the Tervingian homeland, Athanaric was finally brought to bay. The Tervingi were defeated but managed to flee with their remaining forces; soon after they opened negotiations with the Romans. The Tervingi tribes were unable to win a sustained war against the Romans, and tens of thousands must have starved to death. For Valens, the war was a sideshow with little financial gain and fought almost entirely to make the barbarians refrain from supporting usurpers and to pre-empt a Tervingi invasion by the united tribes.

In September 369, Valens and Athanaric made peace. The negotiations took place on a boat anchored in the middle of the Danube, as Athanaric, for obscure religious reasons, refused to set foot on Roman soil. Trade between the Tervingi and the Romans was restricted to two border points. The annual subsidies were stopped, and the Tervingi had to hand over hostages. The Tervingi were allowed to persecute Christians in the Tervingi territories, which they did with a ruthless efficiency. Valens earned the title Gothicus for this war.

The Coming of the Huns

Peace came, but only for a short period, as the powerful Huns had appeared in the East and were on their way from the steppes of Ukraine. Valens's campaign had, however, had several important results among the Goths. The unfortunate Athanaric lost influence and power because of his surrender, and other Tervingi nobles, such as Alavivus and Fritigern (who would play an important part in the battle of Adrianopolis [Edirne in modern-day Turkey] in 378), could increase their power at his expense. For the Greuthungi, the new Roman threat had caused their king, Ermanaric, to create a confederation with the tribe and their neighbors, known around the start of the fifth century as the Ostrogoths. The Tervingi around the same time strengthened their unity by selecting Athanaric as the one leader in the confederation later known as the Visigoths.

When the Huns began their attacks on the Greuthungi in the early 370s, the Goths once again had to face a life-or-death situation. Ermanaric committed suicide rather than submit to the Huns. Vithimir then became king of the Greuthungi confederation and continued the desperate struggle, but fell in battle shortly after. His son, Videric, a minor, then became king under the guidance of two nobles, Alatheus and Saphrax, and was left with a people in chaos.

With a choice between the Romans and the Huns, the Greuthungi were caught between the hammer and the anvil, and had to choose who to submit to. Most of them surrendered to the Huns; the rest, under Videric, the child king, fled to the Roman Empire. But the remnants of the confederation of Ermanaric reached the Danube too late. The Tervingi were already crossing into the Roman Empire, fleeing the Huns.

In the summer of 376, the Tervingian *iudex*, Athanaric, led a strong army all the way to the west bank of the Dniester to determine the truth behind the rumors of the coming of the Huns. A Hunnish force crossed the Dniester during a moonlit night and surprised the Tervingi army. The experienced Athanaric managed to withdraw with few losses. He then retreated and started to fortify the southern flank of the central plateau of Moldavia with an enormous rampart. A Hunnic war band retreating from a successful raid further south once again surprised the Tervingi, and they were again defeated. But they were saved by the Huns' preoccupation with their loot, which kept them from pursuing the Tervingi. Hunnish war bands at the same time ravaged the regions of modern Moldavia and Bessarabia, thereby destroying the food supply for the Tervingi confederation, which was still suffering from the destruction caused by the war with Valens. Beaten and starved, the Tervingi confederation began to dissolve. A large Tervingi group under the nobles Alavivus and Fritigern broke off and sought refuge in the Roman Empire.

When the Roman administration understood the dimensions of the migration, the Danube fleet was dispatched to block the river. No one was allowed to cross; those who tried were turned back with force. Messages explaining the situation were sent to Emperor Valens, who was at Antioch in the east. The case was much debated at the imperial court, but it was decided that the advantages outweighed the disadvantages and that the Tervingi should be allowed into the empire. The permission to accept the Tervingi, disarm them, and settle them in the devastated Thracian provinces arrived in the autumn of 376, and the group under Alavivus and Fritigern were allowed to cross over with their Tervingi. For the Romans, it was a chance to gain cheap manpower for the army and to settle the empty Thracian provinces, while gaining an important buffer at the frontier against future barbarian invasions.

Because Athanaric did not believe the Romans would accept the remaining Tervingi into the empire, he led the starved remains into a region known as Caucalanda in the Carpathians to get out of the way of the Huns. Here they drove out the local Sarmatian tribes from their villages to get enough food to survive the winter. The domino effect of the Hunnic migration was being felt more and more in the region. In the words of Bishop Ambrose of Milan (374–397—the quote is most likely written at the end of 378): "The Huns threw themselves upon the Alans, the Alans upon the Goths, and the Goths upon the Taifali and Sarmatae; the Goths, exiled from their own country, made us exiles in Illyricum, and the end is not yet."

The late arriving Greuthungi envoys asked the Roman emperor for their people to be received into the empire, but without success.

The Roman commander in Thrace, Lupicinus, and the governor, Maximus, tried to stem the growing migration and control it as much as possible. The difficulty of the operation was obvious to the Romans. It was no longer mere barbarian war bands, but entire nations asking to be received into the empire. The immigrants, mainly Tervingi, who had already crossed the river were checked for weapons and dispersed to several camps in the area. The Romans were not unhappy about barbarian immigrants they could use for labor and war, but there were simply too many. The pressure on the local food supplies was growing daily. Gothic groups, mainly Tervingi, had for several months plundered the areas north of the Danube while waiting for the emperor to accept them. Famine among the Tervingi who had already crossed was so great that some parents sold their children to the slave traders rather than see them starve to death. Dishonest Roman officials increased the tensions, and Lupicinus was forced to take away troops from the navy patrolling the Danube to use as escort for the Tervingi. When the navy stopped patrolling, three tribes, including the Greuthungi under Alatheus and Saphrax, crossed the Danube with some of their allies, the Alans.

Around this time, the historical sources begin to distinguish between the two Gothic tribes with the name Visigoths: western Goths, for the Tervingi; and Ostrogoths, or eastern Goths, for the Greuthungi. It is not clear why this change of names happens, but the use of Tervingi and Greuthungi soon disappears from the sources.

The situation was getting out of hand. A group of Visigothic warriors marched to Lupicinus's headquarters at the city of Marcianopolis and demanded food. Lupicinus sought to defuse the situation by murdering the Gothic leaders at a dinner and thereby deprive the barbarians of organized leadership. The result was quite the opposite. Many Gothic leaders, including the leader of the Visigothic confederation, Alavivus, were killed, but several others, such as Fritigern, escaped and organized the Gothic warriors. The Visigoths struck back at the Roman soldiers, and fights erupted in several places. The Goths then started to plunder the province in search of food.

In early 377, Lupicinus had gathered enough of his troops to put an end to the revolt, but they suffered a terrible defeat some nine miles outside of Marcianopolis. The battle destroyed almost the entire Roman army in Thrace and caused other Gothic war bands to rise up, supported by Thracian miners, the overtaxed Roman rural population, and the lower classes in the cities. A Roman military unit stationed near Adrianopolis composed of Visigoths and commanded by the chieftains Sueridus and Colias switched sides and revolted. The Visigoths also attacked the other more peaceful groups of Goths in their rage and to get food. Several Roman weapons factories were captured, and the Goths were able to rearm themselves to some extent using Roman equipment and weapons.

BATTLE OF AD SALICES

Valens was not aware of the seriousness of the situation and reacted slowly. He had been preparing a war against Persia and did not consider the revolt of some unarmed and starving barbarians a great problem. Some Armenian elite troops were dispatched, and Valens asked his nephew and co-emperor in the west, Gratian, for support. Gratian sent the experienced General Frigeridus with some troops to support the suppression of the revolt, but he was himself harassed by the Alemanni tribes, who had heard of the troubles in the Balkan region and were mustering to take advantage of it.

Initially, Valens seemed to have judged the situation correctly. The Armenian units succeeded in pushing the Goths into the mountain region of the Dobruja, where they were expected to surrender from starvation soon. More troops from Gaul arrived under General Richomeres, but the Romans were still outnumbered, and the commanders could not agree on how to fight the Goths.

In the late summer of 377, the Goths were encamped in their strong wagon laager at a place called Ad Salices ("at the willows"). Among the Romans, Frigeridus had fallen ill, and Richomeres had taken command. His plan was to wait for the Goths to starve and therefore be forced to move on. He would then attack the Goths while they were marching and vulnerable with women and children. Fritigern, the Gothic leader, did not appear to move, however, and the impatient Romans decided to attack anyway.

The Roman army opened the battle with the *barritus*—originally a battle cry of the Germanic tribes, but now used by the Roman army. It began quietly and gradually swelled to a thundering roar, revealing just how great the Germanic element in the Roman army was. The battle was fierce, and both sides suffered heavy casualties, but there was no real victor. The Goths retreated to their wagon laager and stayed there, and the Romans retreated to Marcianopolis. The Balkan passes were instead blocked, and the Romans concentrated the food reserves in the cities, which were impregnable to the Goths, who knew little of siegecraft.

The Romans appeared now to have gained the upper hand strategically, so Frigeridus went to Illyria to await new orders, and Richomeres went to Gaul for reinforcements. Valens saw no point in going in person to the region and instead sent Saturninus, a general of cavalry, to support Generals Traianus and Profuturus, who were already there.

It appeared that the Romans had succeeded in starving out the Goths in the triangle between the Danube, the Balkan Mountains, and the Black Sea. But Fritigern was not so easy to defeat and entered into negotiations with the Ostrogoths and their allies, whose forces mainly consisted of heavy cavalry. The Visigoths were essentially an infantry force in this period, but with the addition of the Ostrogoths and their Alan allies, Fritigern could combine a devastating infantry charge with cavalry to follow up a victory. The result of the negotiations was that Alatheus and Saphrax promised to help Fritigern, and so they attacked the Roman forces blocking the passes of the Balkan Mountains and forced Saturninus to withdraw. All of Thrace was now open to the barbarians, who plundered everything in sight and attempted to take several cities, but with no luck. The combination of infantry and heavy cavalry soon destroyed a Roman elite unit—the *cornuti,* under the experienced General Barzimanes—which was surprised and defeated at Dibaltum (Burgas in modern-day Bulgaria).

In response to the changed situation, Frigeridus was ordered to move to Beroea to establish a defensive line, thus continuing the sound Roman strategy of starving the Goths instead of fighting them. If the Goths were to survive the winter of 377–378, they had

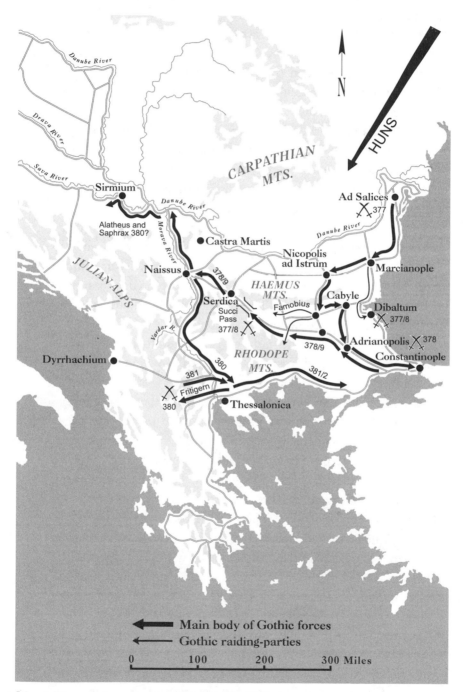

Map 3. The wars in southeastern Europe, 376–382.

to dislodge him from the region of central Thrace. Accordingly they moved toward Beroea from several sides and forced Frigeridus to retreat west. On his way across the mountains, Frigeridus encountered a large group of Ostrogoths and Taifali, who also had crossed the Danube when the Roman fleet withdrew its patrols. The battle ended in the total defeat of the barbarians and the death of their leader, Farnobius. The survivors were settled in north Italy and Aquitania in Southern Gaul. Frigeridus could then fortify the Succi pass between Serdica (Sofia in modern-day Bulgaria) and Philippopolis to stop the Goths from moving west.

Meanwhile, Gratian was gathering his armies to help his uncle, Valens. But the Alemanni had invaded the province of Raetia, so Gratian moved to stop and eventually counterattack the troublesome tribal coalition. In the east, Valens had moved to Constantinople in May 378 with his main army—some thirty thousand to forty thousand troops—and appointed Sebastianus commander of the infantry in Thrace instead of Traianus, who had revealed himself as incompetent.

Sebastianus set about his task with ruthless efficiency. In early June 378, while Valens was troubled with a religious revolt in Constantinople, he moved against the scattered Gothic war bands. It was a general weakness of the Goths that they could stay concentrated for only a short time, and they soon had to disperse to get supplies. Sebastianus attacked a Gothic war band that was returning from a plundering expedition and destroyed it with only two thousand men. Having received news of the Roman armies moving toward Thrace, Fritigern was desperately trying to reconcentrate his troops at the city of Cabyle (Yambol in modern-day Bulgaria). In mid-July Valens reached the city and received news of the victory of Sebastianus and that Gratian, who had won a great victory over the Alemanni, was marching to his aid with the imperial army of the West, and had already reached Castra Martis (Kula in northwestern Bulgaria). Furthermore, scouts reported that the Goths under Fritigern were marching toward the village of Nike, some fourteen miles north of Adrianopolis, with only ten thousand warriors.

To Valens, it was suddenly a question of haste to destroy the annoying Goths before Gratian would arrive and share the glory.

With his junior colleague coming straight from his success over the Alemanni, Valens needed a victory to boost his prestige.

Around August 7, 378, General Richomeres arrived at Valens's headquarters, with the urgings of Gratian to await the Western army before attacking Fritigern. Ostrogothic and Alannic cavalry had attacked Gratian's troops at Castra Martis and caused some casualties. These elements were still at large and might join Fritigern before the battle. Gratian therefore urged caution and to await the Western army. Valens called a war council to decide what course of action to pursue. Sebastianus pointed to his recent victory and urged separate action while Fritigern was weak. Valens was undoubtedly convinced by this and did not want to share the prestige of a victory with Gratian. Accordingly, he decided upon battle.

THE BATTLE OF ADRIANOPOLIS

On the morning of August 9, 378, Valens's army left Adrianopolis, leaving behind its baggage train and the imperial treasure and insignia. The Goths were waiting in their traditional wagon laager. The eleven-mile march in the scorching heat tired the Roman soldiers, who started to suffer from hunger and thirst. Scouts then returned to report that the troops under Fritigern were more numerous than expected.

Fritigern sent envoys to negotiate peace with Valens—probably just to gain time for reinforcements to arrive—and some time was spent in the details of arranging a negotiation with the emperor. Two Roman units then attacked without orders, dragging the rest of the army, more or less disorganized, into a full-scale battle.

The fight had just started when the Ostrogothic cavalry of Alatheus and Saphrax returned from foraging. They charged the right flank of the Roman army and routed the troops there. They then sent another cavalry detachment to attack the opposite Roman flank, with the same results. The Roman cavalry fled along with the infantry reserves, leaving the main body with the emperor surrounded. The Roman army was cut down along with Emperor Valens, most of his generals, and high-ranking officers, among them the gallant Sebastianus. Two-thirds of the imperial army had been destroyed. The contemporary historian Ammianus Marcellinus compared the disaster with the Roman defeat at Cannae in 216 BC against Hannibal, and the death of Emperor Traianus Decius at the battle of Abrittus in 251. As a result of the battle, the Visigoths, who were mainly an infantry force, seem to have changed their troops into cavalry because of the startling success of the Ostrogoths.

Like Hannibal in 216, the Goths were not able to follow up on the great victory. They tried to take Adrianopolis with the imperial treasure but failed; they were still not able to take a fortified city. Fritigern wanted to gain the city through treachery but was voted down by the other Gothic chiefs. In the storm on the city from August 10–12, they suffered heavy casualties, just as they had in their first attack on Adrianopolis in 377, when Fritigern is said to have reminded his troops, that he "kept peace with stone walls."

The Goths then tried to take Philippopolis and Perinthus, to relieve their serious food problems, but again they were repulsed by the local garrisons, supported by siege engines, which terrified the Gothic warriors. Only at Nikopolis (Stari Nikub in modern-day Bulgaria) did they win a victory, when the local garrison did not fight.

To force the Roman authorities to give them food, they finally marched on Constantinople, which was almost devoid of troops. The city's fortifications were daunting, however, and the Goths were soon attacked by a unit of Saracen cavalry stationed in the city. A little Saracen rushed one of the huge Gothic warriors, jumped him, cut his throat with a dagger, and started to drink his blood in the manner of his tribe. To the superstitious Goths it was too much to be attacked by little devils drinking their blood, and they fled in terror.

With the great victory at Adrianopolis and the lack of food, the Goths of Fritigern fragmented in their desperate search for food, all of which the Romans had brought into the impregnable cities. Despite the disaster to the Roman arms, the authorities reacted calmly to the Gothic threat. Their main aim was again to starve out the Goths to prevent their revolt from spreading. In Asia Minor, Julius, the commander of the Eastern army, ordered all Gothic troops within his sphere of command to be killed to avoid a repetition of the revolt of the Visigothic units.

THEODOSIUS

On January 19, 379, Gratian made one of his experienced generals, Theodosius, co-emperor and emperor of the East in Sirmium (Sremska Mitrovica in modern-day Serbia). Although the Gothic war bands had been driven out of Macedonia at this time, and he therefore could enter Thessalonica with no problems, there was still a daunting task in front of him: to re-establish the court army. He did this by enlisting just about anybody, even large numbers of Goths. The primitive and undisciplined Goths were threatening the order of the new court army, and Theodosius had to shuffle around Gothic contingents and exchange them for other units stationed elsewhere in the East. Even a Gothic noble, Modaharius, was recruited. In 379, he destroyed a large marauding Gothic war band. With the dispersal of these bands, it was fairly easy to once again close them up between the Danube and the Balkan Mountains, where they would slowly be starved into surrender. On November 17, 379, victories over the Goths, Alans, and Huns were proclaimed in Constantinople, and the numerous Gothic war bands had either been defeated or shut up north of the Balkan Mountains.

The Ostrogoths were now ready for peace, and Gratian settled them in the province of Pannonia Secunda. Their allies, the Alans, were settled in the province of Valeria. Many of the Ostrogoths were used to further bolster the Roman army.

In 380, Fritigern and his Visigoths were plundering Macedonia, and they came close at one point to capturing Emperor Theodosius. After this they went south and plundered all the way to Thessaly. All through the campaign, Fritigern was well informed of the movement of the Roman army through the Goths in the Roman units. To contain Fritigern, Gratian sent Generals Bauto and Arbogast with an army, which united with the troops of Theodosius and drove Fritigern north into Moesia, where he was once again shut up and starving. Finally, on October 3, 382, the Visigoths of Fritigern surrendered, and a treaty was ratified.

While the peace with the Ostrogoths was important, it was completely overshadowed by the peace with the much more numerous Visigoths and their strong and capable leader, Fritigern. The Ostrogoths in Pannonia were only a fragment of the Greuthungi tribes, most of whom had stayed in their homelands and submitted to the Huns. The details of the treaty of 382 are not known, but the main points were that the Visigoths:

> Became subjects of the empire but were still considered barbarians and foreigners and so would have no right of marriage to a Roman.

> Would be allotted land in the northern part of the dioceses of Dacia and Thrace, between the Danube and the Balkan Mountains; the land would still be considered Roman, but they would be autonomous.

> Would have to supply troops for the Roman army, but their own tribal leaders would only be allowed to hold subordinate commands.

> Would be housed according to the regular rules for billeting Roman soldiers and would initially have to live under the same roof as the Roman provincials.

> Would receive an annual tribute.

It could be said that through their resistance the Visigoths received much better terms than originally planned in 376, when they might have been eliminated as a nation or tribe by being dispersed all over the empire. Now they were settled together and under their own leaders.

It seems incredible to a modern observer that anything but the total elimination of the Visigoths was acceptable to Rome. But the Romans needed trained soldiers for their armies and gold for the treasuries. By recruiting Goths instead of Roman provincials, the emperor could demand taxes paid in gold from the Roman provinces instead of recruits. The frontiers were already deserted regions, destroyed by the many barbarian wars, the plague, and almost constant small raids. The fields were empty, and the once great cities of the Danube, such as Carnuntum (near Petronell in modern-day Austria), stood empty and in ruin. The military presence in the region was strong, as most civilians had fled into the overcrowded cities, thereby creating better conditions for the plague to spread. Into these desolate lands and untilled fields, the Goths would be settled. Barbarian raids and invasions would hurt the Romans much less, and accordingly, the general lawlessness of the Goths was an acceptable trade-off. Army service in those days was extremely unpopular, and recruitment among the Roman provincials created serious problems. Recruits would even cut off their thumbs to avoid military service. With luck, the Visigoths would in time support themselves by growing their own crops and perhaps find peace in their new homeland south of the Danube, as had so many other tribes in the long history of the Roman Empire.

For the Roman provincials in the region, the Goths were an added burden because they generally continued to behave as they had north of the Danube. If the Visigoths felt wronged, they would take the law into their own hands and settle the issue according to their customs, and the few Roman officials at the border could do little against this.

In the coming years, several Gothic groups north of the Danube would try to escape the Huns and enter the empire, with varying success. In 386, thousands of Ostrogoths under Odotheus, fleeing from the Huns, crossed the Danube into the Dobrouja. Promotus, the admiral in command of the Danube flotilla, struck them during their crossing and defeated them decisively. Claudian, the contemporary Roman poet, describes the gory details, with the water of the Danube colored red with Ostrogothic blood and great numbers of corpses strewn along the banks of the river. The pitiful survivors were settled in faraway Phrygia. The Romans did not want a repeat of the disasters of 376–378.

Theodosius would need his new federates in 388, when he no longer could delay the confrontation with Magnus Maximus, who in 383 had usurped the Western throne from Gratian (359–383). The Ostrogoths from Pannonia, the Alans, and the Visigoths fought in Theodosius's army. Their cavalry would decide the initial battles at Siscia and Poetovio (Sisak and Ptuj in modern-day Croatia and Slovenia, respectively). His army defeated, Maximus was executed on August 28, 388. He had, however, bribed various barbarian groups within the Eastern army, and these deserted and formed war bands in Macedonia and elsewhere that troubled the Romans for years.

The Visigoths would soon again trouble the Roman Empire in their hunt for a secure homeland within its borders that could supply them with food for their people. Their quest would involve them in the great struggles between the East and the West. Alaric, the famous Visigothic king, would lead his people on a long and arduous journey through Europe, sacking Rome in 410, until the Visigoths reached Spain, where they defeated the Vandals and Alans and were settled in Aquitania in Gaul in 418. Time and again the Visigoths would be defeated or forced to surrender by the Romans, but each time they would be let free and once again enter the power struggles of the Roman courts. A strong Visigothic kingdom was set up in Tolosa (Toulouse in modern-day France), from where the barbarians would take over parts of Gaul and most of Spain by the year 500.

We now turn to the fate of the Ostrogoths, whom we last left in their homelands under the Hunnish yoke and in Pannonia Secunda.

THE OSTROGOTHS UNDER HUNNISH DOMINATION

The majority of Ostrogoths had chosen to live under the sway of the Huns, a period of servitude that they remembered long after their rebellion following the death of Attila the Hun and the decisive victory over the Huns at the battle of Nedao in 454. Unfortunately, we lack reliable and detailed sources and thus have little knowledge of the history of the Ostrogoths under Hunnish dominion between 375 and Attila's invasion of the Roman Empire in 451. General events can be found in the Ostrogoth Jordanes's history of the Goths and in the few news reports that reached the general and historian Ammianus Marcellinus, who wrote a Roman history of the period.

When Videric, the young boy-king, and his guardians Alatheus and Saphrax fled the Huns with a part of their people, the remaining majority tried to fight the Huns. They won some engagements but were, after a year or two, decisively defeated and became subjects of the Huns. As was the case with other nations under the Huns, they were allowed to have kings of their own govern them—according to the wishes of the Huns. In the first two decades, some of the Ostrogothic tribes broke off and sought refuge behind the borders of the Roman Empire, as the Huns consolidated their power in the region.

Under Uldin (d. 412)—a powerful chieftain of the western Huns during the reigns of Arcadius (394–408) and Theodosius II (408–450)—and later under Attila (406–453), the Ostrogoths had several times been brought along by the Huns on raids and attacks on the Roman Empire. In 439 the Huns had occupied western Pannonia and were plundering the neighboring regions, also with the support of some of the Ostrogoths, although most were still in their traditional areas north of the Danube.

In 449–50, Theodosius had paid Attila not to raid the Eastern Roman Empire, and accordingly he moved instead against the Western Empire. In 451, at the battle of the Catalaunian fields, close to Durocatalaunum (Chalons-sur-Champagne in modern-day France), Goths were arrayed against Goths—Visigoths on the Roman side and Ostrogoths on the side of the Huns. Attila was defeated, and many of his allied Germans and Ostrogoths were left dead on the battlefield. On his way back to Pannonia, Attila died of a stroke. With the death of Attila, the Huns lost their greatest leader, and they disintegrated slowly into warring factions.

Only two years later, in 454, the Gepids, under King Ardaric at the head of a loose coalition of Ostrogoths and other of the submitted tribes, rebelled and won their freedom at the battle of Nedao. What role the Ostrogoths played in the battle is difficult to ascertain. They were not grateful that the Gepids had won the battle, and it is even possible the Ostrogoths fought on the side of the Huns at the battle. However, it is known that after their victory, the Gepids took over the former Hunnish lands, so the Ostrogoths were forced to either submit or seek new lands in the empire. Probably most Ostrogoths remained in their villages and slowly became integrated into the Gepid tribes, as nothing more is heard of the ones who stayed behind. Another large Ostrogothic group, under King Valamir and his brothers Thiudmir and Vidimir, chose to migrate into the province of Pannonia and thus retained their tribal identity.

The Hunnish tribal coalition further disintegrated in 455, when it made a last bid to re-establish control of Pannonia and was quickly defeated.

The Ostrogoths under Valamir and Thiudmir

Despite having gained new lands, the Ostrogoths in the empire were still restless under their new Roman lords, and in 461 the group under King Valamir and his brothers rebelled. Among other things, they felt the emperor favored the more-Romanized Goths under the noble Theodoric Strabo. They had been settled for much longer and had integrated themselves better into Roman society, although they were still considered an Ostrogothic tribe. Again we see that there existed several Ostrogothic tribal groups under various lesser kings and nobles who felt no particular sympathy for each other.

The Ostrogoths under Valamir soon gained a new treaty with the Romans and a subsidy of 300 pounds of gold a year; but Thiudmir had to send his then-seven-year-old son, Theodoric, as hostage to Constantinople. He would remain there for the next ten years. The gold was not enough to keep the peace for long, however, and a few years later the Ostrogoths attacked the Sadagi, one of the hated Hunnish tribes. The Huns were not as strong as they had been and were soon defeated. One of the Hunnic groups, the Bittugures, even submitted to the Ostrogoths and finally migrated with them to Italy in 488–89. Actually, Ragnaris, the leader of one of the few remaining Ostrogothic outposts in the fortress of Campsa in 553, was not an Ostrogoth, but a Bittuguric Hun and still known as such almost a century after their submission.

Now settled without any great danger from the Huns, the Goths embarked upon a period of cattle theft, raids, and rivalry against the other barbarian tribes in Pannonia.

Campaigns Against the Suevi and Sciri

The Suevi and Sciri, tribes in the Alannic confederation, attacked the Ostrogoths around 470. Valamir died in battle, and Thiudmir, his brother, became king. The battles went both ways, but the Sciri, who hitherto had been settled in the neighboring province of Moesia, refused to give up their undertaking, despite heavy losses. The Suevi then called the Sarmatians in as allies. The raids and small fights developed into a regular war between the Ostrogoths and the Suevi, Sarmatians, and Sciri. The Romans had so far kept neutral in the struggle, although all the contestants nominally were Roman subject tribes. In the end, the Eastern Roman emperor, Leo I, sided with the Sciri. This choice was important for the future of the Eastern Empire.

Since 434, Aspar, Leo's powerful *magister militum*, had been the man behind the throne. He was married to the aunt of Theodoric Strabo—the leader of the most powerful Ostrogothic group in the Eastern Roman Empire—and had the command of several Gothic units. By interfering in the war, Leo may have been trying to weaken Aspar.

In 471, the palace eunuchs murdered Aspar. The Gothic troops under his command went burning and looting through Constantinople to the palace, but were defeated and had to flee. The remnants fled to Theodoric Strabo and his Ostrogothic group in Thrace.

Theodoric Strabo soon demanded Aspar's position at the court. Leo was not about to have another Gothic general behind the throne and did the only thing possible: he sent Theodoric, the son of Thiudmir, home from Constantinople, where he had been hostage. His task was to challenge the position of Theodoric Strabo as leader of the Ostrogoths under Roman rule.

Thiudmir was at war with the Sarmatian allies of the Sciri, who had crossed the Danube and taken the Roman city of Singidunum (Beograd in modern-day Serbia), which they used as a base for further raids. When Theodoric Thiudmir, at age 18, returned to his father in 471, he immediately gathered an army to strike back at the Sarmatians. He then crossed the Danube into Sarmatian territory and plundered the villages while the Sarmatian war bands were on the other side of the Danube. On his way back he attacked and took the city of Singidunum, which he kept to himself instead of handing it back to its rightful owners, the Romans. Leo saw this as treason and attacked the Ostrogoths of his former hostage.

The Ostrogoths Settled in Macedonia

The constant war and raiding in the Ostrogothic areas brought starvation to the door, as the fields could not be tended in peace. As seen before, this was often the best—or at least the most cost-effective—way for the Romans to defeat the Goths, as the risk of a major battle was too great for the empire. In 473, King Thiudmir had to move south, further into the Roman regions, to find food for his people, and he attacked the Roman city of Naissus in an attempt to get food for his starving people. Taking a city was his best hope, because that is where the Romans would collect all foodstuffs at the news of a barbarian raid. His brother Vidimir went west and in the end joined the Visigoths in Spain.

Leo, who still hoped to use the Ostrogoths of Thiudmir in the political and military game with Theodoric Strabo, offered the exhausted barbarians land and supplies in the area around Pella in Macedonia, close to the area in Thrace in which Theodoric Strabo was settled with his band of Ostrogoths. This was a clear attempt to start friction between the two groups. After some skirmishes with the Romans, the Ostrogoths accepted the proposal and were settled in the region around Pella. As with all the settlements of barbarians within the empire, the settlement of Thiudmir's Goths would create problems, but neither Leo nor Thiudmir would live to experience them. Before he died in 474, Thiudmir had nominated Theodoric, his son, as his successor, and Zeno became emperor after the death of Leo and the short reign of Leo II (January 18 to November 17, 474).

Struggles between the Two Theodorics

In 473–474, Zeno stopped the annual subsidies to Theodoric Strabo and sent him an ultimatum to renounce his leadership of the Ostrogoths and to send his son as hostage to Constantinople. If this was done, Zeno would allow him to withdraw to his estates and live in peace.

Theodoric Strabo immediately prepared his people for war. Soon after, he and his allied generals—including the Roman Basiliscus, who had returned from a disastrous attack on Gaiseric's Vandals in Africa—forced Zeno to flee Constantinople. For a year and a half, Basiliscus ruled in the capital (475–476) while Zeno fought Theodoric Strabo in Macedonia.

Zeno, however, was wise in the game of politics and asked Theodoric Thiudmir to march with his warriors to Adrianopolis, where he was to unite with twenty thousand infantry and six thousand cavalry from the Thracian garrisons and attack Theodoric Strabo. But when Theodoric Thiudmir arrived with his followers, the Roman troops were not there (most likely by Zeno's order), and the two Theodorics faced each other at Marcianopolis. After some demonstrations of power, Theodoric Thiudmir, who had only brought part of his troops, realized he could not defeat Theodoric Strabo. He was facing a desperate situation. Hunger was threatening again, and the region around Pella had already been plundered. Marching back was impossible.

Humiliated in front of his own people, Theodoric Thiudmir retreated and demanded new land from Zeno, who had betrayed him, as he saw it. Zeno rejected his demands, as his political maneuvering had improved his position greatly. Basiliscus had shown himself to be a useless emperor, and Theodoric Strabo had lost most of his support in the capital. Now was the time to again turn the tables and secure the help of Theodoric Strabo against the usurper Basiliscus. Zeno accordingly offered Strabo the opportunity to take over the position of Theodoric Thiudmir in return for leading thirteen thousand Ostrogothic warriors against Basiliscus in Constantinople. Strabo agreed, and after the defeat of Basiliscus in 476, Zeno was able to return to his capital, which was partly in ruin after a great fire and the confusion of the past years.

ZENO AND THEODORIC

Theodoric Thiudmir was angry at the turn of events, and he started plundering the region. Thessalonica and Stobi (Gradsko in modern-day Macedonia) were sacked. Other cities persuaded the Ostrogoths to move on in return for food supplies. Only after much devastation did Zeno offer peace. The Ostrogoths of Theodoric Thiudmir could receive lands in the province of Dacia Mediterranea and gold to buy supplies until they could grow their own crops. Theodoric refused to be sent so far to the periphery of the empire and instead marched to the west, where he had heard there was good soil for farming.

He moved along the Via Egnatia to Dyrrhachium (Durres in modern-day Albania) and then on to Epidaurus, where the barbarians forced the inhabitants to leave the city, which they then took over. The negotiations with Zeno for a proper area for settlement went on. Back in Constantinople, the emperor was once again facing the problem of Theodoric Strabo, whose support he had used. If Theodoric Thiudmir left the Balkan region or sailed on to Italy, Zeno would have no one to play off against Theodoric Strabo, who was once again in revolt in Thrace.

So again the tables were turned: Theodoric Thiudmir offered six thousand Gothic warriors to help against Theodoric Strabo in return for taking over his position at the imperial court and being recognized as a Roman citizen of Constantinople. Zeno certainly had no intention of bringing another Aspar to the court and so ordered his troops to attack the baggage train of Theodoric Thiudmir, which had not yet reached Epidaurus. The intention was to force better terms when the Goths were starving again. At Candavia the able Roman General Sabinianus won a great victory and captured two thousand supply wagons and more than five thousand Goths. He then blocked the passes to Epirus Nova, the province where Theodoric Thiudmir was camped. Here he was contained until 482. The Goths reacted by plundering the region to the northwest, where they also came into contact with the troops of the Scirian King Odoacer, who held Italy and the province of Noricum. The Scirian tribes were the traditional enemies of the Goths, and several skirmishes were fought.

Meanwhile, the troubled Zeno had to fight the rebellion of Marcianus and was forced to bring in the Bulgars to stave off the growing army of Theodoric Strabo. But Strabo was killed in an accident in camp in 481.

THE OSTROGOTHS MIGRATE TO ITALY

The intrigues at the imperial court caused Zeno to murder General Sabinianus in 482—an unwise decision, as the Goths under

Theodoric Thiudmir saw their chance to break out to the east, where they plundered Greece and sacked Larissa. Without any allies after the murder of Sabinianus and the death of Theodoric Strabo, Zeno once again turned to Theodoric Thiudmir. To pave the way for an alliance, he had Recitach, Strabo's son, murdered, which meant that finally Theodoric Thiudmir could unite all the Ostrogoths in the Balkan region under his leadership. Theodoric promptly supported Zeno against the usurper Illus in return for becoming general of the household troops (*magister militum prae-sentalis*, so named because of their being "in the presence of the emperor") and consul designate for 484. Command of the household troops meant great power, and the position would further bring him the command of the provinces of Dacia Ripensis and Moesia Inferior. Theodoric then pitched his camp at Novae on the Danube, from where his Goths would plunder Thrace in 486, and Thrace and Moesia in 487.

Odoacer in the west now also began to encroach on the western Balkan region. Zeno sent a barbarian tribe, the Rugi, to curb the threat, but they were soon defeated and had to join Theodoric at Novae, with their King Fredericus at their head. Despite many attempts, Zeno could no longer bring Theodoric to follow his orders, and enemies were pressing the empire from all sides. Even Constantinople was under the threat of barbarian attack.

The Goths, however, soon plundered the region around Novae and were once again threatened by starvation. It had become a stalemate, which the Goths were losing. To solve the problem, Zeno finally ordered Theodoric to attack Odoacer in Italy and thus reconquer the province for the Romans. Seeing the difficulties of a continued war against Zeno, Theodoric followed his suggestion and marched with all his people and possessions to Italy. It was only because of dire need that Theodoric took his people on another long march, and he had no intention of handing over Italy to the Romans should he succeed. The pure desperation of the Goths can be seen in the fact that they attempted the expedition at all. They had no supplies and had to survive at least one winter before they reached the Po plain—not to mention that they would be facing Odoacer's veteran troops.

The initial stages of the march—about 280 miles—conducted along the Roman highways in the empire, were probably not so difficult. Food could be obtained at the local markets, and the roads and bridges were probably in good repair, despite the ravages of the Huns and Goths. But from Singidunum on, in the region between the Save and Drave rivers, the archenemies of the Goths, the Gepids, were ruling and were sure to cause trouble. It is estimated that the Ostrogothic column consisted of about forty thousand warriors with a train of around one hundred and sixty thousand noncombatants, encumbered with baggage. This long column must have been hard to defend against Gepidic hit-and-run attacks, and the casualties among the noncombatants can only be guessed at, but the Ostrogoths must have been slowed down by the Gepids and further pressed by hunger. Wounded and ill were left behind to be slaughtered or enslaved by the Gepids.

Battle at the Ulca River

At the end of 488, the Ostrogoths reached the Ulca River at Cibalae (Vinkovci in modern-day Croatia), where the Gepids had lined up their army for a decisive engagement. Turning around was impossible. Theodoric sent ambassadors to the Gepid King Traustila, but to no avail.

The Ostrogoths mustered their warriors and charged across the river, but in so doing took heavy casualties from the shower of lances the Gepids hurled from the opposite river bank.

After a fierce battle that lasted all day and into the night, the Ostrogoths broke the Gepid army. Many were slain; more important, the Ostrogoths captured the supply wagons of the Gepids, which were filled with grain. The way to Italy was now open.

In August of 489, following the terrible trek through the Gepid territory, the advance guard of the Goths was finally coming down from the Julian Alps, and the fruitful Po plain was within their reach. Soon, the herds of animals brought by the Goths were grazing on the lower slopes of the mountains.

3

THEODORIC
IN ITALY

THE KINGDOM OF ODOACER

Italy was not without a ruler who was willing to fight for his dominions. The Western Empire had been in turmoil since the death of Emperor Gratian in 383. Power struggles between emperors and powerful generals of mostly barbarian origin, barbarian invasions, and economic decline had caused the fragmentation of the West. Julius Nepos, a former general in Dalmatia, was proclaimed emperor of the West in 474, after defeating Glycerius, a Roman count who had been made puppet emperor by Burgundian King Gundobad. In 475, Nepos made Roman noble Flavius Orestes, who was a former secretary to Attila the Hun, *magister militum*. This was a bad choice, as Orestes soon deposed Nepos, who fled to Dalmatia. Orestes put his son, Flavius Romulus (surnamed *Augustulus*, or little Augustus, because he was so young) on the throne with the help of the Germanic mercenaries in Italy and their powerful commander, Odoacer, who was of the Scirian tribe. The mercenaries demanded land in Italy in return for their services. When Orestes refused, he was killed on August 28, 476. His son was removed but allowed to live out his life in the south of Italy as a private citizen and given a yearly allowance of six thousand *solidi*, the gold coin of the age.

With Odoacer now in power, one-third of Italy was given to his barbarians, and the Senate sent envoys to Emperor Zeno in Constantinople asking for Odoacer to be appointed patrician and entrusted with the administration of Italy. The envoys brought the imperial regalia and stated that there was no need for a separate emperor in the West, as Zeno's rule was considered sufficient for both parts of the empire.

Zeno, who had only just recovered from the revolt of the usurper Basiliscus, was unable to govern the affairs of Italy along with those of his own Eastern Empire. Conferring the administration of Italy on Odoacer would simply be to accept the existing situation. Unfortunately, envoys from Julius Nepos arrived simultaneously at the imperial court asking for troops and money to regain the throne of the West for Nepos. Being connected to Nepos's family and having crowned him himself, Zeno was in no position to openly put him off. Instead he chose not to take sides in a matter that was of little immediate importance to the Eastern Empire.

He told the representatives of the Senate that Odoacer must ask for the patrician title from the Western Emperor, Nepos, but at the same time addressed him as patrician in a written reply in which he encouraged his actions in bringing peace to Italy. Julius Nepos was killed in 480, and Zeno does not seem to have officially appointed Odoacer patrician. Odoacer instead used the title of *rex*—king—as the other barbarian kings in the West did.

Odoacer initially ruled only Italy and what remained of the provinces of Raetia and Noricum, but he soon took over Sicily from Vandal King Gaiseric in return for an annual payment. After Julius Nepos died, Dalmatia was added to Odoacer's kingdom as well. In all, he *de facto* ruled Italy, the remnant of the Western Roman Empire, for thirteen years.

With the death of Julius Nepos, the Western Roman Empire ceased to exist, having been parceled out to a number of barbarian kings. The Vandals ruled Africa together with Sardinia, Corsica, and Sicily. Sicily was, as mentioned, later turned over to Odoacer for an annual tribute. In Gaul the Visigoths now held the territory between the Durance, the Alps, and the sea. North of the Durance, the Burgundians held all the country east of the Saône and the Rhône. North of the Loire were the independent Armoricans, now reinforced with Britons, and on the lower Rhine were the Franks. Between them an enclave of Roman territory survived in the province of Belgica Secunda, ruled by Syagrius, son of Aegidius, the master of the soldiers in Gaul (*magister militum per Gallias*). It was conquered in 486 by Clovis, king of the Franks. In Spain, the Visigoths had spread their rule throughout the country, except in the northwest, where the Sueves and the native Vascones still maintained their independence.

BATTLES WITH ODOACER

When Theodoric entered Italy, Odoacer had already made his preparations and was waiting for the Ostrogoths at the eleventh milestone from Aquileia at the confluence of the rivers Frigidus and Sontius (Vipava and Soča in modern-day Slovenia). In the distance, the ruins of the once great city of Aquileia, destroyed some forty years earlier by the Huns of Attila, were still standing. Odoacer had fortified his position strongly and held his army of various barbarian contingents, mainly Herulians and Rugi, ready to fight the Goths crossing the Sontius.

Unfortunately, we know almost nothing of the battle that was fought August 28, 489, between the forces of Theodoric and Odoacer. Somehow, the Goths managed to cross the deep Sontius, climb the earthen ramparts, and take Odoacer's fortified camp. Odoacer fled with his surviving troops. There is no doubt that the desperate courage of the Goths played an important part in the battle: there was no turning back, and they were fighting for the lives and futures of their families, who probably watched the battle from the Gothic wagon laager.

Odoacer fled to the line of the Athesis (Adige) River and thus gave up the province of Venetia to the Goths. Later in his reign, Theodoric would count the victory at the Sontius as the start of his reign as king of Italy.

But Odoacer had not been king of Italy for thirteen years and a general of mercenaries for more than that for nothing. He fortified a camp at Verona with the Athesis River behind him, probably to guard against attacks from the rear and to force his followers to face the Goths, as there was no escape in the case of defeat. He still had a large army, and it was said that Theodoric almost lost heart when he saw the myriad campfires of the enemy the night before the battle.

The battle of Verona began September 30, 489, three days after Odoacer had entrenched himself at the city. Again, there is little information about the battle. According to the panegyrist Ennodius, the Goths were wavering in the initial phase of the battle, but a charge by Theodoric and his bodyguard saved the day. It appears that this battle was more closely fought than the one at the Sontius—probably because Odoacer's troops had the Athesis at their rear—and that the Goths took heavy casualties during the battle. But with no room for retreat, Odoacer's troops were cut to pieces, and only the few who dared the waters of the Athesis lived. Odoacer fled to Ravenna.

With Odoacer decisively defeated, Theodoric could take time to consolidate his hold on north Italy. He entered the great metropolis of the north, Mediolanum and there, in October 489, he accepted the surrender of a great part of Odoacer's troops. These troops bolstered the ranks of his victorious Goths. General Tufa was in command of the surrendered soldiers, and Theodoric ordered him to go to Ravenna and initiate a siege of the city. Tufa was high in the ranks of Odoacer's army and had been appointed *magister militum* on April 1, 489. Tufa went by the Via Aemilia to Faventia (Faenza), about eighteen miles from Ravenna, and began a blockade of the city. With Odoacer defeated and shut up in Ravenna, and a large part of his troops on the side of Theodoric, it seemed that the business of taking Italy was almost finished in a few months of campaign. But this was not to be the case.

Odoacer went to speak with Tufa at Faventia and convinced him he had sided with the wrong person. Tufa abandoned Theodoric's cause, along with most of his troops, and even handed over to Odoacer the *comites Theodorici*, part of Theodoric's personal retinue consisting of Gothic nobles. Odoacer had them cruelly murdered.

Suddenly the tables were turned, and Theodoric had to retreat from exposed Mediolanum to the more secure Ticinum (Pavia), where he gathered the Gothic noncombatants, including his mother, for the duration of the war against Odoacer.

Theodoric could no longer offer a *fait accompli* to the surrounding barbarian kingdoms, and so a ponderous but sophisticated power struggle began. The king of the Burgundians, Gundobad,

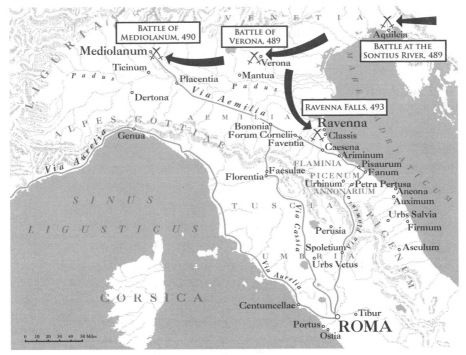

Map 4. Northern Italy at the time of Theodoric's campaigns.

saw the danger of a victorious Theodoric and the shadow of a strong alliance between the Visigoths in Spain and the Ostrogoths in Italy. Accordingly, he gathered a large army and invaded Liguria at the rear of Theodoric. Later, Theodoric would be able to make a treaty with the Burgundians, but in 490 their army ravaged Liguria and brought home long trains of captives and much plunder.

The Visigoths were then also brought into the great struggle and sent troops to Theodoric when the Burgundians entered the scene.

While Theodoric had his attention on the attacks of Gundobad in the western Po valley, Odoacer spent the spring and early summer reconquering the country between Ravenna and Cremona. Mediolanum was punished for the warm welcome its bishop, Laurentius, and citizens had given Theodoric the year before.

With the Burgundians leaving, Theodoric could turn to the business of pushing Odoacer back. The armies met August 11, 490, at the river Addua (Adda), ten miles east of Mediolanum. With the help of his Visigothic kinsmen, Theodoric won a hard-fought battle with heavy casualties on both sides. Odoacer fled and was again shut up in Ravenna. Tufa and his followers again switched sides, but soon after Odoacer again persuaded him to return to his camp. This time, however, Theodoric was wary, and Tufa's actions were discovered. Although Tufa escaped, many of his followers and the followers of Odoacer all over Italy were killed. With the slaughter of the Gothic nobles in Ravenna and the massacre of Odoacer's surrendered followers, the war had become more bitter.

Ravenna had been the capital of the Western Roman Empire since 402 and was perhaps the strongest fortified city in Italy. Swampy areas surrounded it, and the few narrow approaches were strongly fortified. Theodoric knew he could not take the impregnable Ravenna by assault and so settled down to blockade the city. But ships supplied it through the harbor of Classis—the former base of the Roman fleet in the Adriatic Sea—and a blockade could not be effective without mastery of the Adriatic.

So Theodoric made a rampart and ditch three miles east of the city to shut off as much help from the sea as possible. Gothic patrols and the forces in north Italy covered the land route. The blockade must have been quite effective, as the price of grain in the city rose to six *solidi* (a gold coin weighing 4.5 grams) per *modius* (14 2/3 pounds); later during the reign of Theodoric, the price would be 1/60 of a *solidus* per *modius*.

Theodoric now felt secure in his hold on Italy, and sent the Roman noble Faustus, chief of the Senate and consul for the year, to Emperor Zeno to ask for the imperial regalia of the western emperor, which Odoacer had sent to Constantinople. But Zeno was dying, and the negotiations brought nothing for the time being.

The blockade dragged on into 491. Odoacer had somehow received Herulian reinforcements, and in the belief that the long period of inaction signaled that Theodoric was relaxing his guard behind his ramparts, he chose to make a nightly sally in the middle of July 491. The battle was hard fought with heavy casualties on both sides, but again Theodoric defeated Odoacer.

A month later Theodoric left the siege and went to Ticinum, probably to oversee the defense of north Italy against the Burgundians, who were taking advantage of the war in Italy.

In 492, Theodoric went south and took the port of Ariminum (Rimini), some thirty miles south of Ravenna. With the capture of the city, he gained a small fleet of *dromones*, with which he could finally tighten the siege of Ravenna from both land and sea.

But treachery still lurked in the ranks of Theodoric's fickle barbarians. Fredericus, prince of the Rugians in the army of Theodoric, decided to switch sides. This must have surprised everyone. Fredericus's parents had been made slaves by Odoacer's troops, and he had been defeated twice by Odoacer in battle and then come to Theodoric as a helpless fugitive. Theodoric had supported him, and they had fought together during the campaign in Italy. Now Fredericus, when Theodoric seemed only a few months away from complete victory, chose to contact the traitor Tufa, who was still roaming the plains of north Italy with an army of followers. Fredericus then occupied Ticinum with his Rugians and made it his headquarters. It appears that the noncombatant Goths were able to flee before the occupation, as nothing is heard of any massacres.

Fredericus soon quarreled with Tufa about the division of the spoils of Ticinum. A battle ensued in the valley of the Athesis between Tridentum (Trento) and Verona. Fredericus won, and Tufa was killed. The Rugians would continue their rebellion after the fall of Odoacer and were only defeated at the end of 494 by Theodoric.

The year 493 brought the fourth year of the siege of Ravenna and the second of the complete blockade. The inhabitants were desperate from famine and ate whatever they could find. Odoacer could not go on, and on February 25 he surrendered to Theodoric and handed over his son, Thelane, as a hostage. The next day Theodoric entered Classis with his army, and on the 27th a formal peace was made between Odoacer and Theodoric, with the archbishop of Ravenna as mediator. The terms of the surrender were surprising: Odoacer was to rule Italy with Theodoric on equal terms. It can only be wondered why Theodoric would accept such terms, but perhaps he wanted an end to the war before other nations could interfere in the struggle.

The Murder of Odoacer

On March 5, 493, Theodoric rode into the defeated city, which was to become his capital for the next 33 years of his reign. The inevitable murder of Odoacer soon followed.

For the next ten days, the two chieftains held meetings, and on March 15, Theodoric invited Odoacer to a feast at his palace. Odoacer was ambushed during the dinner, and according to contemporary historians, Theodoric himself struck the killing blow while shouting, "This is what thou did to my friends!" referring to the killing of the Gothic nobles in his retinue. The sword hit the 60-year-old Odoacer's collar bone, and the blow continued until the blade reached his loin. Theodoric is said to have remarked, with a brutal laugh, "This wretch does not even seem to have a spine in his body," thereby also implying that Odoacer was a coward. Odoacer's retinue was massacred at the same feast, and his brother and wife murdered. His son was first sent into exile in Gaul, but was killed after trying to escape.

Theodoric's Ostrogothic Kingdom of Italy

Theodoric was proclaimed king by the Ostrogoths in March 493, without consulting Constantinople. This was a strong signal, as the barbarian kings customarily had asked the Romans for their title. Theodoric had already asked Emperor Zeno for leave to wear the purple, but with no success. In 490, when Theodoric's victory seemed certain, Roman Senator Festus had been sent to ask Zeno for permission to wear the royal regalia. Zeno died before deciding, however, and his successor, Anastasius, would not consent.

As such, there was no need to ask, as Theodoric had been king of the Ostrogoths for many years, but the question was for the kingship of Italy. Now, with little power to change the situation, Anastasius simply accepted the usurpation, and in 497, when Festus again was sent to Constantinople, the imperial regalia earlier deposited by Odoacer were finally given to him. Theodoric never took the title of emperor, however, and continued to be called *rex* and *princeps* (first citizen) as had other barbarian kings. Theodoric reigned in Italy from 493 to 526.

Theodoric was perhaps the most civilized barbarian the former Western Roman Empire would ever see. When he took the kingship of Italy he changed his bearing from the earlier plunderer of Thrace, Illyria, and numerous other provinces to that of benevolent ruler, eager to secure concord between Romans and Goths. There is no doubt that the establishment of a proper kingdom, as opposed to a wandering tribal confederation, lured many Goths to Theodoric's standard. Later generations would name him Theodoric the Great, in honor of the prosperity of his kingdom.

Apart from a single incident in 505, when Theodoric occupied the East Roman city of Sirmium during a Gepid war against the Eastern Empire and supported a barbarian attack on Sabinianus, the Roman master of the soldiers of Illyricum, there would be no major clashes with his Roman neighbors.

When in 507 the Franks, in alliance with the Burgundians, attacked and defeated the Visigoths and killed King Alaric II (484–507) at the battle of Campus Vogladensis (Vouillé in modern-day France), Theodoric intervened against the growing power of the Franks and conquered the coast as far as Arelate (Arles), adding this to his Italian kingdom. After the short reign of the Visigothic King Gesalic (507–511), Theodoric decided to champion the cause of his grandson, Amalaric. Gesalic had been ejected from Spain, and young Amalaric was put on the Visigothic throne. In reality, Theodoric governed Spain and the region of Septimania in his name. At the end of Theodoric's reign in 526, the Ostrogothic Kingdom of Italy was the strongest barbarian nation occupying the former Western Roman Empire.

The Ostrogoths changed little of the Roman administration in the time of Theodoric, who had a great esteem and respect for the Roman way of life and Roman civilization. Most of the administration still consisted—perhaps for practical reasons—of Roman citizens. The Senate would also still function and even become more powerful, as both Odoacer and Theodoric were eager to gain the confidence of the senatorial aristocracy. Despite being unwilling to sit in the palaces of the emperors in Rome, Theodoric continued to pay the palace guards and made their positions hereditary, in order to maintain the dignity of the former capital.

Religion in the Kingdom of Italy

The two early persecutions of Christians north of the Danube in
the fourth century seem to have been the only such incidents, and
neither was particularly serious. Theodoric the Great respected the
Christianity of his Roman subjects but kept his own Arianism.
Religion in general does not seem to have played so great a role in
the kingdom of Italy. Theodoric would present himself as a traditional king, supporting the religion of his subjects, and he had
churches built in Ravenna and other places. No doubt the pagan
Ostrogoths living in Italy would also move toward Christianity in
some form because of the great influence of the Roman population.
Apparently, Theodoric even enjoyed listening to religious arguments at court, and the teacher of his daughter, Amalasuntha, was
orthodox. His own mother even converted to orthodoxy, without
censure.

But while the Ostrogoths left their subjects to choose their form
of Christianity, the Vandals in Africa made several violent persecutions of the local Romans and tried to force them toward Arianism.
Only after the death of King Thrasamund in 523 did the persecutions stop.

After their long wanderings and almost constant struggles, the
Ostrogoths finally succeeded in creating the kingdom they wanted,
abundant in food and riches. When the Gothic warriors met the
Roman troops of Justinian, none of the Ostrogoths had ever seen
their homeland north of the Danube. Almost all were born in Italy
and were, therefore, in a way more Roman than the armies of
Constantinople. The war would show that they would be willing to
lay down their lives in the struggle for their new homeland. After
all, where would they go if they did not keep Italy? Herein lies perhaps the reason for the savageness and desperation of the Gothic
War. The Ostrogoths loved Italy more than any of their former
homelands.

4

THE
FIRST STAGES

WITH THE STAGE SET FOR THE GOTHIC WAR, we now turn to the affairs after the Roman victory over the Vandals. Belisarius's services were required for the next stage of the reconquest of the West, for the time seemed ripe for the recovery of Italy.

Theodoric had died in 526, leaving the throne to his ten-year-old grandson, Athalaric, in whose name his mother, Amalasuntha, governed the kingdom. Amalasuntha's position was precarious, for not only did the Goths object to the rule of a woman, but many of them also objected to the pro-Roman attitude she maintained, in conformity with her late father's policy. They insisted that Athalaric should not receive a Roman education but instead be brought up in a proper Gothic fashion under the charge of young Gothic nobles. Amalasuntha thus had to watch her son slowly being alienated from her, but it would only get worse, for under the tutelage of his new masters, Athalaric started drinking, and it became obvious he would not survive long.

To reinsure herself, Amalasuntha entered into secret negotiations with Justinian, offering to resign the kingdom to him in return for asylum. Justinian had sent Senator Alexander to officially complain that the Goths had received Roman deserters, had taken the city of Lilybaeum after the Vandal War, and had attacked the Roman city of Gratiana in Moesia during the war with the Gepids in 530. While making the official complaints, Alexander also negotiated with the queen about the exact terms for her resignation.

But Amalasuntha took courage when she managed to assassinate three of her chief opponents, and on Athalaric's death October 10, 534, she assumed the title of queen, taking as her consort her cousin Theodahad, whom she proclaimed king.

Theodahad was a highly Romanized Goth, and a student of Latin literature and Plato, who had shown no signs of political ambition, contenting himself with increasing his already vast estates. Amalasuntha had expected him to leave the government to her, but Theodahad quickly put himself at the head of the Gothic opposition, deposed her, and imprisoned her on an island on the lake at Vulsena (Bolsena). There she was secretly put to death in April 535.

This was Justinian's opportunity. He delivered a vigorous protest against the murder of a friendly queen and at the same time, hoping to intimidate the weak-minded Theodahad into surrendering, launched two expeditions against the outlying portions of the Ostrogothic Kingdom.

The fleet sailed out pretending it was on its way to reinforce the garrison in Carthage, but with Sicily as its goal. The main southern invasion would be supported by an assault on the northern parts of the Gothic Kingdom led by General Mundus against Dalmatia, and politically through a treaty with the Franks.

Mundus, the Gepid master of the soldiers in Illyricum (*magister militum per Illyricum*), was sent with three thousand to four thousand troops against Dalmatia, the easternmost Gothic province, which lay along the Adriatic Sea. Mundus had already proven his loyalty and ability during the Nika insurrection, when he had crushed the rebellion with Belisarius. After defeating the Gothic troops in the region, the provincial capital of Salona (Solin in modern-day Croatia) was taken without resistance.

While this diversion was taking place, Belisarius would deliver the main attack from the south.

Allies were sought in the form of the powerful Franks, and Justinian sent a letter to the leaders of the Franks citing common religion (the Franks were Orthodox, whereas the Goths were of the Arian heresy) and the traditional poor relations between the Franks and Ostrogoths. The Franks enthusiastically promised to enter into alliance, no doubt also swayed by the large gift of money that came with the letter.

THE ARMY OF BELISARIUS

Belisarius's army was not large, only about seven thousand five hundred men—four thousand regulars, three thousand Isaurians, two hundred Huns and three hundred Moors—but they were all experienced veterans, commanded by able generals. The cavalry had been strengthened after the experiences in the campaign against the Vandals in Africa. In addition, there was Belisarius's personal bodyguard, which during the war rose to about seven thousand elite troops, and the bodyguards of his generals. As was common in this period, the barbarian element in the army was large, as also many of the regulars were of barbarian origin. It was named the Roman army, and the standards still bore the letters "SPQR," but probably not one soldier out of a hundred in the imperial army could speak Latin, and many of them may hardly have known sufficient Greek to function without help in the Greek cities of the Eastern Empire.

Belisarius's generals were also mostly of barbarian stock—the three most important barbarian generals were the Thracian Constantine, the Iberian Peranius (from what is now Georgia), and the Goth Bessas. Their peculiar characters would turn out to be of great importance during the campaign. Photius, the son of Belisarius's wife, Antonina, by a former marriage, accompanied his stepfather as an aide.

Lesser commanders included Valentinus, Magnus, and Innocentius, who were in charge of the cavalry, and Herodianus, Paulus, Demetrius, and Ursicinus leading the infantry. Ennes was general of the Isaurian contingent.

THE SICILIAN CAMPAIGN

The expedition sailed for Sicily with instructions for Belisarius to seize it if he could without a struggle, but if he anticipated resistance to sail for Carthage, as if this was the intention all along.

After Belisarius landed at Catana (Catania) and made it his base, it soon became evident that the Sicilians were eager to become subjects of the emperor again. Belisarius met no opposition except from the Gothic garrison of Panormus (Palermo), and this was quickly overcome by the following stratagem:

After a reconnaissance, Belisarius saw that the fortifications on the land side were too formidable to be assaulted directly. But the walls facing the sea were unguarded, and after collecting his navy in the harbor, he found that the masts of the ships were higher than the battlements. So he hit upon a daring plan. The ships were filled with soldiers who were hoisted up to the yardarms of the vessels that were lying at anchor close to the walls. The men then climbed onto the walls from the boats. If the Goths had manned the walls in any numbers, the plan would have been impossible, but the Romans swiftly took the unguarded walls. From there they could fire arrows down on the Gothic warriors, who soon surrendered. In this way the last Gothic garrison in Sicily surrendered.

On the last day of his consulate, December 31, 535, Belisarius moved into Syracusa after having conquered the island. His soldiers and the jubilant provincials greeted him as he walked in procession through the city, scattering gold coins to mark the occasion. Thus the main corn supply for Italy had been taken without problems. One reason the occupation went so smoothly was that the population was entirely Roman and a few still remembered the times of the Western Empire before Odoacer and Theodoric.

Few Gothic troops had been stationed on the island, and it is reasonable to ask why Sicily, as the most important region for the corn supply of Italy and especially Rome, was not more strongly occupied with Gothic garrisons. Sicily, which was rich and had not been plundered for a long time, had agreed to ensure the corn supply of Italy and Rome if the Goths agreed to not station large forces on the island. The inhabitants feared the Goths would abuse and plunder them. As the Goths knew that the Sicilians derived their main income from the corn trade with Italy, it had seemed a reasonable request, and the agreement was made. Thus Sicily had been garrisoned with only small Gothic forces. Now the defection of the island caused much bitterness among the Goths, who felt they had been deceived. Eleven years later, when there were peace talks between the Goths and the empire and the Goths were in a position

Map 5. Italy and Sicily in the sixth century.

to dictate terms, the Gothic king insisted that the empire not stand between his people and their revenge on the the people of Sicily.

Although there was almost no resistance during the Sicilian campaign, it still took some seven months to take the island.

NEGOTIATIONS WITH THEODAHAD

While Belisarius dispersed his army into winter quarters in Sicily, negotiations between the emperor and the intimidated Gothic king went on. After receiving news of the loss of Sicily, Theodahad entered into secret negotiations with Peter, the imperial ambassador, who agreed to submit to Justinian a draft agreement whereby Theodahad would rule Italy as a vassal of the empire. The conditions were:

> Sicily would be ceded to the emperor.
>
> Each year, Theodahad would send the emperor a gold crown weighing 300 pounds.
>
> Whenever Justinian required it, Theodahad would send three thousand warriors.
>
> Theodahad would refrain from executing, or confiscating the property of, any senator or priest without the emperor's permission.
>
> Theodahad would not grant the patriciate or senatorial rank to anybody without the emperor's permission.
>
> At the Hippodrome, the theater, and all public places, the people were always to shout "Long live Justinian" before Theodahad's name was mentioned.
>
> No statue of bronze or any other material was to be raised to Theodahad alone, but everywhere a statue of Justinian must stand beside him on his right side.

In his panic, Theodahad not only made these humiliating concessions but also confidentially informed Peter that as a last resort he would be prepared to surrender Italy in return for estates in the East with an annual value of one thousand two hundred pounds of gold.

After the initial negotiations, Peter betrayed Theodahad's confidences to Justinian, and the latter accordingly rejected the draft agreement and accepted the second offer of a retirement to the East. Justinian sent Peter and another ambassador, Athanasius, to formalize the details. But Theodahad, encouraged by a Gothic success in Dalmatia, had changed his mind, and he received the Roman ambassadors in a cold manner when they returned to Rome with their master's answer at the end of 535. The envoys were put under guard after having delivered their message. There is no doubt that the strong anti-Roman sentiments among the Gothic nobles had swayed the weak will of Theodahad, who cared little for matters of state.

OPERATIONS IN DALMATIA

After Mundus had taken Salona and the province of Dalmatia, a large Gothic army under Asinarius and Gripas was sent into the province in the autumn of 535. Mauricius, the son of Mundus, was killed during a reconnaissance when he approached too close to the Gothic army. Mundus then became mad with grief and attacked the Gothic army north of Salona. The hastily prepared attack initially broke the Gothic ranks, but Mundus was killed by a spear in the pursuit. At his death, the Roman army lost its momentum and retreated in disorder. Salona was initially left unoccupied by both armies, as the Romans were in disorder and the Goths mistrusted the citizens and the strength of the walls. Only later would the Goths enter the city.

Procopius the historian mentions that an old sibylline prophecy, which had caused some fear among the Romans, had now been fulfilled. The words ran like this:

> First Rome reconquers Africa. Then the World
> Is with its progeny to ruin hurled.

It had appeared to the superstitious Romans that the end of the world was near after the reconquest of Africa, but now they understood that it was Mundus ("world," in Latin) and his son about whom the prophecy spoke.

This success in Dalmatia, which made Theodahad change his mind, was only temporary. Constantianus, the *comes stabuli*, or count of the stables in the imperial household, was sent with an army in 536 to recover Salona and Dalmatia for the emperor. At the approach of the Roman fleet, the Gothic General Gripas was struck by fear, evacuated Salona, and pitched camp in the hills west of the city. On receiving this news, Constantianus landed his troops at Salona, occupied it, and repaired its walls. A force of five hundred men was sent to occupy the narrow western pass, which the Goths would have to use to attack Salona. After waiting seven days, the Gothic general simply marched back to Ravenna, having accomplished nothing. But this would happen later, and we now return to the situation in Italy after Theodahad had rejected the peace offers of Justinian in late December 535.

On receiving the arrogant refusal from Theodahad, Justinian ordered Belisarius to take the war to the Goths and invade Italy. Both sides began preparing for the continuation of the war, and these preparations would take most of the winter of 535–536.

Uprising in Africa

Belisarius was delayed for a time because of troubles in Africa. A few days after Easter 536, at the end of March, a single ship from Africa reached the harbor of Syracusa, where Belisarius was staying. Chief among the passengers was the eunuch Solomon, in whose charge Belisarius had left the city of Carthage two years earlier. Solomon, a brave soldier and efficient administrator, had been forced to flee the newly conquered province, not because of the barbarians, but because of his own soldiers.

The Moors, who had submitted to the Romans soon after the defeat of the Vandals, had in 535 started to make raids on the province. According to Procopius, who was in Africa at the time, the Moorish raiders numbered thirty thousand to fifty thousand. When Solomon reminded the chieftains that he held their children as hostages for their good behavior, they replied that "as for children, that will be your concern, who are not permitted to marry more than one wife; but with us, who have, it may be, fifty wives living with each of us, offspring of children can never fail," and continued their raids. On receiving this answer, Solomon gathered his forces and moved to Byzacena, where the Moorish rebels recently had destroyed a Roman detachment under Aigan the Hun and Rufinus, who had both been killed.

Despite the Romans' winning two great victories in battles against the Moorish armies and defeating their incursions in the province, the Moors in Numidia and their chieftain, Iaudas, had succeeded in encamping with some thirty thousand barbarians on the high plateau of Mount Aurasium, thirteen days' journey from Carthage, from where they kept on raiding the surrounding countryside. Solomon had not been able to dislodge him from this easily defensible base, although he was continually trying to defeat the raids. This situation continued until Easter Day, March 23, 536, when a universal mutiny broke out among the Roman soldiers.

CAUSES OF THE MUTINY

Many of the Roman soldiers had married Vandal widows and had counted on taking over the land the widows inherited from their dead husbands. But the Roman administration decided that the land and estates of the defeated Vandals were to go to the treasury, and that if the husband of a Vandal widow was cultivating them, it would be under the burden of a land tax, no matter if he was civilian or soldier. That is, he would not be the owner of the lands, but a tenant.

The hot-blooded soldiers, with their newly won wives whispering in their ears about the great riches they would miss, were soon disaffected. Had they not conquered the land for the empire, and did they therefore not have a right to the lands, they asked themselves. But as Procopius quotes Solomon:

> While it was not unreasonable that the slaves and all other things of value should go as booty to the soldiers, the land itself belonged to the emperor and the empire of the Romans, which had nourished them and caused them to be called soldiers and to be such, not in order to win for themselves such land as they should wrest from the barbarians who were trespassing on the Roman empire, but that this

land might come to the commonwealth, from which both they and all others secured their maintenance.

This was the law of the empire, and Solomon steadfastly kept to it.

Other troubles stemmed from the fact that most of the soldiers were Arians. Many of the Roman soldiers were Germans by birth and therefore belonged to the Arian heresy of Christianity. In particular, a group of about one thousand Herulian barbarians steadfastly held onto their Arian beliefs. The Vandal priests—also Arians—who remained in Africa preached the suppression and persecution that the emperor exposed them—the victors—to, because of their beliefs. Justinian had even proclaimed that no person could be baptized or baptize others if he did not hold the orthodox faith of Athanasius.

With Easter approaching, the Arian soldiers knew that none of their children would be baptized and none of them would be able to participate in the celebrations without renouncing the faith of their forefathers.

A third problem was that the soldiers had not yet received their pay, which was months behind. While the emperor quickly sent tax gatherers and other officials to the reconquered province, no money to pay the soldiers had arrived. The almost chronic lack of finances during the reign of Justinian, and the inefficient and bureaucratic system of paying the army, would later cause even greater troubles for the Romans during the Gothic War. On several occasions, soldiers would be driven into rebellion or desertion after months or even years without pay. The effect of the mismanagement of the finances of the empire at this time cannot be underestimated; it allowed what should have been a relatively short war against the Ostrogoths to drag on for almost twenty years.

A fourth element increased the tensions that led to the mutiny. The Vandals, whom Belisarius had brought to Constantinople as prisoners of war, had been formed into five cavalry regiments named the Vandals of Justinian and were ordered to the East to garrison the cities of Syria against the Persians. Most of them proceeded to their appointed cities and would serve the empire faithfully in their new life. But during the voyage, after reaching Lesbos, four hundred of them forced the sailors to set the course for the Peloponnesus and then for Africa. When they reached the coast, the ships were set on shore, and the Vandals marched to a fortress on Mount Aurasium. Here they entered into correspondence with the mutinous soldiers at Carthage, and after exchanging oaths, they agreed to support the revolt.

At Easter 536, everything was ready for the rebellion. The signal for the revolt was to be the murder of the governor, Solomon, in the great basilica of Carthage on Good Friday. The attempt on Good Friday failed, as did another attempt the next day, both times because the assassins did not have the courage for the deed. Believing the design now to be generally known, the ringleaders of the mutiny then left the city and started raiding the country districts, while many others stayed in Carthage and pretended not to have known about the plot.

When Solomon realized the danger he was in, he exhorted the remaining soldiers in Carthage to remain faithful to the emperor. Initially, it seemed the rebellion would not develop, but after five days the soldiers in Carthage saw that the mutinous soldiers in the country districts were ravaging without check. They gathered at the Hippodrome, and attempts to soothe them were unsuccessful. The popular officer Theodorus the Cappadocian was sent to calm them, but the soldiers instead chose him to lead their rebellion, as they believed him to be secretly opposed to Solomon. Theodorus, who remained loyal to the emperor, humored them for a while to help Solomon escape. The rebels then went around the streets of Carthage killing everyone who was suspected of supporting Solomon or who had money to rob.

When night came, Solomon and his second in command, Martinus, who had been lying low in the Governor's Palace all day, stealthily went to the house of Theodorus. He gave them food and helped them to a boat in the harbor.

With the rebellion in full flame, Solomon had no option but to flee to Sicily, with five of his officers and the advisor Procopius, who would later record the history of the events. After many difficulties, they reached Belisarius in Syracusa and related the events of the mutiny.

STOTZAS IS PROCLAIMED KING

Meanwhile, the insurgents had assembled a short distance south-west of Carthage on the plains of Boulla. As Theodorus had refused to lead the rebels, they chose Stotzas, a bodyguard of Solomon's second in command, Martinus, and acclaimed him king.

The hardy Stotzas found no less than eight thousand men under his standards. Soon after, a thousand Vandals joined them—the recent fugitives from Constantinople and those Vandals who had escaped the notice of the Romans after the war ended in 534. Numerous slaves from the Roman estates in the region also joined them.

Their goal was to drive out the Romans and make themselves masters of North Africa. They marched to Carthage, which was still held by Theodorus and a few loyal troops, and demanded their surrender, but without success.

With Carthage being the most important city of the region, it is surprising that the soldiers did not initially stay there and make themselves masters of the city. This would prove to be a serious military error. The most obvious reason for this oversight seems to be the rebels' lack of a proper leader and unification in the initial stages.

BELISARIUS ARRIVES

Josephius, a clerk on Belisarius's staff who happened to be in Carthage, was sent to Stotzas as an envoy to persuade him to end the rebellion. The mutineers quickly showed their unwillingness to compromise by brutally murdering him and initiating a siege of the city. The few troops left in Carthage were soon despairing at the hopeless situation and were on the point of surrendering the city to the rebels.

With the army almost ready to march against the Goths, Belisarius could ill afford to have an active and unchecked rebellion in his back. At the same time, he could not jeopardize the Gothic campaign by bringing his entire army against the mutiny. After Solomon's report on the desperate state of things in Africa, Belisarius chose instead to board a single ship with one hundred men picked from his bodyguard and set out for Carthage.

When he arrived, the mutineers were encamped around the city, confident of taking it by surrender or assault on the following day. But by dawn the next day, the news of Belisarius's arrival had filtered outside the city. Awed by the name of their old commander, the rebels broke up their camp and started a disorderly retreat that led them to the city of Membresa (Majaz al-Bab in modern-day Tunisia) on the Bagradas River, about 40 miles southwest of Carthage. Here they finally made camp, probably exhausted from the hasty and long retreat. But Belisarius was already hard on their heels, now with two thousand loyal troops whom he had persuaded to return to the imperial cause with gifts and promises. As Membresa was not walled, neither army dared to occupy it.

Stotzas and his army, which was still four times the size of Belisarius's force, had pitched camp on a hill well suited for defensive operations, while the loyalists made their camp at the river.

THE BATTLE OF MEMBRESA

Because of the impending campaign against the Ostrogoths, Belisarius had to force the decision and quickly led his troops out.

Both commanders harangued their troops in the customary manner before the battle. Belisarius declared that the mutineers had brought ruin upon themselves by their actions and that the slaying of their loyal comrades demanded vengeance. He ended the speech with one of the most important maxims of the Gothic War: "For it is not by the mass of combatants, but by their orderly array and their bravery, that prowess in war is wont to be measured."

Stotzas, in his speech, enlarged on the ingratitude shown to the soldiers after their great victory in the Vandal War. After the freedom they had felt in the past few weeks, a return to slavery would be ten times as bitter. Also, they could not expect pardon from the imperials, after what they had done during the rebellion. They could but die once, so let them die, if need be, as free warriors on the battlefield. The result of a victory over the pitiful band of loyalists would give them the mastery over Africa and their hearts' desires. To the mainly Germanic element in the rebel army, the words rang true.

The battle itself was short. Belisarius had positioned his army so that a strong wind blew in the faces of the mutineers, hindering their use of missile weapons. When the rebels started a flanking movement to get windward of the enemy, Belisarius ordered his troops to come to close quarters at once while the mutineers were in disorder. The unexpected and sharp attack was a success, and Stotzas's army fled in disorder. It did not stop until it reached Numidia, far to the south. The Vandal element in the army seemed to be the only ones who had listened to Stotzas's speech. For the most part they refused to flee and died on the field of battle.

The rebel camp was plundered, and in it was found the great treasures of Carthage and the Vandal wives of the soldiers, the original abettors of the revolt.

With the mutineers either killed or in flight, Belisarius thought the situation to be sufficiently in hand to let the local generals handle the mopping up and left quickly for Sicily. Reports also made him fear that the army in Sicily might follow the example set by the troops in Africa and mutiny. Accordingly, he left his son-in-law Ildiger and Theodorus the Cappadocian in charge of the troops in Africa and sailed away in April or May 536.

The fears of a mutiny in Sicily were unfounded, or perhaps the name of Belisarius also had a magical ring to it there. The worst enemy of an army being idleness, Belisarius immediately started the campaign against the Ostrogoths, as ordered by the emperor.

The Invasion of South Italy

After leaving garrisons in Syracusa and Panormus, he crossed from Messana (Messina) to Rhegium (Reggio), where the inhabitants greeted the Romans jubilantly.

The dissension among the Goths came clearly to the light at Rhegium when Evermud, the son-in-law of Theodahad who was commanding the Gothic army guarding the straits, came into Belisarius's camp with his troops, prostrated himself at the feet of the general, and expressed his desire to be subject to the will of the emperor. He was well rewarded for his treachery: he was at once sent to Constantinople, where he was made patrician and received many rewards from the emperor.

The Romans then took the provinces of Bruttium and Lucania, which were without Gothic garrisons. Everywhere they were received as liberators. As the army marched north, it was supported by the parallel movement of the fleet, which controlled the seas, as the Goths had no navy to speak of.

SIEGE OF NEAPOLIS

The ease of the invasion stopped, however, in front of Neapolis (Naples), which was the center of Gothic power in south Italy. The Gothic governor had a fairly strong garrison, and Belisarius could not risk bypassing the city. He soon initiated a blockade of the city from land and sea, and was rewarded with the quick surrender of one of the outlying forts. The harbor was outside missile range from the walls, so he ordered parts of the fleet to anchor there.

Negotiations with the aristocracy of the city were also soon attempted, but they led nowhere, as they felt quite happy about their Gothic masters. The Jewish merchants in the city, who were anti-Roman, guaranteed the Gothic governor that they would supply the city during a siege. Belisarius then offered the Gothic garrison the choice of fighting for the emperor or marching away unharmed, but they declined.

At the same time, the garrison sent a message to King Theodahad asking for the dispatch of a relieving army. As usual, Theodahad was indecisive, and no help was sent. The garrison, however, seemed able to resist a siege alone. The steepness of the approaches to the walls, the narrow space between them and the sea, which left no room for the movement of troops, and the impossibility of bringing the ships close enough to attack the city all made it difficult for Belisarius to take Neapolis. He had cut the aqueduct that brought water into the city, but there were enough wells within the walls to serve the needs of the garrison and the inhabitants.

Time passed, and several attempts were made to take the walls, but with no success and only heavy losses to show. Belisarius soon became impatient to end the siege. Twenty days had passed with futile attacks, and time was of the essence for the Roman army. If the Romans were to reach Rome before the whole of the Gothic army had been gathered and it became too cold to campaign, the siege had to be ended soon, and without too many losses.

When he was at the point of giving the order to march, thereby leaving a dangerous garrison at his back and making his early gains worthless, one of his bodyguards, an Isaurian named Paucaris, brought a glimmer of hope. One of his fellow countrymen had, out of curiosity, climbed (the Isaurians were from a mountainous province in Asia Minor) up to the end of the broken aqueduct to see the channel in which the water had flowed. He had crept down the channel, which had been imperfectly closed by the garrison and had come to a place where the channel went through solid rock. Here the channel was too narrow for a man in armor to get through, but the Isaurian believed it possible to widen the channel in the soft rock. Quickly Belisarius sent more Isaurians to widen the channel so troops could enter the city.

Before the assault, the garrison and the inhabitants were offered a chance to surrender one final time, but they refused.

Four hundred men were picked and sent to the entrance of the aqueduct, where the plan was revealed to them. Their commanders were Ennes, general of the Isaurians, and Magnus, one of the cavalry commanders, while Bessas stayed with Belisarius. Meanwhile, the rest of the Roman army was made ready to attack the city on all sides the moment the troops had entered it. Initially, it seemed the bold plan would fail, as half the troops that entered the aqueduct tunnel turned back, declaring it could not be done. Belisarius, who was standing at the entrance of the tunnel, then selected two hundred other volunteers. Photius, his stepson, offered to lead the detachment, but Belisarius refused. The example set by the eager volunteers shamed the waverers so that they also returned into the tunnel, thus raising the numbers of the group to six hundred. Fearful of the noise the troops would make while moving inside the channel of the aqueduct, Belisarius sent Bessas to the wall where the aqueduct entered the city with orders to loudly converse with the Goths on the wall.

After some difficulties, the troops exited the tunnel and ran to the northern walls, outside which most of the rest of the army was waiting with Belisarius and Bessas in command. The sentinels in two towers were surprised and killed, after which two trumpeters blew their bugles as the signal for attack. Disaster threatened the plan when the ladders put up against the wall proved too short and did not even reach the battlements. Hastily, they were taken down and fastened together, two and two, and put up again.

The defenders were completely surprised, and soon the north wall was taken. On the south wall, the task was somewhat harder, as the Jews rather than Goths held that section. The Jews had played an important role in the defense of the city and knew that the Romans would not look lightly on their actions. Only when day dawned and they were attacked in the rear by troops from the other parts of the city were they obliged to flee, and the Romans could open the southern gates.

With dawn and victory coming, bands of the Roman troops— almost entirely made up of barbarian and semibarbarian soldiers— were pouring through the town, murdering, plundering, and ravishing the inhabitants. The Huns did not even spare the ones who had fled to the churches for refuge.

Belisarius was able to stop the plundering by explaining to the troops that Neapolis was now a subject city with fellow citizens, and that therefore the victory should not be tarnished by murder and bloodshed. The troops were given whatever plunder they could gather, but the captives were set free. Eight hundred Gothic warriors were captured and were protected from harm by Belisarius, who probably hoped to induce other Goths to lay down their weapons quietly and fight for the emperor.

After the victory, Belisarius left three hundred infantry under Herodian in Neapolis, and the captured eight hundred Gothic warriors were enrolled in the Roman army. Belisarius then continued his interrupted march by the Via Latina toward his main goal, Rome.

5

THE FIRST
SIEGE OF ROME

THEODAHAD DEPOSED

Despite the courageous resistance of the inhabitants and garrison of Neapolis, which had delayed the Romans for three weeks, no help had been sent from Rome. The warlike Gothic subjects of King Theodahad were exasperated by the conduct of the war. His avarice was well known, and they suspected that his inaction was due to treachery. Rumors of his negotiations with Constantinople had reached the ears of his subjects, and the loss of the main city of south Italy and, thereby, the whole region without even gathering the Gothic army, seemed only to confirm the suspicions.

The Gothic nobles met at the village of Regata, a little more than 30 miles from Rome, to deliberate on the perilous condition of their kingdom. There was no doubt Theodahad would have to be deposed, but who was to reign in his stead? The line of Theodoric the Great was practically extinct, with only the young girl Matasuntha—the sister of Athalaric the Visigothic king in Spain—remaining of that great family. None of the nobles seemed an obvious choice either. So they chose Vittigis, an elderly general who had fought his way to the top by his deeds in the Sirmium War against the Gepids and similar campaigns on the borders. The choice of a general as king was perhaps the wisest that could be made at the time.

Theodahad meanwhile tried to flee to Ravenna but was overtaken and killed on the road by a Goth named Optaris, whom Vittigis had chosen to assassinate him. Theodahad's son, Theodegisclus, was soon after imprisoned, and nothing more is heard of him.

VITTIGIS IS PROCLAIMED KING OF ITALY

Vittigis was raised upon a shield in the traditional way and acclaimed as king. On his accession to the throne, he found that no preparations had been made for countering the Roman invasion. Only parts of the great Gothic army had been gathered.

With the Franks (secretly in league with Justinian) pressing the Gothic provinces in Gaul, and the Romans pushing from the south and east, Vittigis made the fateful decision to withdraw to impregnable Ravenna in north Italy and there prepare for the defense of the kingdom. Rome would not be left entirely unguarded, as the officer Leuderis was left in charge of the city with four thousand picked troops, probably with orders to hold Rome or delay Belisarius as much as possible while the Gothic army was gathered. First the Frankish threat would be handled, then the full might of the Ostrogoths would be brought to bear against Belisarius.

Events would later show this withdrawal to Ravenna to be a serious strategic blunder. The Roman forces in Dalmatia were not strong enough to seriously consider a push into north Italy, and the Franks could easily be bought off by land, as they did not want a strong Roman Empire on their own borders. Instead, the main threat was coming from Belisarius in the south. Perhaps Vittigis had been fooled by the fierce resistance of the inhabitants in Neapolis and thought the Romans would meet similar obstacles in the future. After all, the Ostrogothic rule, especially during the golden period of Theodoric, had been benevolent to the conquered Roman population and had earnestly sought to weld a bond between the two peoples.

After explaining his reasons for the move to the army and the Gothic nobles, who agreed with the course of action, Vittigis moved north to Ravenna. Perhaps he was not entirely sure of the fidelity of the inhabitants of Rome, as he took several precautions before leaving. He spoke to Pope Silverius, the Senate, and the people of Rome and bound them by oaths to be faithful to Gothic rule. And, to ensure the loyalty of the Senate, he brought a large number of senators to Ravenna as hostages.

When arriving at Ravenna, Vittigis further secured his position as king of the Ostrogoths by marrying Matasuntha—daughter of the murdered Amalasuntha, sister of Athalaric the Visigothic king, and the granddaughter of Theodoric the Great. After all, Vittigis was a man of lowly origin, and an alliance with the Gothic royal family might make his election seem more than a desperate expedient. The marriage between the old general and the young Matasuntha would not be a happy one, and she made no secret of the fact that she did not love her husband. Later she would even plan treachery against the Goths.

The marriage could also be seen as a diplomatic move to ease the relationship to Constantinople. Soon after, a delegation was sent to Constantinople suggesting that the causes of the quarrel between the emperor and the Goths were gone. Theodahad had paid for his crimes, and the daughter of Amalasuntha was on the throne. We do not know the answers to the delegation, probably received in late autumn 536, but they were clearly negative, as no peace was made and no mention was made of the delegation afterward.

SECRET TREATY WITH THE FRANKS

Since the Franks had conquered the Burgundian kingdom in 534, they had been the immediate neighbors of the Ostrogothic kingdom and the strongest threat to north Italy. One of the first acts of the new king was to buy off the Franks by ceding the Ostrogothic possessions in Gaul (mainly Provence) and paying two thousand pounds of gold. These negotiations with the Franks had actually been initiated by Theodahad but were interrupted by his early death. The Franks in return promised to send some of their subject tribes to support the Gothic cause. All the negotiations were conducted in secrecy, as the Franks wanted to keep up the appearance that they were honoring their treaty with Justinian. The treaty made it possible to recall the Gothic army in Provence—the veteran General Marcias and thousands of the most experienced warriors—to Ravenna and the main Gothic host.

The Franks did not love the Ostrogoths and were otherwise threatened from a union between the Visigoths of Spain and the strong Ostrogothic kingdom of Italy, but much less did they prefer a strong Roman Empire on their borders. Rather, the Franks hoped that the Romans and Ostrogoths would weaken themselves fighting each other and leave the Franks to consolidate their still-young kingdom and then to enter the stage when the opportunity would arise. Accepting gold from the Romans and land from the Ostrogoths while sending away some of their troublesome subjects from conquered tribes shows the adept diplomacy of the one barbarian nation that would truly benefit from the war.

While Vittigis was securing his northern and eastern flanks and his position as king, Belisarius devoted the summer and autumn of 536 to consolidating his conquests in southern Italy. Cumae (Cuma) in Campania, with its strong fortress, was occupied, and a small garrison stationed there.

On the coming of Belisarius, the Gothic General Pitzas, in command of Samnium, surrendered most of his province and his personal followers to the cause of the imperials. The citizens of Apulia and Calabria also surrendered, as there were no Gothic garrisons in the region.

In late autumn or early winter of 536, Pope Silverius, despite his oaths to Vittigis, sent messengers to Belisarius to offer the surrender of Rome. The offer seems mostly to have been made to avoid a repetition of the siege and sack of Neapolis. Considering the fortunes of the Romans and the Goths, it appeared to the nobility of Rome wisest to submit to Belisarius and risk the wrath of the Goths, rather than accept a lengthy siege and sack of the Eternal City.

Belisarius gladly accepted the offer and hurried his march by the great Via Latina toward Rome.

THE CAPTURE OF ROME

When the Gothic garrison of Rome learned Belisarius was coming and the inhabitants were preparing for treachery, the troops concluded it was impossible to hold the more than twelve-mile-long walls of Rome and at the same time guard themselves against a hostile population. They therefore decided to leave the city and retreat north. Their general, Leuderis, would not hear of abandoning their post, but he could not stay his soldiers. So when Belisarius and his army entered Rome by the southern Porta Asinaria, the garrison quietly marched out through the northern Porta Flaminia. The abandoned Leuderis was taken prisoner and sent to Constantinople, together with the keys of the city. The peaceful capture of the great city took place December 9, 536.

Thus, after sixty years of barbarian domination, the Eternal City, the Mistress of the World, Rome, was recovered for the Roman Empire. The impression the capture made in the Roman world was enormous, which was undoubtedly also part of Belisarius's plan. There are many examples of his great understanding of psychology in war. While Rome was not inherently important to the Goths, they now had to—for political reasons—retake the city as soon as possible, thereby surrendering the initiative and creating the best possible tactical circumstances for the Romans.

The city that met Belisarius in 536 was an almost untouched Rome. The Visigoths and Vandals had caused limited destruction in 410 and 455, and the great monuments of ancient Rome were still standing. The imperial palace on the Palatine Hill was still protected by the imperial guard, despite being otherwise empty. The number of inhabitants was somewhat reduced from the empire's heyday but still totaled some 600,000, according to estimates.

Life in the great metropolis had not been altered much either. The citizens were still going to the circus to watch chariot races and still went to the great imperial baths to discuss and debate the issues of the age. But this would soon change.

All of southern Italy and Rome were now in the hands of the Romans, but with his small forces, Belisarius could venture no further. So he started preparing Rome for the inevitable Gothic siege. Belisarius also had the important passes of the Apennines at Spoletium (Spoleto), Perusia (Perugia), and Narnia (Narni) occupied with small garrisons. This move would seriously hinder the Gothic march on Rome and give Belisarius advance warning of any approaching army. This understanding of the strategic situation shows he was already preparing for the next stages of the war.

He would not be able to defeat the enormous Gothic army in the field, as its numbers would make up for its tactical deficiencies. An attack against Ravenna and the entire Gothic army would be impossible with the few troops he had available: in his successful campaign for south Italy, Belisarius had been forced to leave gar-

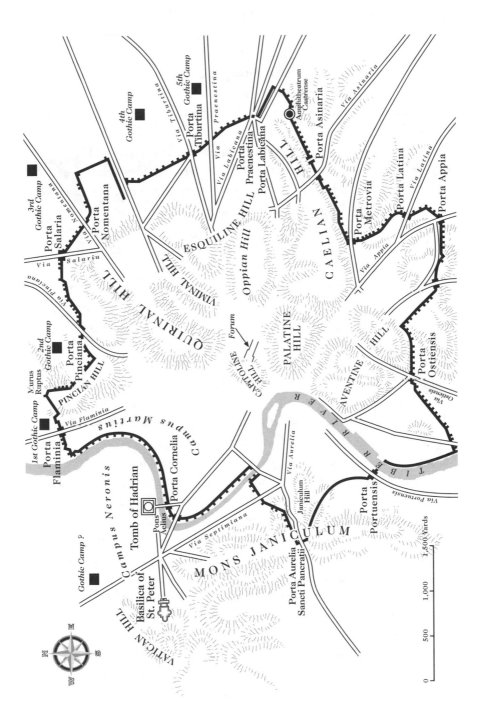

Map 6. Rome during the first siege in 537–538.

risons in strategic places, constantly reducing the size of his army. It appears his plan was to force the Goths to attack Rome—politically it would be impossible not to do this—and thereby force them into a type of warfare with which they had little experience and in which their numerical superiority would be minimized.

Furthermore, the city had the advantage of being practically impossible to blockade because of its enormously long walls. This, however, also meant that a Gothic assault on the walls would have to be held off long enough for Roman reserves to be brought up, as the walls were too long to occupy in strength. At most, the gates and towers could be garrisoned to hold off an attack long enough for other troops to move to the threatened point.

A siege could not be expected to last long, as the huge Gothic army was impossible to supply for any extended period of time, and the Goths did not have anything like the Roman logistical system.

Belisarius's headquarters were set up in a palace, the Domus Pinciana on the Pincian Hill. This position gave a clear view of the northern parts of the city from the Vatican and to the Mons Sacer. It was also only a few minutes ride from the Castra Praetoria, from where the wall all the way to the Porta Praenestina (the modern Porta Maggiore) could be observed. Thus, from these two places, about a third of the whole circuit of the wall, and almost all of what was actually attacked by the Goths, could be observed.

Belisarius's preparations were all a nasty surprise for the citizens of Rome, who had hoped to avoid the terrors of a siege. They had expected that the war soon would be over one way or another and probably decided by some great pitched battle to the north. After all, Rome was most difficult to defend with its long walls, without direct access to the sea and supplies, and with such an enormous civilian population, which had occasionally suffered from famine even in peace. Slowly the inhabitants awoke to the fact that their defection from the Gothic cause by no means would relieve them from the hardships of a siege.

Meanwhile, Belisarius was busily preparing the city for the return of the Goths. Grain was brought in from Sicily daily and stored in the great warehouses, and provisions from the surrounding area were also brought into the city and stored for later use.

Print by Luigi Rossini (1790–1857) of the Porta Praenestina in 1838. The walls of Emperor Aurelian incorporated several earlier tomb monuments and the monumental gate made by emperor Claudius in 52, which can be seen at the back of the scene. Porta Praenestina has now been torn down, revealing the gate of Claudius. (*Author*)

THE WALLS OF ROME

The seemingly desperate defense of Rome was based on the great city walls originally constructed by Emperor Aurelian and further strengthened by later emperors. The walls, which were rivaled only by the fortifications of Constantinople, are perhaps the greatest monument of ancient times left in modern Rome, and large sections still exist. Without them it would have been impossible to defend Rome against the numerically superior Gothic army.

In 271, when Italy was threatened for the first time in centuries by Germanic tribes, Aurelian constructed the first city wall of Rome since Republican times. The old wall of King Servius Tullius (578–535 BC) had long been in disuse, and by the time of Augustus (31 BC–14 AD) it was hard to trace its course at all.

The new wall encompassed the whole city and was twenty-six feet high and twelve feet thick. It was built in the traditional Roman way of the third century, with a core of concrete and faced with the Roman standard bricks called *bipedales*. It was constructed with great gates at the main roads entering the city and also had several postern gates—altogether eighteen gates of various sizes. The towers—on average one for every one hundred feet—were built to house a great number of artillery pieces to deal with any assault.

The towers and walls were provided with *ballistae*—great torsion-driven bows that launched stones or large arrows—that could pierce armor at a range greater than two bowshots, and with catapults called *onagri*, which could smash siege engines and enemy formations. Archers had loopholes all along the wall. It is believed that the total complement of artillery pieces for the first wall was from eight hundred to one thousand. This number was reduced somewhat at the time of Belisarius, when fewer engines and more archers were employed.

It was built in great haste under the direct supervision of the emperor and was finished in only five years. To manage this, old tombs and monuments were reused in the circuit of the wall, such as the Amphitheatrum Castrense, the famous pyramid of Gaius Cestius, and the tomb monument of Eurysaces, which was uncovered at the Porta Praenestina, when the flanking towers at the gate were removed in modern times. The camp of the Praetorian Guard, which was encircled by a low wall, was also incorporated in the new walls. Altogether, about 10 percent of the circuit of the walls was created this way, saving materials and thousands of hours of work time. Even Emperor Hadrian's mausoleum outside the walls was turned into a fortress to protect the Pons Aelius (Aelian Bridge) and to avoid giving an enemy the chance to construct a fortification there.

It is supposed that military engineers supervised the work while the city guilds provided the workers needed to construct the great walls.

The Aurelian Wall was not very high, but it was high enough to keep out barbarians who did not know how to besiege a city. The intention was to avoid a sack of the city by roving barbarian war bands, and not to withstand a proper siege.

The wall was significantly enlarged and repaired in the times of Maxentius (306–312) and Honorius (395–423), when the towers and walls were heightened (in some places the old battlements of

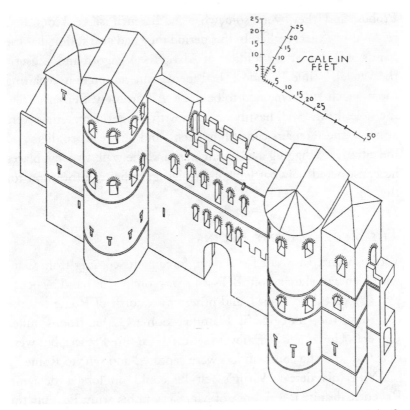

The Porta Asinaria in the time of Belisarius. The windows were mainly for *ballistae*. Based on a drawing in Ian Richmond, *The City Wall of Imperial Rome*.

the first phase can still be seen) and the gates strengthened. It was now able to withstand a real siege by experienced troops.

The increased height meant that more troops could be deployed at any assault point, while fewer men were required to hold the walls. The walls were now up to sixty feet high, and so could no longer be scaled easily, but they remained twelve feet thick. Because the foundations had been made to carry a much smaller wall and it was considered too great a task to tear down the wall and make new foundations, the engineers came upon a brilliant solution. A covered gallery was put on top of the existing wall, and on top of this an open rampart walk, protected by battlements.

By 536, the walls of Rome were already two hundred and sixty years old since their construction by Emperors Aurelian and

Probus, and they were somewhat in disrepair since Honorius's renewal 130 years earlier. In this period they had also suffered at the hands of the invading soldiers of Alaric the Visigoth and Gaiseric the Vandal. While Theodoric had spent some resources in repairing them, much still remained to be done. Accordingly, Belisarius had the holes in the wall hastily repaired with whatever materials were at hand (these repairs can still be seen), and he set his soldiers and the citizens to digging a deep ditch around the wall. In some places he constructed new battlements, which gave better protection for the troops.

THE SIEGE OF ROME BEGINS

Vittigis wanted to wait for the reinforcements coming from Gaul with General Marcias, but Belisarius was forcing his hand by occupying Spoletium, Perusia, and other cities north of Rome to take control of the strategic Via Flaminia. Some Gothic troops under Generals Unilas and Pissas were sent to recapture Perusia, but were defeated, and the commanders were captured and sent to Rome.

With this defeat, Vittigis felt he could no longer delay in Ravenna, despite the absence of Marcias and his army. Possibly the Gothic nobles were also pushing for an advance on Rome.

At the same time, Vittigis sent Generals Uligisalus and Asinarius to recover Dalmatia. Uligisalus went straight for the provincial capital of Salona, while Asinarius went around the Adriatic to gather the barbarian Suevi dwelling in the region of what is now Croatia. Furthermore, Vittigis sent warships to support the army so the Roman fleet would be hindered in supplying Salona.

Uligisalus was defeated by the Romans at Scardona (Skradin in modern-day Croatia) and shut up in Burnum (Ivoševci). The Romans were, however, forced to retreat when Asinarius, who had been recruiting the Suevi, arrived. After this success, probably in spring 537, they besieged Salona by sea and land. The Roman fleet soon attacked the Gothic fleet and put it to flight while destroying or capturing many ships. Despite the naval defeat, the Gothic land forces kept up the siege for some time. Eventually, however, the Gothic army returned across the Adriatic in the summer of 537.

In February 537, Vittigis moved with the entire Gothic army (except the expeditionary forces sent to Dalmatia)—one hundred and fifty thousand warriors—south along the Via Flaminia. This number might seem exaggerated, but it must be remembered that this was the entire host of the strongest barbarian nation on Roman soil. Peace and prosperity for more than a generation had helped to increase its numbers. The proportions of infantry and cavalry are unknown, but the greater number of troops were heavily armored.

Vittigis went in all haste, as he hoped to catch Belisarius in Rome. Procopius relates a story that on the journey, the Gothic army met a priest who had just left the city and who was brought to the king's tent. Breathless with anxiety, Vittigis asked the priest if Belisarius was still in Rome, showing he was afraid he might not catch him if Belisarius already had run. The priest calmly answered that the king should not be concerned about that, for he could guarantee that Belisarius was not planning to run. Evidently, the priest had a better understanding of the Romans' strategy than did the Gothic king.

When Belisarius received news of the advance of the formidable Gothic army, he became uncertain that the recent conquest in Tuscany could be held, so he ordered Generals Bessas and Constantinus to garrison only the most-defensible positions—Spoletium, Narnia, and Perusia—and to fall back on Rome with their remaining troops. Bessas, who was somewhat late in reacting, got into a skirmish with the vanguard of the Gothic army before he retreated to Rome.

Still, Belisarius's position would appear to be pure madness, as he had only five thousand troops to Vittigis's one hundred and fifty thousand.

A small detachment of troops—which Belisarius had tasked with holding the Tiber crossing to buy time to further victual Rome in preparation for the siege—encountered the Gothic host at the Tiber, possibly at the Pons Salaria. The bridge had been fortified with a small fortress to strengthen the defenses.

When the garrison saw the enormous number of campfires in the Gothic camp, twenty-two soldiers of barbarian origin deserted to the Goths. The rest of those in the garrison were so discouraged that they fled during the night. Not daring to return to Rome, they fled south to Campania instead.

As Belisarius received no word of the desertion of the troops at the bridge, he moved out with one thousand cavalry to either support the garrison in their expected retreat before the Goths or to further hinder the Gothic crossing.

SKIRMISH AT THE BRIDGE

The next morning the Goths easily took the fortress, as no defenders were left, and started the crossing.

The Romans met the Goths who were crossing the bridge, and a furious fight started, with Belisarius at its center. Recognizing Belisarius in his armor, the Goths crowded around him and tried to kill or wound him with their lances. Meanwhile, his bodyguard was doing its best to protect the general, who was fighting valiantly. After heavy fighting in which a thousand Gothic warriors and many of the bravest from among Belisarius's bodyguard had fallen, the barbarians fled to their camp across the Tiber.

While the exhausted Romans retreated to a small hill nearby, more Gothic cavalry moved out of their camp in support of their fleeing comrades and attacked the small Roman force trying to catch its breath. The Goths' numerical superiority prevailed, and the Roman detachment fled toward the city.

When it reached the Porta Salaria (later renamed Porta Belisaria because of the day's events), the troops defending the gates refused to open the doors for the fugitives, as a rumor of the death of Belisarius had reached them. In the twilight, it was not possible to recognize Belisarius, who was covered in dust and blood, and with no chance of his voice being heard over the din, there was no way the troops would open the gates, fearing that the Goths also would enter the city.

The situation was becoming desperate, with the Roman soldiers huddled together under the wall, pressing upon each other so much they could hardly move; their comrades refusing to open the gates; and the advancing Gothic army at their heels.

Belisarius, however, managed to keep cool, reformed his troops, and made a sharp counterattack on the Goths, who were already somewhat disorganized by their pursuit in the gathering darkness. Believing a new Roman army to be issuing from the gates in relief, the barbarians turned and fled. After pursuing for a short distance, Belisarius turned his troops around and could now enter the city with them in good order. Amazingly, despite being in the thick of the fighting from dawn till evening, Belisarius escaped without a wound. While the day's action turned out well for the Romans, despite heavy casualties among the bravest and best of their soldiers, it is clear Belisarius made a serious mistake, which could have been fatal to the imperial fortunes in the war, by entering the fight. It is one of the few examples of the otherwise cool and calculating general making what seems a rash decision. If he had been killed or wounded, Rome and the entire Roman army would surely have been lost in this second year of the war.

For Belisarius, the day was not over. As soon as he was inside the city, he collected his soldiers and many of the citizens and stationed them on the walls. As the Goths might attack immediately, they were ordered to light fires along the walls and to stand watch diligently all night. He then went around the walls himself, carefully arranging the defense of each section and each gate.

During the defensive preparations, a messenger from General Bessas arrived from the Porta Praenestina with the urgent news that the Goths had entered the city by the Porta San Pancratius (the gate was formally known as Porta Aurelia Sancti Pancratii) on the other side of the Tiber. On hearing the terrible news, Belisarius's staff begged him to save the army by retreating through one of the other gates. Belisarius, however, did not believe the unlikely report and had a quick horseman sent across the Tiber to confirm the message. He soon returned and reported that there had been no attack on that part of the city.

Belisarius then issued an order to the effect that under no circumstances, not even if they heard that the Goths had penetrated into the city, were the generals entrusted with the defense of the gates to leave them in order to support other parts of the defense. Only then, when night was already well advanced, did his wife and friends succeed in making him rest and eat for the first time since dawn.

The next day, in what was now late February or early March of 537, the Goths began establishing seven camps, six on the east side of the Tiber and one on the west side in the Neronian Plain. This initial blockade was not very effective, but it did obstruct eight of the fourteen major gates of Rome. The Goths, most likely for command and tactical reasons, preferred to keep their main strength together. About two-thirds of the total circuit of the walls of Aurelian and Honorius was covered by the Gothic camps. The camps were well-fortified in the traditional Roman manner. A deep ditch was dug around them, and the excavated earth from the ditch was thrown up to form a rampart in which sharpened stakes were placed. A Gothic officer was put in charge of the troops of each camp. General Marcias, who had by this time arrived with the troops from Gaul, was put in charge of the trans-Tiber camp with orders to control the Pons Milvius and the land all the way to the mouth of the Tiber.

On the Roman side, Belisarius took direct control of the Porta Pinciana and the Porta Salaria, which was where the main Gothic attack was expected and where the best opportunities for a sally existed. The Porta Praenestina was assigned to Bessas, and the Porta Flaminia to Constantinus. The infantry commanders were put in charge of the remaining gates. Several gates were blocked up with stones to avoid surprise attacks or treason from within the city.

Cutting the Aqueducts

One of the first things the Gothic army did was to cut the aqueducts leading into Rome. Remembering their own exploits at the siege of Neapolis, the Romans were quick to block up all the empty water canals. The obvious effect of cutting off the aqueducts—less water being transported to Rome—was not so serious because the Tiber ran through the city and could easily supply enough drinking water. The imperial baths were the main users of the enormous amount of water brought into Rome by the aqueducts (some 150 million gallons each day), and they were closed down.

The most important effect of the cut water supply was to silence the many watermills in the city, which ground flour for the rations of bread given to the soldiers and citizens. In order to make the provisions last, all the animals in the city had been removed or slaughtered (except for the horses needed for war), so there was no opportunity to use draught animals for the mills. So Belisarius hit upon a scheme to solve the problem: Two ships were moored on the Tiber. On them were placed millstones, and between them water wheels, which were then driven by the current. The Goths responded by throwing logs and Roman corpses into the river, damaging the water wheels. To prevent the mills from being destroyed, the Romans stretched a chain across the Tiber to catch the objects. This had the added benefit of guarding against Gothic attacks by boat.

Discontent Among the Citizens

The citizens of Rome were not at all happy about the siege. They received meager daily rations of food, could no longer use the great baths of the city, and were forced to do sentry duty on the walls. Many expected it to be only a matter of time before the city fell. There were murmurs in the Senate, and speeches were made against Belisarius. Vittigis, who was informed of the situation by deserters, sent envoys to Belisarius. They delivered their messages before Belisarius and the Senate. The envoys praised Belisarius for his courage in the war but asked how he could stand against the mighty Gothic army encamped before the walls. Vittigis would allow him to evacuate the city in peace and take away his army's possessions. Belisarius quickly replied with the famous words, "For as long as Belisarius lives, it is impossible for him to relinquish this city." The senators were quiet and did not dare support either party. Only Fidelius, the praetorian prefect and former *quaestor* (treasurer) under King Athalaric, spoke against the Gothic envoys.

With this response, the envoys returned to Vittigis, who eagerly questioned them about the mood in the city. They replied that the Goths were hoping for too much if they supposed they could frighten Belisarius. Vittigis then turned to the preparations for the attack.

Preparations for the Attack

While the defenders were preparing themselves, the Goths were also busy constructing siege engines. They built wooden towers on wheels, which would be drawn by teams of oxen. The required height of the towers was measured by counting the layers of bricks in the city wall.

Four great battering rams covered by wooden sheds were also made, and fascines made of reeds and branches were prepared. These could be thrown into the ditch in front of the walls so the war engines could advance. Finally, great numbers of ladders were produced.

The Romans, meanwhile, equipped the walls and towers with *ballistae* and *onagri* (literally, wild asses, a nickname the machine received because the back of it kicked up when it was fired). The gates were obstructed by a cunning device called a *lupus* (wolf), a kind of double portcullis worked from above and below, thereby appearing like a fanged mouth closing.

The dispositions for the defense were not changed significantly from the initial plan. Generals Bessas and Peranius were in charge of the troops defending the Porta Praenestina, Ursicinus was with the unit known as the *regii*—the kings—at the Porta Flaminia, and Belisarius was at the Porta Salaria and Porta Pinciana, where the main Gothic attack was expected. Constantinus was put in charge of the riverside wall, the Pons Aelius, and the Mausoleum of Hadrian. Paulus commanded the Porta San Pancratius on the other side of the Tiber. Here, as at the Porta Flaminia, with its precipitous position, no Gothic attack was expected because of the difficulty of the ground.

That the Goths did not attack between the Porta Flaminia and the Porta Pinciana, where the wall was damaged from old times, was surprising. A cleft in the wall had caused it to lean in both directions. For this reason, the Romans called that part of the wall the *murus ruptus*—the broken wall. Belisarius had initially intended to tear down the wall there and rebuild it, but the local citizens stopped him, claiming that Peter the Apostle had promised he would ensure the safety of the wall at that place. And indeed, the Goths, strangely, did not attack at this obvious place any time during the siege.

The Attack Begins

On the eighteenth day of the siege, Vittigis gave the order for the assault to begin at sunrise. The main attack, commanded in person by the king, was on the Porta Salaria. The Romans on the walls were dismayed by the sight of the enormous Gothic army and their rams and siege towers drawn by oxen moving toward them. While the soldiers were losing their courage and imploring the general to use the ballistae on the walls before the Goths came any nearer, Belisarius stood calm with a scornful smile on his face and even laughed.

As the Roman soldiers became more and more desperate and even called their general shameless and incompetent, Belisarius waited and still smiled. When the Gothic soldiers reached the ditch dug in front of the walls, he drew his bow and shot one of the Gothic nobles through the neck. The Goth fell dead, and the Romans were much cheered by this lucky omen. Again he shot and killed another noble with an arrow. With this he gave the order for all soldiers to fire, at the same time ordering the closest soldiers to aim at the oxen pulling the siege towers. In a few minutes, all the oxen were slain and the fearsome engines of war ground to a halt at the edge of the ditch, now a hindrance for the advancing troops. The Roman soldiers now understood why Belisarius had held their fire. The engines stood too close to the walls for the Goths to save them, and the Romans could later burn them with little trouble. This incident also shows how ignorant the Goths were of how to take fortified cities, even after so many years inside the Roman Empire. Clearly, no engines drawn by unprotected oxen would be allowed near the walls, which were studded with archers, slingers, ballistae, and onagri.

THE GOTHS CHANGE TACTICS

Meanwhile the archers, slingers, and artillery on the walls and towers were wreaking havoc among the closely packed masses of Gothic soldiers. When the draught animals were killed and Vittigis saw that he was losing troops to no avail, he drew his men back a little from the ditch and ordered them not to attempt further assaults on the part of the wall close to the Porta Salaria. Instead, they were to apply pressure on the defenders by using missile fire and keep the Romans tied down so Belisarius could not give assistance to other parts of the defense—in this case the Porta Praenestina and the Porta Cornelia.

The Assault on the Vivarium

The Porta Praenestina was also the target of a heavy Gothic attack. Here, as at the other gates, the Goths had collected siege towers, battering rams, and ladders. The expected absence of Belisarius and the bad state of the wall gave the Goths some hope of victory. After the arrival of King Vittigis, who went there after the failure at the Porta Salaria, the assault here gained in strength and became a serious danger to the Romans.

The line of the Claudian aqueduct was incorporated into the Aurelian walls, but by the time of the siege it had fallen into disrepair, and the real line of defense seems to have been a lower wall running parallel to it at a distance of less than one hundred yards and skirting the Via Labicana. Between these two walls, which ran parallel for about five hundred yards, was a strip of land used as a holding pen for the wild beasts meant for the shows of the amphitheater. The Romans called this area a vivarium. The lower wall was, therefore, not meant to be a defensive wall but just served to form an enclosure, so it had no towers or battlements.

The terrain was level up to the wall and gave the Goths good opportunity to use their engines of war. Unfortunately for the barbarians, Belisarius had hastened there with his bodyguard as soon as the main attack on his own section of the wall was beaten back. He set only a few men on the lower wall and ordered that little opposition was to be offered to the attackers. When the Goths quickly battered a breach in the wall of the vivarium and pushed into the space between the walls, the fatal flaw in the attack was revealed. Cyprianus and some of Belisarius's best men were at the aqueduct wall, and the unexpected strong opposition caused more barbarians to enter the enclosure, until there was no room to maneuver. At this moment, Belisarius gave the order to throw open the Porta Praenestina so reserves that he had gathered could attack. Now assaulted at the rear and with no room to move, the disorganized Goths panicked and tried to flee through the breach they had made in the vivarium wall. Many were trampled to death by their own friends, and many more were slain by the Romans who fol-

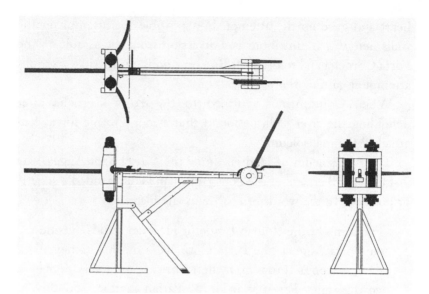

The towers in the city wall were equipped with *ballistae*. Their long range and penetration power made them a feared weapon to the Goths. The drawing is based on Eric Marsden, *Greek and Roman Artillery*.

lowed them in their flight to their distant camp. Their various engines of war were burned, and the rising smoke signaled the end of the Gothic assault on the Porta Praenestina.

Fight for the Mausoleum of Hadrian

Meanwhile, at the Porta Cornelia at the Mausoleum of Hadrian, the Goths had been much nearer to victory. Here, two points were especially threatened: the Porta Cornelia itself and the stretch of wall along the river between it and the Porta Flaminia. The Romans had assumed that the river would make it sufficiently difficult for any serious Gothic attack, and besides, Belisarius could not spare any significant number of men to defend it.

General Constantinus had been put in charge of the defense. When he perceived that the Goths were preparing to cross the river and attack the wall, he rushed off with his small reserves and occupied the wall at the threatened point. When the Goths saw that the wall was occupied and that the landing would be opposed, they lost heart and gave up the attempt. It is possible the attempt on the walls here was meant more as a diversion from the assault on the Porta Cornelia and to draw off Roman troops, rather than a serious attempt at gaining the walls.

When Constantinus returned to the Porta Cornelia after defending the river wall, he found that strong Gothic forces had attacked the mausoleum.

The Mausoleum of Hadrian (now the Castel Sant'Angelo) lay just on the other side of the Pons Aelius and commanded a superior position. In the words of Procopius the historian:

> The tomb of the Roman Emperor Hadrian stands outside the Porta Aurelia [the Porta Cornelia is meant], removed about a stone's throw from the fortifications, a very noteworthy sight. For it is made of Parian marble, and the stones fit closely one upon the other, having nothing at all between them. And it has four sides which are all equal, each being about a stone's throw in length, while their height exceeds that of the city wall; and above there are statues of the same marble, representing men and horses, of wonderful workmanship. But since this tomb seemed to the men of ancient times a fortress threatening the city, they enclosed it by two walls, which extend to it from the circuit-wall, and thus made it a part of the wall. And, indeed, it gives the appearance of a high tower built as a bulwark before the gate [Porta Cornelia] there.

The mausoleum and its commanding position can still be seen in Rome today.

The mausoleum had been garrisoned by the troops of Constantinus with ballistae, and they were awaiting the Gothic attack. The Goths attacked from their camp in the Neronian Gardens. They did not have siege engines, but they had ladders and many archers, and hoped to be able to overpower the few defenders. The Goths moved against the mausoleum in the shelter of a long colonnade, which led from the Pons Aelius to the Basilica of St. Peter. In this way, they managed to come close to the walls of the mausoleum without being noticed by the garrison. When they were discovered, they were already too close for the defenders to use their ballistae, which could not be depressed enough, standing on the high walls of the mausoleum as they did. The Goths were also carrying large oblong shields, which they used to cover themselves against the Roman arrows. The garrison was not strong enough to defend all four sides of the mausoleum, and without the use of its missile weapons, it was hard-pressed by the vigorous Gothic assault. In desperation, the defenders turned to the great number of statues on the mausoleum. The smaller statues were torn from their bases and hurled upon the attackers, and the larger statues were broken into more manageable fragments and used for the same purpose. The Barberini Faun at Munich and the Dancing Faun at Florence were found during excavation of the ditch below the Mausoleum of Hadrian and may have been two of the statues hurled on the heads of the Goths.

The Goths were forced back by the avalanche of marble and retreated, disorganized, a short distance. This brought them into the range of the ballistae, which the garrison manned again, and in the confusion the Goths were unable to maintain a compact shield-wall formation, so the bows of the defenders could no longer be resisted. This repulse was turned into a severe defeat, as Constantinus at this moment appeared on the scene and routed the shaken Goths.

During this attack, sharp fighting was still taking place at the Porta Salaria, where the Goths were pressing the Romans hard with missile fire. One of the Gothic nobles had climbed up into a high tree from which he was shooting at the exposed defenders on the wall. By chance, a ballista bolt—an oversize, arrow-like missile—shot from the gate hit the warrior, pierced his armor, and went straight through his body, pinning the corpse to the tree trunk. At the sight of this the Gothic attackers became demoralized and quickly retreated outside of ballistae range. At this point, the attack on the Porta Salaria ebbed. Shortly after, the Romans who had put the Goths at Porta Praenestina to flight made a sally and defeated the demoralized Goths. The disabled engines of war were burned.

A force of Goths had also tried to assault the Porta San Pancratia on the other side of the Tiber but had been unsuccessful.

The gate and the walls at this point were situated on the slopes of the Janiculum Hill, so little headway was made. Most likely the Goths were only trying to tie down and test the defenses of Paulus, who commanded an infantry detachment there.

Thus, the enormous and confident attack of the Goths ended in defeat. They had succeeded nowhere. The battle had lasted from early dawn until evening put an end to it. All night the burning Gothic engines of war lit the walls. From the city could be heard the cheers and victory songs of the Romans; from the Gothic camps could be heard the screams of the wounded and the lamentations for the many fallen warriors.

According to Procopius, who was present in the city, the Gothic leaders admitted they had lost thirty thousand men, and more than that were wounded. Many of those would later die of their wounds.

The Gothic tactic of overstretching the Roman defense had almost worked, and it might well have succeeded if an experienced and energetic general had not been present to prepare and conduct the defense. But the Goths clearly had little knowledge about taking fortified cities, apart from keeping a steady stream of arrows at the walls while conducting ladder assaults. These were primitive tactics, which were also extremely wasteful in men and equipment, as the number of casualties shows. The fact was, King Vittigis had no idea how to conduct a siege and so continually made many blunders, of which the experienced Belisarius could take advantage.

Belisarius sent a messenger to Emperor Justinian with a letter announcing the victory and asking for reinforcements. Procopius, who probably composed the letter, mentions its contents:

> We have arrived in Italy, as thou commanded, and we have made ourselves masters of much territory in it and have taken possession of Rome also, after driving out the barbarians who were here, whose leader, Leuderis, I have recently sent to you. But since we have stationed a great number of soldiers both in Sicily and in Italy to guard the strongholds, which we have proved able to capture, our army has in consequence been reduced to only five thousand men. But the enemy have come against us, gathered together to

the number of one hundred and fifty thousand. And first of
all, when we went out to spy upon their forces along the
Tiber River and were compelled, contrary to our intention,
to engage with them, we lacked only a little of being buried
under a multitude of spears. And after this, when the barbarians attacked the wall with their whole army and
assaulted the fortifications at every point with sundry
engines of war, they came within a little of capturing both
us and the city at the first onset, and they would have succeeded had not some chance snatched us from ruin. For
achievements which transcend the nature of things may
not properly and fittingly be ascribed to man's valor, but to
a stronger power. Now all that has been achieved by us
hitherto, whether it has been due to some kind fortune or
to valor, is for the best; but as to our prospects from now
on, I could wish better things for thy cause. However, I
shall never hide from you anything that it is my duty to say
and yours to do, knowing that while human affairs follow
whatever course may be in accordance with God's will, yet
those who are in charge of any enterprise always win praise
or blame according to their own deeds. Therefore let both
arms and soldiers be sent to us in such numbers that from
now on we may engage with the enemy in this war with an
equality of strength. For one ought not to trust everything
to fortune, since fortune, on its part, is not given to following the same course forever. But do thou, O Emperor, take
this thought to heart, that if at this time the barbarians win
the victory over us, we shall be cast out of Italy which is
thine and shall lose the army in addition, and besides all
this we shall have to bear the shame, however great it may
be, that attaches to our conduct. For I refrain from saying
that we should also be regarded as having ruined the
Romans [the inhabitants of Rome], men who have held
their safety more lightly than their loyalty to thy kingdom.
Consequently, if this should happen, the result for us will
be that the successes we have won thus far will in the end
prove to have been but a prelude to calamities. For if it had

so happened that we had been repulsed from Rome and Campania and, at a much earlier time, from Sicily, we should only be feeling the sting of the lightest of all misfortunes, that of having found ourselves unable to grow wealthy on the possessions of others. And again, this too is worthy of consideration by you, that it has never been possible even for many times ten thousand men to guard Rome for any considerable length of time, since the city embraces a large territory, and, because it is not on the sea, is shut off from all supplies. And although at the present time the Romans are well disposed towards us, yet when their troubles are prolonged, they will probably not hesitate to choose the course which is better for their own interests. For when men have entered into friendship with others on the spur of the moment, it is not while they are in evil fortune, but while they prosper, that they are accustomed to keep faith with them. Furthermore, the Romans will be compelled by hunger to do many things they would prefer not to do. Now as for me, I know I am bound even to die for thy kingdom, and for this reason no man will ever be able to remove me from this city while I live; but I beg thee to consider what kind of a fame such an end of Belisarius would bring thee.

Preparations had already been made to strengthen the Roman forces in Italy, and the letter caused these to be accelerated. Generals Valerianus and Martinus had already been sent with ships and men in late 536 to help Belisarius, but because of their fear of the winter storms they had lingered on the coast of Aetolia in Greece. The emperor now sent them a message asking them to hasten to the help of Belisarius in Italy. The news of the expected reinforcements soon raised the spirits of the besieged city.

Despite his great victory, Belisarius made further preparations for a long siege. On the day after the first great Gothic assault, the citizens were commanded to send women, children, and old men from the city, to avoid a scarcity of provisions. They were accompanied by all the slaves, except some whom Belisarius had impressed for guard service on the walls. Even the Roman soldiers had to part with their servants. Some went south on the Via Appia to Campania and eventually Sicily, and others went down the Tiber and sailed from the main harbor of Rome, Portus. The Goths did not hinder this exodus and perhaps could not, despite the advantages this gave the Romans in making their supplies last longer. The soldiers were then put on half rations, the remainder now being paid in silver.

THE BLOCKADE BEGINS

Three days after the failure of the major assault, King Vittigis finally made a right step and seized the city of Portus, which was practically undefended, and put a garrison of a thousand troops there. Since the second century, Portus had replaced Ostia as the chief harbor of Rome, and this move greatly aided the coming blockade. Ostia and the smaller harbor of Antium (Anzio) were still in the hands of the Romans, but it was difficult to bring supplies from there along the Tiber to Rome.

It would seem a strategic blunder by Belisarius not to garrison Portus sufficiently, as Procopius states that the walls of the city were so strong only three hundred troops would be necessary to hold it. But Belisarius was so pressed for troops that it was felt even three hundred could not be spared from the defense of Rome, despite the disadvantages in the supply situation.

Another step Vittigis took—and probably the most insensible one, considering circumstances—was to send orders to Ravenna to murder all the senators he had confined there as hostages at the outbreak of the war. A few escaped but most were killed, ending any chance of the Goths' maintaining good relations with the Roman population in Italy.

Meanwhile, the Goths settled down to conduct a blockade of Rome. Again it became clear they were not accustomed to such a war. They clung to their defensive camps, never venturing out by night and only in large companies during the day. This was, indeed, also necessary, for any lone Goth would quickly be slain and stripped of his equipment by the many small bands of Moorish cavalry sent out by the Romans. Disease would also soon become the constant companion of the troops in their unsanitary camps.

Belisarius, on the other hand, was active in organizing the defense of the city to such a degree that little would be left to chance and luck. To prevent his few regular troops from being worn out by guard duty on the walls, he had the remaining citizens and slaves do it. To avoid the ever-present danger of treachery, these companies were shifted every fortnight to guard a new stretch of wall at a distance from the one they guarded before. After every fortnight, he would also have the keys of every gate brought to him, melted down, and recast in a new shape with altered locks. Any sentinel who did not show up for guard duty was severely punished for his delinquency. At night, bands of musicians would play at intervals along the wall to keep the defenders awake and cheerful. All night, too, the Moorish contingent in the army was instructed to patrol the base of the walls accompanied by dogs, in order to detect any Gothic attempt at a nightly attack. This measure turned out to be unnecessary, as the Goths were reluctant to make any attempts on the wall during the night.

Because of concerns over treachery, several senators who were believed to be in negotiations with the Goths were banished from the city.

REINFORCEMENTS ARRIVE

On the forty-first day of the siege, around April 13, 537, the reinforcements under Generals Valerianus and Martinus arrived in Rome. They commanded only sixteen hundred men, but they were all experienced cavalry, mostly Huns, Antae, and Sclaveni from beyond the Danube. The other requested reinforcements would take much longer to arrive. But Belisarius felt that with the added strength, time had come to bring the war to the Goths and take advantage of the Roman tactical superiority. Traianus, one of his bodyguards, was put in charge of two hundred horsemen. Their orders were to sally from the Porta Salaria and occupy a small hill near one of the Gothic camps. When the Goths would come out of their camp to fight them off, they were not to fight hand-to-hand,

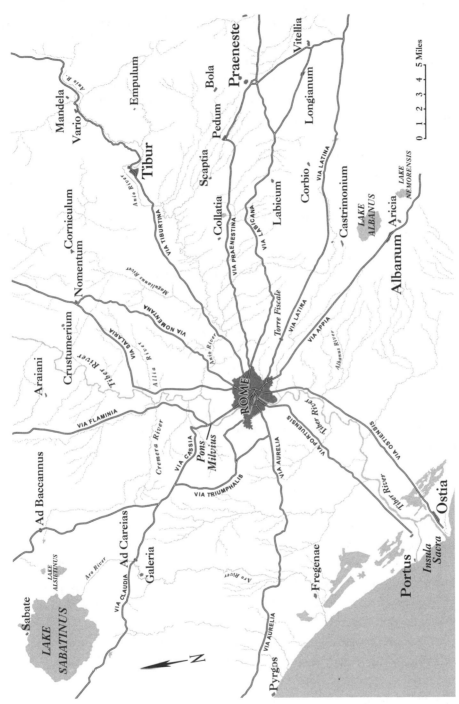

Map 7. Rome and its surroundings.

but to discharge as many arrows as possible, and when these were exhausted they were to retreat to the city.

The tactics were highly successful. The Goths quickly issued from their camp, and the Roman arrows were soon taking a heavy toll. When their quivers were empty, they retreated toward the Porta Salaria. The Goths pursued vigorously, but soon came into range of the ballistae on the walls and towers, and were greeted by a swarm of bolts, forcing them to retreat. The Romans estimated that the sortie caused about a thousand casualties—with not a single Roman soldier lost.

Another sortie with three hundred men under Mundilas and Diogenes—both bodyguards of Belisarius—had the same result. A third sortie commanded by Wilas, again with three hundred horse archers, destroyed another thousand Goths. Altogether, the sorties were believed to have killed some four thousand Gothic troops with no Roman casualties.

When Vittigis saw the success of these operations, he thought he would imitate the Roman tactics. Unfortunately, his understanding of the Roman tactical superiority was lacking, and his logic was that the Roman success was due to making the forces small and easier to control. Accordingly, he sent a troop of five hundred horsemen to occupy a little rise in the ground close to the walls of Rome but outside ballistae range. When the Romans observed this movement, Belisarius sent out Bessas with a thousand horsemen to attack them in the rear. The Goths were soon overpowered and retreated with heavy losses to their camp.

Vittigis upbraided the troops for their cowardice: why could they not win a victory with a handful of men as the troops on the other side did? Vittigis failed to understand the huge difference in training and equipment between the imperial army and his countrymen. While the Gothic soldiers were individually brave and courageous warriors, they did not have the coordination and discipline the Romans still possessed to some extent. Especially the Gothic infantry, while formidable in a pitched battle, simply could not catch the Roman horse archers. Neither could the heavily armored Gothic cavalry, who were equipped with lances and swords, catch the lightly armored, bow-equipped Huns. Attacking or retreating, the Romans could shower the enemy with arrows in the manner of the Persian armies of the East. The Gothic army did not have many archers, and the ones it had were all on foot.

Despite the defeat, Vittigis had still not realized the tactical difference between the armies. Three days later, he collected another group of five hundred horsemen, specially picked from each Gothic camp so he could be sure to have brave men among them. They were sent off with Vittigis's usual vague orders "to make a display of valorous deeds against the enemy." Again the same thing happened: when the Goths were observed from the walls, Belisarius sent out fifteen hundred horsemen under the newly arrived Martinus and Valerianus. The hopelessly outnumbered Goths were quickly put to flight with heavy losses.

Both the Goths and the Romans attributed this series of victories to Belisarius's genius as a commander. Procopius relates that Belisarius's friends later asked him privately why he had been so confident about overcoming the enemy in the war:

And he said that in engaging with them [the Goths] at the first with only a few men he had noticed just what the difference was between the two armies, so that if he should fight his battles with them with a force which was in strength proportionate to theirs [i.e. smaller, but equal in strength], the multitudes of the enemy could inflict no injury upon the Romans by reason of the smallness of their numbers. And the difference was this, that practically all the Romans and their allies, the Huns, are good mounted bowmen, but not a man among the Goths has had practice in this branch, for their horsemen are accustomed to use only spears and swords, while their bowmen enter battle on foot and under cover of the heavy-armed men. So the horsemen, unless the engagement is at close quarters, have no means of defending themselves against opponents who use the bow, and therefore can easily be reached by the arrows and destroyed; and as for the foot soldiers, they can never be strong enough to make sallies against men on horseback. It was for these reasons, Belisarius declared, that the barbarians had been defeated by the Romans in these last engagements.

This clearly shows Belisarius's tactical understanding and ability compared to Vittigis's. The strength of the Roman army was not in its numbers, but in its tactical superiority. That meant the Gothic cavalry had no answer to missile weapons, and the infantry had no defense against a cavalry charge once its own cavalry had been defeated. Because of this, Belisarius believed that all things being equal, the Romans would win any battle.

PITCHED BATTLE

The repeated victories of the imperial troops created as many problems for Belisarius as for Vittigis—in a different way, of course. The Roman officers and soldiers became more and more contemptuous of the Goths, so much so that they started complaining about not being led into a pitched battle. The discipline in the Roman army had only gone down since the early empire, and soldiers and officers would often interfere with their generals' conduct of a campaign, as had happened to Belisarius at the Battle of Callinicum in Mesopotamia in 531.

Belisarius preferred instead to go the safe way and hollow out the Gothic army with sorties, and let disease and hunger do their work among the Goths. A regular battle would only give the Goths a chance to use their still-great manpower superiority. Furthermore, fortune played too great a role in a regular battle, and too much was at stake. Because supplies were not stretched yet, time was a friend for the Romans, and there was therefore no cause to take chances.

But Belisarius would soon find that to keep the army in hand, the only course of action was to yield to its wishes—probably also in the hope that its confidence would carry the day, however unlikely that would seem. With deserters on both sides informing on the plans of the armies, there could be little chance of surprise, so Belisarius resigned himself to fighting a set-piece battle.

The Roman troops were led out of the city and confronted the entire Gothic host. Both commanders gave the customary speeches before battle. Belisarius reminded his soldiers that they had demanded this battle and would have to justify forcing their general's hand. Further, they should maintain their string of victories, and he told them not to spare either horse or weapons in the coming battle, as all lost equipment would be replaced from his own military stores.

The main point of King Vittigis's speech was to assure his people that he did not ask for their help just to keep his throne, but to keep the Gothic race in power. He cited the recently overthrown Vandals as an example of what calamities would come if the Romans won the battle. He assured them of an easy victory, as the enemy was far smaller and weak Greeklings, as he termed them. The only thing that kept them together was their confidence derived from their recent victories; now it was time to pay them back for their insults to the Goths.

Vittigis positioned his army with the infantry in the middle and the cavalry on the wings in the traditional fashion. The line was stationed near the Gothic camps, in order to give them swift shelter if the battle was lost, and to give the Romans a long retreat if the battle was won.

Belisarius decided to make the real attack from the Porta Pinciana and the Porta Salaria. At the same time, a feint from the Porta Cornelia and the Mausoleum of Hadrian would be made toward the Gothic camp in the Neronian Plain to prevent the Goths on the right side of the Tiber from assisting in the main battle. He gave strict orders to Valentinus, who commanded the troops participating in the feint, to not advance into actual combat, but only to harass the Gothic troops. To support this move, Belisarius equipped a large number of the remaining Roman civilians with shields and spears, and stationed them in front of the Porta Cornelia. Because they had no experience in military matters, they were not intended to fight, but only to give the impression of a large body of troops, which would further prevent the Goths from the camp in the Neronian Plain from crossing the Tiber in support of Vittigis. They were told they should not move before he gave the signal, which he was probably not going to do.

According to Belisarius's plan, the main battle was to be fought entirely with cavalry, as this was his strongest arm. Many of his best foot soldiers had also been equipped with horses and practiced in the art of riding to make this arm stronger. At first, it was his intention to station his infantry, which he considered somewhat unreliable and quick to panic, close to the ditch under the walls, to act as support for a retreat of the cavalry. He was persuaded to change his plan, however, by two officers: Principius the Pisidian and Tarmutus the Isaurian, the latter the brother of Ennes, the leader of the Isaurian detachment in the army. They argued that it would weaken the army to keep the foot soldiers, who represented the mighty legions of the old Romans, out of the battle. Any impression of unreliability in earlier engagements was caused by the officers who were mounted and therefore were quick to flee at the sign of trouble. If Belisarius would allow Tarmutus and Principius to lead the troops into battle on foot, they promised they would perform great deeds. Reluctantly, Belisarius agreed to the eager officers' request and stationed the infantry behind the cavalry. If the cavalry was put to flight, the infantry was to open its ranks and let it pass through, engaging the pursuing enemy until the cavalry could reform. A small number of soldiers, with the help of the populace, were set to man the walls and towers with their ballistae.

THE BATTLE COMMENCES

Both sides expected the coming battle to be decisive. Vittigis had brought all his able men, perhaps one hundred thousand, leaving only the wounded and the camp followers in the camps. The Roman forces numbered around six thousand five hundred.

Early in the morning, the battle started. The Roman troops in front of the Porta Pinciana and Porta Salaria were getting the upper hand in the struggle, as row after row of barbarians in their deep columns were falling to their arrows. But the number of barbarians and their courage were too great for even this slaughter to produce a rout. As one rank of barbarians was felled, the next would step forward in its place. Thus, the Romans, who were pressing slowly forward, at noon found themselves close to the Gothic camps, but surrounded by so compact a body of Goths that they began to feel that any pretext that would enable them to return in good order to the shelter of the walls would be welcome.

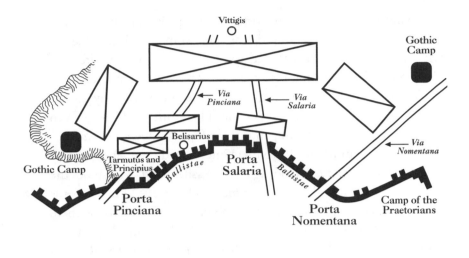

Map 8. The Battle of Rome, 537: initial deployment of Roman and Gothic forces.

While the battle was hotly contested to the northeast of the city, things were developing at a different pace in the Neronian Plain under the Monte Mario. Here the experienced Gothic General Marcias had been asked to remain in waiting, while watching the Pons Milvius, so no Romans would cross the Tiber in support of the main struggle. Because General Valentinus had received a similar order from Belisarius, it would be natural to expect no real fighting to happen—at the most some light skirmishing.

But as the day wore on, one of the feigned assaults of the Romans turned into a real one, as the Gothic troops broke and fled. The fleeing Goths could not reach their camp, so they turned and reformed on a hill close to the Monte Mario. Among Valentinus's troops were many sailors and slaves with no experience or discipline. The success made these troops unmanageable, and Valentinus's orders were disregarded. Instead of slaughtering the disorganized Goths or crossing the Pons Milvius in support of Belisarius—something that might have decided the battle and ended the entire war—they began plundering the Gothic camp of its valuables. As was to be expected, the Goths quickly reformed and waited undisturbed on the slopes of Monte Mario, while observing the Romans plundering the camp. When the Romans could be seen to be without order or leadership, the Goths charged with a great shout and scattered the Roman troops. Hundreds of Roman militia fell during the wild rout toward the city walls.

At the same time, the fortunes of the imperial army to the northeast of the city began to decline. The Goths had been driven to the ramparts of their camp, but there they formed a *testudo* (tortoise in Latin), in which the soldiers interlocked their shields on all sides and on top to defend against missiles, and withstood the Roman attack while slaying many men and horses. As the impetus of the Roman army slowed, it became clear how few troops there were, compared with the Gothic masses. At this critical point, the Gothic cavalry on the right wing wheeled and charged the Romans in the flank. Soon, these Romans broke and fled. When the fleeing cavalry reached the supporting infantry phalanx, it also turned and fled, and soon the whole Roman army was in full flight toward the shelter of the city walls.

Tarmutus and Principius paid for their disastrous advice with their lives. With a little group of stout soldiers they held the Gothic pursuit for a short time, an action that saved countless Roman lives. In the end, Principius fell with forty-two of his foot soldiers around him. Tarmutus managed to hold off the enemy with a javelin in each hand. When he was about to fall from exhaustion and loss of blood from his wounds, a charge by his brother Ennes at the head of a cavalry detachment gave him an opening. He ran at full speed to the Porta Pinciana, which he reached covered in blood and bleeding from many wounds. At the gate he fainted from exhaustion and was carried as dead on a shield into the city by his comrades. It was discovered that he was still breathing, but two days later he died of his wounds, leaving a reputation of great valor among the Isaurians and the rest of the army.

Meanwhile, the fleeing soldiers who had entered the city shut the gates and refused to let the rest of the fugitives enter, as they were afraid that the pursuing Goths would enter with them. The panic-stricken soldiers huddled outside the walls without weapons or shields, which had been thrown away in the flight. The pursuing Goths came to the ditch below the walls and could perhaps have

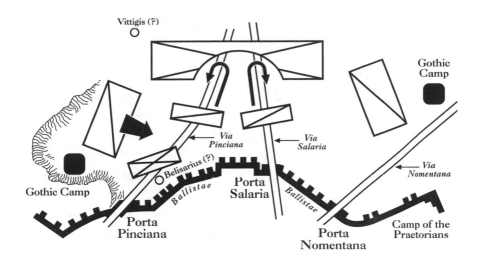

Map 9. The Battle of Rome, 537.

crossed it and annihilated the broken army of Belisarius then and there. However, they had learned painful lessons in approaching the Roman walls and did not dare to come within ballistae range. Instead they taunted the pitiful Romans outside the gates and then retired to their camps.

The result of the battle effectively proved the case of Belisarius and the rashness of the soldiers. The Romans did not have the numbers to fight the barbarians on equal terms and instead needed to take advantage of their superior training and tactical efficiency. Unfortunately, Procopius does not relate the losses in the battle, but the Romans suffered an estimated one thousand five hundred casualties, many of whom were not regular troops but civilians and camp followers killed and wounded in the rout at Monte Mario. The Goths, who suffered a day of constant missile fire, sustained around ten thousand casualties. Despite the disparity in casualties, it was still a great Gothic victory.

THE SKIRMISHES CONTINUE

After the disastrous battle before the walls of Rome, the Romans returned to the proven tactics of making surprise sorties with small bodies of troops, and with much the same success as before. No infantry was used in these skirmishes, and there were many examples of single combat between champions on both sides. If Procopius is to be believed, the Romans won all the instances of single combat and performed all the heroic deeds. Presumably, other tales or versions would be told had a Goth written about these exploits. Nevertheless, it is likely that the Romans had the upper hand when it came to reckless daring, as most of the Roman soldiers were in fact barbarians, whereas every one of the Goths had been born and bred in Italy.

It is worth recounting some of the exploits of the Roman heroes that Procopius relates, to show the importance placed on personal bravery at all levels in the Roman army. Even generals were expected to perform individual deeds of valor, despite the foolishness of putting superior officers in dangerous situations. The Romans already understood this before the Second Punic War in the third century BC, but probably because of the strong barbarian element in the Roman army of the sixth century, many barbarian customs had been taken over.

Chorsamantis was one of Belisarius's bodyguards. Despite being reckless and undisciplined, he was admired as a great warrior. In a skirmish on the Neronian Plain, he pursued some seventy fleeing Goths too far and found himself separated from his friends and surrounded by Goths. The Goths believed the single warrior to be an easy kill and so closed in on him. Bravely, he stood his ground and killed the closest of the Goths and made the rest flee toward one of their fortified camps. When the fleeing band came closer to the camp, they turned on the pursuing Chorsamantis, as they felt ashamed before their comrades in the camp. Again he killed the bravest of them, and again they fled. He then pursued them up to the camp gates before returning unharmed to Rome.

In another skirmish some time after, a Gothic arrow pierced Chorsamantis's left thigh and went as far as the bone. The army surgeons insisted, after removing the arrow, that he rest for some days. He grudgingly accepted this period away from his beloved skirmishes but threatened that he would soon have vengeance on the Goths for his wounded leg.

Soon the wound was healed, and one day at lunch, when he was drunk (as was his custom), he decided he had to make the Goths "pay for my leg", as he was saying over and over again. He told the guards at the gates that Belisarius was sending him to the enemy's camp. The guards did not dare to stop such a famous hero, and so opened the gates. Thus, he rode out alone against one of the Gothic camps. When the Goths saw the solitary figure coming toward the camp, they believed it to be a deserter. They realized their mistake when Chorsamantis started firing arrows at them. Twenty Goths went out against him, but he soon put these to flight. He continued to ride leisurely toward the camp as more and more Goths went out to fight him. Soon he was surrounded, and after a great display of valor he was killed, encircled by the barbarians he had slaughtered.

Also, the generals sought to outdo each other in personal bravery. In one sally, General Bessas singlehandedly killed three of the bravest Gothic horsemen in an enemy cavalry band and put the rest to flight.

Constantinus then went out with some of his Huns from the Porta Cornelia but was soon surrounded by the enemy. To improve the difficult tactical situation, he retreated with his men into one of the narrow streets opening on Caligula's stadium. He then ordered his men to dismount and fire arrows at the barbarians, who were approaching them from both ends of the narrow street.

The Goths believed that the Huns would soon be out of arrows and so waited at a distance, trusting in their armor and shields. After all, they had the Romans blocked from any escape. The Goths' confidence started falling as the expert Hunnish archers found their mark time after time. Soon the Goths had lost half their men, and night was coming. The remaining Goths panicked and fled, while the Huns pursued them, still firing arrows at their backs. The Gothic force was almost entirely destroyed, and Constantinus could retreat with his Huns to the safety of Rome with almost no losses.

Despite the often-barbarian deeds of both sides in the struggle, which became ever more desperate as the war stretched out, there was at the time of the first siege of Rome still an element of chivalry between the Romans and Goths. Some days after the skirmish at

Caligula's stadium, General Peranius was leading a sortie against the Goths. The Goths counterattacked, and a Roman soldier, while fleeing back to Rome, fell into an underground grain-storage vault. He could not get out by himself because of its steep sides, but he was also afraid to call for help, as the Goths might hear him.

During the next day, another skirmish took place in the same area, and a Gothic warrior fell into the same vault. Uniting in their desperate plight, they discussed means of being rescued and bound each other by solemn vows to help each other. They then both shouted and were heard by a group of Gothic soldiers. The soldiers went to the opening and shouted into the dark vault to find out who was trapped there. The Gothic warrior answered alone, told his story, and begged the barbarians to let down a rope. Accordingly, a rope was let down and a man pulled out, and to their surprise it was a Roman soldier. In the vault he had argued that if the Goth was the first to be pulled out, they would not help him also, and so he went up first. The Goth was then hauled up and begged the others to let the Roman go unharmed to Rome. They agreed, and the Roman was allowed to return to his unit.

Battle Before the Walls of Rome

The siege entered its fourth month in June 537. An official named Euthalius landed at Tarracina (Terracina) on the Via Appia, some 62 miles from Rome, bringing much-needed pay for the soldiers. To secure him and the money a safe entrance into the city, Belisarius sent a hundred troops to Tarracina. He also tried to make the barbarians believe he was going to offer battle again so they would not leave their camps to forage or for other purposes, and he could avoid a chance discovery of the little force escorting the money. When he was informed that Euthalius was close and would arrive the next night, Belisarius was ready.

The next morning, Belisarius began to harass the Goths until a large assault was made shortly after the soldiers had eaten their mid-day meal. Attacks were launched from the Porta Pinciana and over the Neronian Plain. The attack from the Porta Pinciana with six hundred horsemen was led by three of Belisarius's bodyguards:

Artasires the Persian, Cutilas the Thracian, and Buchas the Hun. The assault went back and forth, and several times reinforcements were sent from the Gothic camp and the city. At length, the Romans prevailed and drove the Goths back to their camp.

Meanwhile, things were not going well for Martinus and Valerianus, who commanded the Romans on the Neronian Plain. They were being surrounded by the enemy and seemed about to be overwhelmed. Fortunately, Buchas the Hun had just returned with his troops, and Belisarius speedily sent them to relieve Martinus and Valerianus. The charge of Buchas routed the Goths and saved the day for the beleaguered Romans. Buchas especially performed great deeds. At one point, after having pursued too far, he was surrounded by twelve barbarian spearmen. His armor saved him from their stabs, but after a while one of the Goths wounded him in the armpit, and another wounded him in the thigh. By this time the imperials had had time to organize themselves and charged the barbarians surrounding Buchas and rescued him. As it was growing late, this sally also returned to the city.

The object of the day was attained when Euthalius, with the treasure, entered the city by the Via Appia at nightfall. Losses from the battle are unknown, but it was considered a great Roman victory.

Procopius mentions the extraordinary contempt for pain shown by Cutilas and one of his fellow guardsmen during the battle, and we also learn of the high level of surgical skill among the Roman army doctors, who saved many of the wounded with their art. Cutilas had been wounded by a javelin, which had lodged in his skull. This did not hinder him from taking part in the battle, and only at sunset did he ride back with his comrades to the city, the broken javelin waving about with each movement of his body.

Another of Belisarius's guardsmen, Arzes, was hit between his eye and his nose by a Gothic arrow, which had penetrated almost to the nape of his neck. He too rode back, like Cutilas apparently heedless of the arrow lodged in his body.

Procopius later visited the wounded heroes and related the events unfolding there. The Roman physicians did not expect to be able to save Arzes's eyesight. Indeed, it was feared that the lacerations caused by withdrawing the arrow from the wound would kill him. A surgeon named Theoctistus then thought to press the back of Arzes's neck and ask if it caused him pain. When Arzes replied that it did, Theoctistus could assure him that both his eye and his life could be saved. The feathers and the end of the arrow were cut off, after which the surgeons cut through the tissue in the neck until they could grasp the point of the arrow and pull it out through the nape of the neck.

Cutilas was less fortunate. When the deeply embedded javelin was pulled out of his head rather violently, he fainted. The wound soon became inflamed and was followed by an inflammation of the brain. He died some days later.

Buchas the Hun also died, because of loss of blood from the wound in his thigh.

The Romans mourned the two heroes, while lamentations also could be heard from the Gothic camp due to their heavy losses, particularly among their nobles.

Many smaller skirmishes and sorties occurred during the first siege of Rome. Procopius counted sixty-nine large and small.

6

FAMINE AND PESTILENCE

A NEW PHASE IN THE SIEGE BEGAN when both sides realized that the Goths were too inexperienced in the art of sieges to take the city by storm and that the Romans were too few to win a regular battle. The inescapable result was a blockade of the city, in which the first side to be exhausted would lose, and famine and disease would threaten both besieger and besieged. And at the beginning of the spring equinox in 537, famine and pestilence did arrive at Rome. There was still grain for the soldiers, but the stores for the civilians were exhausted.

When Vittigis recognized this he took a step that a more-experienced general would have taken much earlier. He completed the blockade of the city, which until now had been rather ineffectual. About three and a half miles from Rome, where now stand the remnants of the medieval tower of Torre Fiscale, two lines of aqueducts cross and recross one another, making a space between them. Here the Goths filled the lower arches with clay and rubble, and thereby fashioned a crude fortress in which they placed a garrison of seven thousand men. The fortress commanded both the Via Latina and the Via Appia—the two great southern roads that had so far been open to the besieged—so that no communications or supplies would get through this way.

In July, famine had not yet become a serious problem to the Romans, as there were still crops standing in the Campagna that daring horsemen could reap during the night and sell at a high price to the wealthy inhabitants of Rome. But even this resource was now beginning to fail, and the citizens were reduced to living on the herbs growing in the city and close to the walls. Meat was somewhat more readily available in the form of sausages made from the mules of the army, which had died of disease. The soldiers were generally better supplied, as Belisarius had collected stores to ensure the efficiency of the army.

Growing Discontent Among the Citizens

As the difficulties of supplying the army and the population increased daily, discontent also rose. One day a delegation from the hunger-stricken population went to Belisarius to tell him that the loyalty and patriotism they felt when they opened the gates of Rome to his army now seemed utter foolishness to them. They longed for the peaceful times before the army had come. Their estates in the country had been devastated by the Goths, no food was entering the city, and many of their fellow citizens had died, leaving the living envious as their pains had been removed while the survivors still suffered. The delegation begged him to enter into a regular battle to end the misery, a battle in which he would not find them lacking in courage.

Belisarius replied that he had expected all the events that had so far occurred in the siege, including their suggestion. He believed that the populace of a city anywhere was fickle, easily discouraged, and always ready to suggest impossible enterprises and throw away any real advantages. He had no intention of complying with their counsels, which would sacrifice the interests of the emperor and the lives of the citizens. War is not made by a series of ill-considered, spasmodic efforts, but is a matter of calm and serious calculation, he explained. And it was his calculation that waiting would be the winning strategy of the Romans. Belisarius pointed out to the delegation that the populace had no experience in warfare, and he explained that courage alone would not beat the Goths. He respected their zeal and forgave them their ignorant advice, and he finished by informing them that he was expecting strong reinforcements within a few days that would change the situation. With their spirits somewhat revived by the general's speech, they retired.

It was a gamble, as Belisarius had no information of any rein-forcements coming in a few days—only the promises of the emper-or. He therefore sent his secretary, the historian Procopius, with a small bodyguard, commanded by Mundilas the guardsman, to Neapolis to find out the truth about any reinforcements. Procopius was also ordered to gather as many ships as possible and load them with grain for the relief of the city, and to gather as many men as possible from the garrisons in southern Italy.

The small party sneaked out of the Porta Ostiensis (today known as the Porta San Paolo), passed the Gothic garrison at the aqueduct fortress unnoticed, and proceeded to Neapolis. Soon after, Belisarius's wife, Antonina, was also sent to Neapolis, partly to ensure her safety, but also to employ her considerable influence and administrative talents in organizing relief for the besieged city. She was accompanied by Generals Martinus and Traianus and a thou-sand troops, who were sent to Tarracina to harass the Gothic troops besieging Rome from the rear and prevent supplies from being brought to them.

Procopius did not find a huge Roman army waiting for them in Campania in south Italy, but he had not expected he would. Instead he collected unemployed cavalry and troops from some of the gar-risons of Campania and Apulia. As the Romans had complete com-mand of the sea, it was also possible to quickly find provision ships. Procopius alone, before Antonina joined him, had collected five hundred soldiers and many provision ships. Procopius would be engaged in these enterprises from July to November 537.

THE BESIEGERS BECOME THE BESIEGED

After Procopius reached Neapolis, his escort returned to Rome. It again passed the Gothic fortress at Torre Fiscale in safety and brought the good news that the Via Appia was clear by night, as the Goths did not leave their aqueduct fortress after sunset. This infor-mation caused Belisarius to change his strategy. While still avoid-ing a regular battle, which he would have little chance of winning, he felt it was time to bring famine to the Goths. With their great numbers and the region devastated by their foraging, the Goths were having trouble bringing enough supplies to their army. Martinus and Traianus had already been sent with a thousand troops to Tarracina on the Via Appia, and Gontharis with a group of Herulians was sent to occupy Albani (Albano), also on the Via Appia. The Goths soon retook Albani, as it was only fourteen miles from Rome, but the strategy to harass the enemy's supply and make the besiegers the besieged was proving successful. Magnus and Sinthues were sent with five hundred soldiers to occupy Tibur (Tivoli) to further tighten the ring around the Goths. They occupied and repaired the old citadel and used it as a base of operations against the Gothic supply lines.

On the southern side of Rome, the Basilica of St. Paul, connected by its long colonnade with the Porta Ostiensis of Rome and protected on one side by the Tiber, was an excellent stronghold. Here Valerianus was sent with all the Huns of his army, so they could obtain forage for their horses and harass the Goths at the aqueduct fortress. Thus Belisarius dared to further reduce his numbers, but he gained the double advantage of having fewer mouths to feed in Rome and causing the Goths serious supply difficulties.

Because the other great general of war, pestilence, had also come to aid the Romans, the barbarians were hard-pressed in their crowded and unsanitary camps. Apart from hunger, malaria was causing serious problems for the Goths in the aqueduct fortress, and in the end the remnant of the garrison abandoned the stronghold and returned to the camps further north.

Malaria was also plaguing the Huns at the Basilica of St. Paul, and they, too, were forced to retreat, but only after their task had been completed. With the Gothic Via Appia garrison gone, communication and supply lines to the south were under much less pressure.

So the autumn wore on with famine and pestilence pressing ever harder on besieged and besieger, but each hoping to outlast the other.

In October, Antonina returned to Rome from her duties in Campania. An alleged conspiracy in November by Pope Silverius to open the Porta Asinaria to the Goths created a further rift between the local citizens and the Roman army. Silverius, son of a pope and also a Roman noble, was sent into exile on charges probably trumped up by Empress Theodora and supported by Antonina, who had great power over her husband's decisions. Vigilius was appointed pope in his stead.

THE LONG-EXPECTED REINFORCEMENTS ARRIVE

With the month of December came also the happy news of the much-awaited reinforcements. The troops dispatched from the East were gathering in the harbors of south Italy. At Neapolis there arrived three thousand Isaurians under Paulus and Conon, and at Hydruntum (Otranto) eight hundred Thracian horsemen under John, the nephew of Vitalianus, and one thousand regular cavalry under Alexander and Marcentius.

Three hundred horsemen under Zeno had already arrived in Rome by the Via Latina, and the five hundred men collected by Procopius were ready to march from Campania. Altogether there were five thousand six hundred troops—more than Belisarius's entire army, which had been reduced by casualties, hunger, and disease, but still far, far fewer than the besieging Gothic army.

One of the new generals, John, the nephew of Vitalianus, would play an important role in the coming years. He was regarded as a skillful general and a stouthearted soldier who was fearless and well able to compete with any barbarian in enduring hardships and simple living. His actions had earned him the epithet *"sanguinarius"*— "the bloody." Next to Bessas and Constantinus, he was probably the most important imperial general in Italy, and this would later cause serious problems for Belisarius.

The troops under Paulus and Conon were ordered to sail to Ostia as quickly as possible. John, who was joined by the five hundred soldiers Procopius had collected, marched along the Via Appia and was acting as escort for a long train of wagons laden with supplies for the population in Rome. The plan was to create a wagon laager if they were attacked and defend behind this.

While these reinforcements were moving toward Rome, Martinus and Traianus were withdrawn from Tarracina to Rome to take part in a covering operation.

To divert the attention of the Goths from the arriving reinforcements, Belisarius planned a new large sortie against the Gothic camp lying close to Porta Flaminia. The main attack would come from the Porta Flaminia, which had been blocked up by the Romans early in the siege and not used since then. The Goths had therefore regarded it as useless to attack, but also without the menace of a sally. The masonry blocking the gate was torn down during the night, and a large body of Roman troops drew up behind it.

A feint was then made toward the Gothic camps with a thousand horsemen under Traianus and Diogenes from the Porta Pinciana. As had been hoped, the Goths poured out of their camps in hot pursuit of the Roman force. The wild pursuit was disorganizing the barbarians, and when all was ready, Belisarius ordered the Porta Flaminia to be opened and launched his waiting troops into the flank of the unsuspecting Goths. The Romans then charged the Gothic camp nearest to the walls of Rome. Despite their small numbers, the Goths inside the camp managed to hold out for some time because of the strong fortifications. As Procopius describes it:

> For the trench had been dug to an extraordinary depth, and since the earth taken from it had invariably been placed along its inner side, this reached a great height and so served as a wall; and it was abundantly supplied with stakes, which were very sharp and close together, thus making a palisade.

Then Aquilinus, one of Belisarius's valiant bodyguards, mounted a horse and leaped over the rampart and into the camp. There he killed many Goths until he was surrounded and the shower of missiles hurled at him wounded his horse, which fell. Aquilinus, however, escaped unhurt and leaped back over the rampart, where he joined Roman troops who were forming to attack the rear of the barbarians still pursuing the horsemen of Traianus and Diogenes. The Romans showered them with arrows, killing many. The survivors stopped their pursuit and tried to turn around, but Traianus and his men also turned and charged the Goths, who were now caught between two attacks. The barbarians panicked and fled toward the camps while the pursuing horsemen slaughtered them by the hundreds. Only a few succeeded in escaping to the camps, whose occupants did not dare venture out to support them because they feared an imminent attack.

In this battle, Traianus suffered a serious wound. He was hit in the face by an arrow, a little above his right eye and not far from the nose. The whole of the arrow tip, though long and large, entered and was hidden in the wound. The wooden shaft, which was not well-joined to the iron tip, fell off. Despite his wound, Traianus kept up the attack with no serious trouble. No attempts seem to have been made after the battle to extract the arrow tip from the wound. Procopius relates that five years later, the arrow tip worked its way to the surface and began to show itself in his face. This continued for three more years until the arrow tip slowly worked itself out, with no ill effects for Traianus.

PEACE NEGOTIATIONS

The sortie accomplished its goal while causing many Gothic casualties. The troops of Paulus and Conon arrived safely at Ostia, where they fortified their camp with a deep ditch. John could safely rendezvous with them with his great supply train and formed a wagon laager at Ostia.

The sortie also had a more significant effect by deeply discouraging the Goths, who had suffered another heavy defeat.

Famine and disease were now also pressing so hard on the multitude of barbarians that it was difficult to tell who was the besieged party. They were constantly being defeated in skirmishes and had no chance of taking the city by storm. With new reinforcements arriving and more rumored to be on their way, the feared Belisarius had even dared to assault one of their camps, which he almost captured. The question of raising the siege was debated in a gathering of the Gothic nobles and King Vittigis. It was finally decided to send a delegation to Emperor Justinian to seek peace, while another was sent to Belisarius in Rome.

Procopius was present at the negotiations in Rome and recorded the arguments of each side. A Roman official in the service of the Goths initiated the talks:

You have done us an injustice, O Romans, in taking up arms wrongfully against us, your friends and allies. And what we shall say is, we think, well known to each one of you as well as ourselves. For the Goths did not obtain the land of Italy by wresting it from the Romans by force, but Odoacer in former times dethroned the emperor, changed the government of Italy to a tyranny, and so held it [in AD 476]. And Zeno, who then held the power of the East, though he wished to avenge his partner in the imperial office and to free this land from the usurper, was unable to destroy the authority of Odoacer. Accordingly he persuaded Theodoric, our ruler, although he was on the point of besieging him and Byzantium, not only to put an end to his hostility toward himself, in recollection of the honor which Theodoric had already received at his hands in having made a patrician and consul of the Romans, but also to punish Odoacer for his unjust treatment of Augustulus, and thereafter, in company with the Goths, to hold sway over the land as its legitimate and rightful rulers. It was in this way, therefore, that we took over the dominion of Italy, and we have preserved both the laws and the form of government as strictly as any who have ever been Roman emperors, and there is absolutely no law, either written or unwritten, introduced by Theodoric or by any of his successors on the throne of the Goths. And we have so scrupulously guarded for the Romans their practices pertaining to the worship of God and faith in Him, that not one of the Italians has changed his belief, either willingly or unwillingly, up to the present day, and when Goths have changed, we have taken no notice of the matter [The Goths were followers of the Arian heresy]. And indeed the sanctuaries of the Romans have received from us the highest honor; for no one who has taken refuge in any of them has ever been treated with violence by any man; nay, more, the Romans themselves have continued to hold all the offices of the state, and not a single Goth has had a share in them. Let someone come forward and refute us, if he thinks that this statement of ours is not true. And one might add that the Goths have conceded that the dignity of the consulship should be conferred upon Romans each year by the emperor of the East. Such has been the course followed by us; but you, on your side, did not take the part of Italy while it was suffering at the hands of the barbarians and Odoacer, although it was not for a short time, but for ten years, that he treated the land outrageously; but now you do violence to us who have acquired it legitimately, though you have no business here. Do you therefore depart hence out of our way, keeping both that which is your own and whatever you have gained by plunder.

And Belisarius said:

Although your promise gave us to understand that your words would be brief and temperate, yet your discourse had been both long and not far from fraudulent in its pretensions. For Theodoric was sent by the Emperor Zeno in order to make war on Odoacer, not in order to hold the dominion of Italy for himself. For why should the emperor have been concerned to exchange one tyrant for another? But he sent him in order that Italy might be free and obedient to the emperor. And Theodoric disposed of the tyrant in a satisfactory manner, in everything else he showed an extraordinary lack of proper feeling; for he never thought of restoring the land to its rightful owner. But I, for my part, think that he who robs another by violence and he who of his own will does not restore his neighbor's goods are equal. Now, as for me, I shall never surrender the emperor's country to any other. But if there is anything you wish to receive in place of it, I give you leave to speak.

And the Goths said: 'That everything which we have said is true, no one of you can be unaware. But in order that we may not seem to be contentious, we give up to you Sicily, great as it is and of such wealth, seeing that without it you cannot possess Libya in security."

And Belisarius replied with irony: "And we on our side permit the Goths to have the whole of Britain, which is much larger than Sicily and was subject to the Romans in early times. For it is only fair to make an equal return to those who first do a good deed or perform a kindness."

Goths: "Well, then, if we should make you a proposal concerning Campania also, or about Neapolis itself, will you listen to it?"

Belisarius: "No, for we are not empowered to administer the emperor's affairs in a way which is not in accord with his wish."

Goths: "Not even if we impose upon ourselves the payment of a fixed sum of money every year?"

Belisarius: "No, indeed. For we are not empowered to do anything else than guard the land for its owner."

Goths: "Come now, we must send envoys to the emperor and make with him our treaty concerning the whole matter. And a definite time must also be appointed during which the armies will be bound to observe an armistice."

Belisarius: "Very well; let this be done. For never shall I stand in your way when you are making plans for peace."

After these discussions, the Gothic delegates left for their camps, and during the following days arrangements were made for an armistice, and they agreed to exchange hostages to ensure the good faith of both parties.

Armistice

For Belisarius, the truce came at an opportune time. Vast amounts of supplies had been collected in the port of Ostia, but to bring them into the besieged city would be difficult indeed.

It was time for swift action, and on the very evening of the conference with the Gothic delegation, Belisarius and Antonina, attended by a hundred horsemen, rode to Ostia to confer with the generals there. He urged them to take advantage of the situation as soon as possible and prepare for the transport of the supplies to Rome. He returned to Rome early the next morning, having left Antonina in Ostia to consult with the generals on the best way of transporting the supplies.

The only practicable towpath up the Tiber ran along the right bank of the river and was commanded by the Gothic garrison at Portus. Moreover, the draught oxen were in pitiful shape after a long period of little food and much hardship. So Antonina and the generals decided to trust in sails and oars instead, and the lifeboats of the largest boats of the navy at Ostia were selected for the task. These little boats were fitted with planks on the side to function as crude battlements to protect the rowers from enemy arrows. The ships were loaded, and a part of the reinforcements followed on the left bank of Tiber. The winding river was difficult to traverse for ships under sails and oars. Many times the sailors were forced to use the oars to row the heavy ships forward against the current.

Strangely enough, the Goths did not react to this enterprise, despite no truce having been formally concluded. The barges could therefore sail almost under the towers of the Gothic garrison at Portus with no arrows being fired. Neither did the garrisons in the six Gothic camps stir from their fortifications. Most likely, the Goths did not want to risk the results of the conference by doing anything that would anger the feared Belisarius, despite the fact that the expedition would undo much of the results of the last six months' blockade.

So the barges passed and repassed without incident, and the Roman warehouses were refilled. Likewise, most of the reinforcements entered Rome, with only a small Isaurian garrison being left in Ostia under Paulus. With this, the Romans had in fact won the first siege of Rome, and the Goths had lost their chance to retake the city this time.

But the Gothic army stayed before the walls of Rome, most likely in the vain hope that the truce and the delegation to Justinian would bring favorable terms. It was arranged in December 537 that Gothic ambassadors would be sent to Constantinople under Roman escort to plead their case, that a truce of three months should be concluded between the two armies to give the delegation a chance to go and return, and that hostages of high rank should be given on both sides. One of the recently arrived cavalry commanders, Zeno, was given as hostage by the Romans, and the Goths gave Ulias, one of their nobles. Shortly after the negotiations, Ildiger, the

son-in-law of Antonina, arrived from Africa with more reinforcements of cavalry.

Belisarius had, in the course of negotiations, completely outwit-
ted King Vittigis. Nothing had been said about resupplying
Rome—a question Belisarius decided himself. Neither had anything been said about the two armies maintaining their positions, a
problem that soon arose. Without a proper logistical system, and
with the Romans in complete control of the sea, the Goths found
greater and greater difficulty in maintaining their outposts and garrisons. They were soon forced to withdraw their garrisons from
Portus, Centumcellae (Civitavecchia), and Albani because they
were out of supplies. Shortly after the Goths vacated their positions, Belisarius moved Roman troops into the cities and was thereby slowly hemming in the Goths.

Vittigis soon complained about these movements, which, he felt,
were not in accord with the terms of the armistice. Vittigis claimed
he had sent for the Goths in Portus to come to him for a temporary service, and then Paulus and his Isaurians had moved in from
Ostia and taken possession of the empty fortress. The same went
for Albani and Centumcellae. All these places must be given back,
or he would make the Romans regret it. Belisarius simply laughed
at the Gothic threats and told them that everybody knew perfectly
well why these places had been abandoned. The truce still held, but
now both sides were more suspicious of each other.

The Romans Begin Offensive Operations

With his little army doubled by the recent reinforcements and the
Goths clearly on the defensive, Belisarius could spare some troops
for further operations. John, the nephew of Vitalianus, was sent to
the Abruzzi Mountains with the eight hundred cavalry under his
command, four hundred cavalry from Valerianus, and eight hundred horsemen from Belisarius's elite bodyguard. The latter two
bodies of troops were commanded by Suntas and Adegis, who were
ordered to follow John's movements but to camp in other quarters,
probably for reasons of supply. John was to winter at Alba Fucens
(Albe), a city in the Apennine Mountains about 70 miles from
Rome. His orders were to not disturb the Goths as long as they

undertook no offensive operations against him. The moment that news reached him of the truce being broken, he was to move against the Gothic possessions in the territory of Picenum between the Apennines and the Adriatic Sea. He was to spare any Roman villas but to plunder the Gothic farms and to enslave their women and children—an easy task because all the men were serving in the army at Rome. Any fortress or garrison that would not surrender was to be taken, so that no threats would exist against his line of communications. The whole booty was to remain undivided until it could be divided among the entire army, as Belisarius said with a laugh: "For it is not fair, that the drones should be destroyed with great labor by one force, while others, without having endured any hardship at all, enjoy the honey."

MEDIOLANUM REVOLTS

Little happened during the siege in the early months of 538, apart from two events: a visit by the archbishop of Mediolanum and a quarrel between Belisarius and General Constantinus.

Datius, the archbishop, came with a delegation to ask Belisarius to send a small garrison to hold their city, which was ready to revolt against the Goths along with the region of Liguria. Mediolanum was the first city of the Western Empire after Rome and was strategically situated to control the prosperous Po valley. Control of Liguria rested on controlling Mediolanum, so Belisarius granted their request as soon as it was possible after winter ended.

QUARREL WITH CONSTANTINUS

The quarrel with Constantinus arose from small beginnings. Presidius, a leading citizen of Ravenna, had fled to the imperial army because of some troubles with the Goths. Leaving Ravenna under the pretense of going hunting, he made his way to Constantinus's army, then quartered at Spoletium. He brought with him two daggers in golden scabbards set with precious stones. Constantinus heard the rumor of the fugitive and his daggers, and he sent one of his guards, Maxentiolus, to take the weapons in his name. Presidius could do little but hand them over, but he was deeply offended and hastened to Rome to complain to Belisarius as the Roman commander in chief.

Because of the siege, Presidius could not put his case before Belisarius, but with the calm of the truce, he obtained an audience. Belisarius, for other reasons, was not entirely happy with Constantinus, but still he confined himself to urging Constantinus to clear himself of the guilt of the unjust deed and the dishonor it brought him. But Constantinus could not leave it alone and kept taunting Presidius with the loss of the daggers. In the end, Presidius could take no more, and one day when Belisarius was riding through the Forum, he seized his horse's bridle and shouted "whether the laws of the emperor said that, whenever anyone fleeing from the barbarians comes to them as a suppliant, they should rob him by violence of whatever he may chance to have in his hands?" The general's retinue shouted to him to let go of the bridle, but he refused and kept repeating his cries until Belisarius promised that his daggers would be restored to him.

The next day, Belisarius called a conference of generals in his headquarters in the palace on the Pincian Hill. Constantinus, Bessas, and Valerianus were there, as well as Ildiger, who had recently come from Africa. Belisarius presented the case of the stolen daggers to the assembly and urged Constantinus to return the daggers to their rightful owner. Constantinus hotly answered that he would never return the daggers but rather throw them into the Tiber. Belisarius then asked angrily whether Constantinus did not think he was subject to his orders. Constantinus answered that he was willing to obey Belisarius in everything else but this. Belisarius then ordered his guards to enter the room. "In order, plainly, to have them kill me", Constantinus said. "By no means", Belisarius answered, "but to have them compel your bodyguard Maxentiolus, who forcibly carried away the daggers for you, to restore to the man what he took from him by violence."

Constantinus, however, believed he was about to be arrested, so he drew his dagger and stabbed Belisarius in the belly. The general was not fatally wounded and managed to get out of the room while Valerianus and Ildiger restrained Constantinus until the guards could come and help subdue him. He was confined for some days and eventually put to death by order of Belisarius. Constantinus's actions fully justified the death sentence, but the incident was a bad omen for future cooperation between the generals in the Roman army.

THE GOTHS ATTEMPT TO INFILTRATE THE CITY

Not long after this affair, the Goths attempted to enter the city by guile, despite the truce. The Aqua Virgo aqueduct passed through the Gothic lines and passed the Aurelian Wall near the Porta Salaria. Eventually it went under the Pincian Hill and emerged in a deep, well-like chamber connected to one of the palaces on the hill. Because the aqueducts had been cut in the initial phase of the siege, the tunnel of the aqueduct was empty of water. With torches and lamps they crept along the tunnel for one or two miles until they were inside the city, and even close to Belisarius's headquarters on the Pincian Hill. Here a newly built wall made by the Romans soon after the aqueducts had been cut barred further progress. Belisarius was not going to suffer defeat in the same way as the Neapolitans. The explorers broke off a small piece of stone from the wall and returned to Vittigis to tell of their expedition.

While the little party of Goths had been moving along the part of the Aqua Virgo above ground, however, the light of its torches was seen by a guard through a little crack in the walls of the aqueduct at Porta Pinciana. When he told his comrades of the mysterious light, they did not believe him and said he must have seen the eyes of a wolf in the darkness. But on the following day the story reached Belisarius, and he understood immediately that the Goths had tried to get inside the city. At once Diogenes, one of his bodyguards, was sent with troops to examine the channel of the aqueduct. The obstructing wall was taken down, and they entered the tunnel, where they found proof of the Gothic expedition. The Goths soon found out that the Romans were aware of their attempt, and the plan was promptly abandoned.

But the Goths had not abandoned their hopes of taking Rome by stratagem, and two more attempts were made during the rest of the three-month truce. One was against the Porta Pinciana and was planned to take place during the mid-day meal, when few soldiers were expected to guard the walls. The Goths came on in loose order with ladders to mount the walls and torches to burn the gate. Luckily, the active Ildiger was in command of the gate and saw what the Goths were attempting. He quickly gathered his followers and sallied out. The barbarians, who had no time to get into formation, were easily routed and many killed.

The next scheme was somewhat more adventurous in its design. King Vittigis knew that the walls between the Porta Flaminia and the Mausoleum of Hadrian were low and had no defensive towers because the military engineers of Emperor Aurelian had thought the river was sufficient protection. Vittigis therefore concocted a plan to drug the guards on the wall and then send a strong detachment across the river in boats, with orders to climb the wall and open the gates of the city to the waiting Gothic army. He bribed two Romans living close to the Church of St. Peter, who promised to bring wine to the guards on this stretch of wall around nightfall, to keep them drinking, and, when they were getting too drunk to notice, to slip sleeping drugs into the wine.

The scheme was revealed to Belisarius by one of the traitors, who also revealed the name of his accomplice. The latter confessed under torture and revealed the sleeping drugs given to him by Vittigis. Belisarius cut off his nose and ears and sent him riding on an ass to the camp of the Goths to tell of the discovery of the plot.

These three attempts were enough for Belisarius, and he considered the truce broken. Immediately, he sent letters to John to start the planned operations in the Gothic rear.

OPERATIONS OF JOHN

John took his two thousand horsemen through the region of Picenum, burning and plundering the Gothic farms. Vittigis's uncle, the aged Ulitheus, dared to meet him in battle but was defeated and slain with almost his entire army.

On his march of death and destruction, John came to the fortresses of Urbinum (Urbino) and Auximum (Osimo), which were not strongly garrisoned but commanded strong natural posi-

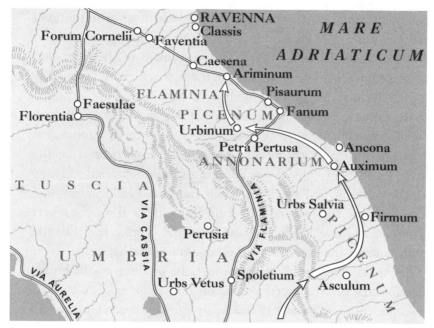

Map 10. The operations of John, nephew of Vitalianus.

tions. Instead of trying to reduce these threats to his communications, as Belisarius had ordered him to, John passed the fortresses and pressed on to the strategic city of Ariminum.

The Gothic garrison in Ariminum was suspicious of the inhabitants, whom they knew had a strong pro-Roman attitude. When they heard that John was coming with an army, they withdrew in haste to Ravenna. The inhabitants could then open the gates to the Roman general, who marched unhindered into the city.

John and his army were now 200 miles in the rear of the main Gothic army and only 33 miles—a day's march—from the Gothic capital at Ravenna. This bold move was the final push to draw the Goths away from the walls of Rome. The Goths began hearing rumors of their farms being burned and their women and children taken into slavery. At the same time, Vittigis received information that his young wife, Matasuntha, in Ravenna, who had never forgiven her low-born husband for marrying her, was in communication with John, promising she would betray the Goths if he married her. So, after three months of truce but with no ambassadors returned from Constantinople, Vittigis decided to raise the long siege of Rome. At dawn one day around the spring equinox, in March 538, 374 days after the commencement of the siege, and after having set fire to all its camps, the demoralized Gothic army withdrew north on the Via Flaminia.

Initially, the Romans considered letting the Goths withdraw without trouble, as much of the cavalry was out on operations, but it was too great an opportunity to inflict more casualties on the still-formidable Gothic army. Belisarius hastily mustered as many troops as were available, and when half the Gothic army had crossed Pons Milvius, he launched his soldiers from the Porta Pinciana and made a furious attack on the Gothic rear. Despite withstanding the Romans in the beginning, the barbarians were soon forced to retreat. As panic ensued, the situation on the bridge became chaotic. Many were pushed off the bridge or killed by their comrades in their attempt to flee. Only a few succeeded in crossing the river to the other half of the army.

In this way the first siege of Rome ended in complete disaster for the Goths. Despite their great numbers and their great courage and hardiness, the barbarian army proved itself useless in the hands of the inept King Vittigis. He did not know how to conduct a siege, a blockade, or anything but a set-piece battle, where the Gothic numbers could be effective. The flower of the Gothic nation had fallen; perhaps more than one hundred thousand warriors were killed or died of disease and hunger, and their courage and determination had been shaken to the roots. Among the countless Gothic graves outside Rome was also the grave for the Gothic monarchy, as such losses could never be replaced. Never again in the war would such a great Gothic army be seen.

7

THE CAMPAIGN
FOR RAVENNA

THE FAILURE OF THE SIEGE OF ROME did not bring about the immediate downfall of the Gothic kingdom. With King Vittigis withdrawing with his remaining troops toward Ravenna on the great highway of Via Flaminia, it is worthwhile to consider the dispositions of the forces in the spring of 538.

With the Via Flaminia running almost straight north from Rome to Ravenna, almost all of the fortresses to the right of it were in the hands of the Romans, whereas the ones to the left were in the hands of the Goths: Urbs Vetus (Orvieto) was held by Albilas with one thousand warriors. Gibimer held Clusium (Chiusi) with another thousand. At Tuder (Todi), Uligisalus held the old Etruscan walls with four hundred Goths. A small Gothic garrison also held Faesulae (Fiesole) above Florentia (Florence). Auximum, commanding the city of Ancona, was held by four thousand picked troops under Wisandus. At Urbinum, Moras commanded two thousand Goths, and Mons Feletris (Montefeltro) and Caesena (Cesena) were occupied by five hundred troops each. In Picenum the fortress of Petra Pertusa, blocking the Via Flaminia, was manned by four hundred Goths. Most of the Gothic strongholds were in excellent defensive positions.

On the other side of the Via Flaminia, the Romans held Narnia, Spoletium, Perusia, Ancona, and Ariminum. But Belisarius thought Ariminum was too exposed, as it was only about 33 miles from Ravenna and surrounded by Gothic garrisons. While John presumably wanted to strike at the heart of the Gothic kingdom, it was Belisarius's plan to push the Goths from all sides and to slowly reduce their territory and resources in a systematic campaign.

Summoning Ildiger and Martinus, who had recently come with reinforcements, Belisarius put a thousand horsemen under their command and had them proceed to Ariminum with new orders for John. The orders were to withdraw his two thousand Isaurian horsemen from Ariminum and leave a small garrison in the city, drawn from the overly large garrison at Ancona, where Conon was commanding his Thracians and Isaurians. As Ariminum was not well provisioned for a siege, a small garrison would be able to hold out much longer than John's two thousand men, who would be too great a prize for the retreating Goths to ignore. Despite the devastating losses to the army of Vittigis, he was still commanding some forty thousand to fifty thousand warriors, more than three times the number of Roman troops in all Italy.

Ildiger and Martinus soon outdistanced the unwieldy Gothic army retreating north, which was slowed by trying to avoid the Roman-held cities close to the Via Flaminia.

Fall of Petra Pertusa

On the fourth day, the Gothic garrison of Petra Pertusa checked the Romans' progress. Here, where the road went through the mountains, with an abrupt mountainside rising on one side and an unfordable river on the other, the Romans in the time of Emperor Vespasian (69–79) had been forced to make a tunnel through the rock for the road. A fortress, named Petra Pertusa, was placed where the gate of the tunnel opened. The pass is now named Passo di Furlo, and nothing remains of the fortress.

The Roman horsemen discharged a few arrows at the fortress, but the Goths were content to remain quiet within it. Then the Romans, some of whom were probably experienced mountaineers from Isauria in Asia Minor, climbed up the steep hillside and started rolling down rocks on the fortress. The avalanche damaged the battlements and towers, and soon the shaken Goths surrendered. They promised to become the faithful servants of Emperor Justinian and to obey Belisarius's orders. A few were left in the fortress as an imperial garrison along with some of the Romans, and the rest followed the army of Ildiger and Martinus, which hurried on toward Ariminum. With this, the greatest obstacle on the Via Flaminia was cleared for the Romans, and at the same time the passage of any Goths was barred.

To the modern eye, it might seem incredible that Goths and Romans often switched sides and fought for the enemy. This was partly because of the morale of the troops—at this point, after the defeat before the walls of Rome, Gothic morale was almost nonexistent—and partly because there was no distinct national attitude in the war. It was more a question of loyalty to a general, who in turn was loyal to the Roman emperor or the Gothic king. If a general could maintain his position and be on the winning side by switching loyalties, he would, especially if he was a Goth, but there was also a Roman example. For the common soldier, fighting for a successful and able general also meant much in terms of prestige and more plunder.

The loyalty of the deserters was, however, often in doubt, especially if put to fight their countrymen. The Romans were adept at receiving deserters and then sending them to the East, where they would fight the Persians—as for example at the Battle of Nisibis (Nusaybin in modern-day Turkey) in 541, where the Gothic pikemen played an important part. Being so far from home, they had no chance of returning or making a rebellion and so would set up a new life for themselves. For the Roman deserters, it was often a question of gain, and only one Roman general—Herodianus in 545—switched sides during the war because of an impending enquiry into some financial irregularities, at a time when the war was going well for the Goths. Again it should be noted that despite being called the Roman army, it consisted of a great number of barbarians who had no particular regard for the Roman Empire as a nation and saw soldiering as a profession like any other.

On the fifth day, the little army reached the imperial garrison at Ancona and collected a number of infantry intended as garrison for Ariminum. On the eighth day after leaving Rome, they finally reached Ariminum and the army of John.

When John received Belisarius's orders, he flatly refused to obey them. Whatever the cause, he would neither part with his two thousand horsemen nor evacuate Ariminum. Instead he asked that Damianus and his four hundred troops stay along with the infantry from Ancona.

All Ildiger and Martinus could do was withdraw the soldiers belonging to the household of Belisarius and leave Damianus and his contingent and the infantry brought from Ancona. They then departed quickly to avoid a skirmish with the approaching army of King Vittigis.

Siege of Ariminum

Before long, Vittigis appeared with his army before Ariminum, and as Belisarius had predicted, he could not ignore the large garrison of the city. In preparation for an assault, the Goths constructed a huge wooden siege tower, high enough to overlook the battlements. The Goths had learned from their failure at Rome: this time they built it so it could be pushed by men from inside, where they would be protected from the enemy's arrows. On the night after the great engine had been built, the Goths went to sleep in expectation of taking the city the next day, an expectation shared by the disheartened garrison.

Their insubordinate general was, however, not ready to yield to despair. With a band of Isaurians equipped with trenching tools and pickaxes, he slipped out of the city in the dead of night. Observing complete silence, the Isaurians excavated a deep trench in front of the tower; they created another obstacle by throwing the excavated dirt up next to the trench, thereby creating an earthen rampart. Just before dawn, the barbarians discovered the trenching party and rushed against it, but John was satisfied with the work done and retreated without a fight.

When Vittigis saw the work of the Romans, he put to death the Gothic guards whose deep sleep had made it possible. But Vittigis was still determined to use the tower, and he ordered his troops to fill the trench with bundles of branches and commence the assault. They filled the trench despite a furious discharge of stones and arrows from the besieged. The tower was laboriously pushed forward, but when the wheels went over the edge of the trench, the bound branches bent and cracked under its huge weight, and the pushing soldiers found it impossible to move further. With this, and the mound of excavated earth on the other side of the trench, it was soon clear that the tower could not be brought up to the wall under the heavy missile fire from the Romans. As the day wore on, the barbarians prepared to drag the tower back, as they feared it would be burned in another nighttime sortie.

John knew the engine could be brought to another unprotected part of the wall, so he collected almost his entire army for a sally. After a stirring speech in which he accused Belisarius of having abandoned them to the enemy, he led all his men out, apart from a few troops guarding the walls, to contest the movement of the tower. The Goths resisted stubbornly, and the battle dragged on until evening, when they succeeded in pushing the tower back to their own lines. But the battle had been so bloody, and they had lost so many of their bravest warriors, that King Vittigis decided not to make any more assaults, but instead to starve out the garrison.

Assault on Ancona

Not long after this Gothic assault on Ariminum was repulsed, Ancona was subjected to a similar assault. Vittigis had sent General Vacimus to Auximum with orders to collect the troops there to commence a siege of nearby Ancona. The fortress of Ancona was strong and situated on a hill above the harbor. Unfortunately, the city below was weak and difficult to defend. In what was a foolish tactical mistake but also a kind desire to protect the populace, Roman General Conon included not only the fortress but the entire city in his line of defense. He drew up his forces about half a mile inland from the city and proceeded to entrench himself and the whole city. As Procopius the historian comments, the ditches might have been useful for hunting game, but they were quite useless for war.

The dispersed defenders quickly found themselves outnumbered by the attacking Goths and forced to retreat in disarray toward the fortress. The first of the fugitives were received without difficulty, but the pursuing Goths had become mingled with the rest of the pursued, so the defenders were forced to close the gates against their own soldiers. Conon himself was among those shut out, and had to be hauled up by ropes let down from the battlements. His fellow soldiers were rescued the same way.

Excited by the initial success, the Goths quickly put up ladders and tried to scale the walls. In the confusion they would probably have succeeded if not for the efforts of two brave men, Ulimuth the Thracian—a member of Belisarius's bodyguard—and Bulgundus the Hun, who kept the enemy at bay while the garrison was organizing its defenses. The two heroes died of their wounds, but the fortress was saved. It is unknown what became of the city, but it was most likely sacked by the Goths.

While these events were taking place, Belisarius was quietly and gradually taking the Gothic fortresses closest to Rome. The garrisons of Tuder and Clusium, with fourteen hundred warriors all told, surrendered at the mere rumor of the approaching Roman army. They were promised that their lives would be spared and were sent unharmed to Sicily and Neapolis. The cities were then garrisoned.

While Belisarius's strategy of methodically taking the Gothic strongholds and pressing the barbarians north toward Ravenna was slow and laborious, it had the advantage of reducing Roman losses in men and material. But it was first of all a safe strategy, guaranteed to win in the end. While Belisarius did occasionally take chances, his plans were always carefully thought through in an almost scientific fashion in which he weighed up costs and benefits. Unfortunately, this was often lost on his generals, who were eager for quick fame and fortune, and accordingly committed many reckless deeds.

Narses Lands in Italy

The arrival in Picenum of fresh and large new reinforcements from Constantinople further encouraged Belisarius to proceed more vigorously with the war. The eunuch Narses, who was destined to have an even greater influence on Italy's future than Belisarius, commanded the seven thousand soldiers in the new army.

The army consisted of several detachments totaling five thousand troops. One was commanded by Justinus, the general of Illyricum; one by Narses the general (so called to distinguish him from Narses the eunuch); and one by Aratius, the brother of Narses the general (both were Persarmenians who had deserted the service of Persia for that of the Romans). There were also two thousand Herulian barbarians, commanded by their chieftains Wisandus, Alueth, and Fanotheus.

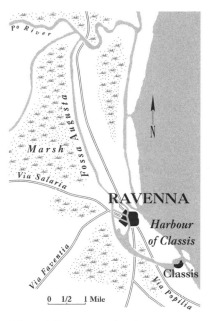

Map 11. Ravenna and vicinity.

Narses the eunuch was born in Persarmenia around 478. By middle age he occupied a high position at the imperial court. After a post as *chartularius*, or keeper of the archives of the imperial bed chamber, he rose some time before 530 to the position of *praepositus sacri cubiculi*, or grand chamberlain. This was one of the most powerful positions in the Roman administration, equal to the masters of soldiery and praetorian prefects, but perhaps even more powerful because of its more continual and confidential access to the emperor.

Narses had shown evidence of his talents during the Nika riots, in which he rendered essential service to Justinian. While the newly proclaimed Emperor Hypatius was being congratulated in the Circus during the chaotic days of the riots, Narses went into the streets with bags of gold from the imperial treasury, met with some of the leaders of the Blue faction, and convinced them to support the cause of the true emperor. With the coalition of the two Circus factions disrupted, and with the soldiers of Belisarius and Mundus, the throne had been saved.

To appoint this man—only trained in the intrigues of politics at the imperial court and already more than 60 years old—general of the new army sent to Italy seems a great error in judgment by Justinian. But the emperor was generally careful in choosing the right man for a job. Yet despite the fact that Narses would show himself to be a capable and at times excellent military leader, this was not the motive for sending the emperor's most powerful civil servant to the Gothic War.

It was the same old problem that had plagued the Roman Empire for centuries. Through his astounding victories in the Persian, Vandal, and Gothic wars, Belisarius had become exceedingly rich and popular—and had thereby become a potential rival to Justinian. Generals much less popular and wealthy had earlier in the history of the empire often usurped the throne. Justinian's own uncle, Justin, came to the throne through his military position despite not being able to read and write, and during the third century in particular there had been a continuous stream of soldier-emperors and usurpers. It was desirable for Justinian to keep Belisarius closely watched by a person whose age and condition meant he could never himself aspire to the throne.

A Council of War is Held at Firmum

A council of war was held at Firmum (Fermo), a town of Picenum about forty miles south of Ancona and six miles inland from the Adriatic Sea. Here were the two major generals, Belisarius and Narses, as well as Martinus, Ildiger, Justinus the general of Illyricum, Narses the general with his brother Aratius, and the primitive Herulian chieftains Wisandus, Alueth, and Fanotheus. There were already disagreements between Belisarius, who did not want to advance further with the dangerous Gothic garrison of Auximum at his back, and Narses's party, which wanted to relieve the troops besieged in Ariminum and end the war as quickly as possible by engaging in a pitched battle with the army of King Vittigis.

The main point of the conference was to determine if Ariminum should be relieved, or John and his army left to their own fate. By relieving the garrison, the Romans would leave the Gothic garrison of Auximum at their rear and thereby endanger the whole army. On the other hand, Ariminum was not prepared for a siege, and soon the provisions would be gone. The majority of the generals were against relieving John, whom they thought had brought his present conditions upon himself by his rashness, vanity, and lust for plunder. He had disobeyed the orders of his commander in chief, so why endanger the rest of the army in relieving him?

When the young generals had voiced their opinions, the gray-haired Narses rose. The question he presented to the other generals was this: Were the problems that would arise from following one course or another of equal magnitudes? If Auximum was left untaken, the garrison could supplement itself from without, but still the taking of the city could be resumed later. But if Ariminum was allowed to surrender with its general and garrison, it would be disastrous for the imperial cause. The Goths were still far more numerous than the Roman army, and what kept them on the defensive was the consciousness of uniform disaster that cowed their spirits and prepared them for defeat. If they gained such a victory as the surrender of a Roman army, they would regain their courage, and the fight for Italy would become so much harder. In conclusion, Narses therefore advised Belisarius to punish John for his disobedience but to relieve Ariminum and not let the cause of the Romans suffer because of one man.

The effect of this speech, coming from Justinian's most trusted counselor, was great and steered the decision. It was strengthened by the timely arrival of a letter to Belisarius from the besieged John. In it he informed the general that their provisions were exhausted, and he was going to surrender in seven days.

Belisarius seriously doubted that Ariminum should be relieved. Any battle taking place before the walls of Ariminum could easily be decided by the Gothic garrison at Auximum, which could lay ambushes or attack the Romans at the rear at the worst possible time.

Finally, after considering all advantages and disadvantages, he decided to relieve Ariminum while standing off the Goths in Auximum.

THE RELIEF OF ARIMINUM

Belisarius was well aware that the Gothic army was much greater than the Roman forces, but hoped to frighten the demoralized barbarians by appearing from all sides at once. If the Goths chose to fight, he would have to retreat and reorganize his troops, and that would mean the end of John and his troops in Ariminum.

With so little time available, it was necessary to improvise. A detachment of one thousand soldiers under Aratius was ordered to camp about 30 miles from Auximum on the seacoast and to watch the Gothic garrison there, but under no circumstances to attack it. The main part of the army, under Herodianus, Uliaris, and Narses the general, was put onboard the fleet, which was under the overall command of Ildiger, and ordered to sail toward Ariminum while keeping abreast of the rest of the army marching by land. When the fleet arrived it was to anchor in front of the besieged city. Another division, under Martinus, was to march on the great highway along the coast through Ancona, Fanum (Fano), and Pisaurum (Pesaro). Belisarius himself, together with Narses the eunuch, led a column that was intended to relieve the city if everything else failed. This column was to move west from Firmum through the ruins of Urbs Salvia (Urbisaglia—destroyed by Alaric the Visigoth in 452) to Nuceria (Nocera), from which it would follow the Via Flaminia through the Apennines.

While marching hastily on the great road, about a day's march before Ariminum and still not out of the mountains, Belisarius's troops met a small company of Goths passing that way, possibly to strengthen the garrison of Auximum. The barbarians were surprised, and Roman arrows were their first indication of the enemy. A few escaped by hiding, and they watched the columns of Romans with the standard of Belisarius move through the mountains. To the fugitive barbarians, the army appeared huge, as it was marching in loose order by many mountain pathways and on the Via Flaminia itself. They fled in terror to the camp of King Vittigis and told of the coming of Belisarius with a great army to surround them. In fact, Belisarius's army would not reach Ariminum before the fighting was over, but the barbarians were expecting to see him exit the mountains any moment.

While the Goths were thus anxiously looking to the north and preparing for battle against Belisarius, they suddenly saw in the night the watch fires of a great army to the south. These were the troops of Martinus, whom Belisarius had instructed to use a tried-and-true stratagem: light many more campfires than were needed. To complete the discouragement of the Goths, the fleet of Ildiger appeared off the harbor of Ariminum in the twilight.

This was too much for the Gothic army, which thought it was about to be surrounded by countless Roman soldiers. The Goths abandoned their camps, leaving all their contents, and fled in panic toward Ravenna. At this point a sortie by the garrison might have ended the entire war, but the soldiers were too exhausted from hunger and hardship.

Ildiger and his men from the fleet were the first to arrive. They sacked the camps and enslaved the ill and wounded barbarians they found there. When Belisarius and Narses appeared later the same day and saw the pale and emaciated bodies of the Roman defenders, Belisarius told John he owed a debt of gratitude to Ildiger, thereby hinting that Belisarius had not hurried to his rescue, because of his disobedience. John answered that he recognized his obligation, not to Ildiger, but to Narses the eunuch, thereby implying that Belisarius would not have come at all if it had been up to him alone. This was the first indication that a serious dissension, which in time would do much harm to the Roman cause, would soon grow up in the imperial camp.

DISSENSION IN THE ROMAN ARMY

The victory and raising of the siege of Ariminum strengthened the already-forming party of Narses the eunuch. Belisarius had laid the plans, but most of the men in the army believed Narses to be the directing brain, as his advice had been followed at the council of war. Accordingly, flatterers and friends of the eunuch began to suggest that it was beneath the dignity of Justinian's chamberlain to follow in the train of Belisarius and take orders from a mere general. The emperor must have sent such a high official to Italy to give him a separate command and not merely to support the actions of an already-too-powerful general such as Belisarius. It was said that if he were to assume a separate command, much of the army would follow him: all the Herulian auxiliaries, all of John's and Justinus's soldiers, the men of the other Narses and his brother Aratius, and his own bodyguard, altogether ten thousand men. This army of Narses, the deliverer of Ariminum, could then reap its own glory and fortune. If these ten thousand men formed a separate army, Belisarius would also not be capable of any independent action, as most of his troops were spread out in garrisons from Sicily throughout Italy.

These counsels, urged at every possible opportunity, affected Narses, elated as he undoubtedly was by his success in raising the siege of Ariminum. Quietly, the generals who supported him began ignorning Belisarius's orders, believing it would please Narses.

When Belisarius understood that Narses seriously meant to challenge him, he called all the generals to a council of war. Without directly complaining about the insubordination and dissent, which was creeping in upon them, he informed them that he saw that their views did not coincide with his in the present crisis. The enemy was, in his view, still much stronger than the Roman forces. So far the Goths had been out-generaled, but if their fortunes and hopes were redeemed by just one lucky battle, caused by the overconfidence of the imperial officers, they would regain their confidence and become very dangerous and perhaps irresistible. In Belisarius's opinion, the war was still hanging in the balance. Vittigis was at Ravenna with thirty thousand or forty thousand Goths, his nephew Uraias was besieging Mediolanum, and Auximum and even Urbs Vetus close to Rome were still in the hands of the enemy. At the same time, the Franks were clearly waiting for an opportunity to interfere in the war. With so many enemies, the Romans could soon be overwhelmed.

Belisarius therefore proposed to divide the Roman army into two divisions: a small part that would march into Liguria and relieve Mediolanum, and a greater part that would stay in Umbria and Picenum with the main goal of subduing the tenacious garrison of Auximum.

Narses arrogantly challenged Belisarius, claiming it was absurd to say the army was capable of attaining only these two goals. Instead, he suggested splitting the army and letting Belisarius have whatever officers and troops he needed to take Auximum and relieve Mediolanum, and to take his own loyal troops to recover the province of Aemilia—the southern bank of the Po from Placentia (Piacenza) to the Adriatic. In this way, he argued, the Goths would lose a prized province while the Gothic army in Ravenna would not dare to cut off Belisarius's supplies—as Narses expected them to do if the greater part of the Roman army marched off to besiege Auximum.

Narses's arguments forced Belisarius to fall back on his imperial commission, in which Justinian had given him supreme and ultimate responsibility for the Roman army in all Italy. That this authority had not been changed by Narses's arrival was proven by a letter from the emperor, which Belisarius read to the council:

> We have not sent our steward Narses to Italy in order to command the army; for we wish Belisarius alone to command the whole army in whatever manner seems to him the best, and it is the duty of all of you to follow him in the interest of our state.

At first, the letter seemed to deny Narses the creation of an independent command, but the eunuch pointed to the last words, "in the interest of our state," and said he did not think Belisarius's plan was for the good of the empire and so declined to follow the general's commands in this matter. It is unclear if this ambiguous line in the letter was intended as Narses chose to interpret it. Belisarius was becoming dangerously influential, but Justinian also seemed to have a genuine wish to recover Italy with as little cost as possible.

It is evident from the further operations that some kind of compromise was reached. Most likely, Belisarius did not want a clear and open break in the command of the army. Peranius was sent with a large army to besiege Urbs Vetus, which both parties admitted was a point of danger because it was near Rome. Belisarius, with the rest of the army, moved off to attempt to take Urbinum, which was about a day's march south of Ariminum. Narses the eunuch, John, and the other generals supporting Narses followed or accompanied Belisarius, but when they got to Urbinum, Belisarius's party camped on one side and Narses's on another.

SIEGE OF URBINUM

In the time of the Gothic War, Urbinum was little more than a fortress. Belisarius sent a delegation to request the garrison commanded by Moras to surrender, but the garrison, which was amply supplied with food and water and believed its stronghold to be impregnable, refused the offer. When Belisarius then seemed intent on besieging Urbinum to the bitter end, Narses and John decided to follow their own counsels. The impatient John had already tried on his first entry into Picenum to take the fortress, with no luck. Since then the garrison had received reinforcements of troops and supplies, so the disobedient generals assumed the siege would take very long. They therefore broke up their camp, despite Belisarius's pleas, and marched away to take the province of Aemilia, and thereby follow the plan of Narses.

The Gothic garrison of Urbinum taunted the Romans when they saw that half the enemy had left. The city was situated at the top of a steep hill, and the approach to it was only anything like level on the north side. On this side, Belisarius intended to make his assault. Accordingly, he ordered his troops to collect wood for making siege engines. But no sooner had the Romans finished their work and made ready to approach the walls of the fortress in expectation of a furious resistance, than they saw the battlements thronged with barbarians begging for mercy and asking to surrender. At first, the astounded Romans believed the Goths were in awe of one of their siege engines, the colonnade, a kind of movable shed under which it was possible to approach the walls without fear of missile fire.

But the sudden change in the defiant spirit of the Gothic garrison was due to the failure of their water supply. For unknown reasons, the spring supplying the garrison had fallen lower and lower for three days until only liquid mud was left. Without water they could not defend themselves, so they surrendered. In this way the strong fortress of Urbinum was taken, and the defenders agreed to become subjects of the emperor and join the imperial standards.

When Narses heard of the surprising—and embarrassing, to him—surrender of Urbinum, he ordered John to attempt to take the strong city of Caesena, about twenty miles inland on the Via Aemilia. John tried to scale the walls with ladders but was repulsed with heavy losses, including the king of the barbarian Herulians, Fanotheus. Philemuth was made king of the Herulians after Fanotheus's death. As he had so many times before, the impatient John pronounced that the city he was attacking was impregnable and moved off with Justinus to the easier task of overrunning Aemilia. Forum Cornelii (Imola) was taken by surprise, and the whole province was soon recovered for the empire. The conquest was quick and easy, but of little strategic value to the Romans.

At the start of the year 539, Belisarius was still intent on taking the strategically important city of Auximum, but he could not expose his troops to the hardships of a long encampment during winter while he was blockading the city. He therefore sent General Aratius with most of the army into winter quarters at Firmum, with orders to watch the garrison of Auximum.

He himself marched with the rest to Urbs Vetus, which had been besieged for many months by Peranius, and the garrison of which was hard-pressed by hunger. Gothic General Albilas had been trying to keep up the spirits of the garrison by promising relief, but they were now reduced to eating animal hides steeped in water to soften them. When they saw the standards of the feared Belisarius under their walls, they soon surrendered. Taking this important fortress was another piece in Belisarius's plan that had fallen into place. That the Gothic garrison surrendered was lucky, as Belisarius estimated it would be impossible to take by storm because of its excellent defensive position.

It was now nine months since the raising of the siege of Rome. The progress of the Roman armies had not been rapid, but it had been steady. Ariminum had been relieved, Urbinum and Urbs Vetus had been taken—and with the latter a serious threat to Rome had been removed—and the province of Aemilia had been retaken.

In the early months of 539, however, the imperial cause sustained a terrible reversal when the Goths retook Mediolanum.

THE LOSS OF MEDIOLANUM

To understand the course of events that led up to this disaster, we must go back a year, to the early part of 538, shortly after the conclusion of the three months' truce between Belisarius and Vittigis at Rome. At that time Datius, the archbishop of Mediolanum, had gone to Rome at the head of a deputation, begging Belisarius to send troops to keep Mediolanum from the barbarians. Belisarius could do little but comply, and after the siege of Rome was raised, he sent one thousand troops to escort Datius back to his city. The small army was composed of a contingent of Isaurians under Ennes and some Thracians under Paulus. Mundilas commanded the whole expedition and brought with him some soldiers from Belisarius's bodyguard. Along with them went the praetorian prefect, Fidelius, because he was a native of Mediolanum and had some influence in Liguria.

The overland route was considered too dangerous and slow, so the troops went by ship from Portus to Genova (Genoa). From there they put the boats of the ships on wagons so the Po could be crossed with no difficulty. Under the walls of Ticinum, Mundilas's troops defeated the Goths in a bloody battle. But the Goths managed to retreat into the city and close the gates to the pursuing Romans. This was unfortunate for the Romans, because Ticinum contained perhaps the greatest store of treasure and arms that the Goths possessed, and was as important as Ravenna in this respect. While the Romans were marching away from Ticinum, Fidelius went into a church to pray. On his way back to the army, his horse stumbled and fell near the city walls. The Goths on the walls saw the fallen Fidelius, went out, and killed him. The loss of the influential Fidelius caused much distress in the Roman camp.

When the little army arrived at Mediolanum, the city immediately surrendered to the Romans and gave them its full support. Most of the cities of Italy considered themselves thoroughly Roman, despite more than 40 years of Gothic rule. Bergamum

(Bergamo), Comum (Como), Novaria (Novara), and other cities in the region also surrendered and were, perhaps unwisely, garrisoned by Roman troops. At Mediolanum, Mundilas stayed with only three hundred men and his officers Ennes and Paulus.

On hearing of the defection of Mediolanum and the other cities of the region, King Vittigis quickly dispatched a large army under his nephew Uraias to retake them. Uraias, brave and energetic, was one of the great heroes of the Gothic nation. The threat to the overextended Roman troops did not come only from the south but also from the west, in the form of the barbarian Franks. The Frankish King Theudebert had been watching the conflict with great interest and was ready to act when the opportunity arose. He was, however, not yet ready to openly break the treaty with the Romans that had been made in 535. Instead, he sought to circumvent it by ordering ten thousand of his semi-independent Burgundian subjects to cross the Alps and camp close to Mediolanum. If Justinian complained of this action, he would simply claim that the Burgundians themselves had decided to enter Italy.

In the spring of 538, Mediolanum was completely blockaded by the Burgundians and Ostrogoths encamped under its walls. With only three hundred men available, Mundilas could not cover the whole city wall and had to call upon the citizens to help.

When Belisarius heard that Uraias had begun to besiege Mediolanum, he sent two generals, Martinus and Uliaris, with a large army to raise the siege. Despite their reputations for bravery and dash, the two generals acted timidly in this operation. When they reached the Po River, they made camp on the southern bank and remained there for a long time while debating how to cross.

Wondering about the delay, Mundilas sent the generals a messenger who passed the enemy lines and swam across the Po River to get to the Roman camp. With strong words, he told them that by delaying the relief they were damaging the cause of the emperor greatly and that they would be traitors if they left the great and wealthy city of Mediolanum, the bulwark against the Franks and the other transalpine barbarians, to fall again into the hands of the Goths.

The generals promised to assist the besieged city as soon as possible, and the brave messenger returned to the city to brighten the hopes of his fellow Thracians and Isaurians. But still Martinus and Uliaris sat in their camp week after week. After some time they sent a message to Belisarius saying they did not have enough troops to engage the great Burgundian and Gothic armies besieging Mediolanum and entreated him to order John and Justinus to come to their aid from Aemilia, which was peaceful. Belisarius straightaway sent such an order, but both the generals refused to obey any command of Belisarius's, saying Narses the eunuch was their leader.

In this way the Roman arms—divided between Belisarius and Narses—reaped the full fruits of insubordination, jealousy, and perhaps cowardice, and all these delays meant that more than six months passed from the beginning of the siege of Mediolanum.

At length, Belisarius sent a frank letter to Narses, explaining to him the dangers of his insubordinate policy to the empire. Finally, Narses gave the order for John and Justinus to support Martinus and Uliaris. John began collecting boats to cross the Po but was taken ill by fever—apparently a genuine, not a feigned illness—and when he finally recovered, it was too late.

During the six months, the garrison and citizens of Mediolanum had been undergoing terrible privations. In the end they were forced to eat dogs and mice to survive. The besiegers were aware of the plight of the city and called on Mundilas to surrender, promising that the lives of the soldiers would be spared. Mundilas tried to have the citizens included in the surrender, but the Goths considered their acts treason, for which there was only one punishment: death. With the terrible slaughter of the citizens in his mind, Mundilas addressed the soldiers in a stirring speech, asking them to join him in a sally for victory or death:

> If it has ever happened that any men before us, though having the opportunity to save their lives with disgrace, have chosen rather to die with fair fame, abandoning their immediate safety for a glorious end of life, such men I should wish you also to be at the present time, and not through fondness for life to pursue it even though it be

involved in shame, and that too, contrary to the teaching of Belisarius, by which you have profited for a long time past, so that to be otherwise than noble and exceedingly courageous is for you sacrilege. For when men have once entered life, a single fate is advancing upon all of them—to die at the appointed time; but as to the manner of death men differ, for the most part, one from the other. And there is this difference. That cowards, as one might expect, in every case first bring upon themselves insult and ridicule from their enemies and then, at the exact time previously appointed, fulfill their destiny no whit the less; but it falls to the lot of noble men to suffer this with valor and an abundance of goodly fame. And apart from these considerations, if it had been possible to become slaves of the barbarians, and at the same time to save the people of the city, that at least might have brought us some forgiveness for saving ourselves so disgracefully. But if, in fact, we are bound to look on while the hand of the enemy is destroying such a great multitude of Romans, this will be more bitter than any form of death of which a man could tell. For we should appear to be doing nothing more or less than helping the barbarians to perpetrate this dreadful deed. While, therefore, we are sufficiently our own masters to adorn necessity with valor, let us make glorious the fortune, which has fallen upon us. And I say that we ought all to arm ourselves in the best possible manner, and advance upon the enemy when they are not expecting us. For the result for us will be one of two things: either fortune will have wrought for us in some way a success which transcends our present hope, or we, in achieving a happy end, shall have rid ourselves of our present troubles with the fairest fame.

But Mundilas's soldiers, exhausted from the hardships of the long siege, did not rise to the stirring speech and insisted on surrendering. The Goths kept their promises and left the Roman soldiers unharmed, but wreaked full vengeance on the populace. All the men were slain—three hundred thousand, according to

Procopius, although that number may be exaggerated. The women were made slaves and handed over to the primitive Burgundians as payment for their services. The city was razed. The praetorian prefect, Reparatus, was caught and cut into small pieces by the barbarians, who then threw these to the dogs. At the surrender of the Ligurian capital, all the other neighboring cities surrendered too, despite their Roman garrisons. The disaster at Mediolanum was perhaps the worst of its kind during the entire Gothic War, especially so as it was as unnecessary as it was terrible.

With the surrender of Mediolanum, Martinus and Uliaris returned with the unhappy tidings to Belisarius, who from grief and anger refused to admit them into his presence. In a letter to the emperor he gave the news and doubtlessly explained the disastrous insubordination, which for twelve months had paralyzed the imperial cause and now had caused the death of untold thousands of Romans and the destruction of the second city of Italy.

The reply from Emperor Justinian came quickly: while none of the insubordinate generals seems to have been directly punished, Narses the eunuch was recalled to the capital, and Belisarius was confirmed in his position as commander in chief of the Roman forces in Italy.

Narses's bodyguard left with him, and the wild Herulians who had come with him refused to serve under any other leader. Accordingly, they marched off into Liguria, sold their captives and beasts of burden to the Goths, took an oath of perpetual friendship with that nation, and marched through Venetia into Illyria, where they again changed their minds and accepted service under Justinian at Constantinople. It was a good example of the behavior of one of the most unstable and primitive peoples who served under the Roman standards.

By May 539, the war had been going on for four years, and central Italy had been particularly devastated by the campaign. Disease and hunger had struck the populations of Tuscany, Liguria, and Aemilia. For two years the fields had not been cultivated because of the movements of the armies. In the summer of 537, a poor self-sown crop sprang up, but with nobody to harvest it, it was rotting in the fields. The following summer there was no more grain. The inhabitants of Tuscany had fled to the safety of the mountains, where they lived off acorns gathered in the forests. The people of Aemilia fled into Picenum to seek their food from the sea, but here also starvation and disease carried off many. During the famine, fifty thousand peasants were said to have died. In some places there was acts of cannibalism.

Procopius relates a story of two women living in the countryside at Ariminum. They were the only ones who had survived in the village, so travelers would often lodge at their house. At night they would kill and eat the travelers. In this way they killed seventeen men, until the eighteenth was roused in his sleep and killed the women in self-defense.

The Romans and Goths seemed more and more evenly matched. The serious disagreements between Belisarius and Narses had given Vittigis some breathing space, and the defeat at Mediolanum had removed most of the Roman threat from the north.

Delegation to Persia

Expecting the arrival of Belisarius before Ravenna in spring, King Vittigis was now looking around for allies to save his kingdom from the Romans. The Franks were too untrustworthy. A delegation had been sent with gifts to King Wacis of the Lombards, but he had refused to break his treaty with the Romans. Vittigis therefore called an assembly of the elders of the Gothic nation, explained the difficulty of their position, and asked for advice. After many deliberations, it was pointed out that the true cause of the disaster that had befallen the Goths, and the Vandals before them, was the peace treaty Emperor Justinian had negotiated with the Persian King Chosroes on his accession in 531. It was only because the Eastern border was untroubled that Justinian could bring so many troops and the terrible Belisarius to bear against them.

It was therefore proposed and decided to send a delegation to Chosroes to stir him, if possible, to a renewal of hostilities against the Roman Empire. Because of the difficulty of Goths making their way through the Roman territories, Romans were chosen as ambassadors. Two Roman priests of Liguria, probably of the Arian heresy, were willing to undertake the daring enterprise for the promise of a large sum of money. One of these pretended to be a bishop to give weight to his representations, and the other accompanied him as his attendant.

Siege of Faesulae

The journey would take a long time, and the results would not be apparent for more than a year after the period we have now reached. The mere rumors of negotiations between the Goths and the Persians were, however, enough to make Justinian, who well knew of the weakness of his eastern frontier, anxious to settle the Gothic War as soon as possible. At once, he sent back the Gothic envoys who had been waiting in Constantinople for a year, to start negotiations. They were asked to return to their king with the offer of a long truce on beneficial terms. Belisarius, who during this period calmly overruled several of the emperor's decisions, refused to allow the Gothic delegation to enter Ravenna until the Goths returned the two Roman ambassadors Peter and Athanasius, the imperial envoys to the now-dead King Theodahad whom the Goths had kept in captivity for almost four years. They were returned and were later given high positions for their devotion to the imperial cause.

These negotiations went on during the winter and early spring of 539. Again in full control of all his forces, Belisarius began in May 539 to take the two remaining Gothic fortresses south of Ravenna: Faesulae and Auximum. Both were strongly situated on tops of almost inaccessible heights, and their siege would take the rest of the year. With these two fortresses taken, there would be no obstacle to besieging Ravenna.

A Gothic garrison of unknown size held Faesulae. To besiege this little town, Generals Cyprianus and Justinus were sent with some of their own soldiers, a band of Isaurian auxiliaries, and five hundred regular troops.

John; another John, called the glutton because of his extraordinary appetite; and Martinus were sent with a large army to cover the siege of Faesulae and to observe around the upper Po. If possible, they were to intercept any communications between Uraias operating north of the Po around Mediolanum and Ravenna. If he was marching to support his uncle Vittigis in Ravenna, they were to pursue the Gothic army and engage it, if possible. The unwalled Dertona (Tortona) by the Po was chosen as their base of operations. The city was well provided with houses for troops, as Theodoric the Great had commanded military barracks to be built there.

Meanwhile, Belisarius marched with the eleven thousand troops of the main army to besiege Auximum.

Several attempts were made to take Faesulae, but the Romans were unable to scale the heights, although they easily surrounded the little town and settled down to blockade it.

Soon pressed by hunger, the garrison appealed to Vittigis for help, and he sent Uraias to assist them. On receiving his orders, Uraias marched to Ticinum, crossed the Po, and made camp some seven miles from the two Johns and Martinus at Dertona. The Romans felt there was no need to engage the Gothic army, because their end was gained just by keeping him away. Because Uraias was afraid that if the battle was lost the Gothic cause would also be lost in one stroke, the two armies waited and watched each other.

The Franks Invade

With the success of their federate Burgundians during the siege of Mediolanum, the Franks felt it was time to reap the harvest from the weakened Goths and Romans. Ignoring the treaties recently made with both nations, King Theudebert gathered his army and marched with one hundred thousand Franks and Alemanni through the pass of St. Bernhard into upper Italy. Apart from a few horsemen attending the king, all the rest of the troops fought on foot, each with a shield, a sword, and a throwing ax, the *francisca*. These axes had short wooden handles and a characteristic S-curve along the top of the head, which made it more balanced to throw. It was their custom to throw these axes at one signal in the first charge in an attempt to break the shields of their enemies or make them otherwise unusable.

When the Goths heard of the great Frankish army coming over the passes of the Alps they rejoiced, thinking they were coming to aid them in their struggle against the Romans. After all, they had given the Franks a large territory and great sums of money for an alliance, but they had so far not come with their armies in great numbers.

The Franks kept up the pretense as long as they still had to cross the Po, and marched as a friendly army, hurting no civilians or plundering. After coming close to Ticinum and quietly taking possession of the bridges there, they revealed their true intentions. Nearby Gothic women and children were slaughtered, and their bodies thrown into the river as a sacrifice to the Frankish gods of war. Despite being nominally Christians, the Franks still kept many parts of their old religion and customarily made human sacrifices to aid in prophecies and in war.

When the Gothic troops at the bridges saw these terrible actions, they fled in fear and surprise to the fortifications of Ticinum. The Franks then went on toward Dertona, where the army of Uraias—who had not received news of the happening at Ticinum and so still believed in their friendly intentions—came to meet them. The Goths became aware of the Frankish intentions, however, as a swarm of axes killed their unprepared warriors. The Gothic army turned and fled through the Roman camp and did not stop until it reached Ravenna.

When the Romans saw the flight of the barbarians, they assumed Belisarius had arrived and won a battle against them, so they advanced to meet him and join in the pursuit. The vast host of the Franks surprised and overwhelmed them immediately. The remnants of the Roman army fled into Tuscany to the troops besieging Faesulae, and others to Auximum to tell Belisarius of the destruction of their army.

The Franks, having won two easy and great victories, sacked both camps and ran wild for a while. But the huge Frankish army was capable of defeating itself. It had no proper supply system to provide for the thousands and thousands of warriors, who could only ravage the country in search of food. They had soon exhausted the provisions in the captured camps and turned to eating the draught oxen of the region and drinking the unhealthy water of the Po. Soon they succumbed to diarrhea and dysentery. It was reported that a third of all the Franks died of disease. Being thus unable to advance, the great army could only stay where it was and continue to use up the food in the region.

When Belisarius heard of the Frankish invasion, he wrote a letter to King Theudebert, charging him with violating the treaty with the emperor to join against the Goths and even turning his Franks on the empire. He recommended that he take care, because the emperor's wrath would not easily be avoided.

The letter reached Theudebert just as his undisciplined troops were complaining of their great losses to disease. The combination of supply problems, disease, and threats from the empire made him hastily turn back to his kingdom with his remaining warriors. Shortly after, Martinus and John returned to their stations at Dertona.

But the damage had been done, and the regions north of the Po had been devastated.

THE SIEGE OF AUXIMUM

While these events were taking place in northwest Italy, Belisarius was conducting the difficult siege of Auximum with his army of eleven thousand troops. The little but important town was situated on a high hill and was almost impossible to assault. In addition, the garrison consisted of brave veteran warriors. In many respects Auximum was the key to the Gothic capital of Ravenna, and both sides realized this. With Auximum gone, nothing could hinder a direct Roman assault on the Gothic capital.

The Romans were quartered in huts below the hill of Auximum, and already on the first day of the siege, while Belisarius was measuring out the Roman camp with some of his bodyguards, the garrison made a sally. They were repelled and took some casualties, but also managed to hurt the Romans.

The day before the Romans arrived, some Goths had been sent out to gather provisions. When they returned in the night and saw the Romans' many campfires, some moved unseen through the

Roman lines and rejoined the garrison, while others hid in the forests, where they were soon found and killed.

After a few unsuccessful skirmishes, Belisarius concluded that the town was unapproachable for any serious attack and settled down to blockade it. But the town was well–stocked, and Belisarius would be tied down for seven months while the Franks were plundering north Italy, and the Goths and Persians were negotiating an alliance.

There was a little green spot close to the walls of Auximum where many bloody skirmishes took place. Both sides used it for forage for their horses and cattle, and sometimes the starving garrison would go there to pick herbs for food. At one time the Goths prepared an ambush in a valley close to the town. By faking flight, they drew the Romans toward the ambush and then turned around and inflicted heavy losses on the besiegers. Because the city was lying on a hill, the Romans in their camp could clearly see the ambush, but they could not warn their unsuspecting comrades because of the distance.

After the defeat in the skirmish, Procopius approached Belisarius with a suggestion drawn from his reading of some treatises on war:

> The men who blew the trumpets in the Roman army in ancient times knew two different strains, one of which seemed unmistakably to urge the soldiers on and impel them to battle, while the other used to call the men who were fighting back to camp, whenever this seemed to the general to be for the best. And by such means the generals could always give the appropriate commands to the soldiers, and they on their part were able to execute the commands thus communicated to them. For during actual combat the human voice is in no way adapted to give any clear instructions, since it obviously has to contend with the clash of arms on every side, and fear paralyzes the senses of those fighting. But since at the present time such skill has become obsolete through ignorance and it is impossible to express both commands by one trumpet, do you

adopt the following course hereafter. With the cavalry trumpets urge on the soldiers to continue fighting with the enemy, but with those of the infantry call the men back to the retreat. For it is impossible for them to fail to recognize the sound of either one, for in the one case the sound comes forth from leather and very thin wood, and in the other from rather thick brass.

Belisarius adopted this suggestion and called together the soldiers and explained the new code of signals, while telling them there was no shame in retreat in this type of skirmishing warfare when the situation required it. When he judged it necessary, he would give the signal for retreat by a blast from the infantry trumpet.

In the next skirmish at the foraging ground, the Romans were successful with their new tactics, and the Goths were becoming more and more hard-pressed by famine. In its desperate situation, the garrison resolved to send messengers with a letter to Ravenna to ask Vittigis for help. On the next moonless night, the Goths crowded the walls and gave a great shout, which made the Romans think a sortie was underway. Fearing a confused and desperate fight, Belisarius ordered his men to stay quietly in their fortified camp. This was, of course, what the barbarians had hoped for, and their messengers were able to sneak through the Roman blockade with little difficulty.

When King Vittigis received the strongly worded letter from the garrison, which accused him of doing nothing to help them in their plight, he told the messengers that aid would be sent quickly. The messengers returned to Auximum, but Vittigis did nothing to fulfill his promise. He was afraid of the army of John and Martinus covering the Po valley, and of the difficulty of supplying his troops on the march to Auximum. For the Romans, issues of supply were rarely a problem, as they had an advanced logistical system while being in full command of the sea. To the Goths, with no properly functioning and organized supply system, moving any amount of troops quickly in a territory that could not supply them was almost impossible. The Frankish invasion provided Vittigis with another pretext for doing nothing. So the garrison of Auximum was left to starve, while Vittigis's options became more and more limited. The garrison of Auximum did not hear of this invasion, and Belisarius, who had received word of the first message to Vittigis, tried to prevent any more messages from going in or out.

In these circumstances the Goths, who were getting quite desperate, began to negotiate with a Roman soldier named Burcentius to carry a message to Ravenna and back. Large sums of money were promised, and Burcentius agreed to bring the letter to King Vittigis.

Vittigis sent back a long letter explaining his reasons for inaction by blaming King Theudebert and his treachery, but he promised speedy assistance to the garrison and begged them to continue their resistance, which had made them the heroes of the Gothic nation. Burcentius brought back the letter, which greatly encouraged the garrison to continue the struggle despite the extreme hardships. But still Vittigis did nothing to help the garrison.

So the garrison asked the traitor Burcentius to bring a third letter to the king, saying that if no help arrived within five days, they would surrender the city. Again Vittigis answered with flattery and promises of help. Again the garrison believed the king would not leave the strategic town helpless and continued to refuse to surrender to Belisarius.

Belisarius was perplexed by the garrison's extraordinary resistance and discussed the situation with his officer Valerianus. Belisarius suggested they try to capture a Gothic officer and question him as to the situation in the town. Valerianus offered the help of some Sclaveni barbarians in his train, who were very skilled in ambushes. A powerful Sclavene was chosen and told he would receive a great sum of money if he captured and brought back a Goth. Accordingly he hid at the popular forage ground until a Gothic noble came to pick some herbs for his meager meal. He was wary of any movement from the Roman camp but did not suspect anything else. While he was stooping down to pick his herbs, the Sclavene jumped out, grabbed him, and, despite his struggles, carried him to the Roman camp.

When questioned, the prisoner revealed everything and pointed to Burcentius as the bearer of the two last messages. When

Burcentius confessed his guilt, he was handed over to his comrades to be dealt with according to their pleasure, which was that he be burned alive in full sight of his former employers in the garrison.

Still the intrepid garrison would not surrender, so Belisarius decided to take active steps to bring the Goths to their knees. He decided to cut off their supply of water, which consisted of a cistern outside the town, but near to the walls. Already the water supply had caused the Goths problems, because each attempt to get water had to be conducted as a sortie, hurriedly and with stealth. Belisarius's plan was to break down the walls of the cistern so that only a little water could gather in it; this would force the Goths to fill their amphorae from the slowly running stream that supplied the cistern, thus exposing them to Roman attack.

To keep the garrison occupied during the operation, Belisarius drew up his entire army as if for battle and gave the impression of making ready to attack the city. Meanwhile, five Isaurians equipped with axes and crowbars sneaked into the cistern. The garrison, however, perceived their intentions and attacked them with many missiles which could be fired from the walls due to the nearness of the cistern. The vaulted roof of the cistern protected the Isaurians, so the Goths made a sally to prevent them from demolishing it. A sharp engagement ensued in which the Roman battle line began to waver before the desperate attack of the Goths. Belisarius ran to the threatened part of the line and exhorted the soldiers to stand firm and fight. While he was thus engaged, a Gothic arrow came whizzing toward him and would have killed him had not one of his bodyguard, Unigastus, put his hand out and blocked it. Unigastus had to quit the field because of his injury and permanently lost the use of his hand, but the general's life was saved. The battle, which had begun at dawn, raged on until about noon, when the Goths were finally repulsed with heavy losses.

After the successful battle, Belisarius received the disappointing news from the Isaurians that despite working for six hours, they had not succeeded in dislodging a single stone in the carefully built cistern. As Procopius writes, "the artisans of old, who cared most of all for excellence in their work, had built this masonry in such a way as to yield neither to time nor to the attempts of men to destroy it."

With his plan unsuccessful, Belisarius chose to poison the well by throwing animal bodies, poisonous herbs, and quicklime into it. Still the brave garrison held out by drawing water from a single tiny well inside the city, while it looked to the horizon for relief.

Soon, however, the siege ended, and in an unexpected way. The garrison of Faesulae, which could no longer endure the famine and other hardships, surrendered to Cyprianus and Justinus on the condition that their lives be spared. The two generals then marched with these prisoners to Auximum, where the sight of their captive countrymen and the words of Belisarius finally broke the endurance of the garrison. They now offered to surrender if they could take their possessions and march to join their countrymen in Ravenna. Belisarius did not agree with this, and his soldiers loudly complained that after such a long siege it would be terrible if they were deprived of the spoils of their labor. For Belisarius, the thought of so many brave and experienced warriors joining their comrades at Ravenna was unacceptable. On the other hand, he wished to be done with the siege and move against Ravenna while the opportunity was there. Furthermore, he was concerned about the plans of the fickle Franks, who might soon return to north Italy.

After some discussions, an agreement was reached: the Goths would surrender half their possessions. So satisfied were they with this arrangement that most of them appear to have taken service with the Roman army—probably also from a lack of faith in their timid king. The siege of Auximum had lasted from May to December of 539.

8

THE CAPTURE
OF RAVENNA

With Auximum taken, Belisarius finally had his back free to attack the Gothic capital and seat of power directly. Ravenna was admirably defended by nature and was almost unapproachable for an army. With command of the sea, it was impregnable; without, it had taken Theodoric the Great three years of land and sea blockade to force the garrison to surrender.

So while preparing for the siege, Belisarius entered into negotiations with the Goths, as the Franks and Persians were restless and eager to take advantage of the situation. He had been told that the Franks were sending a delegation to King Vittigis to propose an alliance for the reconquest and division of Italy. To counter this and to negotiate surrender with the Goths, Belisarius sent Theodosius, chief of his household, as head of the Roman delegation.

Vittigis had been fooled into complacency during the negotiations at Rome in 537, and Belisarius was not prepared to make the same mistake. Generals Magnus and Vitalius, the latter having just arrived from Dalmatia with an army, were sent with two large bodies of troops to operate on both sides of the Po River to prevent provisions being brought into Ravenna.

This effort was helped by a miraculous drop in the water level of the Po, which caused a Gothic flotilla prepared to transport provisions to be stranded on the banks of the river and taken by the Romans. Soon after, the river resumed its usual course and became navigable once more—now to serve the purpose of the besiegers. Ravenna was thus already feeling some effects from scarcity of food when the envoys of the Franks and the Romans arrived.

Peace Negotiations

The Frankish envoys were the first admitted to the presence of King Vittigis and said:

"The rulers of the Franks have sent us to you, in the first place because they are vexed to hear that you are thus besieged by Belisarius, and, in the second place, because they are eager to avenge you with all possible speed in accordance with the terms of our alliance. Now we suppose that our army, numbering not less than five hundred thousand fighting men, has by now crossed the Alps, and we boast that they will bury the entire Roman army with their axes at the first onset. And you, on your part, ought to conform to the purpose, not of those who intend to enslave you, but of those who are entering into the danger of war because of their loyalty to the Goths. And apart from this, if, on the one hand, you unite your forces with ours, the Romans will have no hope left of facing both our armies in battle, but from the very outset and without any effort at all we shall gain the supremacy in the war. But if, on the other hand, the Goths choose to array themselves with the Romans, even in that case they will not withstand the Frankish nation for the struggle will not be evenly matched in point of strength, but the ultimate result for you will be defeat in the company of the most hostile of all men. But to plunge into disaster which can be foreseen, when the opportunity is offered to be saved without danger, is utter folly. Besides, the Roman nation has proven itself altogether untrustworthy toward all barbarians, since by its very nature it is hostile to them. We therefore propose, if you are willing, to share with you the rule of all Italy, and we shall administer the land in whatever manner seems best. And for thee and the Goths the natural course to follow is that one which is destined to redound to your advantage".

It was not difficult for the Roman ambassadors to enlarge on the faithlessness of the Franks:

That the multitude of the Franks will inflict no injury on
the emperor's army—and it is with this that they seek to
scare you—why should one enter into a lengthy proof
before you, seeing that you, certainly, have come to understand by long experience what wholly governs the course of
war, and know that valor is in no circumstances wont to be
overcome by mere throngs of men. For we need not add
that, in point of fact, the emperor surpasses all others in the
ability to outstrip his enemies in regard to multitude of soldiers. But as touching the loyalty of these Franks, which
they proudly claim to show toward all barbarians, this had
been well displayed by them, first to the Thuringians and
the Burgundian nation [conquered by the Franks in 532
and 534 respectively], and then to you also, their allies! And
indeed we, on our part, should take pleasure in asking the
Franks by what god they can possibly intend to swear when
they declare that they will give you surety for their loyalty.
For you understand surely in what manner they have honored the one by whom they have already sworn—they who
have received from you vast sums of money, as you know,
and also the entire territory of Gaul as the price of their
alliance, and yet have decided not merely to render you no
assistance at all in your peril, but have actually taken up
arms thus wantonly against you, if any account of those
things which happened on the Po is preserved among you.
But why need we demonstrate the impiety of the Franks by
recounting past events? Nothing could be more unholy
than this present embassy of theirs. For just as if they had
forgotten the terms they themselves have agreed upon and
the oaths they have taken to secure the treaty, they claim
the right to share your all with you. And if they do actually obtain this from you, it befits you to consider what will
be the end of their insatiable greed for money.

When the Frankish and Roman ambassadors had finished their
speeches, Vittigis conferred with the leading men of the Gothic
nation. After these debates, the Roman offer was accepted and the

Frankish envoys dismissed. There was little Vittigis could do. The Franks' terms were impossible to meet, and they were known for never abiding by a treaty unless it suited them, as the Goths in Ticinum had witnessed firsthand. Contrary to this, the Romans generally went out of their way to honor treaty obligations and had followed this course throughout the war.

Discussions on the exact terms of peace followed, but Belisarius still did not relax his vigil around the city. Furthermore, Vitalius was sent into Venetia to persuade the cities there to return their allegiance to the empire.

During the negotiations, the Romans had an enormous stroke of luck when the large and well-stocked magazines of provisions in Ravenna were destroyed by fire. Among the Romans it was generally believed that Belisarius had bribed somebody inside the city to do it, whereas the Goths suspected domestic treachery by Queen Matasuntha, the unwilling wife of King Vittigis.

Meanwhile, when Uraias had heard about the blockade of Ravenna, he collected about four thousand men, partly Goths from the garrisons in the Cottian Alps and partly natives from Liguria. While on their march, they received news that these garrisons on the Frankish frontier under the command of Sisigis were surrendering to Thomas, a bodyguard of Belisarius's who had been sent there with a small group of troops. The soldiers of Uraias, whose wives and children were still in the fortresses, insisted on marching back. Consequently, Uraias marched back to the Cottian Alps and laid siege to Sisigis and the soldiers of Thomas.

When John and Martinus, who were still operating in the upper Po valley, heard of this they marched as quickly as possible to the area and fell upon some of the fortresses there. Several were captured, and their inhabitants— most of whom were the families of the soldiers in Uraias's army—were taken as slaves. With the threat of the loss of their families, the barbarians refused to fight the Romans. Instead they deserted Uraias and went to John, begging to be accepted as auxiliaries in Roman service. With his troops deserting there was little Uraias could do, so he retired into the fortresses of Liguria with his remaining followers. There was now no hope of outside assistance for the besieged Ravenna.

THE PEACE TERMS

Around this time, probably early in the year 540, came two senators from the emperor, Domnicus and Maximinus, with Justinian's terms of peace. The terms were surprisingly lenient. Vittigis was allowed to retain his title of king and half the royal treasure and to reign over the rich plains north of the Po River. The other half of the royal treasure and all Italy south of the Po, including Sicily, was to be reunited with the Roman Empire.

When taken into the larger strategic perspective of the empire, the lenient terms were carefully considered. Justinian knew that a Hunnish horde was about to swarm into the empire. It would eventually ravage Illyricum, Macedon, and Thrace and even reach the suburbs of Constantinople. So far Justinian had enjoyed peace on the eastern frontier, but Chosroes was becoming increasingly impatient with the eternal peace that bound him to stand by and watch Justinian conquer the West. So in 539, spurred by the delegation that reached him from Ravenna, he began to pick a quarrel with Justinian over a trivial boundary dispute between the federate Saracens of the two powers. The energetic Chosroes and the Persian Kingdom did not want a strong and even greater Roman Empire on their borders. In June 540 he would drive deep into the Roman territories and take Antioch, the Roman metropolis of the East, now the second city of the whole empire. In the West, the Franks were just waiting for an opportunity to invade north Italy.

With these threats from all sides, Justinian had good reason to wish to have his greatest general, Belisarius, and the troops from Italy ready for the troubles ahead, especially because the troops for the Italian campaign had, in large measure, been taken from the other theaters of war. A Gothic buffer kingdom north of the Po could help keep the Franks away, especially if it felt well-treated by the empire. It was better to let the Goths and Franks bleed each other than to face the Frankish hordes alone.

Justinian's western wars had also been making heavy demands on his manpower. Not only was he maintaining large armies in Italy, but he had also been obliged to send reinforcements to Africa because of the rebellion in 534. While Belisarius had prevented the loss of all of the Roman provinces by his swift suppression of the rebellion, it had continued after he left. To deal with this grave situation, Justinian had sent his cousin Germanus as master of the soldiers to Africa. Germanus succeeded by conciliatory measures in winning back a sufficient number of the mutineers to make himself a match for Stotzas, and in 537 defeated him decisively. He was recalled in 539, and Solomon was sent out again with reinforcements. He had to chastise the Moors, who had once more broken loose during the period of confusion that followed the mutiny.

In addition to the wars in Italy and Africa, there had been continued troubles in Illyricum and Thrace. Almost every year from 528 to 535, the Bulgars and Sclaveni had raided these countries in force, and in 537 the Gepids, in defiance of their treaty of alliance, seized the city of Sirmium, which Justinian's forces had just recovered from the Ostrogoths.

In 540, a great Bulgar horde penetrated to the walls of Constantinople and stormed the city of Cassandreia (Kassandra) in Macedonia, after which they returned in safety with their booty.

The obstacle to the peace came not from the Goths, who joyfully agreed to the emperor's proposals, but, surprisingly, from Belisarius. He was not prepared to let the Goths off the hook when they were almost decisively defeated and had no options but complete surrender. He refused to agree with the treaty as put forward by Justinian, and the Goths, who feared some stratagem, would not accept it without his countersignature and oath. Several of his officers criticized him bitterly because he dared to disobey the orders of the emperor and seemed bent on prolonging the war for his own advantage, as they saw it.

Always quick to discuss any dissatisfaction among the troops, Belisarius called a council of war and also asked the ambassadors Domnicus and Maximinus to attend.

With his customary frankness, Belisarius stated that he was well aware of the danger of continuing the war, but that an open debate of the treaty was necessary to decide the best course of action. Should they attempt to recover the whole of Italy, or should the barbarians be allowed to keep part of it? The officers without exception stated that they thought it best to make peace on the emperor's conditions. Belisarius then asked them to sign a paper saying that the emperor's decision was best and that they would be unable to do the Goths further harm, and this was done.

BELISARIUS IS OFFERED THE KINGSHIP OF ITALY

Meanwhile, scarcity in Ravenna had grown into famine. The Goths, however, were determined not to surrender unconditionally to the Romans, as they feared being transported from their beloved Italy, where most of them had been born. Most of the Goths had also become hostile to the rule of King Vittigis, as he seemed inept at carrying on the war. In this situation the Goths conceived the idea of offering the kingship of Italy to their enemy Belisarius, whose generalship they admired greatly. Even Vittigis supported this proposal and begged the general to accept the offer. To the Goths, Belisarius was not only the representative of the emperor in Italy, but also the true power in the region. They saw the reason for the amazing Roman triumphs in the personality and ability of the great general, compared to the incompetent and cowardly King Vittigis. In true barbarian fashion, they wanted a warrior-king to rule and lead them.

Belisarius probably received this highly tempting offer with mixed feelings. Procopius says, "he had an extraordinary loathing for the name of tyrant, and furthermore he had, in fact, been bound by the emperor previously by the most solemn oaths never during his lifetime to organize a revolution." It is not unlikely that he— and many others—thought of himself as the most likely successor to Justinian if he survived him, and he knew of the sad Roman history filled with the disastrous attempts of successful generals to take the throne.

On the other hand, he knew that a feigned compliance would at once end the war. In order not to be accused of aiming at the throne, he ordered the generals who still called themselves anti-Belisarian—John, Bessas the Goth, Narses the general, and Aratius—to disperse in various directions to obtain provisions for the army. Before he sent them away, he held another council of war together with the imperial ambassadors and asked them all what they would think if he succeeded in saving all Italy for the empire and taking the captured Gothic nobility and their treasures to Constantinople. They replied that it would be a deed past all praise and asked him to do it if he could. Accordingly, he sent messengers to the Goths accepting their offer. He gave his word that the persons and property of the Goths would not be harmed, but postponed the oath by which he was to pledge himself to reign as ruler of Goths and Romans until after the entry into Ravenna. As the Goths expected him to be thirsting for more power, this delay did not cause any excitement.

His entry into Ravenna in the spring of 540 can be seen as the crowning moment of an almost fabulous career. The Roman fleet had been gathered in the nearby port of Classis, laden with provisions for the starving citizens. Thus, when the gates of Ravenna were opened to admit Belisarius and the Roman army, he brought with him supplies for the people. He rode through the streets of the impregnable Gothic capital with the Gothic ambassadors at his side and with the victorious Roman army behind him. The streets were crowded with tall and warlike Goths, far surpassing the numbers of the Roman army, and past them marched the soldiers of Belisarius, small compared to the Goths. The Gothic women spat in the faces of their husbands when they saw the Roman army, and, pointing at the victors, they reviled their husbands for their cowardice—for they had heard from their husbands that the enemy were men of great size and too numerous to be counted.

There was no plundering of the city, and the Goths were allowed to keep their private property. But the great royal treasure stored in the palace was carried away to Constantinople. King Vittigis was treated courteously but kept under guard until he could be taken with Belisarius to Constantinople. Some of his greatest nobles were chosen to accompany him, but the mass of the Gothic warriors were told to return to their lands. Thus the Roman soldiers finally became the majority in Ravenna. It is not clear exactly when Belisarius dropped the pretense and let the barbarians see he was not going to accept the offered crown. Probably the process was gradual.

The Romans would make the Gothic capital their stronghold for the next two centuries, until it was taken by Aistolf the Lombard in 752, who soon after lost it to Pepin the Frank.

The Gothic-held cities of northeastern Italy, such as Tarbesium (Treviso) in Venetia, Caesena in Aemilia, and many others surrendered immediately to the Romans when they heard of the fall of Ravenna. Verona and Ticinum seem to have been the only significant cities still held by unsubdued Goths. Verona was held by Ildibad, nephew of Theudis, king of the Visigoths in Spain. Although his children had been taken captive in Ravenna, he still stubbornly refused to surrender to Belisarius. In Ticinum the brave Uraias, nephew of Vittigis, still held out.

When it dawned on the Gothic warriors that Belisarius had no intention of creating a kingdom in Italy, they flocked to Uraias in Ticinum. They called his uncle a coward and claimed that Vittigis had stayed in power only because of the admiration they had for him, his nephew. Despite their many losses on the battlefields of Italy, they said, their king, their nobles, and the Gothic treasure were being taken away. If he would only lead them, they would rather die than have themselves and their families carried away into foreign lands.

Uraias replied that he, too, preferred death to slavery, but he would not take the kingship, by which he would appear to be a rival to his uncle. He therefore strongly advised them to offer it to Ildibad in Verona, a brave and mighty warrior whose relationship to the Visigothic king might prove useful in their desperate situation. The advice seemed sound, and they went to Ildibad and offered him the purple robe of royalty.

Ildibad accepted the offer but urged that they not abandon all hope that Belisarius would ascend the throne, in which case Ildibad was willing to return to a private station. So the barbarians made one more effort to persuade Belisarius.

It was well known in Italy that Belisarius was under orders to leave Ravenna for Constantinople—to take charge of the Persian war, some said; accused of treason by his generals and facing a trial, others said. Both beliefs were reasonable. Justinian needed Belisarius desperately in the East, where the Persians were on the march, but his future actions in Ravenna were also feared. The Gothic delegation went to him, reproached him for breaking faith, and called him a self-made slave to the emperor who could have chosen to be emperor himself, with brave and loyal Gothic warriors to command. He could, however, still repent and receive the purple robe from Ildibad.

But it was to no avail. Belisarius refused to act treasonably toward Justinian. The Gothic envoys returned to Ildibad, and Belisarius sailed for Constantinople at this, the end of the fifth year of the Gothic War, a war that seemed over and won in every respect.

When the ships carrying Belisarius, his noble captives, and the great royal treasure reached Constantinople, there would be no triumph, as in the days of the victory over the Vandals. Despite the fact that the greatest barbarian kingdom in the West had been overthrown—or perhaps because of it—the cautious emperor would not permit such a celebration, which might give the soldiers and citizens too great an opportunity for replacing the studious and secluded Justinian with the famous and dazzling young General Belisarius. Justinian's fears were perhaps unfounded, but certainly not unreasonable: Belisarius, at age 36, was the most celebrated and popular Roman, and through his great wealth and strong bodyguard of seven thousand veteran warriors he was the most powerful man in the empire. Now it must surely have been whispered at court that this was Justinian's future successor.

Although there would be no formal triumph, the greatness of the day was undisputed as Vittigis, the successor of Theodoric the Great, prostrated himself in front of the emperor. With him was his wife, Matasuntha, the great-granddaughter of the greatest of Ostrogothic kings, and the last of the Amals, the traditional Ostrogothic line of royalty. With them was a long train of noble Gothic warriors and the children of Ildibad. The gold and silver of the great Gothic treasure, accumulated in the past fifty years, was exhibited to the Senate.

After having made his prostration, Vittigis was raised up by the emperor and received the title of patrician. After two years in Constantinople, honored by the friendship of the emperor, the old Gothic king died peacefully. It was a strange end to the king who had been elected to save the Goths and ended up offering his kingship to a Roman general. Soon after his death, his young wife, Matasuntha, married Germanus, the favorite nephew of Justinian.

Italy and the old capital of the empire were reconquered for the Romans, and the fearsome Goths who had plagued the empire for three hundred years were finally prostrate. As Procopius relates, despite having been denied a triumph, each day that Belisarius walked through the streets of Constantinople was in fact a triumph, as everyone cheered him. When the stories of the exploits of his bodyguard were told, it was said among the senators that one household had destroyed the kingdom of Theodoric. His popularity among the common people also seemed boundless.

Belisarius was in many respects special as a general. He was greatly loved by his soldiers and the common people. When a soldier was wounded, Belisarius would console him with presents of money, and to those who had distinguished themselves he presented bracelets and necklaces of gold and silver as prizes. When a soldier lost his horse, his bow, or other equipment in battle, Belisarius would immediately replace it. He was loved by the common people for his restraint in warfare, and they would even be enriched by being allowed to set their own prices on everything that was sold to the army. And when the crops were ripe, Belisarius would make certain that the cavalry did not trample them, and no men were allowed to touch the fruit on the trees.

Despite capturing many beautiful women from the Vandals and Goths, he always kept his attentions to his wife, Antonina.

He was remarkably shrewd, and in difficult situations he could swiftly decide the best course of action. He was courageous, but did not take unnecessary risks, and daring, while not losing his cool judgment. He never touched alcohol and rarely seemed out of spirits, despite unfortunate circumstances. He was later criticized for being greedy, although these may have been rumors created by his disloyal generals.

If he was able to command the loyalty of the common soldiers, he had somewhat greater problems in gaining the respect and obedience of his fellow generals, who seemed plagued with jealousy.

While the image of the great general presented by Procopius might be overly flattering at times, there is no doubt that Belisarius was a remarkable general of great ability.

9

AFFAIRS IN AFRICA AND THE EAST

WE NOW RETURN FOR A SHORT TIME to the events in North Africa after Belisarius left, because they greatly affected the conduct of the Gothic War.

After the battle of Membresa in 536, where Stotzas had been defeated, Belisarius left Africa for Sicily to continue the war against the Goths, as the rebellion seemed sufficiently crushed for the local generals to put out the embers. Ildiger and Theodorus the Cappadocian were left to take care of this.

BATTLE OF GADIAUFALA

General Marcellus was in overall command in Numidia and had under him Cyril in command of the *foederati*—the barbarian auxiliaries—Barbatus of the cavalry, and Terentius and Sarapis of the infantry. The five Roman generals quickly moved against the fleeing Stotzas and his small band of mutinous soldiers and brought him to bay at Gadiaufala (Ksar-Sbehi), some two days' journey from Cirta (Ksantina). At the start of the battle, Stotzas went alone among the imperial soldiers and addressed them in a short, vigorous speech, reminding them of the pay that had not been forthcoming for a long period and that they had been deprived of the spoils of the Vandal War, which he claimed the generals had taken for themselves. The imperial soldiers listened to him, and in the end they abandoned their generals and switched sides to support the well-spoken Stotzas. The five generals fled and hid in a church, but were found and killed, after Stotzas lured them out by promising them their lives. Suddenly, the tables had been turned, and the rebellion was again in full flame.

Justinian now took the dangerous situation, which could severely threaten the campaign in Italy and rob the Gothic War of reinforcements, much more seriously. He dispatched his popular nephew Germanus with enough money to pay the rebellious soldiers their wages, which had not been paid for many months. Germanus was furthermore instructed to try to conciliate the rebels rather than striking down hard on them. Two senators went with him: Symmachus and Domnicus—the former to be entrusted with the maintenance of the army and the latter with command of the infantry.

On arriving in Africa, Germanus looked over the registers of soldiers and found that only a third of the Roman army was still loyal to the emperor, while the rest was with Stotzas. Germanus did not move out against him, but instead sought to reconcile the soldiers and granted deserters amnesty. He soon persuaded most of Stotzas's army to cease its rebellion and return its allegiance to the emperor. The deserters were even given backpay for the period they had been fighting for Stotzas.

Now plagued with mass desertions, Stotzas sought to press for a decisive battle with Germanus, and moved against Carthage with his remaining troops. Germanus and his army met Stotzas some four miles from Carthage. Before the battle, Germanus addressed his soldiers and promised them that all that had happened during the rebellion would be forgotten if they were loyal now. He pointed out that he had always treated them well and that now was the time to show their loyalty. The soldiers were enthusiastic, each wanting to be the first to display his loyalty to the emperor.

For a while the two armies remained in position opposite each other, but soon the rebels broke ranks and withdrew into Numidia, where their women and plunder were located, with Germanus in pursuit.

BATTLE OF SCALAE VETERES

Germanus caught up with the mutineers at Scalae Veteres in Numidia at the end of 536 or early 537.

The loyalists deployed their baggage train wagons in a line, with all the infantry under the leadership of Domnicus in front of them, so as to strengthen the infantry's morale by removing any threat to its rear. Germanus, with the best of the cavalry, placed himself on the left wing and the rest of the cavalry on the right wing in three divisions, led by Ildiger, Theodorus the Cappadocian, and John, the brother of Pappus.

The mutineers took their stand opposite the loyalists in a somewhat more scattered formation, in the manner of barbarians. Close to the battlefield, thousands of Moors under their chieftain Iaudas watched the struggle, officially to support Stotzas, but they had also promised their support to the loyalists.

When Stotzas recognized the standard of Germanus, he exhorted his men and began to charge against him. But the Herulian barbarians around him refused his orders and tried to hold him back, saying it was better to attack John's forces, as they were inexperienced. With that wing of the Roman army routed, the troops under Germanus would also be thrown into confusion. Stotzas was persuaded and accordingly went with his best troops against John, leaving his other troops to fight Germanus.

The Herulian plan paid off: John's men were soon routed and their standards quickly captured. The rebels continued to pursue the fleeing men, and some attacked the infantry line, which was already beginning to waver.

At this point Germanus charged the rebels opposite him, and after a hard fight succeeded in routing them, while Ildiger and Theodorus were charging Stotzas on the opposite wing. The armies had by this time become completely mingled, with rebels and loyalists fleeing and pursuing their enemies at the same time. The confusion became great, as they all used the same language, the same equipment, and the same clothes, and friend or foe could not easily be distinguished. The loyalists would ask the watchword of whomever they captured, and if they could not supply the correct one, they were killed immediately.

DEPLOYMENT

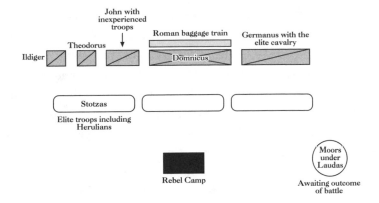

BATTLE

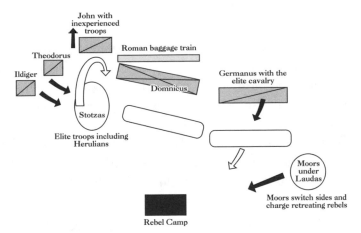

Map 12. The battle of Scalae Veteres.

In the confusion, one of the rebels managed to sneak up to Germanus and kill his horse. Only the swift reaction of his bodyguards saved the general's life.

Finally, Stotzas was put to flight, and the loyalists were able to capture the rebels' camp. With the loyalist victory evident, the Moors launched themselves upon the fleeing rebels, and Stotzas managed only with difficulty to flee along with a hundred Vandals. His retreat ended in Mauretania, where he later married the daughter of one of the local chieftains. The remaining rebels were either killed or went over to the army of Germanus.

The Maximinus Affair

But the troubles in Africa were not over. With Stotzas in full flight
and with no supporters, Germanus had been able to withdraw to
Carthage and attend to the government of the province.

Maximinus, one of Theodorus's bodyguards, had gathered a
large number of dissatisfied soldiers who were willing to join him
in a conspiracy against the government. To gather more followers,
Maximinus explained his plans to others, and particularly to the
influential Asclepiades, a Palestinian and a personal friend of
Theodorus's. After hearing about the project, Asclepiades went to
Germanus and told him of the plot. Germanus did not want to disturb the soldiers in any way, so instead of punishing Maximinus he
tried to gain his loyalty. Accordingly, he summoned him and
praised him for his soldierly qualities and asked him to join his personal bodyguard.

Maximinus was overjoyed by this extraordinary honor and soon
took the oath to protect Germanus with his life, if necessary.
Maximinus did not intend to honor his oath, however; instead, he
thought he could affect his plot more easily now that he was close
to Germanus.

On the appointed day of the uprising, Maximinus's followers
went to the palace, where Germanus was entertaining some friends
for lunch. Maximinus was standing with the other bodyguards
beside the dining couches of the nobles, when someone entered and
announced that many soldiers had come to the palace complaining
that the emperor owed them pay for a long period.

Germanus, who knew about the conspiracy, commanded some
of his most-trusted soldiers to secretly keep watch over Maximinus
so he could not leave the palace, while Germanus went to see the
mutinous soldiers about the disturbance. As planned, the mutineers
proceeded to the Hippodrome, where they were to meet with the
rest of the rebels and Maximinus. Maximinus, however, was unable
to come to them, as he was closely watched, and so Germanus was
able to send loyal troops to the Hippodrome to destroy the rebels.
Without their leader, they were soon either killed or surrendered.
After the defeat of the rebels, Germanus had Maximinus impaled

in front of the city walls of Carthage, as a signal to other would-be rebels.

With the rebellions thus apparently quelled, Germanus could return to Constantinople, and in 539, the eunuch Solomon was again sent to govern Africa. Martinus and Valerianus were also recalled, and Solomon was provided reinforcements commanded by Rufinus, Leontius, and John, the son of Sisiniolus.

Solomon, who was a capable and wise governor, set the army in order, sending away whatever rebellious elements were found among the troops and enrolling new ones in their stead. The remaining Vandals, and particularly all the Vandal women, were also removed from Africa and sent elsewhere in the empire.

The city walls destroyed so many years ago by the Vandals were restored, and Africa was given a chance to recover to its once-prosperous state.

Campaign Against the Moors

Gontharis, one of Solomon's bodyguards, was sent against the troublesome Iaudas and his Moors on Mount Aurasium. After being defeated at the Abigais River, he was rescued by Solomon, who brought the whole army with him. Gontharis was, however, still hard-pressed in his camp after Solomon left. Only the timely return of Solomon saved Gontharis, and the Moors were defeated decisively in a battle near Mount Aurasium.

After this battle, the Moors no longer wanted to confront the whole Roman army in a pitched battle, but instead sought to defeat it by retreating to the difficult terrain around Aurasium. They believed the Romans soon would suffer from lack of water and provisions, and so retreat.

Iaudas accordingly sent most of his troops home to Mauretania and the regions south of Mount Aurasium, and remained with some twenty thousand troops in the forts on the mountain.

But Solomon was determined to reach a conclusion and remove the Moorish threat, so he plundered the fields on Aurasium and began to besiege the forts there. Despite serious deprivations, the Romans defeated the Moors through several skirmishes and sieges, and even wounded Iaudas, who had to flee to Mauretania. After capturing Iaudas's treasure and household, Solomon garrisoned the forts on Mount Aurasium and returned to Carthage.

After the Moorish retreat from Numidia, the province of Mauretania Primus was liberated, while Mauretania Caesarea continued to be held by the Moors, although the Romans held the port of Caesarea (Cherchell in modern-day Algeria). Finally, in 539, the province was at peace—but a peace that would last only four years.

MOORISH UPRISINGS

In 543, Cyrus and Sergius, nephews of Solomon the eunuch, were sent to Africa to govern Pentapolis in Cyrenaica and Tripolis in Libya. The local Leuathae Moors came to Sergius with a great army at Leptis Magna (Al Khums in modern-day Libya), to see if he might give them the customary gifts and insignias of office. Eighty of the barbarians were received into the city, but at the conference, disagreements about complaints lodged by the Moors soon turned into a full-scale fight, and Sergius's bodyguards killed all the Moors.

When the Moorish army heard of the incident, it attacked Sergius, who came out to meet it. In front of Leptis Magna, the Romans defeated the Moors, took their camp, and enslaved their women and children.

Later, the Moors went against the province of Byzacena with an even greater army, and Solomon collected the whole Roman army and summoned Sergius and Cyrus with their troops.

At this time in 543, the otherwise pro-Roman Moorish chieftain Antalas also went into rebellion, allegedly because of some acts of ill faith by the Romans.

The armies met at the city of Tebesta, where Solomon defeated the Moors and captured their booty. The Roman soldiers complained after the battle that the booty was not being distributed, and they were not satisfied when Solomon explained that he was awaiting the outcome of the whole campaign, after which the booty could be distributed more correctly.

Accordingly, when the Moors again offered battle, some Roman soldiers did not enter the battle, and the others fought without enthusiasm. The Romans were soon routed by the great numbers of

Moors. During the rout, Solomon's horse stumbled in a ravine, and Solomon was overtaken by the pursuing barbarians, who killed him.

Sergius Appointed Governor

Solomon's nephew Sergius was then appointed to govern North Africa. Sergius was an arrogant and incompetent governor and general, and known for his avarice. He soon brought the province to its knees through misadministration and inability to handle the Moorish rebellion. Most of the generals in Africa, in particular John, the son of Sisiniolus, disliked him greatly because of his character and were therefore reluctant to take up arms against the raiding barbarians.

Meanwhile, Antalas summoned the old nemesis of the Romans in Africa, Stotzas, who came from Mauretania with a small band of Vandals.

Justinian heard of the useless Sergius but was not willing to remove him from office, out of respect for the dead Solomon.

Antalas and Stotzas had gathered a great army which was raiding Byzacena unhindered. Finally, John was stirred by the entreaties of the provincials and moved his army against the Moors. On his way, he sent a letter to Himerius the Thracian, who was commanding the Roman troops in Byzacena, ordering him to bring his troops to the city of Menephesse, where the armies would join. Later, John was informed that the enemy was already encamped at Menephesse, so he sent a message to Himerius directing him to meet him at a different place. But the message did not reach Himerius, who marched straight into the Moorish army. Himerius was captured, and most of his troops joined Stotzas.

The Capture of Hadrumentum

Antalas and Stotzas then hit upon a stratagem to take the important coastal city of Hadrumentum. Himerius was forced to approach the city walls with some of Stotzas's troops and some Moors in chains and say to the guards that John had won a great victory over the barbarians and would arrive soon. The guards should therefore open the gates for the small party of Roman soldiers. The guards were thus deceived by Himerius and Stotzas's troops, who were allowed to enter the city. The rebels kept the gates open and let the waiting Moorish army enter. The great city was sacked and a small garrison placed there.

A little later, Paulus, a priest in charge of the sick in Hadrumentum, went in secret to Sergius in Carthage, asking him to bring the army to recover the city. Sergius did not want to reduce his garrison in Carthage, however, and spared only eighty soldiers for Paulus. Paulus then collected sailors and provincials and dressed them up as Roman soldiers. They were put on boats and sailed for Hadrumentum. On arriving at the city, Paulus went in secret inside the walls and spread the rumor that Germanus had arrived with a great army. The eager provincials opened the gates for the Roman forces, which soon destroyed the little rebel garrison and recovered the city.

When the Moors heard the false rumor of the coming of Germanus, they fled and only returned after some time.

Soon the Moors and Stotzas were roaming at will throughout the African provinces, plundering the local inhabitants. Because of his hostility towards Sergius, John remained quiet with his army and did not seek to curb the rebels, whose numbers had grown strong from deserters.

With the Moorish rebellion running completely out of control, in 545 Justinian finally sent soldiers and generals to rally the Roman cause. Among the generals was the energetic Areobindus, who was married to Justinian's niece. Their orders were to end the rebellion as soon as possible. The emperor still did not recall Sergius, but instead divided the provinces between the two generals. Sergius was to carry on the war in Numidia, Areobindus in Byzacena.

When Areobindus learned that Antalas and Stotzas were encamped about 100 miles southwest of Carthage at the city of Sicca Venerea (El Kef in modern-day Tunisia), he summoned Sergius and John to join forces with him and end the rebellion. Sergius ignored the request, so only John, with a small army, joined Areobindus. The little Roman army met Antalas and Stotzas outside the city.

Battle of Sicca Venerea and the End of Stotzas

Stotzas and John were mortal enemies and had been trying to kill each other for years. When the battle commenced, they rode between the two armies to fight each other in single combat—an ancient barbarian custom that had long been out of use in the Roman Empire.

As they rode against each other, John mortally wounded Stotzas with an arrow in the groin. He fell from his horse, and the rebels and their allies attacked the small imperial army and swept it away. John was killed when his horse stumbled down a steep incline.

After the battle, Stotzas was found lying under a tree, where his soldiers just managed to tell him of John's death before he breathed his last. His only remark was that now it was most sweet to die, as his mortal enemy was dead.

The End of the Rebellion

The disastrous battle made Justinian realize that Sergius had to be removed, so he was sent to Italy and the Gothic war. In his stead, Areobindus became governor in 545, but was soon slain by Gontharis, a Roman general in Numidia who promised the soldiers he personally would advance them whatever they were owed in pay.

After thirty-six days of tyranny, Gontharis was in turn killed by Artabanes, who then became governor.

Finally, in 546, John, the brother of Pappus, was appointed master of the soldiers and governor of Africa. The Moors were suppressed, and the province once again enjoyed a period of tranquility, after years of devastations, barbarian raids, and the pillaging of the rebels. Africa enjoyed peace for the rest of Justinian's reign, except for one Moorish rebellion in 563, which was quickly quelled. In the end, the province never recovered completely despite having been conquered intact by Belisarius, but was ruined by the misadministration of Justinian.

Affairs in the East

Africa was not the only region in which the Romans were challenged. For a while, we must study the events taking place on the eastern border of the empire. The Persian war would govern affairs in Italy for the rest of the war against the Goths, because of the troops needed there and because this grave threat to the empire occupied Justinian's attention.

In the spring of 541, with all preparations being completed, Belisarius left for the east to take command of the war against Persia. Valerianus was sent to Armenia to organize the defenses there.

THE PERSIAN INVASION OF 540

In 540, Chosroes broke the eternal peace and invaded Syria. Placing too much confidence in Chosroes's good faith, Justinian had neglected the army of the east, and despite recent warnings, he had taken few measures to strengthen it. When Chosroes, acting earlier than had been anticipated, moved with a large army into Mesopotamia in 540, he met no opposition. His object was not conquest but money and loot, and he proceeded methodically to sack, or extract blackmail from, the cities of Sura, Hierapolis, Beroea, Chalcis, Edessa (Sanli Urfa in modern-day Turkey), and Apamea.

Germanus, Justinian's nephew, had been sent with three hundred men in great haste to Antioch but was unable to accomplish anything, as no more troops reached him from Constantinople. The other bodies of troops in the cities were not individually strong enough to challenge Chosroes and so kept quiet behind their fortifications. There were even many deserters from the Roman units who joined Chosroes on the grounds that they had not received their pay for a long time.

It appears that Chosroes's target was the great metropolis of the east, Antioch. Shortly before Chosroes arrived at its walls, six thousand troops had come under the generals of Lebanon, Theoctistus and Molatzes.

With the reinforcements, the garrison of Antioch felt strong enough not to bribe Chosroes to leave, and accordingly he tried to storm the walls. A great rock formation lay close to the walls of Antioch and had not been included in the circuit of the city walls. On this the Persians placed archers and other troops and so could fight almost equally against the soldiers and civilians on the wall at that place. After hard fighting, the Persians broke through and took the city, despite a courageous fight by local gangs of youths in the streets of the city. The valiant street gangs by chance covered the retreat of the Roman troops, who left by an unguarded gate.

After Chosroes made slaves of the inhabitants and plundered the city, it was set on fire. It was a great shock to contemporaries that the great and well-defended city could fall to the Persians.

Soon after, envoys from Justinian reached Chosroes and discussed on what terms he would to return to Persia. The Roman envoys upbraided Chosroes for having broken the treaty, but he listed a number of complaints, some real and some fabricated, against the Romans. It was finally agreed that the Persians would receive five thousand pounds of gold immediately and five hundred pounds annually for all time to cover expenses in maintaining a garrison at the pass of the Caspian Gates. The question of garrisoning the Caspian Gates had long been an issue between the Romans and Persians. In return, Chosroes would depart for Persia, and there he would receive ambassadors from Justinian to agree on final terms of peace.

Chosroes did not, however, go directly back. Instead, he extorted more money from Roman cities along the way. When he came to the fortress-city of Daras, he even began a siege. The city was skillfully defended by General Martinus, who had arrived from the war in Italy. The double walls of Daras and the valiant defenders succeeded in holding off the Persians, who demanded a sum of five hundred pounds of silver, which they received.

When Justinian found out about the assault on Daras, he charged Chosroes with having broken the truce and accordingly refused to honor the peace agreement. So ended the Persian invasion of 540.

Roman Invasion of Persia

Belisarius's first task would be to reorganize the army in Mesopotamia. After having brought the troops from Lebanon and the Saracen Prince Arethas with his men, Belisarius held a council of war in Daras around June 541. It was decided to take advantage of Chosroes's absence on a foray against Lazica and invade Persia. Rhecithancus and Theoctistus, the commanders of the troops in Lebanon, agreed with the invasion but said they would have to return with their troops to Phoenicia and Syria after sixty days. Otherwise the troublesome Saracen chieftain Alamoundaras would plunder these regions, from where their troops had been removed. Belisarius accepted this and prepared for the invasion.

Accordingly, Belisarius moved to the Persian city of Nisibis and camped south of it. He hoped to tempt the strong garrison into attacking him, thereby drawing it so far from the city that it could not retreat to the safety of the walls. But a general named Peter, commanding some of the troops from Lebanon, and John, the commander of the troops in Mesopotamia, disagreed with this strategy and moved closer to the city. Here they were attacked, and after having lost a standard along with many men, they were saved by the timely intervention of the main army, especially the brave Ostrogothic spearmen, who were now fighting faithfully for their Roman masters.

After this debacle, Belisarius considered his army unsuited for conducting a siege of the strongly fortified Nisibis. He therefore moved a day's march past Nisibis and began a siege of the important fortress Sisauranon, which was occupied by eight hundred elite cavalry commanded by the Persian noble Bleschames.

The Romans made camp close to the fortress and soon tried to storm the walls, but they were forced back with heavy losses. Belisarius called together his generals for a conference. Their strategic situation was precarious, as they had the strong garrison of Nisibis behind them, and if they also left Sisauranon in their rear, the danger would be too great. The Persians would then be able to attack them in the rear when they were in difficulty, and any retreat would end in disaster. Accordingly, it was decided to send Arethas with his Saracens, and part of Belisarius's bodyguard under Traianus and John, further inland to ravage the country. The main army under Belisarius would stay and continue the siege of Sisauranon.

The Saracens crossed the Tigris and began to plunder the region, which had been free of war for a long time and so was unprepared for the attack.

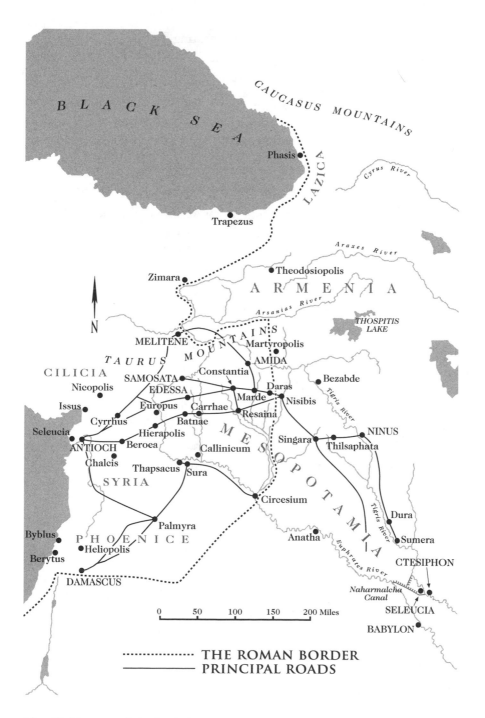

Map 13. Mesopotamia in the sixth century.

Meanwhile, Belisarius succeeded in capturing Sisauranon, as the fortress had exhausted its supplies. The inhabitants, who were Christians of Roman origin, were released, and Bleschames and his Persian troops entered Roman service and were sent to Italy to fight against the Goths.

While this was taking place, the Saracens plundered the defenseless region with no hindrance until Arethas thought he should bring his huge plunder home. He did not want to return to the main Roman army for fear of having to split the plunder with it. The Roman troops accompanying him were scared by a rumor of a large enemy body of troops nearby and so took a long detour back to the Roman Empire, finally arriving at Theodosiopolis.

Because Belisarius received no messages about this movement and none from Arethas, he had to assume the Persians had destroyed the raiding force. This did not improve the already difficult circumstances of the Roman army, which was plagued by disease after taking Sisauranon. As the troops from Lebanon were starting to fear attacks on their province while it was defenseless, Belisarius was forced to retreat to the Roman part of Mesopotamia. But the rumor of his daring invasion and the plundering of his country had reached Chosroes, who was hurrying back from Lazica after having taken its principal fortress, Petra.

At the end of the campaign of 541, Belisarius was recalled to Constantinople.

THE CAMPAIGN OF 542

Chosroes crossed the Euphrates again in 542 and moved into the Roman lands. The weak Roman garrisons kept to the safety of the walled cities, so he met no resistance during his march. Again, he did not settle down to besiege a Roman city, but moved straight through the Roman border defenses toward Palestine and the inner provinces.

Belisarius was quickly sent with a few followers on the imperial post to the region called Euphratesia, which Chosroes had invaded. Here he collected as many of the scattered garrisons as possible in the city of Dura Europos (near Salhiyé in modern-day Syria) on the

Euphrates. But because most of the Roman troops were engaged in Italy, his army was too small to engage Chosroes in an open battle.

Chosroes, however, was not aware of the small size of the Roman army and had only heard the feared name of Belisarius. So he sent one of his secretaries, Abandanes, to him—officially to complain that Justinian had not sent ambassadors to negotiate a peace, as had been agreed upon, but in reality to scout out the Roman troops. Belisarius, however, had his own plan.

He picked six thousand of his best troops of especially fine physique and good stature and sent them to hunt some distance from the Roman camp. Then he commanded his officers Diogenes and Adolius to cross the Euphrates with a thousand horsemen and move along the river in full view, as if guarding the crossing. When he heard that the envoy was on his way, he had a pavilion erected, around which he placed Thracians, Illyrians, Goths, Heruli, Vandals, and Moors in scattered formation. They were then commanded to move about in a casual way, so as to appear as if there were many more.

When the Persian ambassador got into the camp, he explained that Chosroes had invaded the Roman Empire because no Roman ambassadors had come to him, as had been agreed upon in 540. Belisarius upbraided the Persian for the strange behavior of making war when they wanted peace, and dismissed him.

When Abandanes returned to Chosroes, he told him of the huge number of Roman soldiers of great stature and the many barbarians from the whole empire who had gathered to obstruct the return of the Persian army across the Euphrates.

For Chosroes it was a serious risk that a sizable Roman army was at his rear. If the Romans lost a battle, they could easily retreat to their fortresses, but if the Persians lost, there would be no retreat and the entire army would be destroyed. Supposing that the crossing of the river was held in strength by the Romans, he moved his army some way along the Euphrates and there constructed a bridge and quickly crossed. His retreat was possibly hastened by rumors of the coming plague, which would soon reach Persia, too.

After he had crossed the Euphrates, messengers were sent to Belisarius saying he had decided to return to Persia, but he expected ambassadors to be sent as soon as possible. This did not, however, stop him from capturing and destroying the Roman city of Callinicum on his way back to Persia.

Thus Belisarius succeeded in making Chosroes retreat, despite his greatly inferior forces. Belisarius was highly praised for his actions at a time when nothing stood between the Persians and the rich provinces of the interior.

Soon after, Belisarius was recalled to resume command in Italy, where disaster threatened the Roman cause.

In 543, Chosroes moved to the northern sector again, but owing to the plague did not launch any attack; the Roman generals then counterattacked, but were beaten off with heavy losses. The next year Chosroes again turned his attention to Mesopotamia, where he besieged Edessa but failed to take it. By this time he was wearying of the war, which had ceased to bring quick profits, and in 545 he agreed, in return for a payment of five thousand pounds of gold, to sign a truce for five years. He refused, however, to abandon his conquests in Lazica, and there the truce did not apply.

10

THE RISE
OF TOTILA

WHEN BELISARIUS LEFT RAVENNA IN the spring of 540, taking with him his son-in-law Ildiger and the generals Valerianus, Martinus, and Herodianus, Italy appeared to have been recovered for the empire. As it was, the struggle would have to be fought all over again, and twelve years of war, generally disastrous for the empire, had to pass before an impoverished Italy was truly reunited with the Roman Empire.

The generals remaing in Italy to finish the war were John, the nephew of Vitalianus; John the glutton; Bessas the Goth; Vitalius; and Constantianus. The last two had come from Dalmatia, where they were no longer needed when the Goths surrendered. No one was placed in supreme command. Constantianus was in command at Ravenna and Bessas at Rome, and those two positions were the most prominent in Italy. John was, however, the general with the most brilliant military record and perhaps the most likely to have been put in chief command. Each general was therefore left to his own devices, with only the far-away emperor to account to. Accordingly, they began to plunder as much as possible and to fight as little as possible. Discipline was soon nonexistent, as the rapacious generals had their ways with the peaceful population, to whom they were soon a greater menace than any ravaging Gothic army.

Misadministration in Italy

The population was further pressed by the Roman tax system, which soon made itself felt in Italy. Justinian had a huge court, an extravagant building program to finance, and barbarian tribes hovering on the borders of the empire that had to be bought off. He was in constant need of money, and any means were used to obtain it.

In order to deal with the fiscal questions of the newly conquered provinces, Justinian had created the *logothetes*, high administrative officials whose responsibilities included overseeing the gathering of taxes. For the Italians, who had not seen an imperial tax gatherer in more than fifty years, this was quite a shock, as it had also been for the provincials in North Africa. Alexander, the chief of the *logothetes*, especially made an impression. The provincials called him *psalidion*, or *scissors*, for his ability to clip gold coins while still keeping their roundness and so reissue the reduced coin at full value without risk of detection. The *logothetes* received one-twelfth of what they recovered for the imperial treasury. They soon became fabulously rich through their work. While each new month seemed to bring a new tax, almost nothing was done to repair and maintain the infrastructure of the cities and the provinces.

Even the soldiers had to pay their part. The *logothetes* heavily fined every offense—and there were probably plenty of them, given the laxness of discipline and the many Heruli, Huns, Isaurians, and other barbarians who were under the standards of the empire. This policy of financial punishment instead of discipline, and the *logothetes'* wealth, made the soldiers feel that after having reconquered Italy, they were now being treated unjustly and forced into poverty. Another scheme the *logothetes* created also affected the soldiers. The soldiers were paid based on length of service and advancement. Young soldiers received little apart from rations and their arms. After a few years of service, they would be promoted halfway up the rolls of the unit and would be better paid. The veteran who would shortly leave the ranks received a handsome salary. Of course, promotion to these more-favored positions depended on the retirement or death of those who occupied them. The *logothetes* hit upon the idea of keeping all the well-paid positions occupied

by "phantom" warriors. A veteran
might have died or retired, but his
name was kept on the rolls, and thus
no promotion was possible for the
lowly ranked soldiers, while the
armies would also seem to be much
bigger than they were. The *logothetes*
did not appropriate the pay of the
"phantom" soldiers, but it appears they
were rewarded for reducing the cost of
maintaining the army. In his *Secret
History*, Procopius hints that Justinian
himself approved the scheme.

Gold Solidus of Justinian, minted at Constantinople. The coin
has been clipped in antiquity.
(*Author*)

The heavy hand of the tax gatherers was also felt by the population,
which had so greatly aided Belisarius's operations. All provincials
who had made any financial transactions with the Goths or had
held office under them were called upon to produce a strict account
of all money given and received, even money that had passed
through their hands forty years ago in the early days of Theodoric
the Great. The Gothic rulers were legally treated as if they had been
the lawful governors of Italy under Anastasius, Justin, and Justinian,
and therefore charges of embezzlement were prosecuted against all
Roman officials—the Goths had kept the Roman administration
intact—who had not faithfully served the Ostrogothic kings.
Because the *logothetes* would press any case as far as possible, often
with no regard for evidence, discontent was growing rapidly everywhere in Italy.

ILDIBAD AND THE BATTLE OF TARBESIUM

The few remaining independent Goths soon found it possible to
increase their power through the slothfulness of the Roman generals and the abuse of the soldiers and the civilian population.

When Belisarius left for Constantinople, Ildibad only held one
city of importance, Ticinum, and had only one thousand demoralized Gothic warriors. Since then, in less than a year, he had regained

control of all Liguria and Venetia—all Italy north of the Po River—and had collected an army of considerable size, mostly consisting of deserted soldiers, possibly Goths, from the Roman army.

Only one of the many Roman generals stirred at seeing Ildibad building up his strength, while the rest ignored it or watched with apathy. Vitalius, formerly commanding in Dalmatia and now in Venetia, moved—probably in autumn 540—with his Herulian auxiliaries against Ildibad, and a great battle was fought near Tarbesium. The battle ended in a sharp defeat of the Romans, with Vitalius just escaping with his life. Wisandus, king of the Heruli, was killed and left on the battlefield. The victory brought even more discontented soldiers flocking to the standards of the new Gothic kingdom.

Deaths of Uraias and Ildibad

Ildibad would never get the chance to prove how well-suited he was for kingship. If Uraias, nephew of Vittigis, had the nobility to refuse the crown, his wife was of a different type. Known for her beauty and the wealth she lavishly displayed, she was one day going to the baths with her great retinue. On the way she met Ildibad's wife with few attendants and dressed in poor clothes, for Ildibad had lost all his possessions as well as his children in the fall of Ravenna. Not only did Uraias's arrogant wife not show the proper respect to the king's wife, she ignored and insulted her because of her poor looks. Ildibad's wife soon told her husband about this insult, and he was angered at the disrespect. He began to accuse Uraias of disloyalty, claimed he was planning to desert to the Romans, and soon had him assassinated.

With the death of the brave and popular Uraias, Ildibad started losing his grip on his countrymen. Around May 541, six years after the beginning of the war, one of his guards by the name of Wilas, a Gepid whose wife Ildibad had married away to another of his followers during Wilas's absence on some mission, killed Ildibad during a feast in the royal palace. It had not been difficult for him to find accomplices, as many wanted to avenge Uraias's death.

Eraric the Rugian

Eraric the Rugian succeeded Ildibad, although he was not fully acknowledged by all Ostrogoths. When Theodoric the Great entered Italy, part of the Rugian people under their king, Fredericus, had followed his standards and had shared in his victory over Odoacer. Despite the treachery of Fredericus, who switched allegiance to Odoacer, the little nation making up part of the Gothic commonwealth had remained faithful to the Goths since then, but had always kept to itself and remained a separate nationality, marrying only the women of its own tribe and probably having justice administered by its own chieftains. That this little nation could put a king on the throne of the whole Ostrogothic confederacy shows how low the once great Ostrogoths had fallen.

But Eraric proved himself unfit as king and reigned only five months. During this time he succeeded in nothing and took no offensive steps against the Romans, but instead busied himself with negotiations with Constantinople. He called together an assembly of the Goths and proposed to send ambassadors to Justinian, with offers of peace on the same terms as those that had been offered to Vittigis—i.e. all Italy north of the Po.

The assembly approved the suggestion, and a delegation was sent to Constantinople. But Eraric sent with it a secret message in which he offered to sell his people and all Italy to the emperor for the usual fee: the patriciate, a large sum of money, and a splendid establishment at Constantinople.

The Rise of Totila

In the meantime, the Goths were becoming impatient for deliverance from their desperate situation. Ildibad had aroused their hopes, but their Rugian king seemed incapable of any action, apart from meaningless negotiations.

Instead they looked to the house of Ildibad for somebody to take his place. Ildibad's young nephew Totila (or Baduila, as he is known from his coins), who was perhaps in his midtwenties, was known for his courage and capacity. He was in command of the garrison at Tarbesium when he heard of the murder of his uncle. As he thought that the Goths were thus finally defeated, he sent messengers to Constantianus in Ravenna to offer the surrender of the city. The offer was gladly accepted, and the date for the surrender was agreed upon, but before it was handed over, a deputation from the discontented Goths came to offer Totila the crown. He agreed to take it if Eraric was removed from the throne before the day appointed for the surrender of the town. Thus in the autumn of 541, long before the ambassadors to Constantinople had returned, Eraric was slain by the conspirators and the young Totila raised on the shield as king of Ostrogoths.

When the news of the death of Eraric and the resurgence of the Gothic cause reached Justinian, he sent a sharp message to the Roman generals in Italy, charging them with misadministration and sloth. The rebuke made them assemble a council of war at Ravenna, to which all the generals came, as well as Alexander, head of the *logothetes* in Italy. Here it was decided to besiege Verona, the main city of Venetia, and after that to march to Ticinum and put an end to the Gothic hopes. There is little doubt it was the best course of action for the Romans, but due to the extreme rapacity of the generals, it was doomed to fail.

Assault on Verona

The twelve thousand-strong Roman army, commanded by no less than eleven generals, marched into the plains south of Verona, where their cavalry had the greatest advantage.

Marcianus, a Roman nobleman who still favored the imperial cause, sent word to them that he had bribed a guard in Verona to open the gates to the imperials. The generals were unsure of this offer and suspected a trap, so they asked for volunteers to bring a small, picked force to the gate to test the offer. Only Artabazes, an Armenian commanding the Persian troops of Bleschames, which Belisarius had captured in Persia, volunteered.

With one hundred selected men, he went at night to the walls of Verona, where the guard faithfully opened the gate to them. The other sentinels guarding the gate were slain, and the towers at the gate taken. When the Goths soon after found out what had happened, they fled through the northern gate to a nearby hill overlooking the city, where they passed the night. With almost no effort and the smallest fraction of military capacity, the Romans could have retaken the city with ease. But the eleven generals, who had begun marching to the city at the agreed-upon time, began to dispute the division of the spoils when they were about five miles from the city. After much debate, they compromised and continued their march.

By now, however, many hours had been lost, and the sun had risen. With broad daylight, the Goths on the hill could observe the city and see how few men had caused them to retreat. Accordingly, they rushed in by the northern gate and assaulted Artabazes's small band. The

A coin featuring Totila, or Baduila/Baduela, as he is known from his coins, as *Rex* (king). (*Author*)

Romans were soon pushed away from the gate and forced to take refuge behind the battlements of the southern portion of the wall. At that moment the bulk of the Roman army finally appeared under the walls and found the gates barred to them and only a small part of the walls occupied by the imperials. Ignoring the cries for help from Artabazes's troops, they swiftly retreated. Pressed on all sides, the beleaguered troops had to jump from the battlements. Most were killed by the fall, but some, including Artabazes, survived by landing on soft ground. When the pitiful remains of the brave expedition reached the Roman camp, they called the generals cowards and incapable for bringing disaster to such a great opportunity.

With the failure of taking Verona, the Roman army crossed the Po and withdrew to Faventia on the Via Aemilia, some twenty miles south of Ravenna.

When Totila received the news of what had happened at Verona, he quickly took advantage of the situation by gathering his whole army—five thousand warriors and a sad remnant of the great Gothic army—and set off in pursuit of the imperials.

Artabazes begged his fellow generals to attack the barbarians when they were crossing the Po, but each general had his own plan for conducting the campaign, so no common action could be undertaken, despite Artabazes's sound advice. Instead the Roman army stayed at Faventia without doing anything useful.

BATTLE OF FAVENTIA, 542

Before crossing the Po, Totila made a stirring speech to his soldiers in which he called upon them for one supreme effort of valor. They were all aware of the difficult situation. If defeated, the Romans could take shelter in their fortresses and await help from Constantinople, but the Goths had no such hope. If defeated, there would no longer be an Ostrogothic nation. If they won a victory, the Gothic cause would rise again, and there might still be an Italy for them. Blunders and bad generalship had reduced the army of the Goths from two hundred thousand men to only one thousand, and their lands from the whole of Italy, Sicily, and Dalmatia to just one city, Ticinum. But Ildibad's victory near Tarbesium had shown them what victory meant. Since then, their numbers had increased fivefold and they had extended their lands to everything north of the Po River. Another victory now, together with the sympathy of the extorted Italians, who were weary of the tax gatherers and the rapacity of the generals, might restore everything to them, he said.

After his speech, Totila selected three hundred men who were to cross the river at a point two and one-half miles distant and fall upon the rear of the enemy when the battle was joined. The rest of the army crossed the Po without incident and advanced on the many-generaled Roman army, which was more than double the size of the Gothic force.

The Romans went out to meet the Goths, but before the battle began, one of those single combats in which the barbarians in both armies delighted occupied the armies' attention. A huge and fully armored Goth named Valaris rode out into the space between the two armies and challenged the Romans. Only one Roman was willing to fight this fearsome enemy: brave Artabazes. The two warriors charged each other. Artabazes delivered the first blow, and the Goth was killed instantly when the Armenian's spear penetrated his right side.

However, the spear in the dead barbarian's hand had become jammed against a piece of rock below him and prevented him from falling, leaving him erect and making it appear as if he was still alive. Artabazes pressed on to complete his victory and drew his sword to finish the Goth, but because of a sudden swerve by Artabazes's horse, Valaris's upright spear grazed his neck. It seemed a mere scratch at first, and he was able to return in triumph to the Roman lines, but an artery had been pierced and the blood could not be stopped. In three days the gallant and capable Artabazes was dead.

Battle was then joined, and it did not go well for the Romans. When Totila's three hundred men appeared in the rear of the Roman army, they were taken for the vanguard of another Gothic army and created panic among the soldiers. The generals then fled in haste from the battlefield, each to a different city. All the standards fell into the hands of the barbarians—an extremely rare occurrence in Roman military history. Many Roman soldiers were slain, and many were taken prisoner, of which probably not a few afterward joined the Gothic army.

BATTLE OF MUCELLIS

With the main imperial army destroyed and its generals scattered, Totila was now in a position to move south to gain a foothold in Tuscany. A body of soldiers under Generals Vledas, Roderic, and Uliaris was sent to besiege Florentia, as Faesulae was probably deemed too difficult to take because of its superior defensive position. Justinus was in command of the Roman garrison at Florentia but feared he did not have enough men and provisions to hold out against a determined siege, so he sent messengers to Ravenna to ask for relief. A force under Bessas, Cyprianus, and John, the nephew of Vitalianus, was dispatched to his aid.

At the approach of this relief force, the barbarians raised the siege and retreated north up the valley of the Sieve, or Mucellis, as Procopius calls it. After a debate between the generals, it was thought unwise to risk the whole Roman force in the difficult mountainous terrain, and it was decided that one of them, with a picked body of troops, should find and engage the Goths while the rest of the army followed. John was chosen by lot, and he pushed up the valley. The terrified Goths left their camp and ran in confusion to a high hill nearby, where John's troops attacked them.

The Romans began to waver, but John encouraged his men with loud shouts and eager gestures. Unfortunately, one of his bodyguards, a prominent figure in the ranks, was killed, and in the confusion of the battle it was rumored that John himself had fallen. Panic ensued and the Romans fled down the valley from where they had come. When they met the main bulk of the army, they told them of John's death, and the rest of the army was pulled along in a disorderly flight.

Meanwhile, the Goths were pursuing the Romans and killing many of them. As before, many of the captives took service under Totila, and again demoralized and disgruntled Roman soldiers swelled the ranks of the Gothic army. For Totila it was a clear policy to treat all prisoners well, to make others come over freely.

With this great victory, all of central and southern Italy were wide open to Totila and his army. Caesena, Urbinum, Mons Feletris, Petra Pertusa, and all the other fortresses that it had taken Belisarius two years of hard fighting to win were now lost.

Totila pressed on into Etruria. There no fortresses surrendered to him so he marched on, crossed the Tiber, went further south through Campania and Samnium, took Beneventum and razed its walls, so it would be useless to the Romans, who were reluctant to meet the Gothic army in the field. The strategy of razing the walls of conquered cities, as Gaiseric the Vandal had also done, shows he was well aware of the Goths' deficiency in taking fortified cities, but neither did he have the troops to spare for garrisons. The Goths could win an open battle, but stone walls defeated them.

The strong fortress of Cumae with a large store of treasure fell into the Goths' hands, together with some important refugees, the wives and daughters of the Italian senators, who had sought refuge here. They were treated with every courtesy, and Totila dismissed them unhurt to their husbands and fathers, an act that made a deep impression on the Romans.

Meanwhile, the Goths overran all the southern regions of Italy—Apulia, Calabria, Bruttium, and Lucania. Totila did not take all the fortresses in these areas, but he still held the regions so securely that he could collect the revenues normally collected for the emperor and so increase his royal treasure.

Because Justinian had expected the newly reconquered provinces to pay for themselves, the loss of the revenue was a hard blow to the imperial cause. Justinian had no intention of sending more money to the generals in Italy, so the troops could not be paid and desertions became even more frequent. Many soldiers joined Totila, who paid his men well and did not plague them with the tricks of the tax gatherers. In these areas he also recruited many slaves, many of them no doubt of Gothic origin, and methodically collected the regular taxes and also the rents formerly paid by the farmers to their absentee landlords.

Totila then began to besiege the great stronghold of the south, Neapolis, which was held by a garrison of one thousand men, mostly Isaurians, under Conon.

These startling events took place in the summer of 542. Surprisingly, the Roman generals did nothing to prevent Totila's overrunning much of Italy. No concerted actions were taken, and every general sat tight on his own personal treasure, which he had amassed in the past few years of rapacity. Constantianus was at Ravenna, John—who had not been killed at the battle of Mucellis—was at Rome, Bessas the Goth was at Spoletium, Justinus at Florentia, and Cyprianus at Perusia.

Maximinus is Appointed Praetorian Prefect

When the terrible news of the resurging Ostrogoths reached Constantinople, Justinian was filled with sorrow because of all the wasted troops and money. But sending Belisarius back still seemed worse to him than the existing situation. Instead, in the autumn of 542, he acted to remedy the anarchy of the generals by appointing one man praetorian prefect of Italy, who was to have supreme power over all the armies of the empire in that province. This was clearly a wise and necessary action, but the new praetorian prefect, Maximinus, was an exceedingly bad choice. He was completely inexperienced in war, and slow and cowardly, and though he brought with him two capable generals, Herodianus, commander of a Thracian contingent, and Phazas the Iberian, the nephew of Peranius, commanding a band of Armenians, their energy was dampened by Maximinus's feebleness. A few Huns were also sent to Italy at the same time.

After the timid Maximinus had journeyed to Epirus on the Adriatic in November, he lingered there on one pretense or another, afraid to face the crossing during winter. Meanwhile, the distress of Conon and his beleaguered garrison in Neapolis was growing. Demetrius, an officer who had served under Belisarius as commander of a detachment of infantry, had been dispatched from Constantinople after Maximinus, perhaps to quicken his movements. He sailed to Sicily and there collected a large fleet of merchantmen, which he filled with provisions, hoping by the mere size of the fleet to overawe the Goths and reprovision the besieged Neapolis. Demetrius did indeed overawe the Goths, who had been expecting that a great army from Sicily would be coming. The stratagem would probably have succeeded had Demetrius brought the fleet straight into the harbor of Neapolis. He considered the danger of doing that too great, however, and instead sailed to Portus, the port of Rome, to gather more troops. The troops stationed there were completely demoralized and refused to go along on the expedition. So Demetrius again had to steer for Neapolis, but without more troops.

By now Totila had received word of the character and movements of the relief fleet. He had prepared a fleet of *dromones*, and with these he attacked the fleet of unwieldy merchantmen as soon as it rounded the promontory of Misenum. It was hardly a battle: all the ships and all their cargo were taken, and some of the soldiers were killed. Another Demetrius, the governor of Neapolis, who had sailed with the fleet, was also killed in the defeat.

The Fall of Neapolis

Meanwhile, Maximinus had arrived with his troops in Syracusa. Initially, having finally reached a friendly shore, he was unwilling to leave it again, despite the urgings of all the generals for him to relieve Neapolis. Particularly Conon, who was besieged in Neapolis, begged him to raise the siege, as their provisions had been exhausted.

At length, the fear of the emperor's displeasure overcame his own fears and Maximinus sent his whole army to Neapolis under the command of Herodianus, Demetrius, and Phazas, while he stayed safe at Syracusa, as the winter season was drawing near.

A tremendous storm sprang up just as the fleet entered the Bay of Neapolis. The rowers could not draw their oars out of the water, and the roar of the waves and wind drowned any chance of organized command. In the end, the storm dashed almost all the ships onto the shore, where the Goths were calmly waiting to kill any survivors. Herodianus and Phazas escaped with a few others, while Demetrius fell into the hands of the barbarians. He was later led in front of the walls of the city and compelled by the Goths to ask the garrison to surrender.

The soldiers and populace in the besieged city were devastated when they saw the Roman general not bringing relief, but despair. At the same time, Totila offered terms to the city: Conon and his soldiers could leave unharmed with all their possessions, and the citizens' safety was guaranteed by the Gothic king. The terms were accepted, as hunger and pestilence were pressing them, but with the stipulation that they would only surrender if no help came within thirty days. Totila, who was a wise politician, calmly promised that he would abstain from any attack in the next ninety days, thereby dispelling from their minds any hope of assistance from the emperor. Demoralized, Neapolis surrendered in May 543—long before the appointed time—and once again came under Gothic rule.

After taking possession of the city, Totila showed an uncustomary kindness to the citizens. To avoid the consequences of overfeeding after their long abstinence, he posted soldiers at the gates and in the harbor with orders to let none of the inhabitants leave the city. Each house was then supplied with rations of food on a moderate scale, and the portions were increased little by little daily until the people were on a full diet again. This prevented the starving people from gorging themselves and dying of the sudden change in diet, as often happened after long sieges.

Conon and his troops were provided with ships to take them anywhere they chose, and they decided to go to John in Rome. Heavy winds forced them back to the shore, where they feared they would now be treated as enemies, but again Totila offered them protection and told them to mingle freely with his own troops and buy food in the Gothic camp. Because the winds continued to be contrary, he provided them with horses and provisions and sent them on the road to Rome with an escort of Gothic warriors. The point of this lenient policy was, of course, to attract more Roman soldiers to his still-small army. For many, if not most, soldiers, it was not so important whom they fought for, as long as they were paid well.

The walls of Neapolis were razed according to Totila's general policy, to make it untenable for a Roman army. As Procopius says, "For he preferred to reach an outright decision by a battle with them [the Romans] on a plain rather than to carry on a long contest by means of sundry devices of craft and cunning [which belong to the attack and defense of besieged cities]."

Totila's policy of being on good terms with the provincials is illustrated by an event that took place at this time. A local Roman from Calabria came to the royal tent and demanded justice for his daughter, who had been raped by a bodyguard of the king's. The crime was admitted and the bodyguard was put into custody while Totila decided on a fitting punishment. Some of the Gothic nobles in the army came to him to ask for lenience for the brave soldier and not to punish him with death, as was expected. Firmly, Totila refused their request and explained that it was easy to be popular when letting off criminals, but that it was a cheap kindness that would ruin good government and the discipline in the army if it thought crimes would go unpunished. He believed the Goths would win only if they had a just cause, and so the violator was put to death and his property handed over to the daughter of the peasant.

While Totila was reducing Neapolis, the Roman generals with their still numerically superior forces continued to plunder the inhabitants of Italy. Discipline was now completely gone, and common soldiers would wander through the country districts, pillaging villas and farms, and making themselves more feared than the Goths from whom they were supposed to protect the populace.

Map 14. Italy during the campaigns of Totila.

The state of the country became so intolerable that
Constantianus, the commandant of Ravenna, wrote to the emper-
or that it was no longer possible to defend his cause in Italy, and all
the other officers signed this statement.

Meanwhile, Totila continued to make good use of the discontent
among the provincials, and around this time addressed a letter to
the Senate in Rome:

"Such men as wrong their neighbors, being either the victims of ignorance or blinded by some forgetfulness that has
come upon them, may fairly be forgiven by the victims of
their ill-treatment. For their ignorance or forgetfulness,
which led to their wrongdoing, also excuses it for the most
part. If, however, any man does wrong as a result of deliberate intent solely, such a man will have nothing left with
which even to defend his conduct. For it is not the deed
alone, but also the intention, for which this man himself
must, in justice, bear the responsibility. Therefore, since this
is so, consider forthwith what defense you will possibly be
able to make for your actions toward the Goths. Has it
really come to pass that you are ignorant of the good deeds
of Theodoric and Amalasuntha, or have they been blotted
from your minds with the lapse of time and forgetfulness?
No, indeed; neither one of these is true. For it was not in
some small matter, nor toward your ancestors in olden
times that their kindness was displayed, but it was in matters of vital importance, dear Romans, toward your very
selves, recently and in days that are close at hand. But was
it because you had been informed by hearsay or learned by
experience the righteousness of the Greeks toward their
subjects that you decided to abandon to them the cause of
the Goths and Italians? At any rate, you, for your part,
have, I think, entertained them royally, but you know full
well what sort of guests and friends you have found them,
if you have any recollection of the public accounts of
Alexander [the logothete]. For I need make no mention of
the soldiers and the commanders by whose friendliness and
magnanimity you have profited; and it is precisely this con-

duct of these men which has brought their fortunes to such a pass. Now let no one of you think that I am moved by youthful ambition to bring these reproaches against them, nor that I am inclined to boastful speech merely because I am ruler of barbarians. For the overmastery of those men, I say, has not been a work of our valor, but I confidently maintain that a sort of vengeance has overtaken them for the wrongs you have suffered at their hands. How then could it fail to appear a most atrocious act on your part, that you, while God is exacting vengeance from them in your behalf, should cling fondly to that atrocity of theirs and be unwilling to be rid of the ills arising therefrom? Give yourselves, therefore, some ground for the defense you must make to the Goths, and give us, on the other hand, some ground for forgiveness toward you. And you will give this if, without proposing to await the conclusion of the war, now that there is only scant hope left you, and that too of no avail, you choose the better course and set right the wrongs which you have committed against us."

With this letter, Totila hoped the Senate would surrender Rome to him quickly.

The letter was entrusted to some of the Roman prisoners with orders to take it to the Senate in Rome. John, however, forbade those who read the letter to return any answer. Totila then had several copies made and appended to them his promises that he would respect the lives and property of such Romans as should surrender, and sent the letters at night into Rome. When day dawned, the Forum and the major streets of Rome were filled with the proclamation of the Gothic king. John did not discover who had posted the proclamations, but suspecting the Arian priests of complicity, he expelled them all from the city.

Totila then decided to begin a regular siege of Rome. He was at the time engaged in the siege of Hydruntum in the south of Italy, the most likely place for Roman reinforcements to land, but decided to leave only a small force with orders to continue besieging the city while he marched with the main part of the army to Rome.

While Totila was strong in the open field, he was continually threatened by the Roman fleet, which could land troops basically anywhere in Italy it wished and attack Gothic-held territory far from Totila's field army.

For Totila it was paramount to gain a broader and more-solid basis of loyalty among the population in Italy. His army was still small, and there were not many male Goths left in Italy. In many respects, Totila *was* the Gothic cause and kingdom in Italy, as so much prestige was bound in his person. Taking cities and fortresses was all very well, as it often gained more troops for the Gothic army, but if Totila did not succeed in recreating the Gothic kingdom of Italy with a capital, a royal treasure, and a greater army, he could only wait until the Romans sent a new army with new commanders who would in the end defeat him. So despite his astounding victories and the utterly inept Roman generals, Totila and the Goths were in no way safe. The Ostrogoths had truly returned to their status during the fifth century—they were an army, but had no land of their own.

11

THE RETURN
OF BELISARIUS

Finally, in 544, with each message from Italy bringing news of a new disaster to the Romans, Justinian decided that only Belisarius could restore the situation. Despite the fact that the Persians were pressing hard on the eastern borders, Belisarius had to return to Italy.

The situation for the imperial arms in Italy was truly desperate. In two and one-half years, Totila had defeated superior Roman armies in two regular battles and in one sea battle. The Via Flaminia had been opened by the capture of Petra Pertusa in 542, and the Goths could now move freely from one end of Italy to the other. Neapolis and Beneventum had fallen, Hydruntum was threatened, and Rome was under siege. The cowardly and rapacious Roman generals were shut up in their strongholds in Rome, Ravenna, Spoletium, and a few other fortresses, still intent on enriching themselves rather than on fighting the barbarians.

Belisarius was however a different man now in the spring of 544. Two year before, in 542, even the semblance of Justinian's favor had disappeared, and he had become a broken and ruined man.

The Plague

The bubonic plague, which had arisen in Pelusium (Tell el-Farama) in Egypt, spread in 542 to Constantinople, where it hung heavily for four months, with deaths rising at one time to ten thousand people daily. The streets and markets were deserted, and people could no longer even bury their relatives, so the emperor had to undertake this work. All the household troops were employed for this purpose, but still it was impossible to dig graves quickly enough. In the end they were forced to stack the corpses in a large and deserted fortress in Sycae (Galata), which was roofed over when it could hold no more. The stench of decaying bodies wafted over the great city. The emperor himself fell ill, and for a time it seemed that he, like so many others, would fall victim to the terrible plague.

With the emperor ill and expected to die—there was even a rumor that he was already dead—the Eastern army held a hastily summoned military council where some generals said that if a new emperor was made without their consent, they would not acknowledge him.

Justinian's condition changed suddenly, and with this the entire situation. All the officers present at the treasonous council hastened to clear themselves by accusing someone else of treason. They were soon divided in two parties—on one side John the glutton and Peter, and on the other Belisarius and Bouzes, a former consul and master of the soldiers.

Empress Theodora ordered all the generals present at the council to come to the capital for an inquiry into the proceedings, and it was decided—whether rightly or wrongly is not known—that Belisarius and Bouzes had acted in a traitorous fashion.

Bouzes was thrown into the dungeons of the palace, where he would remain for two years and four months in a small room with no light and with no people allowed to communicate with him. The hardship of imprisonment would cost him his sight and his health.

The imperial couple could not go so far against the popular Belisarius, and there may have been little evidence that he had considered treason. In his campaigns he had always appeared extremely loyal to his emperor, despite the temptations of his victories.

Further charges were brought against him that he had appropriated too great a share of the treasure gained in his campaigns. If he could not be thrown into a deep dungeon, he could at least be disgraced, and the emperor and empress proceeded to do just that as thoroughly as possible. His command of the army of the East was taken away from him and given to Martinus. Even worse, his mil-

itary household, his bodyguard of seven thousand of the bravest
soldiers in the empire, handpicked through his campaigns, was broken up. The soldiers were distributed by lot to his rival generals and
the eunuchs of the palace. His friends were forbidden to speak to
him and his wealth taken away. As Procopius says, "And he went
about, a sorry and incredible sight, Belisarius a private citizen in
Byzantium, practically alone, always pensive and gloomy, and
dreading a death by violence."

The plague soon moved on to the rest of the empire and also fell
on the Persians and the other barbarian nations.

In 543, the emperor and empress finally decided that Belisarius
had been humbled enough to be no threat to the throne and so pardoned him of all charges. His treasure was given back to him,
although Theodora appropriated three thousand pounds of gold,
which she gave to her husband as a present. To make certain that
the rest eventually would be theirs, she also began to arrange a marriage between her grandson Anastasius and Belisarius's only child,
Joannina.

Belisarius was made count of the royal stables—a high office,
but still lower than his former one, and despite his entreaties, he
was not allowed to lead the army of the East against Chosroes.

As it became clear to Justinian that the generals in Italy never
would cooperate against the Goths, he graciously gave Belisarius the
task, with the stipulation that he was not to ask for money from the
imperial treasury but provide for everything out of his own pocket.

Thus the Belisarius who arrived on the shores of Italy in 544 was
not the same man who had broken the Goths four years earlier.

THE RELIEF OF HYDRUNTUM AND THE SECOND SIEGE OF ROME

On being put in command of the Italian campaign, Belisarius tried
to enlist some of the veterans from the Persian campaign, but he
was not as popular as before, and all refused. In the end, by moving
around Thrace, he managed by a large expenditure of money—his
own, most likely—to raise some young and inexperienced volunteers. In May 544, he marched to Salona to unite with Vitalius, the
general of Illyricum, but still their forces only numbered four thou-

sand men. Circumstances, however, forced them to move despite
their weak numbers.

The garrison of Hydruntum was sorely pressed by the besieging
Goths and had consented to surrender on a certain date if no help
arrived before then. Hydruntum was very important as one of the
major ports of south Italy, so Belisarius gathered ships and loaded
them with provisions for a year. Valentinus was then sent with some
of the Thracian troops to relieve the defenders of Hydruntum and
to resupply the city. Arriving only four days before the stipulated
day of surrender, he took possession of the unguarded harbor and
succeeded in entering the fortress without fighting. With no hope
of forcing the garrison to surrender, the barbarians raised the siege
and marched to join Totila before the walls of Rome. After relieving the weakened troops of the garrison with fresh soldiers and
leaving a year's supplies in the town, Valentinus returned to Salona.

Belisarius could now move along the coast from Salona to Pola
(Pula in modern-day Croatia) and then on to Ravenna. He wanted
at first to move straight on to Rome, but Totila's forces were too
strong, and Vitalius persuaded him to make Ravenna his base.

Meanwhile, Totila was tightening his grip on Rome. A guard
was set on the Tiber so that no provisions could be brought into the
city that way, and Tibur was taken and its inhabitants massacred.
The garrison escaped with no losses.

Totila also showed his strategic understanding when he formed
a small fleet of *dromones* stationed at Neapolis and the Aeolian
Islands (Lipari Islands) and captured most of the vessels bringing
corn from Sicily to Ostia.

In Ravenna, Belisarius tried to rewin the hearts of the population, but not one Goth or Roman came over to him from Totila's
forces.

Thorimuth, a guardsman of Belisarius's, and Vitalius with the
Illyrian troops, were then sent into the province of Aemilia to try
to capture some of the cities of the rich and populous district while
Totila was at Rome. The move would either force him to raise the
siege of Rome or lose important districts separating him from the
Gothic northern provinces.

Fortress after fortress was surrendering, and they could safely set up their winter quarters in the strategic city of Bononia (Bologna).

But suddenly the Illyrian troops decided to go home and left Bononia for their homeland. Their motives for this mass desertion were not unreasonable. They had served for years in Italy without receiving any pay from the bankrupt empire, and they had few provisions. Furthermore, a great army of Huns was at that moment plundering their homeland and carrying off their wives and children into slavery. When he heard of the defection of the Illyrians, Totila sent an army against Vitalius and his depleted troops in Bononia, but the Goths were caught in an ambush and severely defeated.

The damage, however, had been done, and all of Aemilia had to be abandoned from lack of troops to garrison the gains.

Belisarius's bodyguard Thorimuth was then sent with one thousand troops to relieve the besieged garrison at Auximum. The imperial garrison there under Magnus was holding out almost as stubbornly as the Goths six years ago. The relief force entered the city by night and resupplied it despite the Gothic siege.

Totila knew, however, that they had to leave the fortress again because there were too many mouths to feed, so he set up an ambush with two thousand picked men some three miles from the city. A deserter told him when the withdrawal was to take place, and the barbarians fell on the retreating column during their nightly march, killed two hundred, and captured all their baggage. The rest of the army, including Thorimuth, retreated to Ariminum.

Pisaurum Refortified

Belisarius's next move was to refortify Pisaurum for the sake of the excellent foraging ground for cavalry that surrounded it. This little city, about eighteen miles south of Ariminum, had earlier been taken by Vittigis, who had dismantled its fortifications to prevent its reoccupation by the Romans. The gates had been destroyed and the walls pulled down to half their ordinary height. By night, Roman scouts made exact measurements of the height and width of the gateways. Gates were then made at Ravenna to these measurements and shipped to Pisaurum, which was then reoccupied by some of the troops of Thorimuth and Sabinianus. The gates were put in place and the walls repaired by whatever materials the soldiers could get their hands on. When Totila heard of what was going on, he marched against the fortress with a great army, believing the garrison to be an easy prize. The Goths tried to storm the reconstructed fortress but were unable to capture it and so returned once more to their camp at Auximum.

Since Totila could see that Belisarius had too few troops to march against him, he decided to begin sieges of the cities of Firmum and Asculum (Ascoli), in Picenum.

It was now a year since Belisarius took over command of the war against the Goths, and little had been accomplished. Auximum and Hydruntum had been relieved and Pisaurum refortified. Against this, Totila had taken Tibur, tightened the blockade of Rome, and initiated several sieges of cities. Belisarius felt he was bound on hands and feet. He had no troops, no money, and could expect none in the future. At length, he broke his promise to Justinian to ask for no money for the war and wrote a strongly worded letter to the emperor:

> We have arrived in Italy, most mighty emperor, without men, horses, arms, or money, and no man, I think, without a plentiful supply of these things, would ever be able to carry on a war. For though we did travel about most diligently through Thrace and Illyricum, the soldiers we gathered are an exceedingly small and pitiful band, men without a single weapon in their hands and altogether unpracticed in fighting. And we see, on the other hand that the men who were left in Italy are both insufficient in number and in abject terror of the enemy, their spirit having been utterly humbled by the many defeats they have suffered at their hands—men who did not simply escape at random from their opponents, but even abandoned their horses and flung their weapons to the ground. And as for the revenue, it is impossible for us to derive any money from Italy, since it has again been taken by the enemy into their possession.

Consequently, since we have fallen behind in regard to the payment of the soldiers, we find ourselves quite unable to impose our orders upon them; for the debt has taken away our right to command. And this also thou must know well, my master, that the majority of those serving in thy armies have deserted to the enemy. If, therefore, it was only necessary that Belisarius be sent to Italy, then thou hast made the best preparation possible for the war; for I am already in the very midst of Italy. If, however, it is thy will to overcome thy foes in the war, provision must also be made for the other necessary things. For no man could, I think, be a general without men to support him. It is therefore needful that, above all others, my spearmen and guards should be sent me, and, next to them, a very large force of Huns and other barbarians is needed, to whom money must also be given immediately.

John, the nephew of Vitalianus, was sent with the letter to Constantinople in 545. He promised to return as quickly as possible, but true to his style, other things caught his attention. While Belisarius was waiting at Ravenna, John saw an opportunity to further his own interests by marrying Justina, the daughter of Germanus, the great-niece of the emperor.

So the year wore on with no help for the imperial arms in Italy. With no other option, Belisarius left the command at Ravenna to Justinus and crossed the Adriatic to Dyrrhachium to recruit troops for a new army. On arriving, he wrote another letter to the emperor, explaining the situation.

There, in the course of time, the newly wedded John, who was more difficult to handle than ever because of his new standing and connections to the emperor, met him. With him came the Armenian General Isaac, brother of Aratius and Narses the general, and a considerable army of Romans and barbarians.

The emperor also sent Narses the eunuch to the rulers of the Heruli, in order to persuade them to march to Italy. Many of the Heruli under Philemuth joined him and marched to Thrace, with the intention of spending the winter there and then to march to

Belisarius in Dyrrhachium. They were also accompanied by John the glutton.

Meanwhile in 545, Totila was steadily strengthening his position in central Italy, and the Ostrogoths took Firmum and Asculum.

Herodianus had been besieged in Spoletium on the Via Flaminia for long, and finally agreed to surrender the strategic city if no help came within thirty days. As safeguard for the agreement, his son was given as hostage. Finally, after the thirty days had passed, he surrendered himself, the garrison, and the city into the hands of the Goths. But the real reason for the surrender most likely was the fact that Belisarius had threatened to investigate certain financial irregularities on his part. Herodianus would later continue to fight for the Goths and was reckoned the only deserting Roman general in the war.

Despite a valiant defense of Asise (Assisi) by the allied Goth Sisifridus, this, too, was lost to the Romans. Perusia still held out, but Totila sought to bribe Cyprianus with great sums of money to surrender the city and its garrison. When this scheme failed, he bribed one of Cyprianus's bodyguards, Ulifus, to kill the general. The plot succeeded and the brave Cyprianus was killed, but his soldiers refused to surrender and the Goths raised the siege of Perusia.

12

THE SECOND
SIEGE OF ROME

In the autumn of 545, Totila marched to Rome and commenced a regular siege of the city. His former maneuvers in the region had mainly been aimed at blockading Rome and limiting the movements of the garrison.

Everywhere he went, Totila kept true to his policy of treating the populace well and only demanded the taxes that would otherwise have been paid to the emperor. Provisions were duly paid for, and no plundering took place. It is hardly surprising that the locals viewed his growing kingdom with some favor when they thought of the rapacity of the Roman tax gatherers.

Operations around Rome

Against the orders of both Belisarius and Bessas, commandant of Rome, Artasires the Persian and Barbatian the Thracian—two of Belisarius's guardsmen—had undertaken a sally. The Goths were initially defeated; many were killed and the rest turned to flight. But during the pursuit, the Romans fell into an ambush in which they lost most of their troops. After this defeat, the garrison no longer dared to challenge the besiegers.

With the Gothic fleet in control of Neapolis and the interception of most of the supply ships coming from Sicily, famine further demoralized and plagued the garrison.

While busying himself with the siege of Rome, Totila sent an army into Aemilia with orders to take Placentia, the last Roman-held city in the province, either by storm or surrender. When the garrison refused to surrender, the Goths settled down to besiege the city, which was already in need of provisions.

The year 546 had probably begun when Belisarius—still unable to move himself to the scene of action—sent Valentinus and Phocas, a bodyguard of his, with five hundred men to Portus to assist the garrison there, which was under the command of Innocentius. It was decided that these troops should attack the Gothic camp combined with a sally from the besieged city.

Bessas refused to allow any of his three thousand men to join the operation. The attack, though successful, achieved no decisive result, and the Roman relief force had to return to Portus.

A strong message was sent to Bessas, and he was warned that on a given day and hour the attack would be repeated, and he was asked to support the attack with a sally. Again he refused to commit any of his men. A deserter had informed Totila of the coming attack, and the Roman troops moving from Portus toward Rome soon found themselves ambushed. It was a disaster for the Romans, and most of the five hundred soldiers fell together with their officers.

Soon after this debacle, some corn ships sent by Pope Vigillius in Sicily were intercepted by the barbarians at Portus and taken with their cargoes. It was now clear to the Romans that resupply of Rome by the sea was no longer possible.

About May 546, another of the strategic cities of Italy fell. Placentia surrendered after a siege of almost a year in which the garrison in the end had even been forced to eat human flesh. Totila was now free to move his troops between Ticinum and the Gothic heartland and the valleys of the Arno and Tiber rivers.

Delegation to Totila

Famine was pressing ever harder on the populace of Rome, and the citizens, possibly without the knowledge of Bessas, sent a delegation led by the deacon Pelagius—nine years later to become pope— to Totila to negotiate a truce and eventual surrender of the city.

Totila received the delegation with a great show of outward reverence and affection, but before Pelagius was allowed to speak his intentions, he made clear three points.

First, there would be no pardon for the inhabitants of Sicily. He could not forget the treachery of 535, when this, the granary of Italy, had eagerly surrendered to the Roman troops, despite the respect shown it by the Gothic kings. Furthermore, the island had been the main source of supplies for the Romans ever since.

Second, there could be no talk of preserving the city walls of Rome. Totila argued that the destruction of the walls would also mean greater security for the inhabitants, who would not need to stand more sieges, but instead await the result of a regular battle.

Third, the runaway slaves in the Gothic army would not be returned to their Roman owners.

After Totila's speech, Pelagius replied that it was making a mockery of the ambassador's role if he was not allowed to ask for certain things. If these points were forbidden to be discussed, he saw no point in making any requests whatsoever to Totila. If he insisted on making such truceless war on the Sicilians who had never carried arms against the Goths, there could be little hope for the Romans who had actually fought against them in battle.

Thus Pelagius returned unsuccessful from his mission. The citizens then gathered in large numbers at the house of the generals, possibly the former headquarters of Belisarius on the Pincian Hill, where Bessas and Conon had their offices. They begged the Roman generals in pitiful desperation to give them food enough to at least keep them alive. If that could not be done, then they asked for leave to depart from the city. If that was unacceptable, then they asked that the imperials kill them outright instead of submitting them to the torture of starving to death.

Bessas and his officers calmly and gravely replied to this passionate outburst. None of the three requests could be granted. There was not enough food to issue rations for the entire civilian population of Rome, it would not be in the emperor's best interest to let them depart, and to kill them all would be an unholy deed. They were told Belisarius was expected to relieve Rome soon, and they should patiently await his arrival.

Evidently, Bessas and his fellow generals did not intend to alleviate the suffering of the common people. Indeed, they were even trading on their misery. A large supply of corn had been stored in the magazines of the city, but these supplies were strictly reserved for the soldiers of the emperor. The generals sold these supplies to wealthy Romans at high prices. In the end, the price of a bushel of wheat was seven gold coins—an enormous price. Bran was sold at a quarter of this to the wealthy middle class. Animal food was even harder to come by. Whenever Bessas's bodyguards captured an ox during a sally, they sold it for fifty gold coins.

These prices were beyond the means of most of the citizens of Rome, who were living on the nettles growing everywhere within the walls. Before long these nettles, which were cooked into a soup, became the staple diet of everybody in Rome, as even the patricians did not have more gold to spend. Only the garrison still had supplies.

But before long there were no more military supplies to be sold, as even the soldiers' rations were becoming smaller and smaller. Procopius describes in vivid detail the appearance of the population: their flesh was wasted away, their skin was dark and livid, they moved around like specters rather than men, and many, while still walking among the ruins and chewing the nettles between their teeth, suddenly sank to the earth and died. Even unaccustomed foods such as dogs and mice were becoming rare luxuries, and stories of cannibalism were becoming more and more frequent.

At length Bessas relented and agreed for a large sum of money to allow the civilians to leave the city. The Goths, however, were not prepared to relieve the city of so many hungry mouths and so pursued or killed any people trying to leave the city. Even the flight itself was too much for the exhausted and starved people, many of whom died after having made it safely through the Gothic lines.

Council of War held at Dyrrhachium

But what was actually delaying the relief? In a council of war held at Dyrrhachium, Belisarius had pleaded that the relief of Rome was the most pressing duty of the Romans, and that the best course of action would be to embark the whole army on ships, in which they would be able to reach the mouth of the Tiber in five days. His constant rival John, the nephew of Vitalianus, on the other hand, suggested that they should strike at the south of Italy, where the Goths were vulnerable. A landing should be made in one of the southern ports, and then Totila could be taken in the rear by a rapid march through Samnium and Campania. Belisarius in turn argued that it would take an army forty days at least to reach Rome by a land march from Hydruntum, whereas it would take the fleet only five days to reach Portus at Rome.

Neither general could convince the other, and Belisarius could not force the husband of the emperor's great-niece to obey him. So a compromise was reached—a compromise perhaps worse than either of the two plans because it meant splitting the forces of the already small Roman army. Belisarius and Isaac would take one part of the troops and sail for the Tiber, while John with the rest was to land in the south, retake Calabria, and move north to Rome to unite with Belisarius.

Belisarius set sail but met with contrary winds and was forced to take shelter in the harbor of Hydruntum. The Goths, who had returned to besiege the city, fled when they saw the fleet approaching and were so frightened that the flight only stopped when they reached Brundisium (Brindisi), some fifty miles away. From there they sent messengers to Totila to tell him of the invasion of Calabria. Totila replied that they should hold out as long as possible, but he did not relax the siege of Rome. Soon the winds changed, and Belisarius reached Portus with no further incidents.

Shortly afterward, John crossed the Adriatic and landed close to Brundisium. As luck would have it some of his soldiers managed to take two Gothic scouts prisoner. One of them he killed immediately, but the other begged for his life and promised in return to help the Romans. John asked him to lead them to where the Gothic horses were pasturing. Accordingly the grateful barbarian led him to a plain where the horses were gathered. The Romans took the horses and then attacked the camp of the unsuspecting Goths. The barbarians were completely surprised and easily defeated, and so Calabria was retaken.

Canusium (Canosa) was then taken with no resistance, and Tullianus, a former governor of Bruttium and Lucania, of the family of Venantius, went to John. He spoke candidly of the oppression by the imperial *logothetes*, whose actions had compelled them against their will to accept Gothic rule. But if John would promise to prevent the ravages of his troops, Tullianus would use his influence to persuade the inhabitants of the two provinces to surrender to the Romans. John promised, and so, through Tullianus, Bruttium and Lucania were recovered for the empire.

Here, however, John stopped his advance to Rome. Totila had sent three hundred horsemen to Capua (Santa Maria Capua Vetere) to observe his progress, and despite the urgent messages of Belisarius, John could not be moved. Instead he turned south and defeated Rhecimundus, who was holding Rhegium for Totila with an army of Goths, Moors, and Roman deserters. While it was a crushing victory, it had little importance for the main operations of Rome, where his troops were sorely needed.

After the defeat of Rhecimundus, John moved to Carvarium (Carvaro) in Apulia, where he stayed.

Consequently, Belisarius at Portus had little option but to try to relieve Rome with the troops he had at hand.

ATTEMPTED RELIEF OF ROME

About four miles above Portus, Totila had caused a boom to be placed across the Tiber at its tightest place to block ships bearing provisions for the starving city. This boom consisted of long beams of timber lashed together and forming a kind of floating bridge. It was protected by a wooden tower at either end and further strengthened by an iron chain stretched from shore to shore a little below it, in order to prevent floating objects from damaging and breaking the boom.

As usual, Belisarius prepared carefully for the task ahead. Two broad barges were lashed together upon which was erected a wooden tower sufficiently high to overtop the bridge. Leaving nothing to chance, he had some of his soldiers pose as deserters to measure the bridge and its defenses. To the top of the tower was hoisted a boat filled with a combustible mixture of pitch, sulfur, and resin. Towing and protecting the barges was a fleet of two hundred *dromones* filled with provisions for the garrison and soldiers. High wooden ramparts had been constructed on the decks with loopholes for the archers. Infantry and cavalry were stationed on the riverbank to support the ships and to prevent an enemy attack on Portus.

With the preparations ready, Belisarius left Isaac in charge of Portus, where he left all his reserves, his stores, and his wife. Isaac was given strict orders that no matter what information he received, he was under no circumstances to leave his post. As Portus was the only stronghold in Roman possession in the region, it was imperative that it did not fall into enemy hands. At the same time word was sent to Bessas to support the operation with a sortie from the city against the Gothic camps. But this message, as with so many others, would not stir the lethargic commandant of Rome, so the Goths would be able to focus their full attention on Belisarius's relief attempt.

The fleet was set in motion up the Tiber. The archers on the boats easily defeated the Gothic guards on either side of the river, and the Romans were able to sever the chain across the river and sail on. Here the fighting became intense. At the right opportunity, Belisarius moved his floating tower up to the Gothic tower commanding the north end of the bridge. The boat laden with combustibles was set alight and thrown into the middle of the little fort, which was at once in flames. Two hundred Goths with their leader, Osdas, died in the fire. Encouraged by the success, the Romans pressed the remaining barbarians more strongly. The garrison at the bridge began to panic and was soon in full flight, and the Romans could begin to dismantle the boom. It seemed that the operation was already a success. But that was not to be.

A rumor of the success of the morning's operations, particularly the severing of the chain, had reached Isaac. Envious at having no share in the victory, he forgot all plans and orders, and moved out with a hundred horsemen, crossed the Isola Sacra, and attacked the Gothic garrison of Ostia, commanded by Roderic. In the first rush, Roderic was mortally wounded, and the Goths turned and fled. The Romans immediately entered the Gothic camp and began in complete disorder to plunder it of valuables. While they were thus engaged, the Goths returned and easily routed the Romans. They killed most of them and took the rest prisoner, including Isaac.

That this foolish attack failed was in itself no great disaster, but as fortune would have it, a messenger escaped from the fight and brought the news to Belisarius that Isaac was captured. To Belisarius, who had no knowledge of Isaac's rash expedition, the message meant that Portus, his reserves, his provisions, and his wife were taken too. He gave the signal to retreat, in the hope that he might surprise the victorious barbarians and retake Portus, his only base of operations in the region. When he reached Portus and found it safe, the victory at the bridge was lost. His great anger at discovering Isaac's folly and the missed opportunity of relieving the starving Rome was too much for him, and he fell ill with fever. At one time it was thought he might die, and for some months he could not take any active part in the campaign. Isaac paid for his folly two days later, as Totila was so enraged by the death of Roderic, the commandant at Ostia, that he put him to death.

TREACHERY IN ROME

Meanwhile, in Rome, conditions were becoming more and more unbearable. Bessas was more concerned with making money on his illicit dealings selling the supplies of the garrison to wealthy people than with doing the job of a general. He did nothing to cooperate with Belisarius because each day the siege dragged on, he could make more money. Accordingly, the discipline and morale of the troops were steadily decreasing, and the watch on the walls was becoming more and more negligent. Few soldiers were on guard, and they were not punished if they slept or even did not show up at all. No officers went on rounds to check up on the sentinels, nor did any citizens assist in the watch on the walls, as they were now few in number and too starved to serve.

At the Porta Asinaria, four Isaurians were stationed as guards. They were tired of the siege, tired of the smaller and smaller rations, and perhaps thinking of the kind treatment they had received from Totila after their surrender at Neapolis. These Isaurians decided to betray the city to the Goths. Letting themselves down by ropes from the battlements, they went to Totila's camp and revealed their intention. He thanked them warmly and offered them large sums of money if the scheme to betray the city was successful. When he was convinced of the Isaurians' sincerity, Totila sent the entire Gothic army to the Porta Asinaria at nightfall. While the other Roman sentinels slept, the four Isaurians let up four Goths by ropes. As soon as they were within the walls they hastened to the gate and with their axes severed the great bar of wood that kept the gates closed and shattered the iron locks. The gates were then opened wide, and the barbarians entered the city December 17, 546.

Totila was still expecting some treachery, however, so he ordered the Goths to stay together until dawn. Meanwhile, the city was in an uproar. Bessas and Conon with the Roman garrison of three thousand troops were retreating through the northern Porta Flaminia, just as the Gothic garrison had done ten years earlier.

The civilians, who had no chance of escape, sought shelter in the various churches of Rome awaiting the Gothic wrath. When day dawned and Totila received news of the flight of the Roman army, he let his barbarians loose on the city while he went to the Church of St. Peter to give thanks for his victory. The Goths took all the treasure Bessas had accumulated through his illegal dealings. The most valuable loot was to be given to the king to form a new royal treasure, but the rest the warriors could keep themselves.

At the church, the king met the now-submissive deacon Pelagius, who begged him to spare the population. Totila listened to the request and at once sent messengers through the city saying that the plunder might continue, but no more blood was to be shed. Of course, the amount of blood that could have been shed was limited, as only five hundred citizens were still left in Rome. Compared to the once-thriving city with at least half a million inhabitants, the contrast and emptiness must have been vast.

On the day after the capture of Rome, Totila gave a stirring speech to his army and attributed the victory to his policy of acting righteously toward both Romans and Goths. He gave a speech with quite different content later that day, upbraiding the remaining Roman senators for their lack of faith and their treachery to the Gothic nation. The traitor Herodianus, who surrendered Spoletium, and the four Isaurian soldiers were brought before the

Senate and praised by Totila for their decision to support the Goths.

Later, Pelagius succeeded in calming him and was soon after sent to Constantinople with a Roman orator named Theodorus to propose terms of peace. The letter to the emperor said:

> As to what has transpired in the city of Rome, since I suppose thou hast learned everything, I have decided to remain silent. But as to the purpose for which I have sent these envoys, thou shalt straightway be informed. We demand that thou, for thy part, take to thyself the advantages which flow from peace and also grant them to us. These advantages are recalled and exemplified most admirably in the lives of [Emperor] Anastasius and Theodoric [the Great], who ruled as kings not long ago, and filled their whole reigns with peace and prosperity. And if this same condition should perchance please thee, thou wouldst properly be called my father, and thou wilt also have us hereafter as allies against whomsoever thou mayest wish to use us.

These courtesies were supplemented by a verbal threat that if Justinian would not consent to peace, Rome would be razed and the Goths would invade Illyricum. The emperor's only reply was that Belisarius had full powers for the conduct of the war, and any proposals for peace had to be addressed to him. There would never be peace with the Ostrogoths, who had so damaged the cause of the Roman Empire.

The war could even be intensified, because Justinian had just signed a truce with Persia and so in 546 could begin to transfer troops from the East to the Italian theater.

Meanwhile in Italy, the operations in Lucania, under the guidance of Tullianus, who had gathered the peasants of the province, proceeded with some success. Together with three hundred Antae, a tribe from the area of modern Bosnia, they were holding the Apennine passes against the Goths and successfully repulsed some troops that Totila had sent against them.

The Gothic king wanted to move to the south of Italy but feared either weakening his army by leaving a garrison in Rome, or giving

Belisarius, still lying sick in Portus, the chance of recovering it if it was left unguarded.

Accordingly he razed one-third of the walls of Rome so the city could not be defended and was about to destroy the buildings inside when he received a letter from Belisarius. It must be noted that when the sources speak of the "destruction" of the city wall, it does not entail the complete removal of the wall and its foundations. It appears to mean that the upper galleries of parts of the walls were destroyed and only some few breaches were made, as the lower 20 feet of the wall with its concrete core was almost impossible to destroy.

The letter from Belisarius said:

> While the creation of beauty in a city which has not been beautiful before could only proceed from men of wisdom who understand the meaning of civilization, the destruction of beauty which already exists would be naturally expected only of men who lack understanding, and who are not ashamed to leave to posterity this token of their character. Now among all the cities under the sun Rome is agreed to be the greatest and the most noteworthy. For it has not been created by the ability of one man, nor has it attained such greatness and beauty by a power of short duration, but a multitude of monarchs, many companies of the best men, a great lapse of time, and an extraordinary abundance of wealth have availed to bring together in that city all other things that are in the whole world, and skilled workers besides. Thus, little by little, have they built the city, such as you behold it, thereby leaving to future generations memorials of the ability of them all, so that insult to these monuments would properly be considered a great crime against the men of all time; for by such action the men of former generations are robbed of the memorials of their ability, and future generations of the sight of their works. Such, then, being the facts of the case, be well assured of this, that one of two things must necessarily take place: either you will be defeated by the emperor in this struggle, or, should it so fall out, you will triumph over him.

Now, in the first place, supposing that you are victorious, if you should dismantle Rome, you would not have destroyed the possession of some other man, but your own city, excellent Sir, and, on the other hand, if you preserve it, you will naturally enrich yourself by a possession the fairest of all; but if, in the second place, it should perchance fall to your lot to experience the worse fortune, in saving Rome you would be assured of abundant gratitude on the part of the victor, but by destroying the city you will make it certain that no plea for mercy will any longer be left to you, and in addition to this you will have reaped no benefit from the deed. Furthermore, a reputation that corresponds with your conduct will be your portion among all men, and it stands waiting for you according as you decide either way. For the quality of the acts of rulers determines, of necessity, the quality of the repute which they win from their acts.

Totila read the letter over and over again, and finally dismissed the Roman messengers with the assurance that he would do no further damage to the buildings of the Eternal City. He then withdrew the bulk of his troops to Mount Algidus (Ceraso), about twenty miles southeast of Rome, and in 547 marched into Lucania with the rest of the army to prosecute the war against John and Tullianus. Rome, though not ruined, was left without a single inhabitant. It may seem surprising that Totila left Rome undefended, but his army was never large, and leaving a garrison large enough to hold Rome with its damaged walls would weaken his army too much. Also, Rome had lost most of its strategic significance with the loss of its inhabitants and wealth. It was much more important to Totila to gain more victories over the Roman armies, each of which would swell his ranks.

After the Goths captured Rome, a month or two elapsed with no great operations on either side.

Lucania Lost

In his train, Totila dragged the remaining Roman senators, who were forced to ask their tenants in Lucania to lay down their weapons and return to till the land. In return they would no longer be tenants but receive their own land from their masters. Accordingly the peasants deserted from the Roman army and returned home to their farms. With most of his troops gone, Tullianus fled along with the three hundred Antae, who joined the army of John, now in Hydruntum. In this way the barbarians recovered the whole province. The senators were then sent to rejoin their wives and children in the cities of Campania, where they were living under a strong Gothic guard.

In almost complete control of the whole region, Totila dispersed his army into small war bands, which overran the area. When the Roman troops under John learned of this, he sent a force against them. The scattered barbarians, who did not expect the Romans to leave the safety of their walls, were surprised, and many were killed.

As a result of this, Totila again collected his army and proceeded to make camp on the slopes of Mount Garganus (Gargano) by the Adriatic Sea. Here, according to Procopius, he occupied the same camp that Hannibal's troops had built during the Second Punic War some 760 years earlier. In south Italy, only the strategic port of Hydruntum was now left for the Romans.

SPOLETIUM RECOVERED

Spoletium was at this time lost to the Goths through the treachery of Martinianus, a feigned deserter who won Totila's favor. After the capture of Spoletium, the city walls had been razed, but a fortress had been made out of a nearby amphitheater. There a garrison of Goths and Roman deserters was established to guard the region.

Martinianus was sent to Spoletium, where he succeeded in winning the friendship of fifteen Roman soldiers whom he persuaded to return to the Roman army after having done some great deed against the Goths. At the same time he sent a message to the garrison in Perusia, asking for troops to support the stratagem.

Odalgan the Hun was in command of the troops in Perusia since the assassination of Cyprianus. On receiving the message he brought a force to Spoletium. When Martinianus learned that the Roman forces were close, he, along with the fifteen Roman deserters, killed the commander of the garrison and opened the gates of the fortress to the Romans. Most of the Gothic garrison was killed and the rest brought as prisoners to Belisarius.

John moved from Hydruntum and occupied Tarentum, which was better situated for a strike into Apulia. The city itself was large and unfortified, but part of it was lying on an isthmus, which he fortified and there placed the inhabitants of the city along with a garrison.

As a countermove to this, Totila stationed four hundred Goths at Acherontia (Acherenza), a high hill-city on the borders of Lucania and Apulia, from where it could command both provinces. He then marched away to threaten Ravenna—he knew he could not take it, with the Roman command of the sea—but was soon recalled by unexpected bad tidings.

THE ROMANS RECAPTURE ROME

For six weeks or more after the evacuation of Rome, it had been left completely empty of inhabitants. As soon as Belisarius recovered from his fever, he wanted to see the extent of the damage done to Rome, so he formed a daring design.

He first made a reconnaissance of the city with a thousand soldiers. The Goths on Mount Algidus reacted to this move but were defeated in the skirmish that followed.

A little later, on his second expedition to Rome, he brought his entire army, apart from a small garrison left at Portus, and this time the Goths did not dare interfere. After seeing the damage done to the walls by Totila's troops, he knew they were not completely irreparable. All his soldiers and the populace from the surrounding countryside were put to work repairing the great walls of Rome. There was no lime or other proper building materials, and there was no time to procure any. Instead blocks of tufa from the old city wall of Servius Tullius, rubble, and parts of masonry were put to use. These hasty repairs can still be observed in several places in modern Rome.

The ditch dug around the city just before the first siege had not been filled, and now a palisade of stakes was added to it. In just twenty-five days, the enormous task of refortifying Rome was finished, albeit roughly. Only the gates of the city could not be replaced, as there were no craftsmen left in Rome.

In the same period, Belisarius brought large amounts of provisions into the city.

TOTILA ATTEMPTS TO RECAPTURE ROME

When Totila, on his way to Ravenna, heard of the reoccupation of Rome, he marched there with great speed, hoping to interrupt the work of the Romans. His army made camp by the Tiber, and at sunrise the next day the whole barbarian army assaulted the defenders of the wall. The furious battle lasted from dawn till dusk. To make up for the absence of proper gates, Belisarius had stationed his bravest men in the gateways to keep the enemy away. His other troops were deployed on the walls to provide missile fire. The defense kept up and was further strengthened after the first Gothic attack by planting caltrops in all the gateways. The heavy fighting and constant missile fire from the walls caused great casualties to the barbarians.

But the Goths were not finished. The next day they again made a fierce assault, but were repulsed with losses. The Romans sallied out and were on the verge of being caught when they pursued too far, but another sally rescued the endangered troops.

The exhausted Goths rested for some days and then made their final assault on the walls of Rome. Again a Roman sally threw the barbarians off balance. The standard-bearer of Totila was struck down, and a furious fight took place around the body. By cutting off the hand clutching the standard, the barbarians succeeded in rescuing the royal flag, but the body was taken by the Romans and stripped of its armor while the Goths were fleeing. Again, the barbarians had lost large numbers of soldiers in the unsuccessful attempt to storm the city.

Totila had to admit that Rome was indeed lost. Again the invincible Belisarius held it, and the attempts to retake it had only caused serious losses to the Gothic army. An army that consisted to a large part of Roman deserters was brittle and endangered by defeats that would change the allegiance of the deserters. The Gothic nobles bitterly reproached Totila for not having left any troops in Rome. As mentioned before, this was somewhat unfair, as Totila would have severely limited his offensive options by occupying the now-otherwise unimportant city. It was now little more than a road hub that no longer held the enormous prestige its occupation had entailed earlier in the war.

There was little Totila could do, and he was too wise in the ways of war to waste more time on the empty city. He retreated to Tibur and broke down all the bridges over the Tiber, apart from the Pons Milvius, to prevent Belisarius from following him. The city and citadel of Tibur, which the Goths themselves had earlier destroyed, was now rebuilt and a Gothic garrison stationed there.

Meanwhile, Belisarius had new gates prepared and fitted into the empty archways of Rome. They were fitted with massive locks, the keys of which were sent to the emperor in Constantinople. And so in May 547 ended the twelfth year of the war and the third year of Belisarius's second command.

It can be inferred from Procopius that at this time the north and center of Italy were almost entirely in the possession of the Goths. The only exceptions appear to have been Ravenna and Ancona on the northern Adriatic, Spoletium in Umbria, and Rome and its harbor Portus. Samnium, Campania, and northern Apulia were also for the most part strongly held by the Goths. Calabria was so far dominated by the ports of Hydruntum and Tarentum that it might be considered a possession of the emperor's. In Lucania, the peasants under the command of the family of Venantius were still restless and endeavoring to return to the empire. Bruttium probably, and Sicily certainly, were governed by the empire.

One of the reasons for the languid and desultory character of the war was the determination of the emperor to spend no more money on it than he could possibly help. From the slender remains of Roman-held Italy, Belisarius had to squeeze out the funds necessary to support his own army and that of John. Another cause was the evident want of cooperation between the two generals due to the fact that John belonged to the party of Germanus, the nephew of Justinian, and Belisarius, through his wife, to that of Empress

Theodora, at the imperial court. This discord was also evident to Totila, who took great advantage of the lack of cooperation between the two Roman generals.

For Totila it was also a difficult struggle. His army was so small he could afford only a few garrisons in the most-important cities. Almost every battle he undertook, if lost, would be disastrous to the Gothic cause, as he was the embodiment of the Gothic nation. Most of Italy was completely ravaged from twelve years of war and a lack of provisions was a serious problem everywhere. The Romans could still send provisions to the ports, but Totila had no such option. As mentioned earlier, it was imperative for him to gain recognition from other barbarian nations or from the emperor in some way. While he did succeed in collecting the revenues otherwise sent to the emperor, these had by now dwindled to almost nothing, with much of the population killed in the war and by the plague. Without more recognition and an appearance of legitimacy, he would have a hard time gaining the trust of the provincials and the deserters whom he needed so much. Totila had to appear as a reasonable alternative to the rule of the Romans, as Theodoric the Great had been able to, otherwise he would suffer from constant desertions and treachery. If Totila was not able, who but the Romans could protect Italy from the Franks, the Burgundians, the Langobards, the remains of the Huns, and the other, more-primitive barbarian tribes hovering on the borders?

THE ROMAN SENATE RESCUED

Not long after, Totila lost his other great prize of war, his senatorial hostages in Campania. John, who had been besieging the Goths in Acherontia for some time in vain, made a sudden dash into Campania, marching day and night without stopping. At Capua he met and defeated a body of cavalry sent by Totila. The Goths were almost completely destroyed, and the few barbarians who managed to retreat to Totila brought tidings of an enormous Roman army to remove the shame of their flight.

With these troops in retreat, John could proceed to liberate the senators and their wives from Gothic captivity. The rescued prisoners were speedily sent to safety in Sicily together with seventy Roman soldiers, formerly deserters to the Gothic armies, who had now returned to their old allegiance.

Totila was greatly angered by having suffered another defeat, this time hardly without a battle. While it was too late to prevent the hostages from escaping, at least he could take out his revenge. So he set off in pursuit of the Roman general, who again had retreated into Lucania. He marched rapidly until at nightfall he was close to the Roman camp.

With his ten thousand troops compared to John's one thousand, he could have gained a complete victory if he had but waited to the next morning and surrounded the Roman camp. But impatience got the better of him, and he gave the signal for attack at once. The Romans were surprised and lost about a hundred men, but the rest, among which were John and his right hand, the Herulian chieftain Arufus, escaped into the night. The next day John gathered the remains of the army and retreated to Hydruntum.

Procopius relates an interesting story from the aftermath of the battle. One of John's generals, Gilacius the Armenian, commanded a small force of Armenians. He could not speak Greek, Latin, Gothic, or anything else but Armenian. When he was captured by some Goths in the rout, they asked him who he was. He could only answer "Gilacius, strategos" ("Gilacius, general"), the only Greek words he knew, from having heard them often in the camp. The story shows how large the barbarian element in the Roman army truly was.

A LULL IN THE WAR

For two years after this skirmish, no event of great importance occurred, but slowly the Roman cause was receding. Justinian sent few troops, and only in driblets commanded by incapable generals. Somewhat more than two thousand men were sent in the autumn of 547—a few men under Pacurius, son of Peranius and Sergius, the inept nephew of Solomon; three hundred Heruli under Verus the Herulian; eight hundred men under Varazes the Armenian; and more than a thousand under Valerianus, the general of Armenia. In the summer of 548, two thousand infantry were sent to Sicily.

These troops were too few to enable Belisarius to take the initiative, particularly as there was no cooperation between John and him.

The story of the Herulian chieftain Verus and his three hundred fellow barbarians is worth telling. With little self-restraint—the mark of the primitive Herulians— Verus was constantly in a state of intoxication. He landed at Hydruntum and marched with his band of warriors to Brundisium and encamped near the town. Seeing the warriors thus encamped in an undefended position, Totila exclaimed:

> One of two things must be true. Either Verus has a large army, or he is a very unwise man. Let us then proceed against him instantly, that either we may make trial of the man's army or that he may realize his own silliness.

Accordingly, he advanced with his army and easily routed the diminutive Herulian army, which was only rescued by the accidental but timely arrival of a squadron of the Roman navy. More than two hundred Herulians were killed in the skirmish.

Valerianus, the general of Armenia, lacked courage and soldierly capability. With his thousand men he lingered for months at Salona, afraid to cross the Adriatic. Then, when a council of war was held at Hydruntum and a march north into Picenum was resolved upon, he would not face the perils and hardships of the march but took ship again and sailed to Ancona, where he shut himself up in the city.

SIEGE OF ROSCIANUM

The only item of interest in these two campaigns lies in the defense of Roscianum (Rossano) in 548. In Roscianum there was a considerable number of wealthy and noble Italians, refugees from the parts of Italy occupied by the barbarians, among whom were Deopheron, son of Venantius and brother of Tullianus, the bitter enemies of the Goths in Lucania. To defend this city, John had sent three hundred Illyrians under the command of Chalazar the Hun. Further, Belisarius had sent one hundred troops to assist the garrison.

Late in 547, the emperor ordered Belisarius to unite his troops with the reinforcements sent to Calabria and from there engage the enemy. Accordingly, Belisarius picked out nine hundred men and set sail for Calabria. A storm forced him to put in at Crotona (Crotone), from where he sent his cavalry under Phazas the Iberian and Barbatian to hold the passes into the region.

On the march they met, apparently by accident, a smaller Gothic force sent by Totila to attack the city. In the following skirmish the barbarians were severely defeated and fled, leaving two hundred of their number on the plain. The security of the victory made the Roman force careless, and they pitched their tents wide and wandered off in small groups to forage. Totila, with three thousand warriors, suddenly burst out of the mountains and attacked them. Their general, Phazas, fell in the first onslaught, and his death caused the Roman forces to waver and flee. When the news was brought to Belisarius in Crotona, he appears to have been alarmed for the safety of Crotona itself, which was not properly fortified, and so sailed to Messana in Sicily.

The garrison of Roscianum was now hard pressed by Totila, who had settled down to besiege it. At length the garrison agreed to surrender the city if no help should reach it before the middle of the summer of 548. When the day dawned on the appointed day, the sails of the imperial fleet could be seen in the distance. Belisarius, John, and Valerianus had held a council of war at Hydruntum and decided to send a fleet to the help of Roscianum. At the happy sight, the hopes of the garrison were raised, and they refused to surrender. But a storm arose that the Roman fleet did not dare face, and the ships had to return to Crotona. Many weeks passed, and again the fleet appeared on the horizon. Determined to oppose a landing, Totila stationed troops along the shore. At that sight, the Roman fleet let down its anchors and hovered on the coast for a while. With no place to land, it eventually weighed anchor and returned again to Crotona.

Another council of war was held, and the generals decided to try a diversion. Belisarius was to bring provisions to the garrison at Rome, and the two other generals were to march into Picenum and attack the besieging armies there. It was on this occasion that

Valerianus distinguished himself by not marching, but instead sailing to the friendly shelter of Ancona.

But everything was in vain, and Totila did not raise the siege of Roscianum. In the end the garrison asked for mercy and begged for forgiveness for its unfaithfulness in not surrendering at the appointed time. Totila gave the garrison the benefit of the old capitulation but tortured and then killed the Roman commander, Chalazar the Hun, whom he held responsible for their obstinacy. Totila further let the ones who joined the Gothic army not only keep their lives, but also their possessions. The result was that all but eighty of the garrison enlisted with the barbarians. Totila took all the Italian nobles in the city captive.

Mutiny at Rome

At Rome, the garrison, with long arrears of pay due to them from the bankrupt treasury, could no longer endure the spectacle of their commandant Conon, who had renewed the business of selling corn to the wealthy out of the military supplies. They rose in mutiny in the spring of 548 and killed their greedy general. Knowing the severe penalty of mutiny, they sent a delegation of priests to Constantinople, asking for amnesty for their crime and full discharge of the arrears of pay due to them from the imperial treasury. If these demands were not met, they would surrender to the Goths. The emperor had little choice and complied with the demands, promising to pay the troops.

The Recall of Belisarius

In June 548, Belisarius had now been in Italy more than four years, and little had been done—chiefly from lack of money and support from the emperor. He felt it was time either to proceed with the war with adequate resources or to quit it altogether. Accordingly, his wife, Antonina, was sent in the spring of 548 to her patron at court, Empress Theodora, to get her assurance that Belisarius would receive more resources to carry on the war more effectively. When she arrived at the capital, she found that an event had changed everything at the imperial court: around June 28, Theodora had died.

When Antonina received the news of her ally's death, she at once changed plans. With Theodora dead, her party at court had lost power to the party of Germanus, Justinian's favorite nephew and now indisputably the second person in the state. If somebody were allowed to end the war in Italy, surely Germanus would be the one selected.

The emperor was sick and tired of the Gothic war and was more interested in recovering the eastern kingdom of Lazica, whose king had appealed for aid against Persian oppression. Antonina knew she would therefore be unable to secure troops and money for her husband, and instead she petitioned the emperor to recall him from the war. This favor was granted.

Belisarius returned to Constantinople early in 549. His wealth had increased during his second command in Italy, but his glory was somewhat tarnished by five years of campaigning with little to show for it. He was received with honor and reappointed general of the East, but never took up the position. He was also given the rank of *magister militum praesentalis* and given precedence before all other consuls and patricians, even those who had held the titles longer. With these events, Belisarius, who had played the greatest role in the Gothic War, passes from its history. But it would not be his final battle.

Later Years of Belisarius

In 559, the Cotrigur Huns under the command of King Zabergan crossed the frozen Danube and struck across the provinces of Moesia and through the Balkan passes to Thrace. Here the king divided his troops into three divisions, sending one south against the cities of Greece and another into the Thracian Chersonese, hoping to cross into Asia. The third division—seven thousand cavalry that he commanded himself—struck straight at the capital of Constantinople. By this raid he wanted to show the might of the Cotrigurs, as opposed to the Utigur Huns, who were allied with the Romans.

Constantinople was the most-strongly fortified city of the world at the time, but earthquakes had damaged the Long Walls of Emperor Anastasius, which enclosed the outer suburbs of

Constantinople, and Justinian had not had the money or inclination to restore them. So King Zabergan, perhaps rather surprised, and his seven thousand Huns could easily cross the walls through the breaches. The historian Agathias describes their depredations beyond the walls in all their horror. Vast numbers of civilians were captured and forced to follow the horde on its marches. Nuns were tortured and raped in their monasteries before having to walk along in the great lines of captives, with little food. Pregnant women gave birth at the side of the road, and the newborns were left to be eaten by animals as the famished prisoners were forced to march on.

No enemies resisted the Huns, and they soon pillaged their way to the village of Melantias, some eighteen miles from Constantinople. There were almost no troops defending Constantinople, as Justinian's unwise policies had severely depleted the standing army to one hundred fifty thousand, and they had to fight in Italy, fight in the East, protect against religious rebellions in Alexandria, and watch the long borders of the empire. The *scholarii*, or household troops, had been ruined by eighty years of lack of discipline. During the time of Theodosius (379–395), the household troops contained handpicked soldiers, the bravest of the Roman armies. Later, in the time of Zeno (474–491), and particularly Justinian, it had become fashion among the nobility to offer large sums to have their names on the muster rolls. The smart uniforms and the access to the palace and the emperor were great incentives, and the emperors, who always needed money, were only happy to sell out the quality of the household troops. Thus these splendidly equipped parade soldiers were all that stood between the Huns, hardened through continual fighting since their childhood, and the capital of the Roman Empire.

The aging Justinian, now about seventy-seven, was desperate from fear. All the valuables between the Long Walls of Anastasius and the walls of Constantinople were brought into the city. Orders were given that the *scholarii* and even the senators had to assemble at the city gates, ready to defend the city.

And finally, Belisarius was ordered out of retirement, despite the emperor's still-strong jealousy. Belisarius brought three hundred of his retired veterans who had served under him in the Gothic War.

Though he had been retired ten years, Belisarius accepted the orders of the emperor. Just fifty-four at the time, those around him described him as already worn out with age. The hardship of his life and the fever he had succumbed to in Italy had made him old before his time. But he was still able to don his armor, and it seems his military genius was unimpaired.

Deemed useless as soldiers, the *scholarii* were ordered to man the city walls while Belisarius took his three hundred veterans— mounted on horses hastily brought from the imperial stables and the Circus—outside the city along with a crowd of peasants, who were eager to fight under the command of the famous Belisarius. The peasants were not trained soldiers, but he brought them along to give the impression of great numbers to the enemy and to act as a workforce.

He pitched camp at the village of Chettus, probably about nine miles from the Huns at Melantias. A deep ditch was dug around it, and more campfires than necessary were lit to make it appear that his force was larger than it was. Already his veterans were celebrating the victory, and Belisarius felt it necessary to address them in a speech, in which he explained that while he also believed in a victory, it could only be achieved by observing strict Roman discipline and by obeying his orders to the letter. Otherwise, their small army would not be able to defeat the Huns of King Zabergan.

The next day he ordered the peasants to cut down trees and to trail these behind the army, to raise a cloud of dust, again to make his army appear greater to the enemy.

Two thousand of the Hunnish horsemen advanced on him, but he was prepared. He had placed archers in the woods on both flanks of the Huns along with two hundred of his elite cavalrymen, and the rest of his veterans were in an open area in front of the barbarians. The showers of arrows narrowed the frontage of the Huns and forced them to charge his veterans in the center or turn back. During the battle, the peasants and citizens of Constantinople were ordered not to fight, but to shout and clash their arms, again to fool the barbarians into believing that his forces were more numerous.

With a steady shower of missiles on their flanks and in their back, the Huns were repelled by Belisarius's veterans, who seemed to have lost none of their strength and experience despite their age. The Huns were fleeing so quickly that they even forgot to turn and fire arrows against the pursuing foe, as was their custom when retreating.

Belisarius did not dare pursue them far, but the battle had been a victory, and four hundred Huns lay dead on the battlefield. The fleeing Huns so alarmed their comrades by their tales of the defeat that Zabergan decided to retreat across the Long Walls, and in this way Constantinople was saved.

As soon as it was apparent that Constantinople was no longer threatened, the jealous old emperor curtly ordered Belisarius to return to the capital. At the news of the recall, the Huns stopped their retreat, and in the end they had to be paid to go back beyond the Danube. On his return, Belisarius was again celebrated by the common people, while Justinian and the court saw to it that he was put into retirement again.

Only three years after his great victory, Belisarius was accused of knowing about a conspiracy against the emperor's life. The plot had been set in motion by an obscure civil servant named Sergius, who, upon discovery, indicated that Belisarius and his steward, Paulus, had been aware of the conspiracy. On December 5, 562, Justinian ordered a meeting of the Senate, where the confessions of the conspirators were read aloud. Belisarius was shocked by the charges, which were no doubt untrue. The emperor spared his life, but his guards and servants were taken away, and he was put under house arrest. On July 19, 563, Belisarius was restored to his former position. No doubt the emperor had been convinced of the old general's innocence.

About two years later, in March 565, Belisarius died—some eight months before Justinian. The imperial treasury appropriated his enormous fortune, amassed during all his wars. His only child, Joannina, had already died. According to a later, unreliable source, his wife, Antonina, now eighty-two, retired into a convent.

THE ROLE OF BELISARIUS IN THE WARS OF JUSTINIAN

It is almost impossible to overstate the importance of the person and character of Belisarius in relation to the wars of Justinian, and

in particular the Gothic and Vandal wars. In later ages he was laud-
ed as a hero and one of the greatest generals in history, together
with such names as Hannibal, Caesar, Napoleon, Rommel, and
others.

In many respects there would have been no wars of Justinian if
Belisarius had not been available. The peace on the eastern frontier
that enabled the Vandal War was due to him and his superior leadership and grasp of both tactics and strategy. The Vandal War,
which could easily have ended in disaster at the battle of Ad
Decimum in 533, was instead turned into an astounding victory,
the like of which had not been seen for centuries. The great success
in the Vandal War meant the Gothic War could be initiated with
the expectation of some success. Again Belisarius won a great victory, one that overshadowed even that of the Vandal War. In 540,
the Roman Empire had reconquered North Africa and Italy with
almost undamaged revenues and manpower. If not for the jealousy
of Justinian, who imagined Belisarius coveted his throne and therefore disrupted his general's operations by recalling him and limiting
his material support, there may have been little to stand between
the Romans and the complete reconquest of the empire. The
Visigoths were a broken puppet kingdom that had been ruled by
the Ostrogoths for decades and had little spirit left in them. The
Franks, while a great nation, had only fairly recently established
their power over Gaul and were primitive and ineffective in their
tactics and military abilities. Their kingdom was almost entirely
based on a still fairly intact Roman administration, and they were
outnumbered by perhaps more than ten to one with regard to their
subject Roman population.

The recovery of the empire was not to happen, but with
Belisarius's military ability, it was—in 540—a distinct possibility.
The chance would never come again.

13

THE THIRD
SIEGE OF ROME

W HEN BELISARIUS LEFT ITALY, THE SITUATION for the imperial cause was becoming more and more desperate. The fortress of Perusia, with its brave garrison that had held out for more than three years despite the assassination of General Cyprianus, was now finally overpowered and taken by storm before Belisarius reached Constantinople.

TOTILA REJECTED BY THE FRANKS

With the great general gone, Totila began to press the garrison of Rome more vigorously. The reason for this sudden burst of action, after two years of largely watching and ignoring Rome, was his suit for the hand of a Frankish princess.

Ever since the death of the Frankish King Clovis, and pre-eminently since the outbreak of the Gothic War, the Frankish kings had been advancing steadily toward a position of greater legitimacy than any of the other barbarian kingdoms set up on former Roman soil. With little hope to recover Gaul, the emperor had played along and accepted this, to avoid the Franks supporting the Goths too vigorously. Justinian had therefore formally sanctioned the Ostrogoths' cession of the southeast corner of Gaul to the Franks, and in doing so must inevitably have waived any shadow of a claim the empire might still have been supposed to possess to the remaining nine-tenths of Gaul. The Frankish kings had even begun to strike gold coins bearing their own image and inscription. Until now all the barbarian kings had been content to see their own image on the silver coins, while the at-times somewhat crudely carved image of the Roman emperor was struck on the gold coins.

While the Frankish kings were thus slowly assuming more independence, Totila's messengers came to one of the kings, Theudebert of Austrasia, asking on behalf of their master for his daughter's hand in marriage.

Theudebert refused, saying Totila neither was nor would ever be king of Italy because, having once been in possession of Rome, he could not hold it but had destroyed part of the city and abandoned the rest to his enemies. We do not know what became of Totila's matrimonial suit, but Theudebert's words stung him deeply, and he decided to remedy the situation.

The garrison of Rome now consisted of three thousand hand-picked soldiers commanded by Diogenes, a bodyguard of Belisarius's who had distinguished himself in the first siege of Rome. Under his command the assaults of Totila were repulsed, and the Goths had to begin a regular blockade of the city. With both Ostia and Portus in his hands, Totila could make this blockade the most effective of the war.

Things had changed within the walls, too. With no one living in the city, Diogenes had sown corn on empty ground inside the city. So in the summer of 549, when Totila was blockading it, the corn stood high inside the protective walls, and provisions were not as scarce as before.

The bankrupt imperial treasury was still a serious problem. Either the arrears stipulated for the mutinous garrison had not been sent, or they had not been divided fairly among the soldiers. The little band of Isaurians who kept guard at the Porta Ostiensis deeply resented that for years now they had not been paid. They remembered the great rewards Totila gave their countrymen who betrayed the city to the barbarians three years ago. Accordingly, they initiated secret negotiations with the Goths and promised to open the Porta Ostiensis on an appointed night.

Totila knew that Diogenes was no slothful Bessas, so he prepared a stratagem to ease his entry. On the night of the treachery, he put trumpeters on two little boats and ordered them to creep up the river and blow a loud blast as near as possible to the center of the city. The Romans, who believed an attack was being made by the way of the Tiber, left their various posts and hurried to the threatened quarter. Meanwhile, the Isaurians opened the Porta Ostiensis, and the barbarians entered the city with no trouble.

Many soldiers of the garrison were slain by the Goths in the streets of Rome, and others fled north and east. Some, headed by Diogenes, retreated orderly out through the Porta Aurelia and went along the Via Aurelia toward Centumcellae, the last Roman stronghold in central Italy.

But Totila had anticipated such a move and prepared an ambush on the Via Aurelia. The retreating Romans thought only of the pursuing Goths and rushed straight into the ambush, where most of them were slaughtered. A few, including General Diogenes, escaped and made it to Centumcellae.

Fight at the Mausoleum of Hadrian

A Cilician officer of Diogenes's named Paulus collected four hundred horsemen when the Goths were streaming into the city and with them occupied the now battered and statueless Mausoleum of Hadrian and the Pons Aelius, which it commanded. When dawn came, the barbarians advanced to attack the fortress, but due to its superior position achieved nothing and suffered heavy losses from the Romans' missiles.

On seeing this, Totila called off the attack and let hunger starve the Romans out. The mausoleum had not been stocked with provisions, and through the rest of the day and the following night, the brave little band remained without food. The next day they decided to slaughter some of their horses and eat them, but the idea was so repugnant that they stayed unfed until twilight. They then agreed that it was better to die a glorious death than to die in misery of hunger. So they resolved to make a sortie and kill as many barbarians as possible, and die, if they had to die, in battle.

Totila saw what was going on and, because he did not want to risk the destruction that the desperate Romans might inflict, offered terms of surrender. Either they could depart unharmed to Constantinople, leaving their horses and arms behind them and taking an oath to never again serve against the Goths, or, if they preferred to keep their military possessions and would enter his service, they would in all respects be treated as the equals of their conquerors. The Romans were delighted at the terms and at first were all for returning to Constantinople. But when they thought of returning unarmed and on foot over such a long distance and remembered how the emperor had left their pay so long in arrears, they changed their minds and chose to serve under the standards of King Totila. Only General Paulus and an Isaurian officer named Mindes stayed faithful to the imperial cause. They told Totila that they had wives and children at home, and they could not live without them. So Totila gave them an escort and provisions for the journey home.

There were still three hundred Roman soldiers left in Rome, who had fled to the churches for refuge. Totila offered them the same terms, and all accepted service under him.

In 549, with Rome in his power once again, there was now no talk of destroying the city. The scattered remnants of the senatorial families were brought back to the city from their exile in Campania, and an abundance of provisions was brought into the city. As many as possible of the buildings that Totila had had destroyed after the second siege were restored. No doubt the words of the Frankish king were still ringing in his ears.

After the recapture of Rome, Totila sent a Roman citizen named Stephen to the emperor in Constantinople to propose terms of peace and alliance between the two nations, which had now been at war for fifteen long years. But the ambassador had to return without even being admitted into the presence of the emperor: there would not be peace for the Ostrogoths.

On receiving this news, Totila first marched to Centumcellae and offered the garrison the same terms he had offered the defenders of the Mausoleum of Hadrian. General Diogenes replied that he could not surrender the city entrusted to him without a reason, but that if by a given date no relief had come for the city, he would evacuate it. Thirty hostages were given on each side for the security of the compact. The Goths promised they would not attack during the stipulated period, and the Romans would not defend the city beyond the date agreed upon.

Mausoleum of Hadrian and the Pons Aelius. The Mausoleum functioned as a fortress during the sieges of Rome and protected the northwestern approaches to Rome. Its natural dominant position caused it to also be used by the Popes in the middle ages as a citadel. (*Author*)

The Gothic army then moved south supported by a fleet now consisting of four hundred *dromones* and many larger vessels captured from the Romans.

SICILY RAVAGED

Since the beginning of his kingship, Totila seems to have greatly desired revenge on Sicily. Before an expedition to Sicily could be mounted, he had to remove the threats to his back on the mainland. First he assaulted Rhegium, which was under the command of Thorimuth, one of the former defenders of Auximum, and Himerius, but they so skillfully defended the city that Totila was forced to blockade it. Tarentum was then attacked and taken, and Ariminum was betrayed to the barbarians.

At this time, the almost-comical Verus the Herulian, whose drunkenness had nearly gotten him killed during his first days in Italy, made another of his wild sorties from Ravenna, in which he fell along with many of his followers.

At the end of 549 or the beginning of 550, Rhegium fell when the garrison had no more supplies. Even before this town—nearly the last stronghold left to the Romans in southern Italy—surrendered, Totila had crossed the Straits of Messina into Sicily. He knew he could not hold the island against the Roman fleet, so the campaign was one of plunder and revenge rather than of conquest. He appears to have been unable to take any of the major cities of the island, and only four fortresses were taken and garrisoned. But all the rich Roman villas in the countryside were devastated and the crops in the fields cut down. He spent the whole year of 550 and part of 551 plundering Sicily. Then he gathered his enormous booty—large herds of horses and cattle, grain, fruit, gold, and silver—loaded his ships with it, and returned to Italy. Even though the Gothic troops and king spent more than a year in Sicily, no Roman attempt was made to retake any Italian cities or to force Totila to return to the mainland.

Meanwhile, the appointed day for the surrender of Centumcellae had come and gone. The commandant, Diogenes, had heard the rumors of a great army collected in Dalmatia under the emperor's nephew Germanus, considered himself absolved from his promise, and refused to surrender the city. The thirty hostages were exchanged and returned in safety to the respective sides. It is unknown what later happened to Centumcellae, but it certainly surrendered to the Goths sometime in 551, probably in the spring.

Although Italy was talking about the great relief army from Constantinople, its hopes were put on hold for the present. Since Belisarius's recall in early 549, the emperor had done little to support the war in Italy. In 549, the elderly Patrician Liberius, quite without experience in matters of war, was appointed to command the relief army. The appointment was then canceled. Some months afterward, he was again appointed and actually set sail for Syracusa, where he succeeded in helping the city against the Goths, who were besieging it. He then sailed to Panormus, where he learned that his commission had again been revoked, and the command of the army in Sicily was now entrusted to Artabanes the Armenian. But Artabanes's ships were dispersed by a storm south of Calabria, with the general just making his way to Malta.

Then in 550, the command of the relief army for Italy was given to Germanus, who collected a great army at Serdica. It was this army that people expected to end the long Gothic War in a quick campaign, but these hopes would unexpectedly be disappointed.

Germanus

The noblest and probably the oldest of the nephews of the childless Justinian, Germanus Postumus, was expected to inherit the throne after the emperor. He was a capable general and had struck fear into the hearts of the Sclavenic tribes by a campaign against them in 527. Afterward he had quelled the mutiny of Stotzas in North Africa with great success. In civilian life he was well thought of and was known for always being ready to listen to and help the needy. He also kept away from the troublesome factions of the Circus.

Germanus had two sons, Justinus and Justinianus, by his wife Passara, who had died in the early 540s. Both his sons also had good reputations and had several times been employed against the invading Sclaveni and Gepid barbarians. Justinianus often acted as an officer in his father's campaigns.

Despite, or perhaps because of, Germanus's many qualities, Empress Theodora constantly opposed him in the party politics at the imperial court. Those who wanted to have a good and untroubled standing at court had to avoid his friendship, his sons were rarely employed in the service of the state, and his daughter remained unmarried until John, the nephew of Vitalianus, dared the wrath of Theodora and asked for her hand in marriage.

The Affair of Artabanes

Just before Theodora died in the summer of 548, Germanus was threatened with ruin over a conspiracy. Two Armenian princes, Artabanes and Arsaces, who had risen high in the imperial service, were plotting against the emperor.

Artabanes, who had killed the usurper Gontharis at Carthage in 545 and thus restored the province to the empire, claimed as reward for his faithful service the hand of Justinian's niece Praeiecta. In her gratitude—she was the widow of Areobindus, whom Gontharis had killed at the start of his tyranny—she was even eager to marry Artabanes. There was one problem, however: Artabanes was already married. But he had not lived with his wife for many years and had almost forgotten about her. As his career advanced, however, she had no intention of forgetting him. She implored Empress Theodora to help her, and she in turn insisted that Artabanes take back his wife and gave Praeiecta to another husband.

Artabanes could do nothing against the empress's will and so kept quiet while he rose in the imperial service to count of the *foederati* (the barbarian auxiliaries in Roman service) and even consul. But the honors did not eliminate the wrong he felt at being daily in the company of a woman he hated while having lost the woman he loved.

Arsaces the Armenian knew of Artabanes's misery and eagerly exploited his resentment. Arsaces had been caught in treasonable negotiations with Persia's King Chosroes. He had avoided the death penalty but had been flogged and paraded in shame through the streets of Constantinople on the back of a camel. But the leniency he received was more galling to the proud Armenian, who accordingly planned to assassinate the emperor. At length, he succeeded in convincing Artabanes that Justinian had to be killed, and he asked an Armenian named Chanaranges to help in the plot.

The intention was to gain the support of Germanus, who had suffered so much from Theodora, and make him emperor after Justinian. Arsaces accordingly contacted the eldest son of Germanus, Justinus, who was at the time a young man or teenager. Justinus was bound by oaths to reveal the plans only to his father. He was then reminded of the injustices his family and his father had suffered at the hands of the emperor and empress, and was told that Belisarius had been called home from the Gothic War to profit from Germanus's weak position at court. The names of the accomplices were also revealed to the young man.

Despite the temptation, Justinus refused to cooperate in the plot and said his father also would not be part of such crimes. He then went home and told his father everything. Germanus, who thought of the dangers of a plot against the emperor, revealed the plans to his friend Marcellus, who was commander of the palace guard (*magister officiorum*). Marcellus was a wise man who appreciated the danger of the situation as well as Germanus did. It was too dangerous to enter into the crime, just as revealing the plot would open Germanus up to counteraccusations from the emperor and court. Accordingly, he suggested that Germanus make the conspirators reveal the plot to some unsuspecting witness.

Germanus agreed, and Justinus was sent to reopen the negotiations. Arsaces could not be brought to discuss his intentions, but the eager Chanaranges did not mind speaking with Justinus first and then with his father. On the appointed date, he went to the palace of Germanus. In the room where they met, a thick curtain hung, veiling the couch where Germanus usually dined. It also veiled the hidden Leontius, a friend of Marcellus, who had agreed to come and listen to the conversation.

Chanaranges explained the plan of the conspirators to Germanus. They had decided it was too dangerous to kill Justinian before Belisarius returned, as he would then gather an army and avenge the murder of the emperor. Instead, they would wait until Belisarius had arrived and then, late one evening when Belisarius was at the palace, they would go there and kill Justinian, Belisarius, and Marcellus at the same time.

Leontius, as planned, informed Marcellus of the plot. For some reason, Marcellus postponed reporting it to the emperor. Germanus became more and more troubled, as just hearing of a plot and not reporting it opened him to accusations. So he spoke with two other great officials: Constantianus, the former general of Dalmatia, and Bouzes, who had spent twenty-eight months in Theodora's dark dungeon and so held no love for the imperial couple.

Only when it was reported that Belisarius was close to the capital did Marcellus inform the emperor of the plot. Artabanes and some of his accomplices were arrested and tortured, and the Senate was summoned to the palace to read the statements of the tortured. Naturally, some of the first names to be spoken were Germanus and Justinus. The shocked senators looked to Germanus for an explanation, and it seemed he was already condemned.

Then he told his story and called on Marcellus, Leontius, Constantianus, and Bouzes to vouch for the truth of it. The mood turned, and the senators unanimously voted for the acquittal of Germanus and his son. The decision of the vote was brought to the emperor, but he did not agree and accused his nephew of tardiness in telling him of the plot. The courtiers, who knew how to gain more power, then began to support the emperor's views. The Senate did not know what to say, but Marcellus stepped in and asserted that if anybody was to blame for tardiness, it was him. Germanus had consulted with him at the earliest possible moment, but he, Marcellus, from motives of policy, had insisted that Justinian not then be told of the plot. The emperor finally accepted Germanus's story, and Marcellus was praised for his fearless truthfulness.

Justinian chose to be lenient in dealing with the conspirators, and they were only kept for a time in confinement at the palace. Indeed, the next year Artabanes would be given an important command in Sicily.

Foreign Wars

There were other wars going on in the empire, some much nearer home than that in Italy, which distracted the energies of Justinian. The eternal contest with Persia was transferred to the eastern end of the Black Sea, to the region of Lazica, where from 549 to 557 what was called the Lazic War was being waged with varying fortunes but with a preponderance of success on the side of the Romans.

Late in 548, General Dagisthaeus had been dispatched to Lazica with seven thousand men, but he failed to recapture the principal city of the region, Petra, and in 549, despite two victories over Persian armies, he was recalled. His successor, Bessas, succeeded in taking Petra in 551, and in the same year the five years' truce, which had lapsed in 550, was renewed for a payment of two thousand six hundred pounds of gold; however it still did not apply to Lazica, on which Chosroes refused to relinquish his claim.

In 549, one of Belisarius's guardsmen, Indulph, deserted to Totila and was sent into Dalmatia with a large army of Goths. After taking a few towns and defeating Claudianus, the commandant of Salona, he returned with many provisions and plunder.

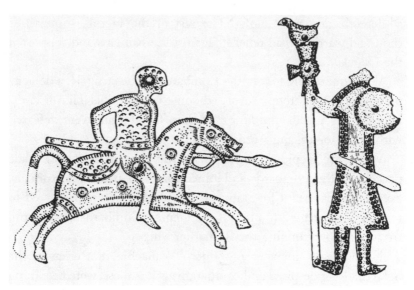

Shield decorations of the seventh century found in Italy, showing a mounted warrior (left), possibly a Goth, and an armored Lombard warrior (right).

North of the Danube there was discontent and a dangerous spirit of enterprise among the fierce neighbors of the empire. Justinian had given the city of Noreia (Neumarkt in modern-day Austria) and fortresses in Pannonia to the Lombards. The Lombards gladly left their homes in the forests north of the Danube and went to live in their new lands, not far from the Gepids, who had held Sirmium and most of the province of Dacia after the battle of Nedao in 454. The Heruli had been given Singidunum and some other cities close by.

Around 550, the Lombards and Gepids had become enemies and were preparing for war. The Lombards, afraid because they were outnumbered, decided to ask the emperor to intervene on their side. When the Gepids heard of this, they also sent envoys to Justinian asking him to support their cause against the Lombards. After hearing their speeches, the emperor decided to support the Lombards, as the Gepids were becoming too strong in the region. Accordingly, ten thousand horsemen commanded by Constantianus, Bouzes, and Aratius were sent. John, the nephew of Vitalianus, also went with them, with orders to march to Italy with his troops after the battle with the Gepids. Fifteen hundred Heruli, commanded by their king,

Philemuth, also went along. The rest of the Heruli, some three thousand warriors, had rebelled against the Romans and supported the Gepids.

While marching to join the Lombards in the struggle, a detachment of Roman troops surprised some of the rebel Heruli commanded by Aordus, the king's brother. The Heruli were defeated with heavy losses, and Aordus was killed.

When the Gepids heard of this battle, they straightaway made peace with the Lombards and joined forces to attack the Romans. So the troops meant for Italy and the Gothic War were forced to remain in the region to prevent the Gepids, Lombards, and Heruli from freely overrunning the Roman provinces.

Further east, in what is modern Wallachia in Romania, the Sclaveni, long despised and comparatively harmless, were becoming a terrible scourge to the empire. In 549, three thousand of these barbarians crossed the Danube, marched to the Hebrus, defeated several greater Roman armies, took captive the Roman General Asbad, and, after cutting off long strips of skin from his back, burned the unfortunate man alive. They then pressed on to Topirus (Paradeisos in modern-day Greece) on the coast of the Aegean, nearly opposite the island of Thasos and only twelve days' journey from Constantinople. They drew out the garrison by a feigned flight, took the city, ransacked its treasures, killed fifteen thousand men, and carried off all the women and children into captivity.

In this way they spread throughout Illyricum and Thrace, ravaging the lands and torturing the inhabitants with great cruelty. At length the Sclaveni retreated across the Danube, driving their endless files of weeping captives before them and leaving Thrace and Illyricum full of unburied corpses.

Two more invasions of these barbarians followed in the next year. It was speculated by some that Totila had hired them to harass Justinian and prevent him from turning his attention to the affairs of Italy.

So we see that Justinian had reasons to hesitate and waver in his decisions on the war in Italy. But now, at the beginning of 550, he finally appointed Germanus commander with absolute powers for the whole war against Totila and the Goths. He gave him a large army and ordered him to increase it with levies from Thrace and Illyricum. He even gave him a large store of treasure for the war. To these already formidable resources Germanus added large amounts from his own private fortune.

Because of the Lazic War, no troops could be released from the east, and only a few cavalry regiments could be spared from the Thracian army, but with funds from the treasury and his own ample resources, Germanus quickly got together a large army.

Germanus's fame and the large amounts of money attracted many recruits, especially barbarians from beyond the Danube. All these flocked to Serdica, where Germanus had made camp. With him were his two sons, Justinus and Justinianus, and his son-in-law, John. Philemuth, king of the Herulians, had also come, and one thousand armored Lombards. But Germanus's power was not only military. He brought with him his newly wedded wife, Matasuntha, widow of King Vittigis and granddaughter of Theodoric the Great. The presence and marriage of Matasuntha meant much to the Ostrogoths, and their morale was steadily declining when the rumors of the gathering of this enormous army came to Italy. How could they fight such an enormous army, with such a commander, and how could they fight one of Theodoric's family? They would be fighting a person married into the family of their greatest royal line, the line that had established the kingdom of Italy—a line with more legitimacy than Totila.

The Roman deserters in Totila's army sent a messenger to Germanus, saying they would change their allegiance as soon as they saw his army in Italy.

But fate would change everything. The first of the Sclaveni invasions of the year 550, in which the barbarians penetrated as far as Naissus, alarmed the emperor, who sent orders to Germanus to suspend his westward march and relieve Thessalonica, which the barbarians threatened. When the Sclaveni heard that Germanus was in the region they became terrified, as they remembered the events of twenty years earlier. At that time, another tribe, the Antae, living close to the Sclaveni had crossed the Danube with a great army and invaded the empire. Germanus was general of Thrace then and so decisively defeated the Antae horde that hardly any returned to their homelands. Accordingly, his name was much feared north of the Danube and was sufficient to turn the Sclaveni horde and to divert their march into Dalmatia.

In two more days the great Roman army would have resumed its interrupted march toward Italy, but Germanus suddenly fell ill, and after a short period he died.

It was an extraordinary end to an extraordinary person who might have ended the Gothic War in less than a year. Had he lived, he would almost undoubtedly have become emperor after Justinian—and perhaps a better one, as far as military ability is concerned.

The emperor then commanded John and Justinianus to take Germanus's army into Italy. The army lacked boats to transport it, so it was decided to march to Salona in Dalmatia and winter there.

When Totila heard of the great army's movements, he ended his expedition to Sicily and began to march north in preparation for the coming struggle.

14

THE RETURN
OF NARSES

In 551, only four cities in Italy were still held by the emperor: Ravenna, Ancona, Hydruntum, and Crotona. There was no actual source of revenue from the province anymore, and the pay of the troops was years behind.

With Liberius hopelessly incapable and the great Germanus dead, the question arose who should be the new commander of the relief expedition. The emperor offered the command to Narses, his grand chamberlain, who eagerly accepted. Appointing this seventy-five-year-old civil servant who had so bungled his first command in Italy with his power games to be the new savior of Italy may seem like the height of folly, but Justinian was known for his capacity to choose the right men to further his own purposes.

Narses—who would live more than twenty more years—was still in good health and very able. He had shown considerable strategic talent in his first command, some fourteen years before, and moreover he had the gratitude of the troublesome John, who was obedient to him as he would be to no other general. Narses's political career and power also meant that no matter where he went in Italy, his orders would be considered as coming almost from the emperor himself. All who hoped to share in the expedition received the announcement that the eunuch was to command the Italian army with a shout of applause, as Narses had always been known for his generosity. Narses was furthermore a devout Christian, and his soldiers believed that because of his piety, he had supernatural visitations from the mother of God, who told him the right moment for his troops to move forward into battle.

Narses's power also meant the expedition could never be starved of resources, as Belisarius had experienced. Accordingly, the long-standing arrears of the soldiers' pay were discharged, and liberal offers were made to all newcomers. Soon eager Romans and barbarians were flocking to the standard of the eunuch.

Despite a Hunnish invasion that stopped Narses at Philippopolis in Thrace, he could soon move across Macedonia to Salona, where he spent the remainder of 551 preparing his great army for the invasion of Italy.

When Totila received the news of the great effort the Romans were preparing for his overthrow, he quickened the pace of his operations. He pressed Ancona on land and sea so the Romans would have no base of operations in the long interval between Ravenna and Crotona, and he did much to try to improve his relationship with the population.

As we have seen in previous chapters, Totila had wisely paid more attention to his fleet than any other Ostrogothic king, and he was by no means disposed to yield the command of the seas to the Roman navy. He sent three hundred *dromones* to cruise off the western coast of Greece with orders to intercept traffic and to plunder and harass the coastal settlements. Corcyra was ravaged, as well as the region around Epirus. Several supply ships carrying provisions from Greece to Narses's army at Salona were also captured.

The Naval Battle off Sena Gallica

The siege of Ancona was the chief operation in which the forces of Totila engaged. With the sea no longer in undisputed control of the Romans, the city was soon hard pressed for provisions. Valerianus, the commandant of Ancona but currently staying at Ravenna, sent an urgent plea for help to John at Salona. John had been ordered by the emperor not to take any initiatives and wait for Narses, but he was so convinced of the seriousness of the situation that he dispatched a squadron of ships to relieve Ancona. Valerianus met him at Scardona on the coast of Illyria, and soon the two generals with fifty ships crossed the Adriatic and anchored off the little town of Sena Gallica (Sinigaglia), sixteen miles northwest of Ancona.

The Goths, meanwhile, brought against them forty-seven ships of war, which they filled with some of their best soldiers under the command of Giblas and Indulph, and sailed to meet the enemy. Indulph was a former guardsman of Belisarius's who had, like countless other Roman soldiers, deserted to the Gothic cause in disgust because of the bad treatment they had received from the emperor.

The two fleets met off Sena Gallica. The wind was light, and as the ships grappled each other the fight became more like a hand-to-hand battle by land rather than a sea battle. But the Goths did not have the long tradition of seamanship of the Greek sailors and failed to keep a proper distance between their ships. In some places a large interval invited an enemy attack, and in others several ships became entangled and lost all maneuverability. The Gothic generals could no longer be heard above the shouts of the steersmen warning their fellows of imminent collision or lack of support. Intent on avoiding collisions by poles and boat hooks, the barbarians could not keep their full attention on the battle.

Meanwhile, the Roman seamen, who had kept their ranks in perfect order, were continually charging into the gaps in the line of the barbarians, surrounding and cutting out the ships that were left defenseless or keeping up a storm of missiles on those parts of the line where the hostile ships were thickly entangled with one another. The barbarians' disorder soon turned into panic, and they began to steer their ships away in flight. Indulph managed to flee with eleven of his ships, but aware that no more resistance could be made at sea, he landed and burned them to prevent the Romans from taking them. All the other Gothic ships were either sunk or captured, and Giblas was taken prisoner.

When Indulph brought the terrible news to his fellow barbarians besieging Ancona, they raised the siege and retreated to the shelter of Auximum. John and Valerianus then landed and plundered the Gothic camp before resupplying Ancona, after which they returned to Salona and Ravenna respectively. This was a further blow to the Goths' morale.

About the same time, the unfortunate Goths suffered another disaster. Liberius had finally been replaced in Sicily by the eager and capable Artabanes the Armenian, the pardoned conspirator, who at once attacked the Gothic garrisons in Sicily with such vigor that they soon surrendered, and so in 551 Sicily was quickly lost to the Gothic cause.

At the same time John, the governor of Africa, sent an expedition to retake Corsica and Sardinia. Totila with his navy had in the last few years managed to take the two islands, and as they administratively were considered part of the African province, John accordingly tried to recover them. The Romans commenced a regular siege of Caralis (Cagliari) in Sardinia, but the powerful Gothic garrison made a sally in which they inflicted such a severe defeat on the Romans that they fled headlong to their ships, and so the reconquest of the two islands was put off until the next year, when a greater expedition was to be mounted.

Despite this success, the Roman victories in Sicily and off Sena Gallica had thrown Totila and his generals into a state of deep dejection. The Romans were again masters of the Adriatic Sea and so could threaten the whole coast of Italy. The loss of Sicily meant a loss of the one comparatively intact and productive region of the Gothic kingdom. For some years, Totila's hold on north Italy had been insecure, and the Franks under King Theudebert had succeeded in annexing Liguria, Venetia, and the Cottian Alps—possibly in return for not attacking the Goths. Only Ticinum, Verona, and perhaps some other fortresses in the region were still held by the Goths. The Goths, who could not fight both the Franks and the empire at the same time, had accepted this state of affairs for a while and even allied themselves with the Franks.

With northern Italy lost to the Franks, and with central and southern Italy almost a desert after seventeen years of war, Totila's situation was—despite his former victories—quite bleak. Again he offered terms to the emperor. He was prepared to relinquish any claim to Sicily and Dalmatia, to pay a large tribute for his remaining lands in Italy, and to ally himself with the empire. But the emperor would not listen to the terms of the Ostrogoths, whose name he now hated. There could not be peace with the Ostrogoths, only their extinction. And so the delegation had to return, as all others of Totila's embassies, with no result.

Roman Delegation to the Franks

About this time a Roman delegation was sent to the Franks to get them to break their alliance with the Ostrogoths. King Theudebert had been killed in a hunting accident, and his young and feeble son, Theudebald, had succeeded him. The Franks were charged with having broken their promises made before the Gothic War and supporting the Goths in their struggle against the empire.

Leontius, the Roman head of the delegation, told the young king he would soon understand the true feelings of the Goths if the Romans concluded a peace with them and ended by asking Theudebald to renew the alliance with the Romans. Theudebald replied that the Franks had thought they were supporting the Roman cause by taking three important provinces from the Goths that he did not consider Roman. If it could be proven that he had taken anything from the empire, he would immediately return it. A Frank named Leudard was sent with the Romans back to Constantinople, but nothing appears to have resulted from this. With these negotiations, the winter of 551 wore away.

Early in 552, Crotona was relieved. Its garrison had been hard pressed by the besieging Goths and had sent a message to Artabanes, the governor of Sicily, to send help with all speed. Artabanes was not in a position to help, but when Emperor Justinian heard of the garrison's distress, he sent orders to the garrison at Thermopylae in Greece to set sail for Crotona and raise the siege. The sight of the ships filled the besieging barbarians with terror, and they fled from their camp. Perhaps they thought this was the great army gathered for their destruction, as soon after several Gothic governors of cities in south Italy began negotiations for surrender—including Ragnaris, a Gothic noble commanding the garrison at Tarentum, and Moras, commanding the troops in Acherontia. Both surrendered with all their troops.

Despair now gripped the Goths, who could see only enemies everywhere—enemies who, no matter how often they were defeated in battle, still came back. It was now clear to them that the great and mighty Roman Empire did not want peace but only their destruction.

Narses Marches to Italy

Meanwhile, the great and well-equipped host of Narses was at last on its way to Italy. We do not know how large the army was, but we know its composition.

The two armies of John and the dead Germanus were the core of the host, but also John the glutton was there with many Roman soldiers. Asbad, a Gepid prince, was there with four hundred of his warriors. Aruth the Herulian led a large band of his countrymen. Philemuth the Herulian, a veteran of many of the campaigns in Italy, led three thousand of his barbarians, all on horseback. There was General Dagisthaeus, who had been thrown into prison for his mismanagement of the war with Persia and was being allowed to vindicate himself by serving the emperor. Cabades, the estranged nephew of Persian King Chosroes, was there leading a band of Persian deserters. Also Audoin, king of the Lombards, was in Narses's service with five thousand five hundred fierce and heavily armored men. Many Huns had also come on their swift little horses. Narses's army was a perfect example of the many races and composition of a "Roman" army in the sixth century AD. It was somewhat paradoxical, as mentioned before, that all the Ostrogoths had been born in Italy.

Furthermore, Narses had been given huge amounts of money, both to pay the troops in Italy, who had not been paid for many years, and to bribe deserters and Goths into changing their allegiance.

The imperial army marched around the head of the Adriatic Gulf, but when it came to the confines of Venetia, it found its passage barred by the order of the Frankish King Theudebald. More to the west, Teias, one of the bravest of Totila's young officers, barred the Brenner Pass at Verona. Furthermore, he had so obstructed the bridges in the region that Narses would be incapable of passing him without fighting a battle.

The Roman army was so great that it could not be transported across the Adriatic, but John, the nephew of Vitalianus, suggested a scheme for using the few ships he had available. The army would march along the coast, and where the rivers Piave, Brenta, Adige, and Po were met, the ships could be used as ferries to bring across the army. John's suggestion was adopted, and accordingly Narses managed to bring the army to Ravenna with no skirmishes with either the Franks or the Goths. At Ravenna, Justinus and Valerianus joined their forces to those of Narses.

After a stay of nine days at Ravenna, an insulting message came from Usdrilas, the general holding Ariminum for the Goths, challenging Narses to battle:

> Though you have filled the world with talk of you and have already captivated the whole of Italy with the visions of your power, and have assumed an air of supercilious pride quite above the level of mortal men, and though you have in this way frightened the Goths, as you fondly imagine, you nevertheless now sit in Ravenna without at all showing your own forces to your enemy, through your policy of keeping hidden—no doubt as a way of guarding still this proud spirit of yours—but using a heterogeneous horde of barbarians with which to ruin the land which belongs to you in no sense whatever. But arise with all speed and henceforth essay the deeds of war; show yourselves to the Goths, and do not tantalize us longer with mere hope, since we have been awaiting the spectacle a long time.

Narses could only laugh at the words of the insolent barbarian before setting out with the bulk of his army, leaving only a small garrison under Justinus at Ravenna.

On his arrival at Ariminum he found the bridge over the Marecchia River blocked by the enemy. Some of his soldiers crossed the river and were looking for a ford convenient for the passage of the whole army when Usdrilas, with some of his troops, fell on them. A skirmish followed in which Usdrilas was killed. The Goths were so discouraged they did not prevent the Romans from throwing a pontoon bridge across the river and proceeding south on their march. It was Narses's plan to seek a regular pitched battle with the Gothic king and not let himself be tied down in lengthy sieges or other such operations.

After passing Ariminum, he departed from the Via Flaminia and went to the east, as the fortress of Petra Pertusa was held by the

Goths and so effectively blocked the Via Flaminia. Accordingly, he had to keep south along the Adriatic Sea until he could strike inland again and return to the Via Flaminia south of Petra Pertusa.

While crossing the Apennines to return onto the Via Flaminia, Narses received information that Totila and the Gothic army was close.

The Battle of Taginae, or Busta Gallorum

Meanwhile Totila, after receiving news that Narses had bypassed the defenses in Venetia, waited some time in the neighborhood of Rome to give the outflanked Teias in Verona time to rejoin his forces. When all but two thousand of these reinforcements had arrived, he started on the northward march through Etruria and Umbria. His movements were hurried by the news of the death of Usdrilas and the unsuccessful attempt of the Ariminum garrison to impede the imperial army. He knew the Romans would not try to pass Petra Pertusa, but he was not aware of exactly where Narses would attempt to cross the Apennines. Awaiting news from his scouts, he made camp at the little town of Tadinum (Gualdo Tadino), or as Procopius calls it, Taginae, close to a place called Busta Gallorum. Here, high up in the Apennines in the early summer of 552, would be fought the great and deciding battle of the war.

As soon as Narses had made camp some fifteen miles from the Goths, he sent a delegation to Totila asking him to lay down his arms and abandon the hopeless task of opposing the full might of the Roman Empire. If, however, he was eager for battle, then he was to name the day. Totila haughtily rejected any question of surrender and replied that he would fight in eight days. Narses was wise, however, and suspected a trick, so he prepared for battle the next day.

And he was right. The next day Totila suddenly appeared with his whole army and encamped at a distance of two bowshots from the Roman camp.

A hill of moderate height, probably an outlier of the main Apennine range, looked down on both armies and commanded a path by which the imperial army could be taken in the rear. Both

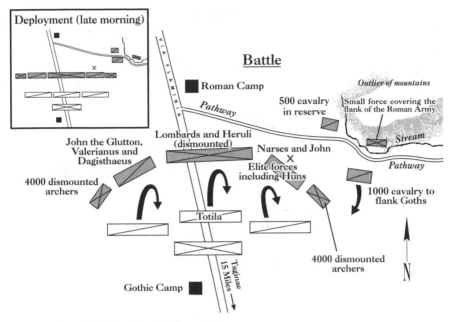

Map 15. The battle of Taginae, 552.

sides recognized the hill's strategic importance, but Narses was quicker than Totila in seizing it. Fifty picked foot soldiers were sent to occupy it during the night, and when day dawned, the Goths saw these men drawn up in serried array. A stream running parallel to the path protected their front.

A squadron of Gothic cavalry was sent to dislodge them, but the Romans kept steady and by clashing their weapons on their shields so frightened the barbarians' horses that they were able to inflict heavy losses on the attackers. The cavalry then retreated.

Totila tried again and again with fresh horsemen to dislodge them, but the fifty Romans kept their ground. Conspicuous among the Romans were the soldiers Paulus and Ansilas, who were at the front of the battle. They had stood before the ranks of the Romans and had shot a barbarian or horse with each of their arrows until their quivers were empty. They then drew their swords and chopped off the attacking Goths' spearheads. After a while, Paulus's sword became bent from use. He threw it on the ground and started seizing the spears of the barbarians with his bare hands, breaking four of the weapons. With such soldiers against them, the Goths lost heart and abandoned their attempts to take the hill. After the battle Paulus was promoted into Narses's bodyguard.

Now the two main armies were drawn up in battle formation, and both their leaders harangued them.

Narses congratulated his troops on their evident superiority to the band of robbers and deserters who composed the Gothic army. The soldiers of Totila were simple runaway slaves with a king of no royal line, who had only succeeded by tricks and stratagems to harass the Romans for so long. Lastly, he spoke on the passing nature of all barbarian kingdoms, as contrasted to the enduring and eternal might of the Roman Empire.

Totila, perceiving that his troops were shaken by the great imperial army and the ineffectual attacks on the strategic hill, called upon them to make one last effort of valor, one last effort to win against the Romans, who were weary of the war and with a victory here would give up the struggle. The Roman army was only a motley host of barbarian tribes—Huns, Heruli, and Lombards with no coherence or bond of unity, and who had only come because of their pay.

Narses, who evidently had superior numbers and equipment, perhaps twenty to twenty-five thousand soldiers, drew up his troops in the following order. In the center he stationed his barbarian allies, the Lombards and the Heruli, and, as he was not overconfident of their stability, he directed them to dismount and fight on foot so that flight would not be easy. All his best Roman troops with picked men from among the Hunnish allies, men who had been selected as bodyguards for their prowess, he stationed on his left wing, where he and John were in command. This portion of the army was covered by the hill. Under the hill and at an angle with the rest of his line, Narses stationed two bodies of cavalry, numbering respectively one thousand and five hundred. The five hundred were to watch the Roman line and strengthen any part that might seem to be wavering. The thousand were to wait for the commencement of the action and then get into the rear of the Goths and so place them between two attacks. On the left wing were the rest of the Roman troops, under John the glutton, Valerianus, and

Dagisthaeus. On each flank was a force of four thousand archers, fighting on foot, contrary to the usual custom of Roman archers in those days.

Looking at Narses's tactics, we can see a clear disregard for what might happen in the center. He was determined to win with the wings of his army and was waiting for Totila to attack so he could outflank and surround the Goths.

We do not know any details of the Gothic order of battle. Procopius says Totila "arrayed his army in the same way opposite his enemy" and relied on his cavalry to decide the issue. The infantry was to remain at the rear, ready to support the cavalry if it was routed. Furthermore, he ordered his warriors not to use any other weapon than the spear. The reason for the order seems somewhat unclear, but the gist must have been that, as soon as possible, he wanted them to get into hand-to-hand combat, where they would be most effective.

There was a long pause before the armies clashed. Knowing that the remaining two thousand troops of Teias were on their way, Totila postponed the signal for attack. Various demonstrations of valor or martial ability took up the morning. Totila rode along his line cheering his men. Narses also rode along his army, not to appeal to their soldierly instincts but to dangle golden armlets, twisted collars, and bridles before their eyes. Narses probably chose the right appeal to his men.

Then Coccas, a Roman soldier but now serving Totila, rode out and challenged the bravest of the Roman army to single combat. An Armenian named Anzalas accepted the challenge. Coccas rode on, couching his spear and aiming for Anzalas's belly. With a sudden swerve at the right moment, Anzalas made his opponent miss and in turn made a fatal thrust into Coccas's left flank. Coccas fell dead from his horse, and the Roman army gave a great shout.

The two thousand Gothic horsemen had still not arrived, and to further postpone the attack Totila, who had been practiced from his youth in all the arts of horsemanship, gratified the two armies with an extraordinary performance. Richly dressed—with gold lavishly displayed on his helmet, mail, and greaves, with purple favors fluttering from his cheek strap, javelin, and spear—he rode forth between the two armies. Now he wheeled his horse to the right, then sharply to the left. He threw his heavy spear up into the air, stretched out his arm and caught it again. Then he tossed the spear from hand to hand, lay back in the saddle, bent to one side then the other, displaying all his ability in arms.

To further delay the battle, Totila sent a message to Narses inviting him to a conference, but the eunuch declined the offer, saying Totila had professed himself eager for the fight and now might have his wish.

Just at the time of the noon meal, the expected two thousand Gothic warriors arrived. Totila, who had drawn back his army within their entrenchments, commanded them and the newcomers to quickly eat and put on armor, then led them hastily out, hoping to catch the imperial army in disorder during its lunch. He himself changed into the armor of a private soldier, so as not to be recognized too easily on the battlefield.

But Narses had expected such a move, so the men had been served their meal while they were still keeping rank and under arms. Moreover, he had turned his straight line into a crescent by drawing back his barbarian center and so made ready to receive the Gothic attack.

Narses's tactics succeeded. Only a remnant of Totila's cavalry reached the Roman center because of the eight thousand Roman archers on the wings, shooting them in the flank. The Lombards and Heruli, whose disposition for fighting had been uncertain up to the moment of battle, now threw themselves into the fray with unexpected eagerness.

For some time the Gothic cavalry kept up the unequal fight, but toward evening it staggered back to its protecting infantry. It was a disorderly retreat, with some infantry even trampled by the fleeing cavalry, and they had no fight left in them. With the cavalry in full flight, outnumbered and outflanked, the barbarian infantry fled in disorder. The Romans pursued, killing six thousand men. Some of the barbarians asked for quarter and obtained it for a time, but they were soon after slain by their captors, as were the many Roman deserters in Totila's army. No barbarians or deserters were left alive, apart from the ones who escaped. It had now truly become a war of extinction.

Totila, unhurt, fled at nightfall with a few followers from the battlefield. Some Roman soldiers pursued them closely, and during the pursuit one of them, Asbad the Gepid, thrust a spear into the king's back. The Goths hurried on in their flight and only stopped at the village of Caprae, thirteen miles from the battlefield, to tend to his wound. But it was too late, and in a few minutes the king was dead. His escort buried him there and quickly departed.

One version of the events says Totila was wounded by a Roman arrow during the retreat, made it to Caprae, fainted, and soon died.

TOTILA THE GOTH

Totila had reigned for eleven hard and troublesome years. It was said that his end did not compare with his actions. At the time he gained the crown, the Ostrogothic nation had been brought to its knees, and few expected that more would be heard of the Ostrogoths. His kingdom could have been brought to a short end, if not for the rapacious and inept Roman generals. Instead he succeeded in retaking most of Italy, apart from a few coastal cities. He won almost all his battles, and several times against the odds. He was a wise politician and understood how to take advantage of the Roman misadministration and so accordingly treated the provincials well. In the same way he gained the loyalty of great numbers of Roman deserters, and to a large extent based much of his military power on this fact. In many ways he pursued the course that Theodoric the Great had set in forging a bond between Goths and Italians.

As mentioned before, Totila's driving force seems to have been his quest for legitimacy and acknowledgement, which he never achieved. That was not his fault—he did everything he could—but the fault of circumstances. The Ostrogoths had had their back broken by Belisarius and had lost their foremost leaders. Their losses before the walls of Rome during the first siege were perhaps five times as great as those in the rest of the war combined.

With the dragging out of the war, the encroaching Franks were given time to further establish their kingdom, and again Vittigis's errors shine forth. If lands had not been given to the Franks in return for the illusion of a treaty, Totila would not have faced the same uphill struggle as he did.

In many respects the war was already decided when the Franks and Justinian did not acknowledge Totila. There was perhaps no way Totila and the Ostrogoths could win the war after Vittigis's defeat. Totila might win battles and take cities, but he did not have enough troops to hold them, and Italy was so ravaged that it had a hard time providing enough food for its remaining inhabitants. Totila could only wait for a new imperial army to come to Italy, and at each battle the war could be decided, as it was at Taginae.

In August 552, messengers arrived at Constantinople to tell of the great victory of the Romans, attested to by throwing the blood-stained robe and jewel-encrusted helmet of the Ostrogothic king at the feet of the emperor.

Teias, the Last King of the Ostrogoths

Narses's first concern after the battle was over and he had thanked heaven was to remove as quickly as possible the most barbaric of his federates. The most savage were the primitive Lombards. Everywhere they passed they would burn and plunder the farms of friend and foe alike, and make slaves of the local population. With large sums of money he persuaded these unstable allies to promise to return to their own land. To ensure their faith, Valerianus and his nephew Damianus were sent with a body of troops to watch over them on the journey to the Julian Alps. When this duty was accomplished, Valerianus commenced the siege of Verona, whose garrison was soon ready to surrender.

Now, however, the Franks appeared, and in the name of King Theudebald they forbade the Romans from taking Verona. Because they held so many fortresses in upper Italy, they considered all the lands north of the Po River to be Frankish territory and would not allow any city there to surrender to the Romans. With only few troops, Valerianus was not strong enough to challenge the Franks, so he moved across the Po and stayed there to prevent any Frankish or Gothic attempts at crossing the river.

Meanwhile the few remnants of the Gothic army that had escaped from the Battle of Taginae made their way to Ticinum, where again, as twelve years earlier, it was the last bastion of Gothic power. By common consent Teias, son of Fritigern, the bravest of Totila's generals, and probably still a young or middle-aged man, was raised on the shield and acclaimed king of the Ostrogoths.

The defeat and Narses's full purses made the remaining Ostrogoths desert in large numbers. Having learned nothing from the past events of the war, Teias did all he could to obtain an alliance with the Franks, as he knew he could not face Narses alone. The royal treasure in Ticinum was expended in great gifts to Theudebald and his court to obtain this alliance. The Franks took the money of the dying Gothic nation and decided not to assist the Goths, but instead to let the Romans and Goths fight their battle to the end so Italy would be easier for them to take afterward.

For some time, Valerianus seems to have prevented Teias and his little army from crossing the Po. Meanwhile, the Gothic garrisons all over Italy were surrendering to the Romans. This was indeed Narses's strategy from the beginning. If the Gothic field army could be defeated, all the garrisons would soon surrender. Thus he avoided tedious and lengthy sieges of the numerous fortresses and cities in Italy, for which his barbarian army did not have the patience. Narnia, Spoletium, and Perusia quickly fell into the hands of the Romans. Tarentum fell after a battle, and soon after the extremely important fortress of Petra Pertusa surrendered, and so the strategic route of the Via Flaminia was reopened.

These various sieges and surrenders across Italy took place throughout the summer and autumn of 552.

ROME FALLS

With Valerianus keeping Teias on the other side of the Po, Narses marched to Rome with a great army, chiefly composed of archers, and camped before its walls. The Gothic garrison concentrated its strength in a small area around the Mausoleum of Hadrian, which had been rebuilt and fortified after the destruction of the city. The walls of Rome were too long for the Gothic garrison to defend properly, but it was also impossible for Narses to attack everywhere, so he attacked at three points. He commanded one force, John another, and Philemuth, with his Herulians, the third.

But it was General Dagisthaeus who succeeded in entering the city first. With a small force carrying scaling ladders, he appeared at an unguarded portion of the walls and mounted unresisted. He could then hasten through the ruined city to open the gates for his fellow generals. With the Romans inside the city, the Goths fled—some to Portus and some to the Mausoleum of Hadrian, where they soon surrendered.

Before long the harbors of Portus and Centumcellae also fell to the Romans. The keys of Rome were again sent to Justinian, a ceremony that must have brought a bitter smile to the emperor, who remembered that this was the fifth capture of Rome in his reign and who knew what a desolate ruin the once great Mistress of the World now was. The remains of the Roman Senate were dispersed across Italy, mainly in Campania, and were lodged in fortresses garrisoned by Goths. With little hope for their nation, the Goths killed their hostages and any provincials they came across, with Teias putting to death three hundred children of Roman nobles.

With only a few thousand warriors, Teias could do little, and the war was becoming a race to secure the remainder of the Gothic royal treasure. The hoard at Ticinum was gone, used in persuading the treacherous Franks, but Totila had accumulated a greater treasure in the fortress of Cumae in Campania. Aligern, the brother of Teias and the Roman deserter Herodianus, commanded this fortress. In order to capture the treasure, Narses had sent a considerable force to take the fortress. At the same time he sent John and Philemuth into Tuscany to hold the passes and keep Teias away. But Teias took a great detour through Picenum and the provinces by the Adriatic Sea, and by twice crossing the Apennines, succeeded in bringing his little army into Campania. When Narses was told of this move, he summoned all his generals—John, Philemuth, and Valerianus—to join his army and moved south to crush the remnants of the Gothic nation.

Narses's speedy movement frustrated Teias in his attempt to join up with his brother at Cumae. He had reached Campania, but the great Roman army was before him. Near Nuceria, with the Sarno River between the two armies, they met. Teias's army was caught in this little peninsula for two months, possibly December 552 and

January 553. The Goths still commanded the sea in this region and so could obtain provisions with few problems. They had fortified the bridge across the Sarno with wooden towers on which they had placed *ballistae* and other engines of war, thus barring the Romans' approach. The Goths do not seem to have used such engines of war before, and it is believed that Roman deserters had probably manufactured them.

BATTLE OF MONS LACTARIUS

At the end of the two months, a traitorous admiral surrendered the Gothic fleet to the Romans, who had already been collecting many ships from Sicily and other parts of the empire. The Goths, who were becoming desperate, fell back from their previous line and took up positions on the Mons Lactarius (Milk Mountain), an outlier of the St. Angelo range, which rises abruptly above the valley of the Sarno. They were safe there, as it was too rocky for the Romans to follow them, but they soon found that starvation was an even greater enemy. With a sudden resolve, and hoping to catch the Roman army unprepared, they rushed down into the plain, and the last pitched battle between Ostrogoths and Romans began.

The Romans were somewhat surprised by the Gothic move and could not position themselves in their accustomed order, nor could they gather around the standards of their respective generals. The Goths dismounted from their horses and formed themselves into a deep phalanx, and the Romans also dismounted, possibly because of the difficult terrain. The Goths were strongly outnumbered. King Teias fought bravely in the front together with the common soldiers and performed many deeds of valor.

A third of the day had worn away in the battle when Teias's shield became heavy with the weight of twelve Roman arrows in it. He called for his squire to bring him another shield, but at the moment of the change of shields, a javelin pierced Teias's breast and he fell, mortally wounded.

Roman soldiers rushed to the body and cut off his head, which they paraded along the battle lines to bring courage to their comrades and strike panic into the hearts of the barbarians. But the

Goths had entered the battle with little hope and so fought on, despite the death of their leader. The battle continued until nightfall and was renewed the next day. At length, during a pause, the Goths sent a message to Narses that they now understood that God was against them and they would end the war if given terms. Their conditions were that they:

> Would not serve under the banners of the hated empire.
>
> Would be allowed to leave Italy and live as free men in some other barbarian kingdom.
>
> Would be allowed to collect their movable property from the various fortresses and take it with them to cover their expenses on the road.

Narses and his generals considered the proposal, and he accepted it to avoid losing more troops to the obviously desperate barbarians. His only stipulation was that they should swear to leave Italy and never again engage in war against the Roman Empire. One thousand Goths who refused to accept these terms broke out of their camp and, under the command of Indulph, evaded the imperial troops and marched to Ticinum. That city, as well as Cumae, held out for a few months longer against the emperor's troops, but all the other Goths marched sadly over the Alpine passes and never returned to the land of their birth.

The Gothic War was over.

15

AFTERMATH
AND
CONCLUSIONS

THE FIGHTING DID NOT COMPLETELY CEASE with the end of the Ostrogothic kings, for there were still Ostrogoths holding out in a number of Italian towns, and in the north the Franks, who had some years past taken advantage of the struggle to occupy large parts of the Alpine provinces and Venetia, now became more aggressive. In 553, a vast horde of Franks and their Alemannic subjects swept through Italy, but in 554 they were decisively defeated at Capua and withdrew. The sieges of the northern towns dragged on for some years more—it was not until 561 that Verona and Brixia (Brescia) fell—but from 554, Italy enjoyed peace.

In 554, Justinian issued a pragmatic sanction settling the affairs of the country. The acts of the "tyrant" Totila were annulled, and those who claimed they had sold property under pressure during his reign were permitted to recover it on refunding the amount they had received. Returned exiles and prisoners recovered their rights and property; slaves were restored to their former owners, and tenants to their landlords. Various administrative abuses were corrected. At Rome the issuing of free corn to the citizens and the salaries of the professors and doctors were restored, and funding to repair the aqueducts and public buildings was re-established.

Narses remained in Italy as commander in chief and virtual governor-general. The Alpine passes were again garrisoned.

RECONQUEST OF SPAIN

In the same years Narses was completing the conquest of Italy, Justinian embarked on the reconquest of Spain. On the death of Theodoric the Ostrogoth, Spain had become an independent kingdom once more, with King Amalaric having attained maturity. Five years later, in 531, Amalaric, having been defeated by the Franks in battle, was lynched by his troops, and Theudis, the Ostrogothic general who had commanded Spain under Theodoric, became king. After a reign of seventeen years, he was assassinated in 548, and his successor, Theodegisel, suffered the same fate eighteen months later. His successor, Agila, promoted a rebellion of his Roman subjects by violating the shrine of a local martyr at Corduba (Cordoba). The provincials soundly defeated him, and in 551 he was challenged by a pretender named Athanagild, who asked Justinian for aid. The emperor seized the opportunity and sent an army, which conquered a part of southern Spain in Athanagild's interest. In alarm, the Visigoths killed Agila and accepted Athanagild as their king. Having achieved his ambition, Athanagild had no further use for the Roman troops, but they held on to the area they had occupied, which included Carthago Nova (Cartagena), Malaca (Malaga), and Corduba (Cordoba).

Thrace and Illyricum continued to be harried by periodic barbarian raids. The Bulgars invaded Illyricum in 548, and in 550 swept over Thrace, Dacia, and Dalmatia. They passed the winter in Roman territory, and it was not until the spring of 551 that the Roman army succeeded in making them retire beyond the Danube. After this we hear of no invasions until 559, when a new enemy, the Cotrigur Huns, together with the Bulgars and the Sclaveni, crossed the Danube. One group ravaged the Macedonian diocese and was only halted by the defenses of Thermopylae in Greece. The makeshift army of Belisarius in front of Constantinople defeated another group. In 561, a more-formidable tribe, the Avars, advanced to the Danube and demanded to be settled in the province of Scythia, but they were ultimately persuaded to accept a subsidy instead.

THE WAR IN THE EAST

After the second five-year truce of 551, there was some desultory fighting in Lazica between 554 and 556, but the next year, when the truce was renewed, it was extended to Lazica also. In 561, a peace of fifty years was agreed on. Chosroes relinquished his claims to Lazica and evacuated the remaining positions he held there. He also agreed to prevent barbarians from crossing the Caucasus through the pass of the Caspian Gates, which had often been a major issue in former peace negotiations. In return, Justinian agreed to pay him thirty thousand gold pieces a year. The first seven payments, which amounted to three thousand pounds of gold, were made in advance, and the next three were to be paid in the eighth year. Other parts of the peace agreement probably only confirmed existing arrangements:

> The federate Saracens of both parties were included in the peace.
>
> Trade was restricted to certain towns.
>
> Provisions were made for the settlement of disputes between Persians and Romans.
>
> Deserters were not to be received by either side.
>
> Persian objections to the border city of Daras were withdrawn, but no large force was to be stationed there, and no new forts were to be built near the frontiers.

Justinian also obtained from Chosroes a promise not to persecute his Christian subjects.

One point remained unsettled. Suania, a dependency of Lazica, had in the last few years revolted and come under Persian rule. Justinian claimed it should be given back, but Chosroes refused to surrender it.

Italy was not to remain at peace for long, and the exhausted provincials once again faced a barbarian foe in 568, when the Lombards invaded.

Conclusions

It is not easy to draw up a balance sheet of Justinian's wars. Territorially, he greatly increased the empire by the recovery of Dalmatia, Italy, Sicily, Sardinia, Corsica, North Africa, the Balearic Isles, and most of Spain south of the Baetis River. But it is possible these conquests weakened rather than strengthened the empire. Justinian's aggressive wars in the West may have so seriously exhausted Eastern finances and manpower as to weaken the defense of the Danube and the Eastern border. And the recovered provinces of the West may have been a liability rather than an asset, requiring Eastern troops to garrison them and yielding insufficient revenue to pay even for their defense.

The wars of reconquest were undoubtedly long and exhausting. It took twenty years of continuous fighting to subdue the Ostrogoths, and though the Vandals were quickly defeated, the pacification of Africa required an additional twelve years of warfare. These wars were so prolonged largely because the expeditionary forces received meager reinforcements and were consistently starved of money. It does not, however, follow from this that men and money were not available. It would seem rather that Justinian, encouraged by Belisarius's brilliant initial success against the Vandals and the Ostrogoths, persisted in underestimating the diffi-culties that faced later commanders in Africa and Italy, and that, having been informed of the conquest of the two regions, he expected them immediately to pay for themselves. The latter mis-take was particularly disastrous, since with their pay in arrears the troops in the field became mutinous and deserted; and the pro-longed troubles in Africa were due as much to mutinies of the Roman troops as to the revolts of the Moors, and in Italy insubor-dination and desertion became so rife that a new army eventually had to be sent out.

The fact that in 551, Narses was supplied with enough money to pay a large new army and to settle all arrears in Italy shows that by then the financial resources of the empire were not exhausted. The composition of his army does, however, perhaps suggest that man-power was running low, for it contained a high proportion of barbarian allies, whom Justinian so far had used sparingly, and the bulk of the regular troops seem to have been drawn from Thrace and Illyricum, where they could ill be spared.

The diversion of the empire's resources in manpower and money to the West inevitably weakened the Danubian and Eastern borders. Against Persia, Justinian managed to hold his own with remarkable success, despite the fact that he faced a king of exceptional ability and energy who exploited his opportunities to the fullest. Apart from the disastrous year 540, when Chosroes sacked Antioch, the Eastern provinces suffered little damage, and in the end Justinian was able to make good his claim on Lazica. These results were achieved less by military operations than by diplomacy and the payment of gold, but this policy at least enabled the emperor to conserve his manpower on the Eastern border, and it was probably not more expensive than the large-scale military effort, which was the only alternative.

On the Danube, Justinian was less successful. No territory, it is true, was actually lost, and from Singidunum to the river's mouth, the chain of fortresses was maintained intact. The emperor moreover fortified Illyricum and Thrace in depth, improving and repairing the defenses of the cities and building a vast network of small forts over the whole area. But he relied too much on purely passive defense, assisted by diplomacy and subsidies to the tribes beyond the frontier. He frequently withdrew troops from the Illyrian and Thracian armies for service in Italy, and exploited the area as a recruiting ground for his Italian wars. As a result, the Roman armies were rarely able to meet the barbarian invaders in the field, and the whole country from the Adriatic to the Black Sea as far south as Dyrrhachium and Thessalonica and Constantinople itself was subject to perennial devastation.

Africa was finally more or less pacified in 548, the Spanish province conquered in 552, and the taking of Italy completed in 554; the same year saw the end of hostilities in Lazica. So far the finances of the empire had stood the strain. The manpower situation was more precarious. To supply enough troops for the Western campaign, the armies of Armenia and the East had been reduced to such a dangerously low level during the successive truces that they too could offer no serious resistance to invaders. But the shortage of men cannot have been acute, for in the same years Justinian was able to send an army to Spain strong enough to win and hold a considerable province against the Visigoths.

For the last decade of Justinian's reign, there was peace in the West, but the condition of the reconquered provinces was far from happy. When Italy was finally recovered, it was exhausted by the long years of fighting. In 556, Pope Pelagius declared to the bishop of Arles that the estates of the Roman see were so desolated that no one could achieve their rehabilitation, and in a letter to the praetorian prefect of Africa he asserted that "after the continuous devastations of war which have been inflicted on the regions of Italy for twenty-five years and more and have scarcely yet ceased, it is only from the islands and places overseas that the Roman church receives some little revenue, however insufficient, for the clergy and the poor."

Africa was in a rather better state, but the Roman government never recovered from the Moors the large areas they occupied in the last years of the Vandal kingdom, and even within the area effectively under Roman administration, the many fortifications erected by Solomon and his successors suggest that prosperity was greatly reduced and conditions highly insecure. Even in the northern parts of Numidia and Byzacena, and in Africa Proconsularis itself, every town was fortified; in most the length of the walls was drastically reduced, and in many the forum was converted into a stronghold. Only Sicily and Sardinia had peace, except for Totila's brief incursion in 550–51, and enjoyed some prosperity.

Financially, the Western provinces can hardly have paid their way during this period; they certainly can have contributed nothing toward the general expenses of the empire. In manpower they were undoubtedly a drain on the resources of the Eastern parts. Italy was depopulated by the war and could furnish no recruits, and only a limited number of Ostrogoths took service under the empire. Africa made some contribution; not only were a substantial number of Vandals transported to the Eastern front, but Moors were also recruited for service overseas, and some African regiments were raised—two, for example, are later found in Egypt. But these cannot have compensated for the large number of Eastern troops required for the garrison of Africa.

Religiously the war caused the destruction of the two greatest Arian kingdoms, the Ostrogoths and the Vandals. While Arianism would survive some centuries yet, it would now be no more than an antiquated heresy. In 589, at the Third Council of Toledo, King Reccared of the Visigoths announced their conversion to the orthodox faith of Athanasius. The Lombards and Heruli continued in their Arian beliefs, but by the early eigth century, no Arian nations remained.

It is interesting to observe that while Justinian took great care to protect the Christianity of his subjects, religion rarely had any direct impact on the war. His appeal to the orthodox Franks had no effect, and the population in Italy was well-treated by its Ostrogoth overlords and had no cause for complaints. Only in the Vandal war did religion play some part, particularly among the Germanic soldiers who were punished for their Arian beliefs. However, Justinian does not appear to have continued the harsh treatment of his Arian subjects later in the war.

In the last decade of Justinian's reign, the armies shrank to a total of barely one hundred fifty thousand. These had to cover Italy, Africa, Spain, Lazica, Egypt, and the Eastern border, where few were left because the truce was deemed to be sufficient protection. Justinian did construct and restore a great number of forts to improve security, which to a certain extent would reduce the need for troops, but the overall effect was a weakening of the empire's military strength. Thrace was denuded of troops, and because of this the Cotrigurs were able to penetrate to the walls of Constantinople during the invasion of 559.

At Justinian's death in 565, he left the empire enlarged by Italy, North Africa, and southern Spain. But the new conquests did not endure. Within four years, Roman Spain was attacked by the neighboring Visigoths, Africa by the Moors, and Italy by the Lombards. The Lombards who invaded in 568 had the greatest success, taking north Italy and most of the interior of the Italian peninsula by 572.

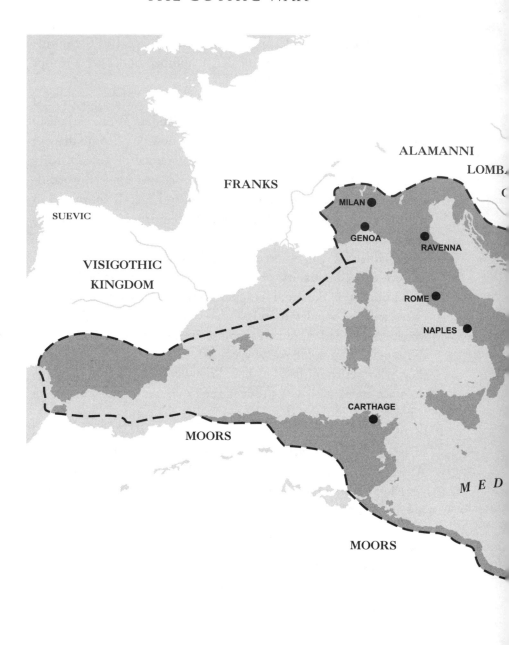

Map 16. The Roman Empire in 565.

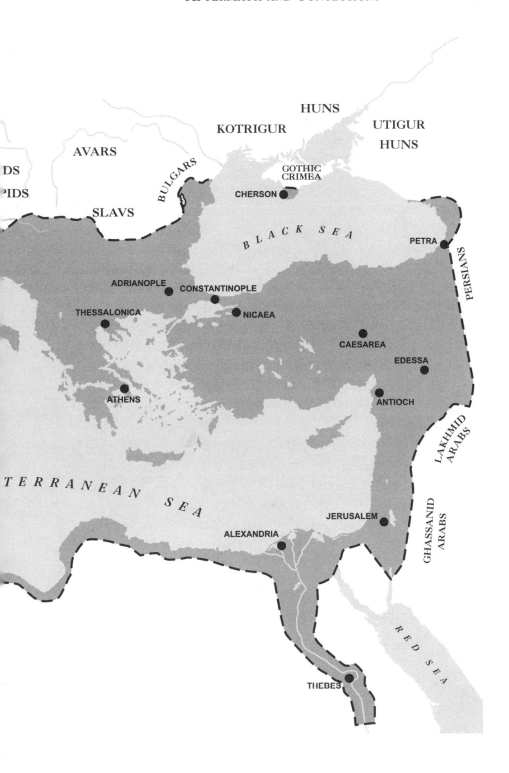

HUNS

KOTRIGUR

UTIGUR
HUNS

AVARS

DS

PIDS

BULGARS

GOTHIC
CRIMEA

CHERSON

SLAVS

B L A C K   S E A

PETRA

PERSIANS

ADRIANOPLE

CONSTANTINOPLE

THESSALONICA

NICAEA

CAESAREA

EDESSA

ATHENS

ANTIOCH

LAKHMID
ARABS

T E R R A N E A N   S E A

JERUSALEM

GHASSANID
ARABS

ALEXANDRIA

RED

JERUSALEM

S E A

THEBES

The early seventh century brought even more desperate conditions to the exhausted empire. Avars, Bulgars, Slavs, Persians, and others reduced the empire to little more than Anatolia, Africa, and Egypt along with small parts of Thrace, Greece, and Italy. Emperor Heraclius did win back large parts of the lost territory, but in the 630s, the Arabs, newly converted to Islam, erupted, and the empire once again had to fight for its life—a fight from which it never recovered.

APPENDIX

MEN, EQUIPMENT, AND TACTICS: THE ROMANS

The Roman army in the early sixth century was no longer the well-disciplined citizen force of heavy infantry that had conquered the vast Roman Empire under the early emperors.

Between the third and sixth centuries, the army changed its character completely. The high-quality Roman legionnaires of earlier times were gone, and the army consisted of many different nationalities—many from outside the borders of the empire—armed in many different ways. The heavy, all-around capable cavalry was now the most dominant and decisive troop type. Discipline was, to a large extent, gone, although the average Roman soldier still adhered to the long military tradition of his forefathers, which had made the Roman Republic a great empire. The morale of which the Romans could boast earlier was now no longer superior to that of the barbarians they fought, and in many cases it was inferior, in particular with regards to the infantry. But the Romans could still put well-equipped and well-supplied troops on the field and still maintained a greatly superior military organization, which gave them a strategic advantage.

The roots of the sixth century Roman army were in the military reorganization of the defense of the empire at the end of the third century, made by Emperor Diocletian (284–305).

From an offensive strategy based on a well-defended border system of troops and fortresses, he turned toward a defense in depth. The borders were garrisoned by static, low-status troops, the *limitanei* or *ripenses*, while more-flexible field armies were created of elite troops. These field armies were ready to handle threats that the border troops could not, such as full-scale barbarian invasions. The local troops were to handle the suppression of smaller war bands and brigands, and to perform what we now call police duties.

The whole concept of central reserves combined with a linear defense of the borders was aimed at protecting against everything from robbers and raiders to a massive barbarian invasion. The great number of fortresses and depots, strengthened by, among others, Emperors Valentinian (364–375) and Valens (364–378), meant there would always be some that could support the mobile field army. Furthermore, they could prevent barbarian war bands and individuals from filtering back into their homelands with loot and slaves.

The barbarians could choose between wasting time and supplies—their weakest point—trying to take a fortress, and moving into the empire with a more or less intact system of fortresses at their backs. To the Romans, the loss of a fortress was of little concern as it could easily be reconstructed, since the barbarian wars generally were not aimed at acquiring territory but at plundering.

By besieging fortresses, the barbarians would quickly run out of provisions brought by the war bands, and new supplies could only be gained by living off the land. The foragers could then easily be attacked by the Roman troops, and barbarians returning to their homelands would be attacked by the local garrison troops. If the barbarians were defeated in a regular battle inside the empire, they were even worse off, as they would not be able to retreat past the border garrisons. When functioning, this system of defense was proof against all but the greatest barbarian invasions. In fact, the situation was somewhat less than ideal. Some fortifications or garrisons were not kept at full strength because of the financial pressure on the state, and occasionally usurpers would remove the field armies for use in civil wars, leaving the borders wide open.

We have a fairly good idea of what the reorganized army looked like from a document dated around the end of the fourth century, *Notitia Dignitatum*, which contains a list of all military units in both parts of the empire.

COMITATENSES AND PALATINI

The core of the new army were the mobile field armies—*comitatenses*—which were raised by recruiting new units and pulling away parts of the border troops. Later, some elite units were termed *palatini*, and they formed the core of the central army of the emperor, later termed the praesental army. *Palatini* and *comitatenses* were soon mixed in the field armies, but the *palatini* continued to have a higher status than the *comitatenses*. Some of these regular units survived even to the Gothic War, where, for example, the unit called the *regii* (the kings) is found among the imperial units during the first siege of Rome. The *regii* were originally an *auxilia palatina* unit.

THE FIELD ARMY

The new units created for the field armies were much smaller than the old legions, which consisted of around five thousand or six thousand men. The new units seem to have been around one thousand to one thousand two hundred strong. Most of the foot soldiers were grouped in units of about five hundred men called *auxilia*, like the allied troops of the early imperial armies.

The old distinction of legionaries being citizens and auxiliaries noncitizens disappeared with the general enfranchisement of all inhabitants of the empire in 212. Furthermore, by the fourth century, legions and *auxilia* were accepting recruits from beyond the empire's borders—primarily the warlike Germans. Also, the differences in armament and equipment seem to have been smaller and smaller. In historian Ammianus Marcellinus's description of the Battle of Strasbourg in 357, the *auxilia* units *Batavi, Bracchiati,* and *Cornuti* all fought in the main line and were similarly armed as the *Primani* legion.

Against this is the testimony of Vegetius, the fifth century writer, who says in his treatise on military matters, *De Re Militari,* that the legions were more heavily armed and more disciplined than the *auxilia*.

There were also a number of specialist light infantry, such as archers, crossbowmen, javelin men and slingers, often raised from regions that traditionally favored these special weapons.

As the cavalry increased in importance in the fifth and sixth centuries, the infantry began to decline. Already in the fifth century Vegetius, who was suggesting a return to the ways of the old legions, says "the name of the legion remains to this day in our armies, but its strength and substance are gone." Slowly, the cavalry element in the field armies was increased, and more focus was put on training the cavalry rather than the infantry and making the cavalry the decisive instrument.

LIMITANEI AND RIPENSES

The remains of the old Roman legions and federate troops were combined and became static garrison troops, protecting the borders. They were called *limitanei*, because they defended the fortified border (*limes*), or *ripenses*, because they defended the great rivers (*ripa*) such as the Rhine and Danube, which made up the border. Their task was to keep small barbarian war bands out of the empire, to garrison fortresses and supply points, and to take part in collecting toll and the general surveillance of the border.

As time passed, these troops turned into a form of part-time militia that was only rarely on campaign. There is a story of a Christian soldier in Egypt who wove baskets and prayed all day, then late in the afternoon put on his uniform and went to drill with his fellow soldiers. When the *limitanei* were used on campaign— such as after the disastrous losses at the Battle of Adrianopolis in 378—they were renamed *pseudocomitatenses*.

While Justinian did make use of *limitanei*—for example in 545 after the recapture of North Africa—he did not pay them if there was no war. Because it was impossible to live on their salary, most of the *limitanei* turned into a form of peasant militia that probably only drilled in times of war.

FOEDERATI

Foederati—federates—in the sixth century mainly consisted of barbarian war bands that, for pay, participated in the Roman military campaigns under their own leaders, such as King Philemuth of the Herulians and King Audoin of the Lombards, who led their forces in the campaign against Totila.

Often a treaty had been made, settling a barbarian tribe on Roman lands with the stipulation that it had to supply a number of troops for the emperor's campaigns. In other cases, defeated barbarian nations were forced to send troops for the emperor's wars.

Generally, the federates would fight for a year, or a short campaign, or just until they had enough booty, then return home. Fighting for the Romans did not always mean an expression of general allegiance, and particularly the Huns would gladly fight for one side, then fight for another side the next year. In other cases loyalty and allegiance were, in the traditional Germanic way, tied to an individual. The best example is Narses's special relationship with the Heruli, who went home after Narses was recalled from the Italian campaign in 539 because they would serve no other leader. When Narses called for the final campaign against Totila, the Herulians again joined in large numbers.

The federates were generally difficult to control, but at the same time they brought some military specializations that were of great use. The Herulians were light infantry and excelled at ambushes and moving in difficult terrain. The Huns were superb horse archers. The Moors were excellent skirmishers, and the Lombards were brave and expendable heavy infantry. And to a certain extent the keyword is expendable. Heavy losses among the federates were of little relevance to the Romans. They would often be placed in the center of a battle line—to ensure their loyalty and to be used in situations where it would be a waste of Roman troops.

The quality of the federates varied, and they could generally be bought by the highest bidder and had little or no discipline. But they gave the Roman army a flexibility that is perhaps most evident in Narses's campaign against Totila in 552.

Narses wanted to end the war in one great battle, but the Romans could not concentrate enough troops to do so as no nation could live with such a surplus of troops waiting for the next major campaign. To collect such forces, the Romans would have to denude the units in other regions, as Justinian had done for the Vandal campaign and the initial stages of the Gothic War. But this meant inviting disaster elsewhere. So instead, Narses hired a great number of federates, who were sent home as soon after the campaign as possible. By far the most economic solution, but it was also the safest solution for the empire.

It is important to emphasize that the main concern of the Roman Empire in military matters was the financial cost. There could be no idle troops waiting for the next major campaign. Also, why equip a recruit, train him for a long period (the great flexibility of the Roman troops in this period demanded a great amount of training), supply him with rations during his training, and then lose him on the battlefield? Why not prefer a barbarian, who had practiced himself for many more years, brought his own equipment, was responsible to a large extent for his own supplies, and whose loss was insignificant and even in a way in the interests of the empire? And the barbarian could be dismissed just after the campaign, whereas regular Roman troops were almost never stricken from the roll. The use of federates was basically good economy, but also a danger if the proportion was too great to the number of Roman soldiers.

ROMAN CAVALRY

By the third century, the Roman army was already increasing the size of its cavalry. This was not because the cavalry had shown itself to be more successful than the heavy infantry, but it was more able to quickly deploy from the strategic reserves to any trouble spots while the Roman depot system was still functioning. The fourth century army, as described in *Notitia Dignitatum*, shows that there were several specialized types of cavalry, such as *equites sagittarii* (cavalry horse archers); *mauri, dalmatae,* and *cetrati* (probably lightly armed skirmishers); as well as *clibanarii* and *catafractarii* (heavily armored lancers in the Persian style).

Particularly the Vandal War proved to the Romans that more cavalry was needed for the Gothic War. While the forces sent to North Africa numbered fifteen thousand, of which only five thousand were cavalry, the infantry played no part in the battles.

During the Gothic War, cavalry played an even greater role and was the deciding factor. Garrisons consisted mostly of infantry because they were a waste of cavalry, but whenever a sally or a regular battle took place, the outcome depended on the cavalry. It was also the mainstay of Belisarius's tactics in hitting hard where the enemy was vulnerable and retreating as soon as the Goths could bring their numbers to bear. These tactics would have been impossible with the heavy infantry of earlier Roman history.

The cavalry offered increased mobility—in particular tactically—and flexibility. The Roman cavalryman of the Gothic War was equally well-suited for all military tasks: he could function as an archer, as shock cavalry, as a mobile scout, as skirmisher, but could also guard city walls and function as infantry or as a marine on ships when needed.

Sixth century ivory relief showing Roman troops of the V Macedonian legion. Notice the armored horse archer in the center. (*Rheinisches Landesmuseum, Trier, Germany*)

The strategic mobility of the cavalry has sometimes been over-rated. During the Gothic War, the armies do not seem to have marched further or quicker than earlier Roman armies—perhaps even the contrary because of their lack of discipline and physical training. Rarely did they bother to make a proper camp every evening, for example, which the legionnaires of earlier times had to do on top of marching. There are examples of great speed—John's dash to rescue the senators in Campania in 547—but they are rare. It must not be forgotten that not only were supplies for the men needed, but also food for the horses, who otherwise would have to spend most of the day grazing. Furthermore, if the train of the army with tents, smithies, camp followers, etc. was brought, they were brought on ox wagons that travelled very slowly indeed.

As the cavalry became more important, it gained more prestige and morale. While the infantry at best was unreliable, the cavalry could generally be counted upon to do the job. There were even examples of infantry acquiring their own horses and learning to ride in order to gain prestige and be among the cavalry.

The usual tactic for the cavalry was to shower the enemy with arrows until they wavered, at which point a regular charge was put in to rout the enemy.

By the sixth century, the cavalry specializations of earlier Roman history seem to have disappeared. Nowhere is there mention of specialized cavalry, whose roles on occasion are taken over by federates, and it is evident from the sources that the cavalry was expected to handle all the specializations. This meant that the tactical options available to a Roman commander were great indeed.

ROMAN INFANTRY

The regular Roman infantry of the sixth century had little in common with the proud legions of imperial Rome. It invariably had a bad reputation, and on the few occasions it was used in battles, there generally were disastrous results, as in the battle before the walls of Rome in 537, when the infantry demanded to be led out against the Goths. Despite being placed behind the cavalry with orders to stay out of the fight and only to protect the cavalry if it was routed, the infantry fled immediately when the cavalry was routed. Only at the Battle of Callinicum in Mesopotamia in 531 and at Nisibis in 541 does the infantry show spirit, with the spearmen saving the Roman army from total defeat.

Belisarius almost always used his infantry to garrison cities or to act as a screen for his retreating cavalry, behind which they could reorganize. On some occasions he mounted them as cavalry. It would be surprising, however, if ordinary infantry could so quickly learn to fight on horseback. More probably they were used as mobile infantry, who dismounted before going into battle.

The infantry was almost always deployed in a phalanx formation, as deep as possible, and forming a solid shield wall against the missiles of the enemy.

BUCELLARII

As the reliability and coherence of the regular field armies decreased, military commanders and wealthy individuals started hiring bands of armed retainers, the *bucellarii* (biscuit eaters). The great warlords of the fifth century such as Stilicho, Aetius, and Aspar all maintained large armed personal followings—a regular bodyguard attached not to the state but to them personally. Attempts were made to limit such private armies, including a law of 476 that made it illegal for individuals to maintain "gangs of armed slaves, Bucellarii or Isaurians." But the ban did not work: Belisarius, for example, maintained up to seven thousand highly trained *bucellarii*, although they were taken from him in 542 when it was felt that he was becoming too powerful.

By the sixth century, the *bucellarii* had been institutionalized, and Roman field armies had partly evolved into large followings of mounted warriors, mostly barbarians, who owed allegiance to powerful generals.

The *bucellarii* were an elite force, and only soldiers who had shown great bravery could be promoted to the status of bodyguard. Most likely the status brought increased pay as well as great prestige. In the period of the Gothic War, the bodyguard was composed of horse archers in the Roman style with heavy weaponry and armor, as well as a bow.

The bodyguard was mainly used to protect the general. It was, however, also used as the elite force it was—for special missions requiring the best troops. At other times a single, particularly respected member of the bodyguard would command other troops, or join a general on a mission. Belisarius's bodyguards are conspicuous in the Gothic War for being given such tasks, and it seems they were meant to be his representatives who would make sure everything happened according to his will.

The Navy

The Roman navy, while rarely mentioned, was incredibly important during the war.

The great navy made ready for the Vandal War is the best-recorded example. Five hundred ships were required to move the Roman army to Africa, and the fleet was protected by ninety-two small warships called *dromones* manned by two thousand marines. Most, if not all, of the transports were probably hired for the job, but the administrative task of bringing together such a large number of vessels is staggering. The ninety-two *dromones* were probably only a relatively small part of the regular Roman navy, as many other tasks had to be done at the same time.

The *dromon* was a light galley with two tiers of oars, with each tier composed of about twenty-five benches, with two rowers on each bench. It was fast and capable of ramming. The ship was commanded by a captain and had two steersmen and a couple of officers. The crew performed the double service of marines and rowers and were provided with arms, including bows and arrows, which they could use from the upper deck, and long pikes, which could be used either for combat or for pushing away boarding enemy ships.

The main task of the navy during the Gothic War was to supply the armies through the ports of Italy, move troops and reinforcements, and to some extent maintain a military superiority in some regions. This meant that the supply situation of the Romans was very good all through the war, although Totila did manage to challenge this for a period. After Totila built his fleet of four hundred *dromones,* and until the Roman naval victory at Sena Gallica in 551, it appears the Roman navy was not in the region, or perhaps it was so engaged in escorting supply ships that it could not gather in greater numbers.

Unfortunately, Procopius tells us little about the fleet, despite its great impact on operations. Basically, the Goths could not take an adequately defended port while the Romans retained naval superiority because the port could constantly be resupplied and reinforced. This same situation existed during the later Lombard invasion, when almost all the interior of Italy was lost but the Romans held onto the ports. This also gave the Roman generals great flexibility, as they could strike anywhere they wanted along the coast of Italy. It was only the lack of initiative among the Roman generals that prevented them from keeping Totila away from south Italy and Sicily.

Later, at the time of Narses's invasion, the fleet made it possible for the Roman army to get to Ravenna fairly quickly. It was probably only the lack of the required ships for horse transport that kept the navy from ferrying them across the Adriatic straightaway.

TRAINING AND DISCIPLINE

The new recruit was generally drafted into existing units, some of which dated back several hundred years. A unit would rarely be completely destroyed in a battle, and it would soon be filled up with new recruits who could learn from the surviving veterans.

From the fourth century on, soldiers are regularly depicted in the sources as debauched, soft, and undisciplined. But this was not entirely true. The soldiers were continually instructed in weapons handling and drilled in unit maneuver. Training seems to have been continually declining in the fifth and sixth centuries, and the standards varied much from army to army. The demands of the generals for setting drill standards were especially important, as seen after the recall of Belisarius in 541, when the Roman armies fall apart.

It is also clear from events of the war that if the troops were not paid, they would not fight or put themselves into danger. Although they would stay on for years in the hope of being paid eventually, they would in the end rebel—with disastrous consequences for the empire. In all regions—Africa, Italy, or Mesopotamia—Justinian seems to have been a lax paymaster, and this was one of the major causes for the lack of durability of his conquests.

The increasing barbarian element and thus the decreasing discipline of the soldiers also meant a decrease in the hated drill. But the culture of the barbarians put a great emphasis on the fighting ability of the individual warrior, so many soldiers were probably roused to practice as individuals and less as a unit.

Drill and weapons practice seem to have had little impact on the lives of the soldiers of the *limitanei*, particularly after Justinian reduced their pay in 545. The writer Vegetius also criticizes the decline in training and discipline in the fifth century.

While the discipline of the sixth century was quite low, the standards of practice probably had not fallen as much as was claimed by some ancient writers. It took great practice to function properly as a horse archer who was also capable of hand-to-hand fighting and knew difficult formations and feigned flight tactics, and Procopius on several occasions praises the training of the soldiers.

One of our main ancient sources for the military in the sixth century, *Strategikon,* by Maurice, says the heavy infantry "should be trained in single combat against others, armed with shield and staff, also in throwing the short javelin and the lead-weighted dart a long distance."

The soldiers' power had become great since the time of the early empire, and sometimes the unruly troops would more or less force their general into battle against his better judgment, as happened twice to Belisarius: at Callinicum in 531 and before the walls of

Rome in 537. At the same time, it is also possible that defeats were explained away by blaming the rashness of the soldiers.

The lack of discipline caused the troops to react somewhat irregularly to orders during battle, and often they would take the initiative themselves. During sieges and other static operations, it seems, the troops would go out and forage on their own initiative without necessarily reporting it.

Desertion was general if morale was low, and the common troops would often desert when the opponents seemed to be able to pay better or were winning. Totila, for example, was able to gather many disgruntled Roman soldiers after his first successful battles. This general lack of discipline meant generals had to be more charismatic and generous to keep the loyalties of their troops.

The heavy infantryman was taught to use the spear (*lancea*), sword (*spatha*), javelin (*veruta*), and weighted darts (*plumbatae*, or *mattiobarbuli*).

The cavalry was taught to jump onto and down from their horses and to hit targets with bow and lance with great accuracy. Further, whole units practiced drill and cooperation with other units on the battlefield. Musical instruments, such as various types of horns, were used to signal the troops.

MEDICAL SERVICES

While the area of medical services is often somewhat overlooked, it was very important to the morale and efficiency of the Roman soldiers. There was at least one surgeon, with his various helpers, per unit of five hundred men. The standard of medical treatment in the Roman army was, even in the declining years of the empire, at a level surpassed only in modern times.

While some serious wounds could not be treated, as was the case with Buchas the Hun in 537, most light wounds would have been quite easy to treat. But some of the more serious cases, such as Arzes the guardsman, who had been hit with an arrow in the skull that had to be surgically removed, show the skill of the Roman doctors. Unfortunately we know little of what kind of treatment they used to avoid infection, which was probably the biggest killer of the wounded, but they seemed overall to be quite successful. Proper treatment could save most of the lightly wounded.

Knowing that a wound would be treated was important for morale, and the warriors could therefore worry less about exposing themselves to injuries.

Camp Building

The Roman army no longer built the famous temporary march camps every evening before resting. But occasionally it was still needed, and Belisarius reintroduced the march camp at the start of the Vandal War:

> As for me, then, I say that we must disembark upon the land with all possible speed, landing horses and arms and whatever else we consider necessary for our use, and that we must dig a trench quickly and throw a stockade around us of a kind which can contribute to our safety no less than any walled town one might mention, and with that as our base must carry on the war from there if anyone should attack us.

This is the traditional Roman field camp, but rarely afterward do we see it constructed even when marching in enemy territory. It seems to have been more common to camp in an easily defensible spot and then put out scouts. Later in the war, for example, at Portus in 537, the Romans made greater use of the traditional barbarian wagon laager, where the supply wagons were placed in a circle around the camp to create a defensive position. Although this type of camp is not mentioned often in Procopius, it was probably the most used because of its convenience.

Supply Systems

While Procopius does not describe the Roman logistical system in detail, it seems it was well-functioning in the sense that the Romans could supply their troops everywhere during the entire war. During the reign of Totila, several Roman cities and fortresses do seem to have lacked provisions, but that may be because the inept patrician Liberius did not arrange for them to be supplied, or the Goths challenged the Roman navy. Most provisions for the troops were shipped from Sicily, which was capable of supplying most of Italy with grain, and from Greece.

Generally, the Romans paid great attention to issues of supply and made sure the grain silos of the cities were well-stocked in expectation of sieges. During long sieges, rations were slowly reduced and finally withheld from the civilian population as great care was taken to ensure the efficiency of the garrison. In such cases the civilians were forced to live on herbs, dogs, and other such foods—in a few cases, the besieged resorted to cannibalism.

One of the main reasons for the defeat of the enormous Gothic army during the first siege of Rome was the Goths' lack of a proper supply system. While the Romans could disperse or concentrate their forces at will because of their efficient logistical system, the Goths had no such option.

The Romans maintained command of the sea through most of the Gothic War, and this also eased supply problems. When Procopius mentions that the Romans collected a fleet of merchant ships and brought grain into the harbor of Classis, it is easy to forget the enormous planning and work that lie behind such undertakings. There is no doubt that enterprising merchants offered themselves at every opportunity for a price, and that most of the supply ships were privately owned. This gave the Roman army a flexible supply of merchant ships that could be reduced or increased according to the strategic situation.

RECRUITING

Conscription had never been popular in the Roman Empire, and increased losses to the approximately five hundred thousand-man army (estimated in the fourth century) meant recruits were constantly needed. The Roman civilian population was intentionally kept nonmilitary so as to avoid unrest, and the authorities looked more and more to barbarians to fill the ranks, including the officer corps. By accepting money instead of a reluctant draftee, the army could use that money hire a willing barbarian. Such foreigners gave loyal service to the empire, at least before the practice of hiring tribes *en masse* under their own leaders became commonplace. The troubled times of the fourth and fifth centuries only aggravated the problem of finding enough recruits for the army. As most Romans were not used to carrying or using weapons, and because of the essentially nonviolent nature of the Christian society, Roman recruits had to be trained far more than, for instance, a Goth who had grown up in a warrior culture that was constantly engaged in tribal skirmishes.

The solution was sought in the wholesale recruitment of elements of barbarian tribes, often tribes already troubling the outlying regions of the empire. The tribes were basically bought off and hired as federates. Land and money were given in return for military service. This was the pattern for the fifth century and, to a certain extent, the sixth.

In 394, Emperor Theodosius brought twenty thousand Gothic federates to battle a West Roman army led by a Frank and containing large numbers of Alans. Buying a fully trained, if rather undisciplined, army of soldiers under its own commanders was convenient for fighting the empire's constant wars. The loss of a Roman field army, such as at the Battle of Adrianopolis in 378, was disastrous and took years to replace, as recruits would have to be drafted, collected, equipped, and trained. And in those years, the empire's enemies would not be idle. The loss of a federate army would mean little and even be somewhat convenient—that particular group of barbarians would no longer be fighting the empire, and other tribes would take the lands and money the Romans would offer.

The barbarians were easier to recruit than peasants, and the process did not interfere with the interests of the landowners who were emerging as more and more powerful in this period. Besides, some tribal groups had the reputation of being good warriors.

At the same time, the Roman recruits were often from the hardy provincials living in the border regions, and these often had a barbarian ancestry or were taken from the less civilized regions of the empire, such as Isauria in Asia Minor. Their more-warlike traditions also made them more interested in joining the military.

Unfortunately, as when Odoacer deposed the puppet Emperor Romulus Augustulus in 476, the barbarians eventually found out that they had little need of the Romans and could mind their own affairs. Even the loyal federates were often like enemies and always ready to enter the field of politics with their military might.

While the Western Empire eventually fell to foreign mercenaries, the Eastern Empire had learned its lesson after 476 and kept the federates out of politics as much as possible.

In the time of Justinian, the army had reached an all-time low of about one hundred fifty thousand troops. The reduced number was the result of heavy losses and Justinian's lack of interest in the army, as well as having a shorter border. It was also not uncommon to have many "phantom" soldiers—dead soldiers who were still on the rolls so the officers could illegally appropriate their pay and rations. There is a similar example from Italy, where Alexander the *logothete*, in his search for new ways to make money, kept the dead soldiers on the rolls so recruits could not advance into higher pay scales. This reduced the cost of maintaining the army, for which Alexander was rewarded. While this practice was not illegal, it gave the appearance of the army being larger than it was. The high rate of desertion when the troops were not paid also caused the units to be hollowed out. In 536, when Germanus went to Africa, he found that only one-third of the soldiers on the rolls were present. The rest had deserted.

It worked the other way around in the periods when it was going well for the Romans and many Goths deserted Vittigis when he proved to be an inept leader. At times whole garrisons would switch allegiance and be put on the Roman rolls. After the Vandal War, five regiments of Vandal cavalry were created and sent to the East. After the surrender of Vittigis, the same happened with some of the Goths, who also were shipped to the East, where they fought faithfully for their new masters.

OFFICERS

The Roman army had a large number of officers compared to the barbarian armies. During expeditions, a general who would lead the forces would be appointed from among the commanding officers of the units, or from without. This would occasionally create serious problems if there was no superior officer present, or if the prestige of a certain general was higher than his superior officer's. A good example is John, the nephew of Vitalianus, who, after he married into the imperial family, had such great prestige that he accepted only Narses as his superior.

The situation in Italy after the recall of Belisarius in 540 was characterized by there being no overall commander, or the commander not being present. Accordingly, command structures dissolved into a struggle for prestige and power, with disastrous results.

A marked difference from the old Roman military system was that many of the generals were professionals who held no civilian posts. While a civilian would occasionally be appointed general—often with bad results, as the elevation of Liberius showed—it was most common to shift around generals from one theater of war to another. While this professionalism meant the Roman generals were more experienced, it also meant they could create their own little spheres of power and at times become semi-independent warlords. This would later trouble the Byzantine Empire greatly. As with most other ancient armies, this focus on the person of the general resulted in a tendency for a Roman army to stop and await new orders when its general was killed, rather than to carry on their orders.

The *Strategikon* of Maurice from the late sixth century describes an ideal regiment of five hundred twenty troops with the following grades:

1 *tribunus* (commanding officer)
1 *vicarius* (lieutenant commander)
1 *primicerius* (chief of staff)
1 *adiutor* (clerk)
5 *hecatontarchs* (commanding 100 men each)
1 *campidoctor* (drill sergeant)
1 *actuarius* (quartermaster)
1 *optio* (quartermaster)
1 surgeon
2 heralds
2 *draconarii* (standard-bearers)
1 cape bearer (assistant to the tribune)
1 trumpeter
1 drummer
50 *decarchs* (commanding 10 men each, including themselves)
50 *pentarchs* (commanding 5 men each, including themselves)
50 *tetrarchs* (commanding 4 men each, including themselves)
350 common soldiers

While this is probably not exactly the way the army was structured at the time of Justinian, it offers a good picture of the number of officers in a regiment. This number had changed little since the time of Emperor Diocletian (284–305).

The number of officers in the Roman army provided greater flexibility of command and control. It also added extra cohesion to the units, as there was theoretically always somebody to take over when an officer was killed.

As with all ranks in the Roman army of the sixth century, some of the officers were of barbarian origin: Bessas was a Goth, for example, and Narses the general and Aratius were Persarmenian deserters. This did not appear to influence them, and most, if not all, officers of barbarian origin conducted themselves well as with regards to loyalty and ability.

SIEGECRAFT

While the Romans were the undisputed masters of siegecraft—rivaled only by the Persians—they rarely made use of it in the Gothic War. Most fortifications in Italy made an admirable use of the terrain and were often unassailable. In such cases the Romans would simply starve out the garrison, attempt a stratagem, or try to make the garrison surrender. Only in the East, where the cities and fortresses were placed on level land, did the Romans occasionally use their knowledge of siegecraft.

Starving out the Gothic garrisons was most likely used because a regular assault wasted men and was less certain to be successful. While starvation might take a long time, the Goths generally seemed inefficient at providing their fortresses with enough provisions, and because the Romans generally had no reason to hurry, this was the optimal choice.

Because of their "scientific" approach to warfare, the Romans rarely failed when they wanted to take a city or a fortress.

FORTIFICATIONS

Fortresses and the fortified cities were the mainstay and backbone of the Roman strategy until the invasion of Narses in 552. The Romans were simply too few to fight a regular battle with the

Goths and so had to use a system of fortresses and fortified cities as their base of operations. There they could keep their provisions safe and make good use of their tactical superiority against the blundering Gothic army.

The first siege of Rome is the best example: an army of five thousand troops won decisively against an army of one hundred fifty thousand fierce Goths. Because the Goths never learned the art of siegecraft and do not seem to have employed their many Roman deserters for it (as Attila the Hun, for example, did in his campaigns), the small Roman garrisons could generally feel safe behind their walls. If the Goths could not take the walls by storm—which, no matter the outcome, was very wasteful of troops—they had to starve out the garrison. Unfortunately for the Goths, their supply system mainly consisted of living off the land, whereas most of the Roman fortresses were well-stocked with provisions. Accordingly, only treachery or some stratagem would allow them to take a fortress quickly.

For Belisarius, the conquest of Italy was a series of jumps from one fortress to another. This was very cost effective and forced the Goths into a type of warfare at which they were simply not very good. The strategy was, however, also time-consuming, and this would later create problems when the Persians felt they could not stand idly by while Justinian was enlarging his empire. But how else to fight the formidable Goths with an army so small? The choice of this strategy again showed Belisarius's genius, and despite a few blunders, mostly caused by his own generals or soldiers, the campaign of 535–540 was based on this strategy and was executed brilliantly.

The Goths soon understood the Roman strategy and so Totila began to raze the walls of the captured cities and fortresses. Despite the criticism of his own people after the recapture of Rome by Belisarius in 547, Totila's strategy was quite sound. He did not have enough troops to garrison all the captured cities and could only win the war by keeping a sizable army together. Again Belisarius defeated him, by retaking the empty fortifications and refortifying them. Despite Totila's speed at reacting to these operations, he never succeeded in retaking the refortified places.

By using the system of fortifications against which the barbarians could do little, Belisarius was following a strategy of defense that had been used by Emperors Diocletian and Constantine the Great and that had proven its worth time and again—for example, in the campaign following the Roman defeat at Adrianopolis in 378.

When Narses returned to Italy in 552, we see an entirely different strategy, which he had also thought to employ in 537 when he first came to Italy. In 552, Narses had a superior army and avoided getting bogged down in sieges. Instead he sought a confrontation with the Gothic king as soon as possible. For political reasons, Totila could not avoid the conclusive battle, although a better strategy would have been to make Narses chase the Goths around Italy. The Roman army would have had more and more supply problems, and more and more desertions from its large barbarian contingents. But Totila had to show himself as king of the Ostrogoths and of Italy and so had to fight Narses, despite the latter's numerical superiority.

When Totila was defeated at Taginae in 552, most of the troublesome allied barbarians were sent home, as Narses believed there was no need of such a large army to destroy Teias and the remaining Goths. Again, Narses seeks a quick confrontation with Teias, which he does not fully achieve, because of Teias's reluctance to engage.

After the battle of Mons Lactarius and the destruction of the Ostrogoths, Narses reverted to the strategy of fortification, refortified cities and fortresses in Italy, and garrisoned them. When the Franks invaded in 553, just after the end of the Gothic War, they were in the end defeated in the same way as the Goths and also lost great numbers of warriors. The Roman use of horse archers and fortifications was even more devastating against the Franks, who were primarily an infantry army. The horse archers especially caused many casualties, as the Franks rarely used armor, apart from wooden shields.

The fortifications varied greatly, but the most modern ones were built so that as few men as possible would be needed to defend them. The walls were built high so they could not be scaled easily, and they had towers with interlocking fields of fire and various siege engines. In the sixth century, the tendency was to move away from siege engines and employ the more-flexible archers for a strong defense.

A ditch was dug around the walls of most cities with level access so towers and rams could not be brought forward easily. The gates were heavily defended with artillery, as they were naturally easy to access. Most fortresses and cities in Italy made much use of the terrain in their defenses, which would be constructed accordingly. In the East, where many cities were on level ground, sometimes double walls were constructed, and they were more strongly fortified.

TACTICS

With the flexibility inherent in the Roman army of the sixth century, a wide range of options were available to the general. He could choose exactly what formation to use and how to put up the battle line according to the tactical needs of terrain and the enemy.

At Rome, Belisarius based his defense on a combination of fortifications and sallies. The cavalry would engage the Goths, showering them with arrows until they began to lose cohesion, at which point a regular charge would be made to break them, or the cavalry would retire while continuing to shoot arrows at the enemy. The inability of the Goths to react to these tactics caused heavy casualties—usually with no Roman troops lost. The Huns were particularly adept at this type of fighting because of their unparalleled experience in riding and their skills at archery from horseback. The destruction of Gibamund's detachment in North Africa in 533 was a clear example of the efficiency of the Huns, who were greatly feared for their abilities.

At Rome, if the sallying troops were too outnumbered, they would retreat within *ballistae* range of the walls and so end the enemy pursuit.

Pitched battles were generally avoided, and the Gothic War can boast of only a few, though they were generally important. To the Romans, with their educated attitude toward warfare, a regular battle was too risky. They rarely had the numbers to challenge the barbarians in a stand-up fight, and the financial costs of a lost battle were enormous. Furthermore, the outcome of a battle—no matter the odds—was considered uncertain and up to chance.

Only if the gain from the battle was comparable to the risk did the Romans engage. In battle, infantry was mainly set up in a spear phalanx behind the cavalry or in the middle of the battle line. Their task was normally to hold back the barbarian charge and to receive the friendly cavalry if they were routed. Generally, barbarian federates would be placed in the center of the battle line, where their loyalty could be better ensured. The cavalry was customarily placed on the flanks—mostly if expecting the enemy to attack—or on a broad front if the Romans planned to attack.

The Romans generally sought the solution to the battle on the flank, by either flanking the enemy charge or by charging the enemy flanks. Initially, the cavalry would shower the enemy with missiles and then make the decisive charge. These tactics were mainly used against the Western barbarians, whereas against the Persians, who had a more-developed military, other, more-sophisticated tactics were used.

When the enemy was broken, a general pursuit would take place with the whole army. Generally, the Romans were wary of pursuing too far because of the danger of ambushes and feigned flight.

The Romans knew the different tribal abilities of the barbarian federates and used them accordingly. Maurice devotes an entire chapter ("Characteristics and Tactics of Various Peoples") of his *Strategikon* to describe optimal ways of fighting various nations such as the Persians, Scythians, Germans, and Slavs.

WEAPONS AND EQUIPMENT

Procopius describes the basic equipment of the Roman cavalry in this war:

> [T]he bowmen of the present time go into battle wearing corselets and fitted out with greaves which extend up to the knee. From the right side hang their arrows, from the other the sword. And there are some who have a spear also attached to them and, at the shoulders, a sort of small shield without a grip, such as to cover the region of the face

Roman long sword (*spatha*), originally used by the cavalry, but in the sixth century, it was used also by the infantry.

and neck. They are expert horsemen, and are able without difficulty to direct their bows to either side while riding at full speed, and to shoot an opponent whether in pursuit or in flight. They draw the bowstring along by the forehead about opposite the right ear, thereby charging the arrow with such an impetus as to kill whoever stands in the way, shield and corselet alike having no power to check its force.

The corselet would either be chainmail (*lorica hamata*); lamellar (*lamellae*), an armor made of narrow vertical plates laced together horizontally and vertically; or scale armor (*lorica squamata*), which was particularly popular in the East. Scale armor consisted of little scales of bone or metal linked with wire and attached in rows to a lace, which in turn was sewed to a fairly stiff linen backing. Each row overlapped the one below it by about a third.

Helmets were of the *spangenhelm* type. They probably originated from Sarmatian helmets and were made up of several plates, usually six, held together in conical form by reinforcement bands. The Roman version usually had cheek pieces, neck guards, and nose guards added. Another helmet of the period, called the ridge helmet, was characterized by two bowls held together by a central ridge.

The most common sword was the long sword (*spatha*), used for stabbing and cutting.

The bow was much superior to earlier bows. The composite recurved bow consisted of a wooden core with a layer of horn on the inside and sinew on the outside. The tips were reinforced with bone. Maximum range was about 325 yards. The arrows were constructed from cane or reeds.

The infantry was equipped with the spear (*lancea*), which could be thrown or used for close combat. Some infantry carried javelins (*veruta*) for close fighting. Their range was about 100 feet. The infantry also used darts (*plumbatae* or *mattiobarbuli*). While their range was greater than the javelin, they did not cause serious wounds and probably could not penetrate armor. Their main purpose was to stick in the shields of the enemy and, by their weight, make the shields clumsy to use. The infantry also used slings and bows.

Various shields were in use, mostly small ones for the cavalry and larger ones for the infantry. It appears they were mainly oval for the infantry, and about 43 inches high by 35 inches wide. They were constructed of wood not quite a half-inch thick and covered with leather. A hollow iron boss covered the central handgrip.

The barbarian federates came with their own traditional equipment, which varied greatly according to their chosen tactics. Procopius describes the wild Heruli this way:

> And the Persians, shooting into great masses of the enemy in the narrow alleys, killed a large number without difficulty, and particularly of the Heruli, who had at the first fallen upon the enemy with Narses and were fighting for the most part without protection. For the Heruli have neither helmet nor corselet nor any other protective armor, except a shield and a thick jacket, which they gird about them before they enter a struggle. And indeed the Herulian slaves go into battle without even a shield, and when they prove themselves brave men in war, then their masters permit them to protect themselves in battle with shields. Such is the custom of the Heruli.

So the army that Belisarius brought to the war in Italy was nothing like the legions of old, but instead a modern response to the changes in warfare. The Roman army of the sixth century was professional, hard-hitting, and able to adapt its tactics to almost any type of foe, terrain, and weather. The Goths, Vandals, and Franks would time and again be defeated by much smaller Roman forces because of their tactical superiority and adaptability.

While the discipline of old times was lacking, the Roman soldier was still highly trained for his job and very motivated, if he was treated well. In many ways, the armored horse archer of the sixth century was the epitome of centuries of development of Roman military institutions.

MEN, EQUIPMENT, AND TACTICS: THE GOTHS

When Theodoric the Great invaded Italy in 489, he did not lead the entire Ostrogothic people, but a federate army composed mainly of Ostrogoths. What is referred to as the Ostrogoths contained other barbarian elements, and being Goth was not only a question of ethnicity. Within this framework were also the Rugi of Fredericus, who maintained a high degree of independence. They did not intermarry with the Ostrogoths when they settled together in the north Italian districts. After the debacles of 540 and 541, they even felt strong enough to proclaim one of their own, Eraric, king of the Ostrogoths, although the tribal alliance was still named the Ostrogoths and not the Rugi.

Smaller groups and splinter groups of other tribes were of course integrated more quickly into Theodoric's people. This fundamental polyethnic character of the Gothic army was intensified after the defeat of Odoacer's army. Considerable contingents of the Western Roman army joined Theodoric, whereby additional Rugian, Herulian, Scirian, Turcilingian, as well as Suevic, Sarmatian, and Taifalian elements became "Ostrogothic." No doubt the victory over Odoacer also increased the number of Romans in the Gothic army. There were even Romans who saw themselves as Goths and belonged to the Gothic army. Furthermore, there existed a regional military organization. For the construction, maintenance, and garrisoning of the cities and fortresses, not only the locally settled Gothic landowners were called upon but also the Romans.

To be a Goth and to march in the Gothic army was the same thing. If a Goth was threatened with loss of his rights and liberty, proof that he had served in the army was sufficient to protect his personal freedom. Whoever belonged to the Gothic army was automatically of age. We also know the name of honor of Gothic freemen from their songs: they were called *capillati* (the curly-haired or long-haired ones).

The Ostrogothic army held out the promise of social mobility and attracted the Roman underclasses. At the time of migration this attraction was useful, for it helped the Goths relieve the chronic shortage of manpower. But in Italy the tenants were needed in the fields, not on the battlefields. Because Theodoric had staked his future on the consolidation of his kingdom, he prohibited the Roman tenants from joining the Gothic army. It was also possible he did not consider them to be loyal and that their addition would undermine the morale of the army. But the old attraction was still alive when the Ostrogothic kingdom was fighting for its survival. Totila not only accepted Roman slaves and tenants into the Gothic army but even mobilized them against their senatorial masters, promising them freedom and the ownership of the land they were tilling. This is perhaps one of the central reasons for the poor Romans to see a future in being Goth—simply out of despair over their economic situation.

War was a characteristic part of early Ostrogothic history, but it rarely turned into major warfare that involved the whole tribe. Even the history of the Goths, written by the Ostrogoth Jordanes in the sixth century, makes it clear that large wars were rare and short. Cattle raids, plundering expeditions, and military competition between war bands were, on the other hand, commonplace.

Theodoric was a fierce and respected warrior, as may be remembered by the story of the murder of Odoacer, but nobody could claim the same of his many grandsons or his inept nephew, Theodahad.

Even Vittigis, who was raised on the shield and proclaimed king because of his military experience, failed as a general. Eraric, Ildibad, and Teias did not even get a chance to prove themselves. Only Totila deserved his reputation as a good and effective general, perhaps mainly because of his great understanding of the psychology of the troops in both armies.

Despite the Goths' being a warlike nation, most of their history is about honorable defeats rather than glorious victories. They were decisively defeated by the Huns and quickly submitted. The Ostrogoths fought bravely for Attila the Hun at the battle of the

Catalaunian Fields in 451, but lost the battle. The defeats incurred at the hands of Belisarius and Narses were great indeed, particularly in the early years of the war, when Belisarius broke the back of the mighty Gothic kingdom.

Even in their victories they are sometimes defeated, such as the battle at the Pons Milvius in 537, when Belisarius's small cavalry force was caught but managed to escape and inflicted heavy losses on the Goths. The same is true for the battle before Rome in 537, when the Romans were decisively defeated but managed to flee to the city and, despite great losses among the inexpert militia of Rome, caused much greater losses to the Gothic army.

The victory at Adrianopolis in 378 was also complete, and mainly due to the Greuthungi cavalry charge on the Roman flank, but they failed to take the imperial treasure or to follow up the victory. The same could be said for the victory at Abrittus in 251, when the Goths swiftly retreated home after the battle.

Nevertheless, if the Goths differed from the other Germanic peoples it was in their tenacity and their ability to make use of the surviving Roman administrative systems and defenses. They succeeded in preserving the defense of the Alpine regions, the Rhône valley, and thereby Italy until the crisis in the war against Emperor Justinian. They were able to defend against their hostile barbarian neighbors, against whom they won practically all conflicts. Before the Gothic War they had defeated Sarmatians, Sadagi, Suevi, Gepids, Franks, and the barbarians of Odoacer. None of these tribes was weak, and neither were Odoacer's mercenaries.

But the two decades of the Gothic War destroyed the Ostrogothic nation and, to a large extent, the Ostrogoths themselves. Countless thousands had fallen on the battlefields of Italy, and countless thousands had starved to death, or were killed or enslaved in barbarian or Roman raids. It is incredible that the Goths stubbornly kept up the fight for so long.

The war against the Huns after Attila died was probably bigger, and memories of these battles are reflected in Germanic sagas. Nevertheless, details of the actual battles are too few to be of value.

Theodoric's campaigns against the Sarmatians and his long feud with Theodoric Strabo have been recorded in the same fashion as the sagas. Even his last operations from his base at Novae in

486–487 appear only to be large raids rather than actual battles and warfare. Only at the confrontation with the Gepids at Cybalae on the Ulca River during his long march to Italy in 488–489, and in the war of Sirmium in 504–505 against the same tribe, do the sources show Theodoric's ability to translate political power into military power.

One of the Ostrogoths' main wars was against the Gepids in the Sirmium area. In 504–505, a new war began there, at the fringes of Theodoric's kingdom of Italy. Sirmium was geographically and strategically important. The Gepids had captured the city in a campaign sometime after 454, when the fortifications were in disrepair. After establishing themselves in the formerly important administrative center, they used the city as a base for raids in the region.

Theodoric saw no option but to move against the Gepids, the archenemies of the Ostrogoths who were threatening the eastern Gothic provinces and the roads leading into Italy. Theodoric appointed the Goth Pitzia from his following to take command of an army from Italy with orders to capture Sirmium.

The Gepids were soon defeated and Sirmium taken, but the easy victory motivated the Ostrogoths to move further east, thereby violating Roman territory. To support this move they had allied themselves with a local warlord named Mundo.

Mundo, a Hun by birth, had put together an army of barbarians and bandits from beyond the Danube and threatened Roman-Gepid control of the region around the city of Singidunum and the province of Dacia Ripensis. The Romans responded by sending Sabinianus, general of Thrace with their newest allies, the Bulgars. They defeated Mundo and his makeshift army, but he joined Pitzia at an abandoned fortress called Herta by the Danube. Jordanes writes that Pitzia had two thousand infantry and five hundred cavalry. Here the Ostrogoths defeated the Bulgars, but otherwise the battle was a tie. Reluctantly, Sabinianus accepted Ostrogothic control of Sirmium, and the Goths gave up their plans to expand their control over the regions east of Sirmium. No more was heard of Pitzia. When Vittigis gathered the army to retake Rome from Belisarius in 537, the troops from Sirmium were also summoned. The Gepids soon recaptured the city, which became their capital.

The Sirmium War illustrates Ostrogothic political and military structures under Theodoric better than any other event. The eastern border was of vital importance for the Ostrogothic kingdom, but there were no plans of a massive garrisoning or Gothic settlement. There were simply too few Ostrogoths, and the region was too far from the center of the kingdom, for any military pressure to be put there. Instead, the Ostrogoths had to rely on the local Romans and put the the defense and civil administration in their hands.

The northern Alpine regions, roughly modern Austria and Switzerland, were also a problem for the Ostrogoths. Here too there were not enough Goths and only smaller military units, and the defenses were also largely in the hands of the local population. The security of the region and, in the end, the security of north Italy lay in Theodoric's attempt to build buffer kingdoms along the northern border, particularly to keep the Franks out. Garrisons were established at key passes and crossroads. The Rhaetian provincials were the core of the defense system, which was to ensure the delay of invading northern barbarians until the Goths could muster an army to relieve them. Also here, as in all the kingdom, the Roman population was part of the civil administration. As he had experienced in the Roman Empire, Theodoric also used tribal remnants and war bands, such as after Clovis's victory over the Alemanni in 507, to settle on the borders to help in the defense as federates. In 508, the Gepids were induced to join the Ostrogothic kingdom, and some of their troops served in Gaul.

Theodoric kept diplomatic relations with the Thuringians, Burgundians, and Alemanni, who were the main buffer kingdoms. Several villages also had a small Gothic element who functioned like the Roman *limitanei*: peasants in peace, soldiers in war. They were unable to stop an invasion on their own, but they could harass the invading army and limit plundering. Their daily function was to keep bandits away and ensure the safety of traffic and trade.

The settlement of federates and other defensive measures show that Provence and the western Alpine regions demanded constant attention. At the creation of the Ostrogothic kingdom in Italy, the Burgundians had caused so many problems for northwestern Italy that Theodoric had to buy peace and buy back captives from their raids. Behind the Burgundians was the growing Frankish kingdom, which was also ready to fight for more land. In 509, the Ostrogoths and Burgundians had made an alliance against the Franks. The same year, Ostrogothic Duke Mammo invaded Provence and thereby started a long period of Ostrogothic activity in the region—often in alliance with the Burgundians. In 534, the Franks saw their opportunity to eliminate the Burgundian kingdom and gain control over the region. All the way until their withdrawal, the Goths had kept the Roman administrative system in place.

To conclude, before the war against the Romans, the Ostrogoths had made considerable advances in developing a military strategy and defenses—particularly under Theodoric the Great. They managed to keep the borders free while winning the struggles in the Rhône valley and at Sirmium. That is not to say that the basic technological aspects of warfare had changed. The Ostrogoths were still fighting with the same weapons and in the same way as their ancestors at Adrianopolis in 378.

Against the Romans they fared much worse, especially during long campaigns, such as those of Emperor Constantine in the early fourth century. That is how Sabinianus kept the Goths fenced in at Epirus Nova until he died in 481, and it was generally a favored Roman tactic to starve the barbarians into submission rather than risk an open battle.

In the end, all Ostrogothic men were warriors. Individual prowess in battle was an important trait for determining position in Gothic society. Weapons and armor differed from individual to individual, but their quality and beauty showed who were the nobles on the battlefield. Totila died after having exchanged his magnificent armor for a common soldier's, in order not to be too conspicuous on the battlefield. The importance of courage and ability on the battlefield is also exhibited by a law of Theodoric's that any Gothic warrior who was sent home from a campaign for anything but serious wounds lost his yearly donation and was severely rebuked.

Maurice, in his *Strategikon*, sums up the barbarians' deficiencies: they lacked a cohesive military command and control, as well as technological elements such as efficient siege techniques, and they did not have the patience needed to use tactical reserves.

Their technological deficiencies could be neutralized for a short while through stratagems and possibly through the use of Roman mechanics, shipbuilders, sailors, and even Roman soldiers and bandits—all of which was seen through Gothic history. But they never approached the military organization of the Romans.

GOTHIC INFANTRY

Belisarius is said to have attributed the decisive weakness of the Goths to the lack of heavily armed mounted archers. The Goths had only foot archers with limited mobility and hence were very vulnerable. But we should not underestimate the Gothic foot warrior. The Crimean Goths once resisted a Hunnic cavalry charge by forming a shield wall and thrusting their long lances against the attackers. In mountainous Moesia, Theodoric the Great employed a large number of infantry against Bulgarian horsemen and was just as successful as his father, Thiudmir, who had conducted a victorious winter campaign with an army on foot.

But because it was mainly the socially disadvantaged who fought on foot, they depended for the most part on the supply of public weapons. When Theodoric's system of training and supply collapsed after Vittigis's capitulation, the training and equipment of the infantry became irregular and insufficient. Perhaps this was one reason why the Gothic infantry failed in the Battle of Taginae in 552, even though it had fought valiantly under Vittigis before Rome.

The almost total absence of weapons in Ostrogothic graves prevents a detailed reconstruction of their weapons and equipment, but many aspects of their military life are evident. A Lombard shield decoration of the seventh century might give us an idea of the appearance of the Gothic foot soldier: he had a long spear or lance (*contus*), a sword with a buckler, and a battle tunic that reached below the knees and served as protection against long-range weapons. The wealthier would have owned a chainmail and a helmet. The helmets were similar to the Roman types of the period: the *spangenhelm,* or ridged helmet.

The Ostrogoths appear to have used weapons produced at Roman factories or similar workshops. Based on the sources, it seems that the Roman pattern-welding methods that increased the carbon content and thereby the strength and flexibility of blades was unknown and somewhat mystical to the Goths.

In his *Strategikon*, Maurice recommends that the Roman soldiers wear the Gothic long tunic and Gothic shoes with thick, hobnailed soles, broad toes, plain stitching, and fastened with clasps. Despite the disappearance of the Ostrogoths and the severe defeats of the Visigoths, parts of their traditional war gear had clearly made an impression on the Romans.

In battle the Gothic infantry was much more active than its Roman counterpart. Its charge could be as devastating as the charge of the cavalry, and only late in the war was the infantry relegated to the role of acting as a screen behind which the cavalry could reorganize.

Gothic Cavalry

The famous cavalry under Alatheus and Saphrax in 378 does not seem to have been a large force. Initially, the cavalry probably consisted of the nobles following the young King Videric, some noble Visigoths who had found some horses, and the allied Huns and Alani.

Like the Greuthungi in southern Russia and the Visigoths in Gaul and Spain, the Ostrogoths in Italy were primarily horsemen. The mounted warrior enjoyed the highest esteem. Theodoric Strabo could heap no greater insult on the Goths of his cousin Theodoric Thiudmir than to ride up in front of their camp dressed in splendid armor, reminding them that they all had once owned two or three horses but now had to go on foot like slaves. This mockery does not mean that a "real" Gothic army was composed exclusively of horsemen who only in an emergency switched to fighting as infantrymen. In Theodoric's army, as in those of his successors, there were foot warriors who had specific tactical tasks. But even when the infantry fulfilled its tasks in a disciplined manner, it was the cavalry that dealt the decisive blow.

The Gothic horseman was much like the lance rider of other nomadic peoples. A warrior of this kind ideally wore a helmet with protection for his neck and cheeks and was dressed in a flexible suit of armor—not necessarily of metal but sometimes made of bone or leather—that reached down at least to his knees. Their shields were bigger and appear to have been mainly round, with a central grip protected by a hollow shield boss or a small buckler. Most likely they did not wear greaves. Their helmets were of the *spangenhelm* type. The horseman wielded with both hands the extra-long thrusting lance, the *contus*, to which a pennant was affixed, and he carried a long sword (*spatha*) as a secondary weapon for close combat on horseback or on foot.

The Navy

As seaworthy as the Goths may have seemed in the third century, the sea was not of interest to them after their admission into the Roman Empire. As king of Italy, Theodoric the Great did without a fleet until shortly before his death. In naval matters he relied on the Vandal kingdom until that doubtful ally deserted him for good. After the murder of his sister by the new ruler of Carthage, Thrasamund, Theodoric ordered a campaign of revenge. Construction began on a great fleet, but Theodoric died before it was completed. Thereafter, Ravenna had at its disposal only light sailing ships.

Totila soon recognized the value of a fleet in the war against the Romans, but this did not turn the Ostrogoths into real seamen. Even if the crews were made up of active warriors commanded by an officer corps of Roman deserters, such as Indulph, the guardsman of Belisarius, they nevertheless remained Goths, who disliked the sea. It is therefore not surprising that they acted as infantry and tried to fight land battles at sea. The outcome of the naval battle off Sena Gallica was correspondingly disastrous. They did, however, have some success in capturing Roman supply ships and scored an important naval victory at the siege of Neapolis in 542–543.

In the end, the last Gothic admiral deserted to the Romans and handed over the fleet that was protecting King Teias and the rest of the Goths in the bay of Neapolis, and in so doing sealed the fate of the last Gothic king.

While the existence of a stronger Ostrogothic fleet might have greatly affected the war, it was not possible. The Ostrogoths were not seafaring people and would have had to rely on Roman sailors and man the ships with Gothic warriors. To challenge the formidable Roman fleet on such a shaky basis would only have been to invite disaster, as seen by the sea battle off Sena Gallica, where the Gothic navy was outfought and outmaneuvered.

CAMP BUILDING

The Goths, like the Romans, often neglected to build camps while on the march, but occasionally they did construct proper fortified camps. At the first siege of Rome in particular, their camps, constructed with ditches and earthen ramparts with sharpened stakes in them (in the traditional Roman fashion), kept away the Roman assaults and saved many a Gothic life. Their normal march camps consisted of wagon laagers, behind which they could spend the night in safety. Indeed, the Goths seem to be one of the barbarian tribes who brought this type of march camp to the Romans.

SUPPLY SYSTEM

One of the main problems for the Goths was their lack of a proper and developed supply system. The Goths were defeated all through their history by the Romans, who starved them and attacked their foragers. Their armies and war bands had to be constantly on the move to find enough provisions. This was one of the major causes for the failure of the first siege of Rome. Despite being in almost absolute control of Italy, the Goths did not supply their enormous army at Rome, and soon they suffered more than the besieged Romans. Several times during the war they had to disperse their troops to forage, and King Vittigis could not supply the expedition to relieve the brave and tenacious Gothic garrison of Auximum. Generally, the Goths could not properly provision large forces during the war, despite being in their own country. In the time of Totila, after the virtual destruction of Italy by famine and more than a decade of war, it became even more of a problem.

Supplying the Gothic fortresses was less of a problem, as the garrisons were not large and the provisions were mainly based on gathering foodstuffs from the surrounding lands.

While it would have been of great advantage for the Goths to have a fixed and functioning supply system, they can hardly be blamed for not having one. They had never fought a war that required them to supply large numbers of troops for any extended period. The gathering of the whole Ostrogothic army under Vittigis was something that had not happened since the exodus of Theodoric the Great more than forty years earlier.

OFFICERS

The Ostrogoths took over many Roman military institutions when they became masters of Italy. While they did not have anything like the command structure of the Romans in the units—indeed, in most cases there were no units as such, for the Goths were a nation in arms—they did have higher levels of command.

The military and social structures of the Gothic army were almost identical. The rich and powerful were the dukes and counts. In war the title *dux* (duke) entailed an independent command in place of the king, who, since the capture of Ravenna in 493—and probably following the imperial model—did not lead the army in person. Only when the threat of the Gothic War became so great that it was thought to threaten the existence of the nation did the Gothic king again campaign.

Wealth and position determined an individual's rank, which was based largely on how close the individual was to the king. The personal style of the king's rule, however, aimed at addressing every free Goth and every warrior of the army (*millenarius, mediocris, capillatus*), and dealing with him directly. Although this was often nothing more than a good intention, the possibility of getting to know capable men "among the common people" and of recruiting them into royal service existed and was utilized. But the best way for a Goth to make an illustrious career for himself was to go to court at a young age. There he was first employed as a page. If he proved himself capable, he rose in the ranks of the palace.

Dukes were the highest military leaders in Gothic society, and their presence at a border showed how serious a situation was viewed to be. In addition to having military authority, they could decide legal matters. Their power was almost unlimited—a subject that was often debated. Dukes were often appointed from among the nobles in the kingdom.

The second-highest rank was the *comes Gothorum*—a Gothic count—who had the right to use the staffs of the Roman authorities. He was charged with military tasks and possessed the judicial power that accompanied them, but in disputes between Goths and Romans he could exercise such authority only in consultation with Roman lawyers. In times of peace a Gothic count was usually responsible for a city, but if a city had few or no Gothic barbarian settlers and instead military units, the count's sphere of influence could be extended to include the entire province.

The *saiones* were the personal messengers and bearers of direct orders from the Gothic king and could perform civilian and military tasks in the king's name. Under certain circumstances, they could direct and control any official. *Saiones* came onto the scene especially when the king had something to discuss with his people; the movement of troops, interference in Gothic practices and customs, and various civilian affairs—all came under the purview of the *saiones*.

We have virtually no information about the commanders of the smaller divisions of the Gothic army. In one source they are given the rather nondescript name *duces et praepositi* (commanders and superiors). Nor can we say what the units under their command were called, assuming they had a fixed name.

Because military ability was central for leadership among the Goths, service at the borders was viewed as an important road to promotion. An example is Tulum, who began his career as a young man fighting under Pitzia in the Sirmium War. After that he commanded in several campaigns against the Frankish King Clovis, where he distinguished himself during the fighting around Arelate. Later he was sent back to Gaul to overhaul the defenses against the Franks. When it became evident that the western border with the Franks demanded constant attention, Tulum was given large lands there so he could settle with his Gothic followers.

Siegecraft

The Gothic tactics mainly consisted of a human-wave attack with much shouting, throwing of rocks and spears, and shooting of arrows, or a massive cavalry charge. These tactics had little chance of success against city walls, of course, so for sieges they used different tactics—almost always without success.

At Marcianopolis in 248, the Goths collected large stones and put them up against the walls in heaps, but this primitive attempt at building a siege ramp was unsuccessful, and they failed to take the city.

At Philippopolis in 250, they succeeded in crossing the walls with the help of a ramp of wood and earth, but not before the defenders had crushed their rough and unprotected siege towers with boulders.

At the siege of Side in Lycia in 269, the Goths pushed armored towers against the walls but failed anyway. The same year, they again used armored towers, this time against Thessalonica. The battle raged back and forth while the defenders threw fireballs of wicker soaked with olive oil against the towers. The Goths responded by building water reservoirs behind the towers so they could quickly extinguish the flames. But this meant the towers could not be moved at night. Thessalonica was not taken.

Despite their experiences in the third and fourth centuries, the Goths do not seem to have learned much. During the first siege of Rome, they used unwieldy siege towers pulled by unprotected oxen. Generally throughout the war they were unable to take a well-defended city by siegecraft and had to starve the defenders or attempt some stratagem.

Besieging Roman cities was a particular problem. Gothic siegecraft was inadequate and poor in practice, but to blockade a city and starve it out meant months and possibly years during which the besiegers had to live under field conditions and with growing logistical problems in hostile territory. Often the besieger—particularly the Ostrogoths, with no proper functioning logistical system—would starve before the besieged. This happened even to the troops of Emperor Maximinus at Aquileia in 238, and almost again for Attila in the fifth century in the same place. None of these many military problems could be remedied unless central changes occurred in the political and social areas of Gothic society. Such developments took time, more time than the Goths had.

FORTIFICATIONS

The Goths had no tradition of using fortifications of any advanced type. Several earthen walls have been found in the Gothic territories beyond the Danube, but only a few have been carefully examined. Unfortunately, there are almost no written sources on Gothic fortifications. However, much can be reconstructed through other sources, such as archaeological excavations. Illyria shows a quite complex defense system, which was typical for the Ostrogoths, during the period of the Sirmium War in 504–505. Many similarities can be observed in the defense of the Italian kingdom on the northern borders against the Alemanni and Franks. The same goes for the Rhône valley, but there the Goths were forced to commit themselves more after the Frankish King Clovis began to put pressure on the Burgundians in 534.

Historian Ammianus Marcellinus mentions a wall built by the Greuthungi at the time of the Hunnish invasion, and that further west Athanaric had another wall built, also against the Huns. There are several walls in the Dniester River area. Some historians believe that Athanaric built the wall between modern Brăhăsesti at the Seret River and Stoicani at the Pruth River—a length of about 53 miles. The Greuthungi probably also constructed the wall and ditch between Leova at the Pruth and Chircaesti at the Dniester. This so-called wall of Moldavia Inferior has been excavated, and it appears to be a traditional earthen rampart, with a ditch in front from which the earth was excavated. While this is one of the greatest ramparts in the area, its form was not new to the Goths.

It is unknown what the Goths sought to achieve by constructing the wall of Moldavia Inferior against the Huns. It was too long to be manned in strength, and it presented a limited obstacle to the Hunnish armies. Such earthworks seem more often to have been used to mark boundaries rather than to serve a military purpose.

The need to defend Italy from invasions across northern Pannonia, particularly along the Drava (Drau) and Sava (Save) rivers, and the Roman road system along the rivers, was not a new problem.

In the reign of Diocletian (284–305), the Romans had established a series of fortresses and constructed walls across the main passes through the Julian Alps. When Theodoric conquered Italy, he began to stabilize the region in much the same way as the Romans and perhaps also Odoacer. The fortifications in the Julian Alps stretched from Tarsatica (Rijeka in modern-day Croatia) at the head of the Adriatic, to the north through Nauportus (Vrhnika in modern-day Slovenia) and up to Zarakovec, to northwest of Forum Julii (Cividale), but not all elements of the defenses were manned. Archaeological surveys show that only some were manned by Goths—and for that matter, only some by the Lombards who came after them in the second half of the sixth century.

At any rate, we know of several measures by the Gothic king to construct fortifications and supply camps at the Gallic Durance, in the Cottian Alps, in the Val D'Aosta, and near Comum and Tridentum. The fortress with the telling name "Wart" (*verruca*) was constructed on the hill Dos Trentos, which Gothic coin finds also identify as a stronghold. This Verruca and the Ligurian fortress of Dertona are the best-known constructions of Theodoric's time. Forum Julii was kept as the strategic center for the northern defense sector. Aquileia, devastated by Attila the Hun in 452, and then little more than a village in the midst of the ruins, was still an important road hub in the region and received an Ostrogothic garrison.

The Ostrogoths also established garrisons in key positions along the Save River, including at the modern cities of Kranj, Dravlje, and Rifnik. At the eastern Ostrogothic border lay the important city of Sirmium.

Generally, the northern and eastern areas of Pannonia were in chaos, with a number of more-or-less abandoned cities containing a mix of barbarians and Romans, and the region was without interest to Theodoric. So in central Illyricum, the Ostrogoths controlled a wedge of land covered by the Drau and Save basins and along this corridor almost to Sirmium.

South of this area was Dalmatia, which was loosely influenced by the Ostrogoths and whose main city, Salona, had an Ostrogothic garrison. In these border areas there was a symbiosis between traditional Roman administration and Gothic military power. The citizens of Salona were instructed in the use of weapons and were armed by the Ostrogoths as militia. Such a strategy worked well against barbarians but proved to be double-edged sword against the Romans, whom the local inhabitants favored.

Italy's wealth of cities was an advantage to the Goths. Verona, Theodoric's second residence, and the royal city Ticinum, where as late as 552 Totila stored part of the royal treasure, remained Ostrogothic until the end of the war. Aligern, Teias's youngest brother, defended himself in fortified Cumae with the remaining part of the royal treasure for more than a year, even after the death of the last king. The fortifications of the peninsula, some of which were excellent, derive from Theodoric's efforts to preserve and improve the system of defenses. The main fortress, Ravenna, was also the most important residence; but he also spent considerable sums maintaining Rome's city walls, although they were in some disrepair when Belisarius took the city the first time in 536.

TACTICS

The Ostrogothic military had a strong reputation of doing well against other barbarians built mainly on its own tribal traditions, but it also used some Roman organizational and supply systems.

Because of disunity, however, the Goths could not sustain invasions for an extended period, and generally they did not develop anything more advanced than the "hurrah and charge" tactics of their ancestors. Because manliness was synonymous with military prowess proven on the battlefield, who would wait in reserve and miss so many opportunities to prove his courage? Neither did a leader have the power to order another free man to remain in reserve, even one from his own war band. It was therefore not surprising that Gothic tactics differed so little, without regard to the individual tribe or geographic circumstances.

The warriors sat on armored horses and galloped toward the enemy with their long lances held in close formation. One of their common battlefield tactics was a cavalry charge. If the enemy wavered, they would continue the charge; if not, they would throw spears and retreat to form up for another charge. In close combat they would use their swords or lances.

Gothic attitudes, such as their great esteem for horses; their weapons; and the tactics of the Gothic armies remained relatively unchanged during their entire history. The Italian weapons factories, which maintained their skilled production under Theodoric's special care, and the royal stables, which even in times of crisis remained remarkably productive, may have provided war material in larger quantities and especially of better quality than what the Ostrogoths were used to, but a fundamental change in the type of armament or in the attitudes and tactics did not occur. The tactics Totila used at the Battle of Taginae in 552 were no different from those the Ostrogoths used successfully for centuries.

Procopius's books on the Gothic War are full of stories that do not differ fundamentally from the best-known examples of success or failure of Gothic cavalry attacks: the Battles of Adrianopolis in 378, when the Goths struck down the Roman army and killed Emperor Valens, and in 507, when the Visigoths were decisively defeated by the Franks at Vouillé. The many duels Procopius describes were fought in the same manner. They usually took place as single combat between a mounted Gothic barbarian and an identically armed Roman barbarian. Both charged and tried through skillful maneuvering to pierce the enemy with a lance.

The characteristic elements of Gothic tactics were the quick attack, preferably launched from an ambush and accompanied by loud war cries; outflanking maneuvers to attack the enemy's infantry from the rear; riding the horses hard and fast in the hope of dealing a decisive blow before the horses were exhausted; quick retreat behind the lines of one's own foot warriors in case the attack failed; and gathering new forces for another attack. The strength and weakness of the Gothic army lay in its one-dimensionality. The relatively simple manner of fighting could be easily practiced and thoroughly trained. If the enemy neglected the necessary reconnaissance or lacked discipline, a Gothic cavalry attack could easily cause the intended panic. If the enemy lines wavered or even broke, there was soon no way of stopping the attackers.

Gothic horsemen served in other armies as well, especially in the Eastern Roman armies of Belisarius and Narses, which were characterized by a high degree of specialization in fighting techniques and tactics, the various tasks being carried out by different ethnic units. In the polyethnic confederation of such an army, Goths were often more successful than under Gothic leadership. Even the great Theodoric could never defeat a Roman army that was well put together from different military branches—that is to say, different peoples—and led with determination.

Procopius's description of the Gothic style of warfare appears to contradict that of Vegetius from the beginning of the fifth century. He describes as a Gothic tactic mounted archers showering their enemy with arrows. But Vegetius is describing the three-tribe confederation of Goths, Huns, and Alans, and he does not distinguish between three tribes. At that time, the Gothic cavalry already relied on the lance, and its allied Alan and Hun tribes were mounted nomads who had become horse archers. According to Jordanes's history of the Goths, this was also the arrangement at the Battle of Nedao in 454.

Artillery and Engineering

Only late do we read about Ostrogothic artillery. It could be that Roman deserters were manning it, as the Goths do not seem to have been disposed toward military engineering.

At the time of Totila and Teias we find evidence of more-strategic warfare when the Via Postumia along the Po River and other roads were blocked with the help of dikes, ditches, and flooding while the bridges were destroyed. Taking advantage of natural barriers must have been easier for the Goths than the city-hopping that the Romans forced upon them and that required good siege engineers. Starving out the enemy, hoping for treason within city walls, and cutting off water lines—these were almost the entire repertoire of Gothic siege techniques. The greater the size of a city—after all, the Goths twice captured Rome, and only Ravenna remained closed to them after 540—the greater the difficulty in holding it once taken. When Vittigis lifted the siege of Rome in March 538, he dealt his kingship the fatal blow. And when in April 547, the imperial forces captured Rome for the second time, Totila's reputation among the Goths and the other barbarian tribes suffered irreparable damage.

CHRONOLOGY

528–535: Bulgars and Sclaveni raid Illyricum and Thrace.

531, September 13: Death of Cabades. Chosroes made king of Persia.

532, January: The Nika Uprising.

532, Spring: Treaty of "Eternal Peace" made with Persians.

533, Early: Revolt of Pudentius in Tripolitania and Godas in Sardinia. Roman troops sent to support the revolt. Justinian declares war on Vandals.

533, Late August or September: Belisarius lands in Africa.

533, September 13: Battle of Ad Decimum, Belisarius defeats the Vandal king Gelimer.

533, September 15: Romans take Carthage.

533, December 15: Battle of Tricamarum, Belisarius defeats the Vandal king Gelimer. End of the Vandal kingdom.

534, Spring: King Gelimer is captured and brought to Constantinople.

534–535: Negotiations with Amalasuntha and afterwards Theodahad for surrendering Italy or parts of it to the Romans.

534, October 10: King Athalaric dies. Theodahad made king.

535, January 1: Belisarius enters the consulship.

535, April: Assassination of Amalasuntha. The Gothic War begins.

535: Romans invade Sicily and Dalmatia. Moors raid Roman Africa. Romans make treaty with the Franks.

535, Autumn: Goths send army to Dalmatia. Romans defeated.

535, December: Goths reject peace offer of Justinian.

535, December 31: Sicily is taken by the Romans.

536, probably Spring: Roman army sent to Dalmatia and defeats the Goths.

536, Spring: Theodahad is assassinated. Vittigis is made king.

536, March 23: Mutiny led by Stotzas begins in Africa.

536, April: Battle of Membresa. Belisarius defeats Stotzas.

536, Summer or autumn: Battle of Gadiaufala. Stotzas defeats Roman loyalists and the mutiny in Africa is rekindled.

536, Autumn: Goths offer peace, but are rejected.

536, December 9: Rome is captured by the Romans.

536, Winter: Germanus, nephew of Justinian, lands in Africa and rallies loyalist Roman troops.

536–537: Ostrogoths make treaty with the Franks.

536, Winter or early 537: Battle of Scalae Veteres. Loyalists victorious. Stotzas flees to Mauretania.

537–539: Moorish raids on Africa.

537, Late February, early March: Skirmish at Pons Salaria. Vittigis begins first siege of Rome.

537, Middle of March: Assault on Rome, Goths defeated.

537, Late March: Vittigis murders Roman senators confined at Ravenna.

537, Early: Gepids take Sirmium and makes it their main city.

537, April or May: Battle of Rome, Romans defeated.

537, June: Major sortie by the besieged Romans results in Roman victory.

537, July: Goths construct fortress south of Rome, thereby tightening the blockade.

537, November: Pope Silverius exiled for treason. Vigilius appointed pope in his stead.

537, December: Peace negotiations.

537, December or 538, January: Armistice.

538, Spring: Mediolanum revolts.

538, March: Goths abandon siege of Rome, Romans defeat their rearguard at Pons Milvius north of Rome.

538, Spring: Narses the Eunuch lands in Italy.

538, Spring: Burgundian subjects of the Franks invade Upper Italy.

539, Early: Mediolanum is captured and sacked by Goths and Burgundians. Narses is recalled to Constantinople

538: Goths send delegation to Persia seeking alliance.

539, Summer: Franks invade North Italy, defeating both Roman and Goth armies. Frankish army devastated by disease and retreats.

540, January or February: Franks offer alliance to Goths, but are rejected. Peace negotiations with Goths. Vittigis surrenders. Ravenna taken by Romans and made capital of Italy.

540, Early Spring: Ildibad made king of Ostrogoths. Belisarius leaves for Constantinople.

540: Bulgars invade Thrace and Macedonia.

540–551: Franks slowly take parts of North Italy.

540, Summer: Chosroes invades eastern provinces and sacks Antioch.

540, Autumn: Battle of Tarbesium, Goths under Ildibad defeats Roman army.

541, Spring: Belisarius leaves for the East to take command of the war against Persia.

541, May: Ildibad assassinated, Eraric the Rugian made king of Ostrogoths.

541, June or July: Belisarius invades Persia, while Chosroes is raiding Lazica.

541: Peace negotiations between Goths and Romans.

541, September or October: Eraric assassinated, Totila is made king.

542–545: Persian invasions of the eastern provinces.

542: The plague ravages Constantinople.

542, Spring-early summer: Totila defeats Roman armies in battle of Faventia and battle of Mucellis. Goths begin retaking Italy.

543–544: Moorish raids.

544, Spring: Belisarius is sent back to Italy.

545: Stotzas returns. Battle of Sicca Venerea, Stotzas is killed and the mutiny ends. Moors are subdued. Armistice, Justinian transfers troops to Italy.

545, Autumn: Totila begins siege of Rome.

546, Summer or early autumn: Attempted relief of Rome fails.

546, December 17: Rome captured by Totila through treachery.

547, February: Belisarius captures Rome after skirmish with Gothic troops. Totila unsuccessfully tries to recapture it.

548, June: Belisarius recalled to Constantinople. Death of Empress Theodora.

548: Bulgars raid Illyricum.

549: Goths raid Dalmatia. War with Persia erupts again.

549–550: Sclaveni raid Illyricum and Thrace.

549, Summer: Totila captures Rome through treachery. Goths offer peace, but are rejected.

550: War with Lombards, Gepids and Heruli.

550–551: Sicily ravaged by Totila. Bulgars invade Illyricum and Thrace.

551: Huns raid Thrace. Justinian invades Spain in support of Visigothic pretender Athanagild. Romans take Southern Spain.

Goths offer peace, but are rejected.

551, Spring–summer: Narses takes command of great Roman relief army meant to end the war in Italy.

551, Autumn: Naval battle off Sena Gallica results in Roman victory.

551: Five year armistice concluded with the Persians, but Lazica is excepted. Justinian attempts to renew alliance with Franks without success.

540–551: Franks slowly take North Italy.

551, Summer: Sicily retaken by the Romans.

552: Justinian tries to bring silk worms to the Empire to reduce silk trade through Persian lands.

552, June: Narses enters Ravenna.

552, June–July: Battle of Taginae. Death of Totila. Teias is made king. Teias attempts unsuccessfully to gain alliance with the Franks.

552, Autumn: Rome is captured by the Romans.

552, October: Battle of Mons Lactarius. Death of Teias.

553–554: Franks and their Alemannic subjects invade Italy. They are defeated by Narses at the battle of Casilinum.

555: Capitulation of the last Goths in Italy.

556–557: Armistice with Persia.

559: Huns invade Thrace. Belisarius defeats Hunnish army outside Constantinople.

561: Peace is concluded with Persia.

565, March: Belisarius dies.

565, November 13 or 14: Death of Justinian.

568: Lombards invade Italy.

SOURCES

The number of ancient sources and modern studies on the Goths, Romans, and the wars of Justinian is vast, and I have therefore only thought it relevant to select some of the most important ones. For a more complete bibliography, I refer readers to the various major studies below.

GENERAL LITERATURE ON THE PERIOD

The basic narrative of the Eastern Roman Empire in the fifth century is *The Later Roman Empire*, by A.H.M. Jones, which covers the period very well and looks into several aspects of ancient society such as trade, the church, education, culture, and the army.

There are many books on the church and religious matters. Peter Brown's works, including especially *The Cult of the Saints*, are useful, as is his collection of essays *Society and the Holy in Late Antiquity*. J. Richards's *The Popes and the Papacy in the Early Middle Ages, AD 476–750* gives a good introduction to the growing power of the papacy.

For settlement patterns, trade, and archaeological evidence in general, see K. Greene, *The Archaeology of the Roman Economy*, and M. Hendy, *Studies in the Byzantine Monetary Economy ca. AD 300–1450*, which contains a great deal of important material about the fiscal and economic workings of the late Roman state.

For a general treatment of the reign of Justinian and the period, see Averil Cameron, *The Mediterranean World in Late Antiquity AD 395–600*; R. Browning, *Justinian and Theodora*; and J. Barker, *Justinian and the Later Roman Empire*. For the history of mainly Western Europe, see Roger Collins, *Early Medieval Europe 300–1000*. See also the recent work of James Evans, *The Emperor Justinian and the Byzantine Empire*.

Roman Military Equipment—From the Punic Wars to the Fall of Rome, by M.C. Bishop and J.C.N. Coulston, is the best general treatment of the arms and armor of late antiquity. *Byzantium and Its Army 284–1081*, by W. Treadgold, is very good for its discussion of the organization and size of the late Roman army, as well as giving a good overview of the financial burden of the army in the days of Justinian.

I. Richmond's *The City Wall of Imperial Rome* is a detailed study of the development of the fortifications of the Eternal City, and describes both the state of the defenses before Belisarius and the changes made during the Gothic War. Despite its age, it is still the main book on the subject.

For architecture, see R. Krautheimer, *Early Christian and Byzantine Architecture*.

The Cambridge Ancient History also provides much general information on the period.

CONTEMPORARY SOURCES

The reign of Justinian is one of the best-documented periods in the history of the later empire. The military and diplomatic history of his reign up to 552 is told in great detail by Procopius in a generally accurate and well-informed account of contemporary history. His usefulness lessens, however, the further the events are distanced in time and geography. His work was continued by Agathias, who, after the death of Justinian, wrote a history of the years 552–558. Under the later Emperor Maurice, Menander Protector carried on the history until 582. The gaps in the history of Procopius regarding events in North Africa are filled by a Latin epic by Flavius Corippus, which describes in detail the exploits of John, the unfortunate *magister militum* in Africa from 546 to 548.

The historians of the period mainly looked into the many conflicts or religious matters of the age, and less into the internal affairs of the empire. Procopius does mention some of the more striking events in his *Wars*, such as the plague, and in a separate book gives a detailed account of Justinian's great building program. His *Secret History* of the reign down to 550, though difficult to use, also gives good insight to the functions of the court at Constantinople. Much of it appears to be based on gossip, and many of the emperor's activities are presented in an overly hostile way and must therefore be regarded with suspicion. The chief value of the work lies in the occasional details and information about the administration of the empire. Procopius as a source is covered in Averil Cameron, *Procopius and the Sixth Century*, and E. Stein, *Histoire du Bas-Empire*, Vol. 2. All the works of Procopius—*The Wars*, comprising two books on the Persian War, two books on the Vandal War, and four books on the Gothic War; *The Buildings*; and *The Secret History*—are translated into English in the Loeb edition.

The only other historian of the reign is John Malalas, whose chronicle, although uncritical and somewhat childish, has at least the merit of being a contemporary record. See also the studies on the same in Elizabeth Jeffreys, Brian Croke, and Roger Scott (eds.), *Studies in John Malalas*, Sydney 1990.

John Lydus, a clerk in the administration in Constantinople in the first half of the sixth century, wrote the treatise *De Magistratibus*, which offers great insight into the internal affairs of the administration. For John Lydus see A.C. Bandy, *On Powers, or, the Magistracies of the Roman State* and Michael Maas's *John Lydus*.

The Histories of Agathias, which continued the work of Procopius, are translated by Joseph D. Frendo (Berlin and New York: 1975). See also Averil Cameron, *Agathias*. The parts of Menander Protector that have survived are translated in *The History of Menander the Guardsman*, by R.C. Blockley.

Among the other important surviving sources is the Greek Zosimus's *New History* from the late fifth or early sixth century, drawing on the earlier history of Olympiodorus. The *Notitia Dignitatum* is very interesting for military matters despite the difficulties of determining the exact period described.

Roman Senator Cassiodorus's works are translated in several editions and provide detailed insight into the workings of Ostrogothic Italy at its height. Jordanes's history of the Goths, written in Latin in the middle of the sixth century, is fundamental to Gothic history but must be used with great care because of the author's preference for the Ostrogoths and his shortcomings as a historian. See also Arne Søby Christensen's work on the *Getica*.

Gregory of Tours, who wrote *History of the Franks* in the late sixth century, offers excellent insight into the workings of the Frankish kingdoms. Isidorus of Seville's *History of the Goths, Vandals, and Suevi*, written in the early seventh century, is also of great interest.

The lack of good historians is amply compensated for by the legal sources. Imperial legislation is found in *Codex Theodosianus* and *Codex Justinianus*, which are both greatly interesting if one remembers that there could be quite a gap between legislating and actual behavior in late antiquity.

There is no continuous ecclesiastical history apart from that of Evagrius. The personal reminiscences of John, the Monophysite bishop of Ephesus, and his lives of the Monophysite saints, are valuable as a source on religious matters and contain much information about the conditions of the period. The ecclesiastical histories of Socrates and Sozomen provide good insight into religious matters of the age. There are also many documentary sources for church history, including the important acts of the Second Ecumenical Council of Constantinople.

The Strategikon, written by Maurice in the late sixth century, is an invaluable source of information on the art of war of the period (translated by George Dennis, Philadelphia: 1984). Although written years before the Gothic War, Vegetius's *Epitome of Military Science* (translated by N. P. Milner, Liverpool: 1996) is interesting regarding the Roman army and its equipment.

Literature on the History of the Ostrogoths and Other Barbarians

Although the Goths, their culture, and their impact on Roman society have been discussed for a long time, the main works were published around 1990, when the results of extensive new archaeological material could be included. Herwig Wolfram's *History of the Goths* is the main work. Thomas Burns's *A History of the Ostrogoths* has a detailed bibliography. Peter Heather's *Goths and Romans 332–489* has an excellent treatment of Jordanes's history of the Goths and discusses the formation of the Visigoths and Ostrogoths in the migration period. I refer readers to the bibliographies in these three works for more sources on the Goths in general and the Ostrogoths in particular.

Despite its age, Thomas Hodgkin's *Italy and Her Invaders* remains a significant work on the Ostrogoths in Italy. Much new research has been done—mainly in the field of archaeology—and the style of writing is old, but it gives a full and detailed account of the war, with excellent comments on the military and religious affairs of the age.

For the Huns and their impact on Europe, see Otto Maenchen-Helfen, *The World of the Huns*, which remains one of the best books on the subject. The Alans, who rode with the Goths and the Vandals, are well-treated in B. Bachrach's *History of the Alans*. Hanno Helbling treats the Vandals and the historical tradition in his *Goten und Wandalen*. For the Franks and their kingdoms I refer readers to Edward James, *The Franks*, and Bernard Bachrach, *Merovingian Military Organization 481–751*. For relations between the Persians and the Romans, see Beate Dignas and Engelbert Winter, *Rome and Persia in Late Antiquity*.

Selected Ancient Sources

For a complete list of ancient sources and their translations, see Herwig Wolfram's bibliography in *History of the Goths*.

Agathias. *The Histories.*

Ammianus Marcellinus

Anonymous Valesianus

Boethius. *De consolatione philosophiae.*

Cassiodorus. *Chronica. Variae epistolae. Historia ecclesiastica tripartita.*

Claudius Claudianus. *Carmina.*

Codex Justinianus

Codex Theodosianus

Cornelius Tacitus. *Germania.*

Dexippus. *Chronica. Scythica.*

Ennodius. *Opera.*

Eunapius. *Historiarum Fragmenta.*

Flavius Corippus. *Johannis.*

Flavius Renatus Vegetius. *De Re Militaris.*

Fredegar. *Chronicon.*

Gothic Bible

Gregory of Tours. *Historia Francorum.*

Herodianus

Isidorus of Seville. *Historia de regibus Gothorum, Vandalorum et Suevorum.*

Jerome. *Chronicon.*

Joannes Lydus. *De Magistratibus.*

John Chrysostom. *Epistolae.*

John Malalas. *Chronographia.*

Jordanes. *Getica. Romana.*

Lex Romana Visigothorum

Libanius. *Opera.*

Marcellinus Comes. *Chronicon.*

Maurice. *Strategikon.*

Menander Protector. *Historia.*

Notitia Dignitatum

Orosius. *Historiarum adversum paganos, libri VII.*

Passio sancti Sabae Gothi.

Paulus Diaconus. *Historia Langobardorum.*

Priscus

Procopius. *History of the Wars. The Secret History. The Buildings.*

Scriptores Historiae Augustae

Sextus Julius Frontinus. *Strategemata.*

Sidonius Apollinaris. *Carmina. Epistulae.*

Sozomen. *Historia Ecclesiastica.*

Victor Vitensis. *Historia persecutionis Africane provinciae.*

Zosimus. *Historia Nova.*

MODERN LITERATURE

Amory, Patrick. *People and Identity in Ostrogothic Italy, 481–554.* Cambridge Studies in Medieval Life and Thought: Fourth Series. Cambridge: Cambridge University Press, 1997. Reprint, Cambridge: Cambridge University Press, 2003.

Bachrach, Bernard. *A History of the Alans in the West.* Minneapolis: University of Minnesota Press, 1973.

———. *Merovingian Military Organization 481–751.* Minneapolis: University of Minnesota Press, 1972.

Bandy, Anastasius C. *On Powers, or, the Magistracies of the Roman State.* Philadelphia: American Philosophical Society, 1983.

Barker, John W. *Justinian and the Later Roman Empire.* Madison: University of Wisconsin Press, 1966.

Bichir, Gheorghe. *The Archaeology and History of the Carpi.* British Archaeological Reports. Suppl. Series 16. Oxford: Archaeopress, 1976.

Bishop, Michael C., and Jon C. N. Coulston. *Roman Military Equipment from the Punic Wars to the Fall of Rome.* London: Oxbow Books, 1993.

Bona, Istvan. *The Dawn of the Dark Ages: The Gepids and the Lombards in the Carpathian Basin.* Budapest: Corvina Press, 1976.

Boss, Roy. *Narses, Belisarius, and Justinian's War.* New York: Montvert Publications, 1993.

Brand, C. E. *Roman Military Law.* Austin: University of Texas Press, 1968.

Brown, Peter. *The Cult of the Saints.* Chicago: University of Chicago Press, 1981.

————. *Society and the Holy in Late Antiquity*. Los Angeles: University of California Press, 1982.

Brown, Thomas S. *Gentlemen and Officers: Imperial Administration and Aristocratic Power in Byzantine Italy, AD 554–800*. Rome: British School at Rome, 1984.

Browning, Robert. *Justinian and Theodora*. London: Praeger, 1971. Reprint, London: Gorgias Press, 1987.

Burns, Thomas. *A History of the Ostrogoths*. Indiana: Indiana University Press, 1984.

Bury, John B. *The Later Roman Empire*. London: 1889. Reprint, New York: Dover Books, 1958.

The Cambridge Ancient History.

Cameron, Averil. *Agathias*. Oxford: Oxford University Press, 1970.

————. *The Mediterranean World in Late Antiquity, AD 395–600*. New York: Routledge, 1993.

————. *Procopius and the Sixth Century*. New York: Routledge, 1985. Reprint, New York: Routledge, 1996.

Cheesman, G. L. *The Auxilia of the Roman Imperial Army*. Oxford: Clarendon Press, 1914. Reprint, Chicago: Ares Publishers, 1975.

Christensen, Arne Søby. *Cassiodorus, Jordanes, and the History of the Goths: Studies in a Migration Myth*. Copenhagen: Museum Tusculanum Press, 2002.

Collins, Roger. *Early Medieval Europe 300–1000*. New York: St. Martin's Press, 1991. 2nd ed. London: Palgrave Macmillan, 1995.

Delbrück, Hans. *Geschichte der Kriegskunst im Rahmen der Politischen Geschichte*. Vol. 2. Berlin: Verlag Georg Stilke, 1921.

Dignas, Beate, and Engelbert Winter. *Rome and Persia in Late Antiquity: Neighbours and Rivals*. Cambridge: Cambridge University Press, 2007.

Evans, James A. *The Emperor Justinian and the Byzantine Empire*. Westport, CT: Greenwood Press, 2005.

Ferrill, Arthur. *The Fall of the Roman Empire: The Military Explanation*. London: Thames & Hudson, 1986.

Finley, M. I. *The Ancient Economy*. London: Chatto and Windus, 1973. Reprint, Berkeley: University of California Press, 1999.

Gibbon, Edward. *The Decline and Fall of the Roman Empire*. London: Strahan & Cadell, 1777–1788. Reprint, London: Wordsworth Editions, 1999.

Goffart, Walter. *Barbarians and Romans, AD 418–584: The Techniques of Accommodation*. Princeton, NJ: Princeton University Press, 1980.

Gordon, C. D. *The Age of Attila: Fifth-Century Byzantium and the Barbarians*. Ann Arbor: University of Michigan Press, 1959. Reprint, Ann Arbor: University of Michigan Press, 1966.

Greene, Kevin. *The Archaeology of the Roman Economy*. London: Batsford, 1986.

Grosse, Robert. *Römische Militärgeschichte von Gallienus bis zum Beginn der byzantinischen Themenverfassung*. Berlin: Verlag Weidman, 1920.

Haldon, John. *The Byzantine Wars*. Charleston: Tempus Publishing Inc., 2001.

Heather, Peter. *The Goths*. Oxford: Blackwell Publishers, 1996.

———. *Goths and Romans 332–489*. Oxford: Oxford University Press, 1991.

Helbling, Hanno. *Goten und Wandalen*. Zurich: Fretz & Wasmuth Verlag, 1954.

Hendy, Michael. *Studies in the Byzantine Monetary Economy ca. AD 300–1450*. Cambridge: Cambridge University Press, 2008.

Hodgkin, Thomas. *Italy and Her Invaders, 376–814*, Vol. 3, *The Ostrogothic Invasion 476–535*, Vol. 4, *The Imperial Restoration*. London: Clarendon Press, 1885.

Hoffmann, Dietrich. *Das Spatromische Bewegungsheer und die Notita Dignitatum*. 2 vols. Dusseldorf: Rheinisches Landesmuseum Bonn, 1969–70.

James, Edward. *The Franks*. London: Wiley-Blackwell, 1988.

Jeffreys, Elizabeth, Brian Croke, and Roger Scott, eds. *Studies in John Malalas*. Sydney: Australian Association of Byzantine Studies, 1990.

Jones, A. H. M. *The Later Roman Empire: A Social, Economic, and Administrative Survey*. Norman: University of Oklahoma Press, 1964. Reprint, Baltimore: Johns Hopkins University Press, 1992.

Kaegi, Walter. *Byzantine Military Unrest, 471–843: An Interpretation*. Amsterdam: Hakkert, 1981.

———. *Byzantium and the Decline of Rome*. Princeton, NJ: Princeton University Press, 1968.

Krautheimer, R. *Early Christian and Byzantine Architecture*. Harmondsworth: Penguin Books, 1965. 4th ed. Harmondsworth: Yale University Press, 1984.

Llewellyn, Peter A. B. *Rome in the Dark Ages*. London: Praeger, 1970.

MacMullen, Ramsay. *Soldier and Civilian in the Later Roman Empire*. Cambridge, MA: Harvard University Press, 1963.

Maenchen-Helfen, Otto J. *The World of the Huns: Studies in Their History and Culture*. Berkeley: University of California Press, 1973.

Marsden, Eric W. *Greek and Roman Artillery*. Oxford: Oxford University Press, 1971.

Mattingly, Harold, C.H.V. Sutherland, and R.A.G. Carson. *The Roman Imperial Coinage*. London: Spink & Son, 1972.

Meier, Mischa. *Justinian: Herrschaft, Reich, und Religion*. Munich: Verlag Beck, 2004.

Moorhead, John. *Justinian*. London: Longman Publishing Group, 1994.

Musset, Lucien. *The Germanic Invasions: The Making of Europe. AD 400–600*. University Park, PA: Pennsylvania State University Press, 1975. Reprint, New York: Barnes & Noble Books, 1993.

Richards, Jeffrey. *The Popes and the Papacy in the Early Middle Ages, AD 476–750*. London: Routledge & Kegan Paul, 1979.

Richmond, Ian A. *The City Wall of Imperial Rome*. Oxford: Clarendon Press, 1930.

Starr, Chester. *The Roman Imperial Navy, 31 BC—AD 324*. Cambridge: W. Heffer and Sons, 1960. 3rd edition reprint, Chicago: Ares Publishers, 1993.

Stein, Ernest. *Histoire du Bas-Empire*. Vol. 2. Amsterdam: Desclee De Brouwer, 1949. Reprint, Amsterdam: Desclee De Brouwer, 1968.

Sulimirski, Tadeusz. *The Sarmatians*. London: Thames & Hudson, 1970.

Thompson, E. A. *The Goths in Spain*. Oxford: Clarendon Press, 1969.

———. *A History of Attila and the Huns*. Oxford: Clarendon Press, 1948.

———. *Romans and Barbarians: The Decline of the Western Empire*. Madison: University of Wisconsin Press, 1982.

————. *The Visigoths in the time of Ulfilas*. Oxford: Clarendon Press, 1966.

Treadgold, Warren. *Byzantium and Its Army 284–1081*. Stanford, CA: Stanford University Press, 1995.

————. *A History of Byzantium*. Stanford: Stanford University Press, 1997.

Wallace-Hadrill, John M. *The Barbarian West 400–1000*. London: Wiley-Blackwell, 1967.

Wolfram, Herwig. *History of the Goths*. Munich: C.H. Becksche Verlagsbuchhandlung, 1979. 2nd revised edition, Berkeley: University of California Press, 1987.

Wroth, W. *Catalogue of the Coins of the Vandals, Ostrogoths, and Lombards, and of the Emperors of Thessalonica, Nicaea, and Trebizond in the British Museum*. London: 1911. Reprint, Boston: Adamant Media, 2002.

INDEX

ACKNOWLEDGMENTS

Many people helped me in discussing the subject and the making of this book, for which I am thankful. The greatest help perhaps came from Dr. Marion Brüggler of *Bodendenkmalpflege im Rheinland*, Germany, who read an early draft and gave me many good ideas on how to improve it. The great patience of my family during the six years it took to write *The Gothic War* was also a great help, particularly that of my wife, Katerina, to whom this book is dedicated.

I am also grateful to the Danish Academy in Rome, where I received much help during my stays there. The opportunity to study the walls of Rome in detail and the battlefields and cities of Italy—as well as the stimulating academic environment—meant much to me.

My thanks also go to Bruce Franklin of Westholme Publishing, who accepted this book for publication and gave me many good suggestions for improving it, as well as to Ron Silverman for his great support during the copy editing, and Tracy Dungan for his excellent maps.

My final thanks go to professor Jens-Erik Skydsgaard, formerly of the University of Copenhagen, who was always inspiring in his teachings on ancient Rome, and assistant professor Arne Søbye Christensen, who first introduced me to the Goths, Franks, and other tribes of the Dark Ages.

17